CW00820911

SPECIAL THANKX

To Those Who Gave And/Or Fell In The Line Of Duty . . .

Jason

Barry Reid

Will Low

Robert Lewalski

Dan

Mark Robinson

Robert Martin

Stephen Hayes

Dale Seago

plus various members of agencies, firms, and governments that prefer, probably wisely, not to be "thanked."

Art Director Cindy Garrison

SpyGame:
Winning Through Super Technology
By Scott French and Lee Lapin

ISBN 0-87364-614-2
Printed in the United States of America

Published by Paladin Press,
a division of Paladin Enterprises, Inc.
Gunbarrel Tech Center
7077 Winchester Circle
Boulder, Colorado 80301, USA
+1.303.443.7250

Direct inquiries and/or orders to the above address.

Visit our Web site at www.paladin-press.com

MORALITY

We have just concluded an interview with a newspaper reporter, and, as in most of these situations, the question of morality reared its ugly head. Should we be giving away information like the details in this book?

Should the "general public" realize such things go on in this almost perfect world? Worse yet, should they know how to perform or even protect themselves against such actions?

How do we justify publishing this book?

We have two answers; one, the Constitution of the United States, and two, the Bill of Rights, both of which declare all men to be created equal as well as suggest that the power should rest in the hands of the people. Look around the world today; how many governments do you trust as much as your next door neighbor?

Finally, I'd like to relate a story that occurred in Germany a few years ago. A man was on trial for molesting and then choking to death a five-year-old girl. He had raped and killed one other child in the past, was put in prison, and then was castrated and released. The court had just re-sentenced him to a few years (or less) in a mental institution.

The child's mother was in the courtroom at the time. She stood up and shot the son-of-a-bitch six times, killing him on the spot.

What if that had been your daughter?

Lee and Scott

A WORD FROM LEE

It may sound a bit corny, but I would like to take a moment, or a couple of inches in this case, and thank everyone who purchased and/or enjoyed my last book, *How To Get Anything On Anybody.*

At this time we have received over 200 (!) letters complimenting this effort. The readers have included people from almost every aspect of professional investigative and security work (including a large group of intelligence agencies) to talented "amateurs."

The book has been reviewed in some 30-odd publications from the N.Y./L.A. newspapers to *Security Journal* and *Police Times.*

Two of the highest honors came from unlikely sources: *The National Enquirer,* who decided the book was "material unsuitable for advertising in the *Enquirer,*" and *New Woman* magazine, yes *New Woman . . .* They did a nice profile of one of the country's top P.I.s (who happens to be a woman) and she is pictured reading my book.

Thanks to all of you for helping make it a success.

Lee

See pages *505-506* for a listing of updated address information for the companies and organizations referenced in this book.

SpyGame: What is it?

First of all, what it is *not.*

It is not a book that is going to teach you to become a "Ninja." Neither Scott nor myself is a ninja. There is one real instructor in the art of ninjutsu in America. Stephen Hayes. If you wish to spend the time and effort, he *can* teach you to become a ninja. He is very good at what he does.

In a way we apologize for the original title; "ninja" is fast becoming the buzzword of the 80s . . . just like judo in the 50s, karate in the 60s, and "kung fu" in the 70s, ninja is being used to sell everything from instant death touch books to toothpaste.

So why did we use the title? When I first began planning this book several years ago, the term *ninja* was relatively unknown and the concept fit the contents.

Basically, we will show you how to begin to understand the ninjutsu way of thinking and duplicate much of their technology, instead of you having to go through thirty years of training.

This concept will upset some purists. How can anyone cheapen a martial art by substituting technology for study? In the first place, ninjutsu is not a martial art, per se. Yes, it kills, when killing is necessary, but that is not the idea. Both Scott and myself have been involved in the martial arts for many years. I have studied under some great karate players and top wing chun artists, including some of Bruce Lee's students and partners. I have also attended seminars with Stephen Hayes. They are all great. There is no comparison; the martial ends of ninjutsu simply cannot be used in any tournament-type play.

Apples and oranges.

It is also necessary to remember that ninja schools, throughout history, were always the first to incorporate the latest technology into their repertoire. This practice of using skill plus technology to defeat much larger numbers of more traditional warriors (samurai) earned them a nasty reputation (remember, history is generally written by the survivors and the many samurai did outlast the handful of ninja).

But the ninja had their own code of honor, often more rigid than that of the samurai. They chose to apply their skills only when they felt the cause was just and the "client" outnumbered.

So if not a martial art, what is ninjutsu?

Simply stated, it is the art of winning. The practice of skill and technology application to accomplish a given set of goals. Using whatever approach necessary to *really win,* sometimes without the other side even realizing they have lost.

So watch Chuck Norris and Bruce Lee. They are (were, in Bruce's case) very skilled at what they do. But also remember what Bruce Lee said -- after spending his entire life in the arts -- in his one major Hollywood film, *Enter the Dragon,* when asked to infiltrate a martial arts stronghold and kill the leader with his bare hands. "Take a .45 and shoot him."

You see, that approach would have done it.

Won.

This book is the art of winning.

Lee/Scott

INTERESTING MOMENT

Writing this book provided me with one of the most interesting moments of my short life. I was in the middle of a photo session when there was a knock on the door and I yelled, without thinking, "Come in" . . . What I did not know was there had been a burglary next door the previous evening, and the nice local cop was asking the neighbors if they heard anything. When he walked in -- as best I can reconstruct the scene -- on my counter were: one camera, three crossbows, nine crossbow bolts, one wrist crossbow and arrows, three pistols, two AR-7 rifles (one with silencer), modified stock, auto crank and extended clip, one set of ninja claws, several ninja darts, one electric blaster, one pair of sap gloves, six extendable batons, one Sipo, two slingshots, several boxes of ammo, two cammo overalls, a bunch of shot-up targets and test logs, three holsters (ankle and underarm), one hypo, one bulletproof vest, and assorted minor weapons. The cop took it well. Except for the in initial mouth drop and grab for his holster (he never did actually remove the gun), he controlled the situation admirably. First, he backed toward the door and suggested I not make any sudden moves. Then he calmly asked if I was planning a major revolution within or without the country. I tried to explain the idea without any hand movements at all -- a difficult procedure -- and ended up promising him a book. A calm man.

Lee

ET CETERA

Some thoughts while reading;

For you do-it-yourself bulletproof garment makers, Nam flak jackets are available from Quist's Trading Post, 111 W. Robert St., Crookston, MN 56716. They have other things of interest also.

Fingerprints -- the magic cyanoacrylate process we've detailed works great BUT a brand new product, called PRINT LOCK, is the same idea in a spray can and will lift latents off damn near anything by JUST SPRAYING IT ON!!! Try it out. They may want a letterhead (security at least), Print Lock Co., 8055 West Manchester Ave., Suite 405, Playa Del Rey, CA 90293.

The TSU 3000 Countermeasures unit we tested does more than I thought in the way of covering noise. It either injects some nice ultra-freq harmonics and/or does some sort of random clock rate sweep making it almost, if not actually, impossible to "decode" from a tapped (and taped) source.

The National Directory, published by Central Directory and Information (listed) contains a yearly listing of some 30,000 investigators, process servers, polygraphy examiners, repossessors, etc.

EDEN PRESS, Box 8410, Fountain Valley, CA 92728 is publishing a newsletter on privacy/IDs entitled PRIVACY HINTS that gives the up-to-date scoop on the new laws, tricks, and trials. Also has new and very good information on passports.

DELTA PRESS features, in their latest catalog, a do-it-yourself ID kit that looks pretty good.

Most states use a code in the license number of a vehicle to indicate a rental vehicle. These codes vary from state to state but might be worth learning in your area.

The Reliance Co., Box 4582, Stockton, CA 95204 also sells some nice ID cards.

Kenwood Associates, Box 66, Long Green, MD 21092 offers a wide variety of ID cards.

MEREDITH INSTRUMENTS IS LOCATED AT: 6403 N. 59th Ave., Glendale, AZ 85301.

DIRIJO CORPORATION, 2505 Woodbridge Drive, Gastonia, NC 28052 furnished a couple of the best circuits in the back of this book. They also have designed a remarkable LASER beam reader and supply some very hot items in the electronic surveillance and countermeasures field. Their LASER was recently featured in RADIO ELECTRONICS magazine.

PASSPORTS -- As of Jan. 1, 1987, federal regulations regarding new passports have taken a hard turn for the worse. Under the new laws, Social Security numbers, along with certain income tax information and proposed trip details, are required on the application form. The "new" passports (including renewals) are probably going to include built-in magnetic strips, which will help government computers keep track of the user anywhere in the world as well as allow airport metal detectors to expose anyone attempting to "smuggle" a passport on his person. It will also become easy to encode stop-and-search flags onto this strip, replacing the system(s) now in use, which include the placement of a red "X" in ultraviolet visible ink on suspect passports.

One should also be aware of the fact that almost all states now cross reference birth and death records, thus making it very risky to attempt the original paper trip of assuming the identity of a dead person. Many, if not most, passport applications now include a check on the offered birth certificate to see if it really was issued where and when the applicant claims it was. *However,* expect a possible quick check of offered information, including -- but not limited to -- a phone call to any relatives listed, to verify the physical description of the person who is applying for the document.

PRIVATE INTERNATIONAL MONEYLINE, 357 S. Robertson Blvd., Beverly Hills, CA 90211 publishes a monthly newsletter that updates information on taxes, offshore banking, passports, etc. It is expensive ($94.00 a year), but is easily the best ongoing source of information on worldwide money situations, IRS crackdowns, banking procedures, customs regulations, and so on.

If you are not already aware of it, the U.S. is planning to issue new paper money within the next couple of years. The design of the new bills has already been approved and will incorporate such details as a 3-D hologram to frustrate counterfeiting attempts and metal fibers interwoven in the fabric to limit the undeclared passage through airport and mail metal detectors. One of the official justifications for the changeover is to allow the government to control the flow of drug profits. Best believe there will be a limited amount of time "given" to change in the old bills for new before the current currency becomes worthless. Best believe the IRS is going to monitor any changes. Watch what happens to the price of gold when this idea becomes law.

As this is written, a perfect, gem-quality diamond has just been created under laboratory conditions. It will be interesting to see how long the international diamond cartel can support the price of pretty carbon.

The newest items in electronic surveillance are mini-transmitters that do not use any RF to relay audio but send a carrier wave of IR light to a waiting receiver. This procedure limits the range and angle of transmission greatly but avoids detection by conventional bug finders. Several of these units are available from our German suppliers and at least one U.S. general mail-order house offers a unit that can be adapted to surveillance purposes.

In an upcoming video, we (CEP) will demonstrate IR transmission, signal boosting, and detection methods.

CONTENTS

I've always said that while I might die in bed, it wouldn't be doing anything boring.

SpyGame was a kick to write. I still feel it is probably one of the best works I've ever written and/or collaborated on. I mean, when we tested the effects of Glaser cartridges against "state-of-the-art" body armor in the African bush, or detailed the collection and use of the most advanced electronic surveillance methods around at the time, it was an experience that I have really never duplicated in 20+ other books.

This book ain't history; it's valid and surprisingly still quite current, more than 15 years after its publication.

Maybe, right after I finish the follow-up series to *Shogun* and *Lonesome Dove*, I'll go back and do another *SpyGame*."

—Lee Lapin, May 2001

"What Lee said!"

—Scott French (written from San Jose, Bolivia; signed in his absence)

TRADITIONAL NINJA DEVICES

Throwing Stars (Shuriken)

One of the most often portrayed ninja tools is the star. These are effective weapons, and are/were used by ninja. However, as with most of the items discovered by slick magazines and screenwriters, a number of misconceptions exist about the use and effectiveness of shuriken.

These were not (or hardly ever) killing weapons. Instead they were employed to hurt, harass, and distract one or more enemies, often in order to then escape or throw off the adversary's timing so a killing weapon/technique could be brought into play.

Believe me, it is distracting to have one or more razor sharp pieces of metal hurtling at your face...

There was no traditional (or "correct") shape for the stars. Remember the original ninja were farmers and other poor types. They did not shop thru Black Belt magazine for endorsed products, and as such, had no idea they were not doing things according to form...

However their units worked...

Even the best stars, and most purchased today are far from that ideal, will not do serious damage through a leather coat or other heavy clothing.

The stars do NOT have to be thrown to be effective weapons. There is an entire sub-"major" in some ninja schools that produced shuriken experts both in close combat as well as in throwing.

THROWING

The correct method of throwing shuriken, like many ninjutsu techniques uses the entire body NOT JUST THE ARM.

The star is gripped as shown and then the body is "aimed" at the target. The arm is brought forward from the chest and the star is released at the last second. The star will spin directly towards the target on an almost horizontal path if done correctly.

Notice the star is NOT thrown overhead like a baseball, nor is it spun out sidearm style from the side of the body using the arm's strength.

The correct throw (note "throw,", not "fling") comes from the center of the body and is much, much more accurate than any other type of throw.

A few practice throws should convince you of the validity of this technique.

Notice how the automatic aiming incorporated in this method closely resembles instinct shooting.

A good idea to save furniture, trees, friends and relatives is to employ one of the heavy rubber practice stars available from martial arts suppliers while learning accuracy.

It is also important to realize that these weapons, like most ninjutsu philosophy is based on the theory of winning through adaption and initiative.

Most ninja practitioner do NOT carry darts with them, yet their training allows substitution of the actual darts by available objects...

To quote Mr. Hayes, an ashtray, among many other common objects, makes an ideal throwing star...

The ability to improvise is a necessity to any campaign.

FANGS

The ninja used to delay their enemies as well as cause untold pain and confusion by tossing small, multi pointed tacks known as calthrops into the suspected path of any pursuers.

These spikes were made so that one point would stick upright no matter how they landed. They were very sharp and people in those days tended to run about in straw sandals, making calthrops a very effective measure.

Although most people no longer wear sandals sharp calthrops can pierce gym shoes and thin soled shoes quite effectively. Traditional calthrops can be purchased from NINJA SUPPLY SYSTEMS.

A more common occurance in today's world is chase by automobile. These beasts too can become easily confused and thrown into pain by the right form of "calthrops".

The best commercial version we have seen are ROAD FANGS, from LEA among others...

These hollow spikes are mounted on a flexible track (or on a rolled drum) which allows rapid deployment. Several of the spikes will pierce the tire of any vehicle that passes, the hole in the tip of the spike allows extra fast air escape, deflating the tire almost at once.

These hollow spikes have the added effect of a controlled deflation, thereby allowing the victim, ah, driver, to retain control of the vehicle.

If you are not quite so concerned with a controlled deflation you can put together your own version of auto calthrops by going to a farm supply store and purchasing a box of mower blades (used when harvesting grains).

Now take the blades to a welding shop and have them brazed (not welded) along the edges so one blade points straight up, resting on the flat of another as shown.

These will shread any tire that passes over them stopping even heavy vehicles. They can be painted gray or black to blend in with the road top or partially buried in a gravel roadbed.

If the top blade has a ridge, grind it off leaving a sharp point before camouflaging.

HOOKS AND SUCH

Ninja were feared for many reasons, some of which were real and some of which were either false or at best, wildly blown out of proportion.

One of the rumors was that ninja could make themselves invisible and pass through solid walls. At least part of this belief was fostered by the fact that they were experts at climbing and grapling.

The ninja grapling hook was usually black iron and utilized both as a weapon as well as a true grappling hook which could be flung onto roofs or trees and then used as a climbing anchor.

The best hook we found is provided by NINJA WARRIOR ENTERPRISES and is a sharpened nine inch black three-armed hook with a loop connector for attaching a climbing rope.

NWE's hook is sturdy, dark and sharp enough for use as a weapon or for climbing. At $25.00 it is a useful addition to any tool kit...

Another interesting source, if only by default, is PIGEON MOUNTAIN INDUSTRIES. PMI is a climbers/rescue equipment source that sells the highest quality ropes, harnesses, hooks etc.

They have a very interesting line which features flexible rope made of kernmantle and figure 8's, pulleys and carabiners...

All are done in a non-reflective black finish...

Great devices for perspective ninja or cat burglars...

SHUKO

Invented by the Togakure school of ninja these iron bands fit around one's hands and then are secured by a wrist band. The bands usually have four very sharp iron spikes protruding outward which allowed the shuki to be used for climbing walls, tearing the hell out of an unprotected enemy, or surprising a attacker by actually grabbing his sword with "bare" hands and wrenching it from him with no visible harm.

They are still effective weapons and climbers. Ours were gotten from Ninja Supply Systems, a small outfit run by one of Mr. Hayes' blackbelt instructors.

They are perfectly constructed, sharp as hell, fit, and do what they are supposed to do.

The major problem is that wearing hand claws gives one a certain "aura" when viewed by normal people or police...

They also make it hard to preform some normal functions like driving, or tying a shoe; never shake hands with anyone and for god's sake do not slap your thigh at a good joke...

On the other hand, if concealed correctly and then applied for climbing or hurting someone badly/quickly in a most surprising fashion (fighters do not expect open hand slaps to do much damage) the shuko can be very effective.

ESCORT

Also secured from Ninja Supply Systems, the Escort is a kind of combination weapon. It is a Lexan handle that supports a triangular blade of blued steel.

It is not made for cutting your dinner steak; more like an ice pick or joint shank, this razor sharp weapon is worn around the arm or leg where it is instantly available.

Not made for throwing, this is strictly a close range entry weapon that does major damage.

Velcro straps hold the sheath and pure friction holds the escort making it a fast draw weapon.

NINJA SOURCES

SHADOWS OF IGA
PO Box 1947
Kettering, OH 45429

JUSTIN CONCEPTS
PO Box 142
Germantown, OH 45329

NINJA SUPPLY SYSTEMS
PO Box 28222
Atlanta, GA 30328

SCORPION ENTERPRISES
PO Box 774
Tucker, GA 30084

BEAVER PRODUCTS
PO Box 1700
Anna Maria, FL 33501

SHADOWS is the offical, and real, society for Togakure ryu ninjutsu the ONLY authentic (34 unbroken generations of teachers) ninja society open to any outsiders. For $25 a year one gets the quarterly journal, NINJA RELM, membership card, schedules of seminars with Mr. Hayes and his instructors all over the country, articles, product reports, etc.

The other folks are suppliers of some REAL ninja equipment including honest shuriken, suits, tools and weapons. Most of them are endorsed by Mr. Hayes and/or run by his students. Our ESCORT and Stars were from SCORPION SCORPION and NINJA SUPPLY SYSTEMS.

These are not toys.

Ninja Kyoketsu Shoge
Hook blade weapon. Used for cutting, climbing and striking.

Ninja Stars
Authentic replicas of shurikens used by ninja centuries ago.

Ninja Steel Bakuhatsugama
Black finish steel handle and blade with weighted chain hidden in the handle.

Ninja Kasari Fundo
Authentic ninja chain weapon. All black with 3" weights.

Ninja Walking Staff
8' chain inside with weight and hook on each end. Used for grappling, binding and striking.

Ninja-To
Authentic steel replica of ninja sword, 24" long.

NINJA SLIPPERS - Low cut canvas slippers with quiet, rubber soles. Light weight and durable. Sizes 6 - 12.

THE ESCORT - Rugged, dependable ... disposable - when you need to make a point. The Escort features a blued steel, non-reflective, triangular ground blade and a dark grey Lexan compound handle. The overall length is less than 7" and it's furnished with a sheath that adapts to leg or arm carry. A horizontal belt sheath is available as an optional extra.

MINI-DERRINGER RIG - Black suede pocket will hold mini-derringer pistols or other small items on the ankle or arm.

BANDIT - A commando watchband and wrist sheath made for the Sting la and other similar low profile knives. Designed for concealment rather than speed.

SCORPION ENTERPRISE'S RAZOR SHARP STARS AND DEADLY ESCORT

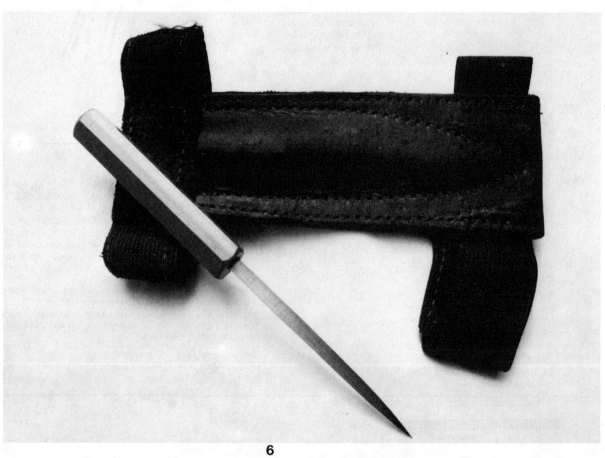

6

How many weapons can you spot on our overdressed friend?

Pen gun in right pocket along with COBRA rod, poison spray bottle in opposite pocket, strap on back pack with nunchauku, poison ring on right hand, sap glove and steel claws from SCORPION ENTERPRISES on left hand, escort (also fro SE) strapped on left leg, WESTERN CUTLERY book knife clipped on right ankle, steel stars in belt pack under shirt.

If these items were properly concealed most would pass all but the most minute inspection, and most are very, very deadly.

Don't invite this man to your party.

NIGHT CLOTHES

Traditional ninja (and all of those that make magazine covers) employed black suits and often hoods as most of their operations took place under the cover of darkness.

It is good to remember the real ninja were usually farmers, supporting a family, and did not rush out and buy fancy karate suits, but simply made their own uniforms from dark cloth.

There are a flood of ninja and ninja-like outfits on the market, many of which ARE simply karate gi's dyed black and upped in price, or constructed of inferior materials.

Personally I like a pair of simple drawstring tied "kung-fu" pants and a black T-shirt, if I am in a fancy dress mood I tend to wear my SHADOWS OF IGA T-Shirt and dark shoes.

Day time work out or operations tend to be simple camo...

A couple of our suppliers on the ninja page make good suits and if you wish an authentic version I would suggest you go to them.

Another alternative is the NIGHTSTALKER made by:

GEMINI INDUSTRIES
P.O. Box 20064
Oklahoma City, OK 73156

They produce a set of black combat fatigues that go for $55 a full set.

This includes a four pocket Nam type jacket but made from a cotton- poly fabric that is tough and durable.

The pants are six pocket GI style with full cargo pockets and a tab waist coupled with drawstring ties for the leg blousing.

A full set of extras can also be ordered including a black assault load harness that supports 2 magazines in pouches, a hip holster a canteen and a first aid kit.

One can also add various other mag pouches, black canteen and cover, black equipment belt and black cartridge belts.

Three different SWAT type hats (also black) are also available as well as various gear bags.

We were given a full NIGHTSTALKER set up for testing purposes and quite frankly I will not return it...

It is the perfect set up for ninja practice; after wearing out one of my favorite T shirts in one evening's practice I switched to their outfit...

It is heavy enough to keep you reasonably warm in most nights, fits perfectly, is large enough to put things on underneath if necessary, the pockets are perfect for carrying anything needed.

The fabric stands up to rolling around on hard ground with no wear and actually help take up some shock and makes small pointed objects seem a little less sharp...

Really no complaint about this product, it can be a trifle noisy when new if the operator rubs his legs together, but this soon passes with practice and age (either yours or the suit's).

A perfect package for practice or running around waterholes in the African night, believe me...

AMERICAN MILITARY INDUSTRIES
1204 Princess Anne st.
Fredericksburg, VA 22401

Makes a nylon jump suit with velcro waist, wrist and leg closures for a tight fit. The suit is one piece, rip stop nylon with two breast pockets, velcro closing cargo pockets, and zipper legs (if ordered) for over boot fits.

The jump suit, along with a fairly large line of hats, packs, bags, holsters, rain suits, mag cases, etc, is available in camouflage, black or drab.

YOU DON'T LOOK LIKE YOU SOUND-

Electronic Voice Altering Devices

There are a number of devices available for altering the characteristics of the human voice. All in all the devices do work.

This is the good news.

The bad news is many people are not happy with said devices after purchase (of same)...

Why?

The problem lies in the concept of voice changing. All the devices now available to the public alter the original input electronicly but only on the telephone. It is not reasonable to expect a unit, hidden on your chest, to amplify, alter, and reproduce your voice without anyone being the wiser...

Understanding this guideline still does not satisfy many would-be aural alters...

Many people assume a voice changer simply makes them sound like someone else, say Orson Wells, for example...Or say, their wife to a not-so-friendly bank teller looking over a joint account..

No, No; after all the sales brochure said it would alter your voice, it did NOT say per your ideal model.

They do alter, no disput here. Some do it by simple distortion, as if one was listening to an off frequency radio station. Some do it by fancier means but by and all every unit induces an alien factor that can drop volume, make the resulting audio almost (or completely) unintelligible,or at least make the other party wonder if he has mistakenly dialed into a new AT and T information robot that has twisted its chips and is freaking out.

The devices I tried tended to make people I called ask if;

    A. I was really that sick, should they call a doctor?
    B. I was back into old, old, drug induced bad habits?
    C. They knew me?
    D. I had been reported to the phone company for obscenity?

E. There was anyone on the line. Click. Dial tone.

By the way, never, never leave an altered message on a machine; it's bad enough in first person, reproduced there is no hope...

So why would anyone consider such an investment?

A couple of reasons come to mind.

Any of the devices can/will make you totally non-recognizable to your mother, say nothing of casual friends...

Done correctly, altered voices screw up any attempt at both PSE type (voice "lie detection") analysis and voice pattern idenification.

You know, the kind they use in court...

Uses? Obscene phone calls to close friends or ex-wives, tips, threats, or advice to any agency (or private party) that may be taping the conversation, avoiding PSE problems.

TESTING

We tested two different alteration units, chosen for their operating principles and low price:

Viking Electronics ECV
New Horizons Voice Changer

The Viking unit uses a digital method of breaking voice down into small frequency units and then rearranging the total structure. Power is from a 9 volt battery and a variable control allows infinite variations.

The unit fits over the standard phone mouthpiece and the user talks into a small microphone situated in the front of the unit.

Volume is decreased and the resulting audio can be difficult to decipher depending on the control setting.

It does alter and render PSE/voice print units useless.

It will not sound human.

New Horizons' choice (or their latest choice-they have sold several) actually fits between the phone handset and the body of the telephone with modular AT and T type plugs allowing ease of installation.

This unit is also powered by a 9 volt battery, however instead of the variable control it uses a combination of buttons and a rotary switch to produce several modes of change.

NH actually attempts to label each setting with choices like "will sound long distance", "makes your voice higher", "makes it lower", these descriptions are open to dispute.

Does it work?

Yes, but with the addition of much distortion, some low frequency motorboating, and many complaints from listeners.

Also, the damn battery doesn't last very long...

This unit does provide a "hold" feature which works and is priced in the $100 range.

Viking is in the $300 range.

CONCLUSIONS

Compared to the $1,000 and units on the market these two are bargains. The Viking is a better choice but neither device is going to convince anybody an unaltered voice (or person?) is at the other end of the magic line.

At times, especially when using long distance services, the party of the second part may not even understand the conversation, much less believe it emanates from a human being...

PERIMETER AND PREMISE SECURITY

This section will concentrate mainly on effective, cost efficient devices that can (for the most part) be used in a couple of different situations.

In CEP's book, No Cause For Alarm ALL types of alarm and security devices will be closely examined.

Perimeter Security

One of the simplest, and best, perimeter security devices is also the simplest. Like most of these devices a direct link to the military, Veitnam in particular, is obvious.

INTERTEK
1626 N Wilcox Suite 130
Los Angeles, Ca 90028

Makes a couple of units that are of interest. The first is called CAMPALERT, is a delightful little unit that consists of a 9 volt, battery powered control unit and a trip wire.

The control box has both an audio and visual alarm and can adapt to an earphone if a silent indication is desired.

The trip wire comes on a 1,000 foot spool and is about as thick as a human hair. It is attached to the control unit by slipping both ends of the wire into springs on top of the control unit.

The wire is then strung around a campsite, in a back yard, in front of doors or across stairs.

The trip wire is damn near invisible to the naked eye and breaks when anything goes through it. Even when the wire is broken the intruder will not notice the wire...

The unit can also be used in a briefcase as a opening alarm by carefully attaching the trip wire to the case cover so that the owner can reach inside and disconnect the alarm before the wire is broken.

If a wider alert area is desired an optional alarm horn can be plugged into the earphone jack.

Under $30 and a bargain.

INTERTEK also makes a larger and more sophisticated system; the CAMPALERT 2000.

Based on the same break-the-tripwire principle this unit incorporates a transmitter and pocket sized receiver.

Instead of an audible alarm the transmitter sends off a signal if the the wire is broken to the matching receiver at up to a 5 MILE distance.

Instead of a trip wire any break (normally closed) switch can be used such as window foil, reed switches, magnetic breakers etc. This extends the unit's operations so it can be used to guard a remote vehicle, RV, boat, campsite, etc.

This systems sells for $239 complete...

Quick And Dirty

Based on a Nam trip wire unit a device known as, yes, the TRIP-IT, is available from:

KEYSTONE SECURITY
Box 1028
Keystone Hgts, FL 32656

The TRIP-IT is an adjustable pull-pin spike that contains a primed .223 cartridge. 3 or more units can be driven into the ground and a wire strung between them in any perimeter shape desired.

When the wire is "tripped" the pin pulls out and a spring driven firing pin fires the cartridge.

We used the TRIP-IT in a game situation and discovered it has several immediate effects upon activation:

1. Pinpoints the intruder's location.
2. Alerts and awakens anyone who is not dead.
3. Scares the hell out of the intruder...

A couple of other suppliers feature units that explode and send up a flare to visually mark the unit that fired, but we found it was fairly easy to tell which spike had activated and at $15 a shot, excuse the pun, this is hard to beat.

STANO COMPONENTS carries a couple different types of Nam surplus seismic intrusion detectors.

These units are similar to the ones planted in operation Igloo White in Viewnam.

Each unit comes with four detectors which are buried around the perimeter in question. Any vibrations made by a man, vehicle or large animal within 30 feet or so of the detector will trigger the alarm signal.

One unit uses wires to communicate the alarm signal signal to the master, one is wireless...

The devices are rugged and sensitive and will work under difficult conditions.

Some problems with freezing ground, or marshland, transmitting the vibrations have occured...

SCRAMCO
832 W 1st st.
Birdsboro, PA 19058

Markets a unique electronic alarm system called the INTERCEPTER 1010, that actually stops crimes before they can progress...

As most criminals realize, after a burglar alarm goes off one normally still has several minutes to grab a few interesting items before vacating the premises.

Police hate to respond to alarm systems as they are susually false alarms and, if not, they face an unknown and possibly dangerous situation.

Neighbors are generally used to an alarm going off and will ignore it until it begins to bother them.

The above is doubly true in large cities...

The SCRAMCO control box is mounted (indoors) and set with any combination of normally closed switches and/or breakable foil.

When the circuit is tripped a loud alarm goes off for 20 seconds.

This gives the owner time to use a keyor trigger the hidden cut off switch.

If this is not accomplished, it will flood the entire area with CN stun gas...

Those of you that missed the Berkeley protests of the seventies, or army gas mask training have no clear grasp of the pain this lovely invention can cause.

It WILL cause anyone to leave the premises NOW!

It will not harm furniture or other inside equipment but will make the place unhabitable for some time.

It will save valuables.

Cost is about $300.

Simple Version

SECURITY CONTROL RESEARCH
Box 3660
Reading, PA 19605

Produces a little toy known as BURGLARMIST which is a mechanical version of the above unit.

The BURGLARMIST is a sealed plastic container with a nozzle at one end and a lever running up the side. A safety pin is inserted at the end of the lever and protected by tape.

One screws the unit onto a solid surface and then runs a trip cord across a hallway (not really a good idea) or onto a piece of valuable equipment such as a stereo, computer, typewriter, etc.

The pin is then removed.

A one inch movement of the lever (5 ounces of force) will empty enough CN gas to saturate 2,000 square feet.

We have also installed the unit (shown) into a briefcase to protect its electronic contents from prying eyes.

As their is no warning alarm on this device it is wise to remember placement details...

About $30.

At last, a security system that can actually STOP a burglar!

TWO BURGLAR ALARMS THAT ACTUALLY WORK

HARAGEI

The Shadow had the ability tocloud men's minds, but even he couldn't read them. While ninjutsu training may not actually develop the ability to read another person's mind, it can atune one to "feel" emotions, or intent. I have seen Stephen Hayes demonstrate this technique by sitting down crosslegged while a student stood behind him with a raised sword (wooden in this case, but real in Japan), he could not see any part of the student, nor were there any shadows or reflections.

His attacker was allowed to keep the sword poised for as long as he wished, 2 seconds to half an hour, and then strike as fast as possible with no prior warning.

As the sword began its blinding descent Stephen would spring to the side, avoiding the blow.

How is this possible?

Mr. Hayes would explain it as the trained ability to pick up the sudden emotion of rage (the student was told to strike with all the emotion of a real attack-to hold nothing back) and then react without thinking.

In THE NINJA (novel) the author speaks of "haragei" the evolved sensitivity that allows a person to enter a dark room and "feel" the presence of other people in a room.

Agents (and one would assume, burglars) are taught to rest silently after entering a strange room and "feel" the pulse of the area. Is anything different? Is there an unusual "presence" in the air? Does it feel at peace or is there tension there?

Try this next time you come home at night. Before turning on the lights wait a few seconds and take the pulse...

In fact I would advise doing this EVERY time you come home.

Any business negotiator will tell you he can "sense" changes during a meeting. Hippies used to speak of "vibes" (vibrations) coming from people when they were in an emotional state.

Almost every type of meditation allows for this "reading" of emotions or even thoughts. Even con artist "psychics" learn to pick up physical and some mental hints. Lie detector operators can often do as well or better without out their machines as they can with them simply by a practiced alertness.

MECHANICAL HARAGEI

Are there devices on the market which will duplicate these sensing skills? Can a machine read a mind?

Yes, and sort of...

A number of years ago two seperate projects were set up to utilize computers to "read" brainwaves.

One project was at Stanford Research Institute, the other at MIT. Both worked independently of their counterpart.

The idea was to invent a foolproof way of telling who was your enemy and who was your friend. At the time of this noble idea we were still involved in the Nam war and the fact that both friend and foe looked, dressed, and talked in the exact same fashion led to some Americans dying from "friends" and other Americans simply shooting anything with a yellow skin...

What a great concept; aim a reader at anyone and "sense" their thoughts. Think of the uses in business, government and poker...

I spoke to one of the people employed at the SRI project and the progress was startling, to say the least.

First they started with electrodes glued to the subjects scalp, as with a conventional EEG. The resulting brainwaves were then amplified and fed into a computer for analysis.

Once this was old hat, receivers were used to pick up the same weak waves without any connection to the subject.

How good were they?

Well the war ended and both projects were "disbanded". The PhD at Stanford was able to receive thoughts at a distance and pick out most emotions as well as some words.

As well as some words...

This was 10 (or so) years ago; a few years after this the same Dr. tried to sell a small machine to banks all over the country that would instantly identify anyone from his brain wave pattern.

And you thought fingerprints were bad...

After both projects were "shut down" the two scientists became very difficult to find, much less talk to. Think how far technology has come since that time...

Can the government "read minds"?

No solid evidence, but I would not bet my life savings against it...

Can you buy such a device?

No, but you can get one that will do many of the things the hero in NINJA was able to do...

Made by Polaroid it's called the Rangefinder and is a sound based personal radar system. An ultrasonic generator feeds high frequency sound waves through a transducer which radiate out in front of the Rangefinder and bounce off any solid objects in its path.

The returning sonic waves are picked up and "read" by the unit. This means you can enter a room and immediately know the location of every object in the room as well as their exact distance from you.

The device can also be utilized to detect motion, allowing a portable alarm system to be constructed, or to allow you to follow any moving target.

The range on the unit is 35 feet and it is very accurate. Stronger versions may be released soon, but even 35 feet is very useful for most enclosed spaces or campsites.

Under $200 from Polaroid or many dealers.

BECAUSE IT'S THERE...

Traditional ninja were thought to be able to go through walls as if they did not exist as solid objects. One of the main reasons for this was the ability to climb straight up slick walls that were considered to be totally safe.

The two inventions that allowed this illsion to continue were the shuko and the ashiko, needle sharp claw-bands for the hands and the feet.

The shuko were steel/iron bands that fit around the hands and then were secured by a leather wrist strap.

They usually had four claws that curved downward providing both leverage and grip.

Shuko were used for climbing everything from trees to rock walls, as well as allowing the the ninja to actually grab a sword and rip it from the hands of the wielder.

They were also employed as weapons to rip the hell out of unprotected enemies.

Ashiko provided solid grip on most any surface, gave footing in wall climbing and could also deliver a ripping kick...

These devices are still available in their original formats, see our supplier's section.

Personally I will climb a tree or wooden structure with these two ninja helpers. I do not like heights and have a very unnatural fear of early death.

I will NOT climb any hard or slick surface with them.

So, now what?

There are a whole number of devices used by glaziers to transport heavy sheets of glass from one area to another. The things in question must not slip from slick surfaces, and be able to hold heavy weights.

They are known as hand vacuum cups and operate in several different ways.
They all consist of a rubber cup with some sort of device for creating a vacuum, thereby sticking the cup to the surface. They are designed to supply a sticking pressure of 500 to 1,000 pounds per unit.

Most are designed to operate on a smooth surface, although a few will grip irregular surfaces also.

A good second story man will establish the vacuum, use the cup as a holding point while placing the second cup a few feet above, then the vacuum is released and the process repeated.

Some of the "climbers" I spoke with liked the triple positive lock unit for the safety factor, others liked the pump up models for the additional suction but pointed out that if one's knee hit the release lever by accident, it was an unhappy experience.

A number of human "flies" have climbed tall buildings using exactly these units.

Like I say, I harbor a fear of high places, I would have been the ninja they let in the back door after someone else did the up the wall number, but if this is you, carry both, maybe use foot spikes and hand vacuum; whatever works...

Don't look down...

The other climbing methods such as the grapling hook, are described elsewhere.

It must have been a scary feeling to wake up to four black suited gentlemen in a room in a castle thought to be totally safe...

These suction cup devices are available from glazier's supply stores in major cities, or from the source we have listed.

They work well, but there is no fallback in case of failure.

No pun intended...

STRAIGHT UP

A Look At Playing Spiderman...

Who hasn't at least dreamed of climbing unclimbable walls, scaling Guns-Of-Navorone cliffs, leaping tall buildings (or fences) in a single bound?

Ninja of old were thought by many to be able to go through solid walls, a tale they did little to down play.

In reality, the ninja were excellent climbers and, aided by several secret devices, could scale almost any wall no matter how steep or slick it appeared.

Coupled with the fact that this was often done in total blackness while wearing a black uniform, led to the through-the-wall stories.

Nobody could come up with any other answer to their sudden appearances in "secure" areas...

A set of good, sharp, strong, ninja claws and footspikes can be a great aid in scaling trees, wooden walls, sheet rock, and some walls made of hard rock or brick (this is usually done by utilizing the softer mortar) in between the individual rocks.

Practice on a soft wood tree USING A SAFETY BELT OR OTHER PROTECTIVE DEVICES, to get the idea of digging the claws in to the correct depth to allow support but still let one remove the hand or foot when desired.

Nothing is more embarrassing than to have the local fire department pull one from a tree in full ninja garb...

Also, try to pick a tree that not too valuable.

Technology has come to the rescue here by adapting a product from another field.

Glaziers, people who risk life and limb by installing huge sheets of glass that can break into shards and cut people to cat food for no reason, (one of our editors had his 1 and 1/2 year old girl sit in front of the local grocery store and tap on the main window with her plastic AIR FILLED hammer. It came down in a million pieces) use a form of vacuum cup that can securely grab onto slick surfaces and withstand a pull of several hundred pounds.

These cups are operated by closing a front pump, or pumping our the air by pushing on a side button. When the grip is over the vacuum is emptied by releasing the pump switch.

A number of people have made headlines by scaling slick, modern style skyscrapers by using two or more of these units to grab and then release, increasing their climb by an arm's reach each time.

The surface to be climbed must be very slick and unbroken for this idea to work properly.

Several types of units are available from the traditional front loading single units to triples that give better odds of staying gripped if one unit fails...

Some people tend to like the side pump units because a stray knee can not hit the release accidently and provide a sudden "surprise".

These can be purchased directly from the factory:

> CR LAURENCE
> 800-421-6144 or in California 800-372-6361

Or from:

> COBEL GLASS, INC.
> 400 Franklin st
> Oakland, Ca 94607 no catalog, please don't bother unless serious

Or from your local glazier's supply company.

- **Pump Actuated**
- **Quick Release**
- **Red-Warning Indicator**

CRL Double Cup

- **No. 1 Seller**
- **Industry Proven**

Two 5″ one-piece rubber bases make this double vacuum cup lifter the most practical way to put a handle on glass, marble, granite or any smooth surface material. Used for setting mirrors, removing salvage, handling structural glass, etc. Weighs only 3½ pounds.

NINJA MEETS SPIDERMAN

Modern day glazier's suction cups that have been used to climb some of the tallest buildings in the world and SCORPION ENTERPRISES' great ninja claws.

Both work for the correct application.

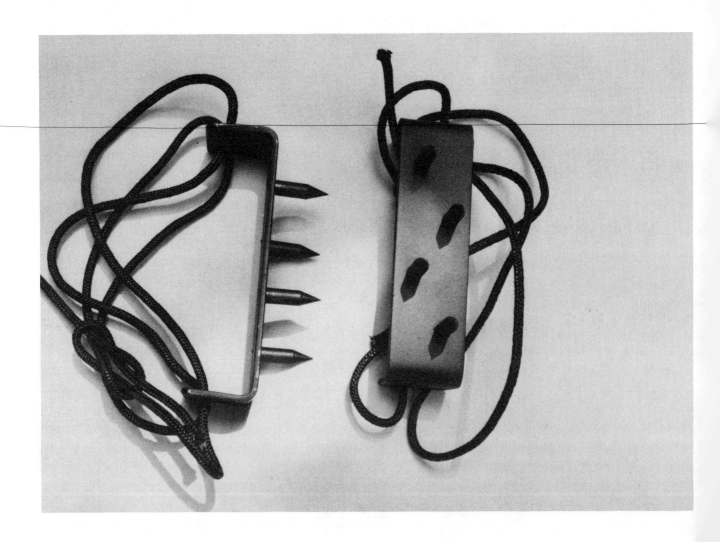

LOGIC, MAGIC AND INTENTION

One of the great "secrets" of ninpo has been their use of "magic" hand symbols coupled with a drive and follow through that seemed to let them accomplish things no "mortal" man could accomplish.

What were/are these techniques and how do they apply to today's modern world of mental and physical hassles?

Each particular ninja "school", or more likely, family, had its own set of "magic" hand symbols, chants, mental image reinforcement and accomplishment tricks.

Even so, most of these can be looked at from a bottom rung level and one can gain much...

Now do not take this as an all-encompassing explanation of ninja mind techniques; that would be, quite frankly, far above me, or most anyone else, especially those that would claim to have such knowledge.

As Stephen Hayes has said, "think of ninjutsu as a multi-petaled flower (actually he said a Chrysanthemum, but I can't spell that), and each of these techniques is but one petal of the total flower."

Now each petal may be pretty and complete within itself, but it is not the total flower.

Okay, so much for the philosophical end of things, down to the above bottom rung.

One the the main ninja secrets is one of the simplest.

And like many simple things, it works...

Most things in life, whether they are physical wants or needs, or less tangible items can be achieved by following a "ninja" formula.

Oddly enough, it is one that holds up to modern science also...

One can get almost anything in this life if a three pronged approach is used:

1. Intention
2. Intelligence

3. Physical

Let's look at each one on an individual basis;

Intention is just that. DEFINE YOUR GOAL. One must state (or write) exactly what is the desired end result. This seems so bloodly simple, and is so often over-looked.

Many goals remain cloudly or ill-defined in one's mind. Wanting to be rich and famous or beating one's enemy is not a clearly defined goal.

State the actual intent, analyze it and then use one or more symbols to reinforce that intent when it gets pushed to the back of the mind by current, but more trivial pursuits.

It sounds like a joke, but when I started writing, more years ago than I care to admit, I decided it was for fortune, not fame.

Writing is NOT a glamour edged job unless you are in charge of the PLAYBOY foldout interviews ("well, I want to be President and bring love and joy to the whole world and drive a Porsche"), and it gets damn boring at times.

When I had defined my goal and things started getting diffused, I would use a technique from The Book Of Five Rings called Rat's Head/Ox Neck, which simply translated means to step back from yourself and your situation and see what is really happening.

What is bogging one down.

Then I would go down to the local Ferrari dealer and look at the Dino's. Sometimes I would even sit in one or drive one. I bought a Ferrari key chain (I am not making this up, as poetic license oriented as it sounds).

This became my symbol of intent and brought me back to this damn keyboard many times.

No I never got the Dino.

Today I drive a 365 Ferrari and a Cosworth Lotus, two of the fastest cars on the road...

Intelligence does not refer to one's IQ, rather to the ninja habit of always gathering and then assembling all possible facts on any situation before formulating a plan of attack.

Intelligence gathering is the world's second or third oldest occupation, although it has been called by less flattering names.

It does not mean (not necessarily mean) spying. It means research in whatever form is necessary to get information directly related to the problem at hand (achieving one's intention).

As an editor of mine once said, "copying from one source is plagiarism, from two is research."

Ninja's were experts at intelligence and this ability was one of the main reasons they survived and defeated enemy forces many times their strength.

Ninja of old often did this by blending in, becoming farmers, actors, merchants, whatever it took to assemble the necessary facts.

So should today's.

Remember the word "ninja" means, roughly, "to prevail".

This takes a combination of intelligence and intention.

Now as to the nuts and bolts on intelligence gathering, The Big Brother Game, How To Get Anything On Anybody and this work of art all deal with various ways to accomplish this.

Any complied intelligence is only as good as its method of access. Talk about luck, and the perfect place for the second plug in as many paragraphs, How To Get etc. details a very nice system of information storage and access.

The final leg of our three pronged tier is physical, or performance.

If the first two legs have been completed correctly this should be the easiest, yet it often is the hardest in reality.

It is one thing to plan, dream collect facts and be ready. It is quite another thing to act.

Removing this gap between intention and action is best accomplished by the use of timing. Being "in phase" in electronics is best explained when each part of the supply signal is moving in the same direction at the correct time.

So it is with life.

Timing is not easily learned; sometimes it must be a gut instinct as when to move, sometimes it can be the occurance of expected actions which trigger a natural opening, sometimes it comes from practicing ninjutsu until "motion becomes no motion" and the time is just there.

This whole process is an interlocking unit. If any leg fails the triangle fails. The three legged stool collaspes.

It is necessary to constantly reinforce each and every part of this three pronged approach. This can be done with the use of physical reminders, as already detailed, or by the use of "magic ninja hand signs".

These signs, consisting of various positions of interlocking fingers are used for several reasons, the primary one being an instant method of association with previous conditioning (or hypnosis, if you will) to bring back a feeling in all five senses of a set of circumstances.

This instant replay is set up by an excerise in meditation, breathing and body position. The student is encouraged to close his eyes and visualize, with all five senses an event, real or not, that produces a feeling of power or peace, or intent or anger.

When one can totally experience this vision and the feeling that goes with it, a hand positioning exercise can be employed so the total experience is coupled with this physical action.

If this is repeated until it becomes natural one can bring on the same experience by simply recreating the hand position.

This aligns one's energy to a given situation in an instant.

This ability to bring on a fire, or attack condition by folding one's hands into an unusual position had a secondary effect on the enemy of believing the mysterious hand folding produced a magic effect on the user as well as the target.

Which, in effect, it did...

This is not a metaphysical event but a practical application of total recall. If you can already use hypnosis (self or otherwise) to create a needed situation try to couple it with this idea.

If you never have experienced this try attending some classes, reading books on self hypnosis or use some of the conditioning tapes we have listed along with hand position recall.

Again the "secret" system can be listed as:

1. Visualize/intention
2. Seek details/research/investigate
3. Movement/action/physical with timing

Reinforce by meditation/practice.

Use symbols.

It works.

I apologize to Mr. Hayes for "borrowing" (research) many of his ideas and statements for this section.

BETTER LIVING THROUGH CHEMISTRY

Chemicals, those wonderous harbingers of fun, artificial sweeteners, and nylons play an interesting role in our unfolding story.

For obvious reasons it is impossible to include every chemical that might fall into our relm, so we will concentrate on some of the most interesting...

RICIN

A distilled product of the common castor bean, ricin is one of the most deadly poisons known to man.

When a 1/1 millionth part of ricin is introduced to the human blood stream several unusual things occur; after a three day delay nausea, vomiting, diarrhea, pain, drowsiness, stupor, pain hemorrhaging, asthma...

Followed by death.

The ricin can be introduced by eating, but the most potent reactions seem to occur when the compound is either breathed into the lungs or imbedded under the skin as in a projectile or injection.

In such cases 1/2000th of a GRAIN can be fatal.

When ricin poisoning takes effect the reaction is almost impossible to identify.

There is no antidote in either case. It is always fatal in the proper quantity. It strikes three days after ingestion and is im- possible to trace or cure.

Several years ago a number of legioniares at a convention in San Francisco California all came down with a mysterious disease with the same outward symptoms as ricin poisoning.

Most of the ill died at a local hospital. The mysterious disease was named "legioniares disease" after the victims.

A year or so later the FBI came out with a clouded statement that the "disease" was caused by a foreign substance in the air conditioning system of the hotel where the victims were holding their convention.

Ricin is most effective when ingested through the air...

Did they die of some bizarre experiment? I don't know, but ricin does cause "legionaires disease".

One can make this daedly poison by a fairly simple process (there is a US patent on the subject and various people have done more specific follow-up research) but it is a process that should not be attempted by anyone not trained in chemistry.

With death from as little as 1/2000 of a grain, it is just too easy to slip and break a beaker or have a tube explode...Neither one of us really wants to be the target of a number of lawsuits from Mothers Against Poison (MAP) and one of us does have some semblence of a conscience...

On the other hand, one can actually purchase pure ricin from at least one of the suppliers we have listed and our old friend KURT SAXTON details the manufacturing process quite well in his publication, THE WEAPONEER.

Be certain to read the entire publication before starting any experi- mentation as several updates are printed in the latter end...

Bullets can easily be enhanced with ricin by wetting a small portion and loading it into a hollow point bullet and then sealing the mess with glue.

IT IS A FEDERAL OFFENSE TO POSSESS POISONED BULLETS!!

DMSO

Good old dimethylsulfoxide, once illegal (except for animal use with a script) this "wonder drug" is used to break down clotted blood, help the healing process and ease the pain of internal or bone diseases.

DMSO is one of the most powerful solvents known to man and will pene- trate skin and muscle tissue like it was a sponge.

DMSO also has the ability to "carry" anything which can be entered into its solution. If one mixes lemon juice in DMSO and applies it to the body, the lemon will "appear" on the tongue in a few seconds...

Any poison or drug that will mix with the solvent will also be carried into the body.

This means DMSO/bad stuff can be applied to steering wheels, after shave, perfume, hand rails, shoes, you see the possibilities...

Of course, once it dries the thrill is gone...

VENOMS

A number of vile animals stock their own form of protection as organic poisons. The various snakes are a good example of this practice.

If one attends cocktail parties with poison snakes and happens to get bit death usually occurs within a couple of minutes at the outset.

Examples of this are the cobra, krait, coral etc. Those with nero poisons are usually the deadliest.

Venoms can be mixed with DMSO, placed in foods stuffs, packed in bullets, glued to darts, injected, mixed with toothpaste, on and on.

Now all one has to do is catch a cobra...No there is an easier but less fun method of obtaining the mucus output of our furless friends...

Buy it.

Several of the suppliers...you know the rest. It ain't cheap but it is effective.

NICOTINE

Yes, a deadly poison, can be purchased or "soaked" from common tobacco, several books detail the process including THE POOR MAN'S JAMES BOND.

Can also be extracted from a very efficient insect poison known as Black Leaf 40. See the WEAPONEER for process.

CYANIDE

Cyanide, (usually potassium) is a deadly poison which is often mixed in with food and fed to barking dogs or barking spouses.

It usually proves deadly.

This chemical can be easily purchased alone or is often found in rat poison mixtures. When mixed with sulphuric acid a very deadly gas is formed that will flood the immediate area wiping out all life.

Both Black leaf 40 and cyanide can be mixed with DMSO at a ratio of about 4 (DMSO) to 1 for effective aabsorption.

FORMALDAHYDE

Easily purchased at chemical supply houses or even drug stores (used to perserve lab animals; dead, lab animals that is) formaldahyde is an extremely bothersome chemical when sprayed into someone's face from a nasal inhaler bottle, hypo, or plastic squeeze bottle.

At close range this treatment is more effective than tear or stun gas...

If one mixes form with cyanide and DMSO and then sprays it onto an attacker, death and destruction is the immediate result.

It is important to remember that if one's trusty nose spray bottle leaks while enclosed in one's trusty pocket, one's death will be the immediate result...

DOA.

CHEMICAL SUPPLIERS

City Chemical Corp 132 W 22 st New York, NY 10011

Sells only to "companies", so please don't pencil them a letter on lined paper...1 lb minimum, good prices.

CASTOR BEANS Available from any good nursery. 1 bean is considered poisonous to a human.

D&R ENTERPRISES Box 14741 Cleveland, OH 44114

Cyanide, various explosive powders, lumps, metal powders.
Price list $1.00.

AARDVARK INDUSTRIES PO Box 35066 Louisville, KY 40218

"We must emphasize these chemicals are for research only and in no instance should be used as pharmaceuticals or drugs or food additives or household chemicals nor in the manufacture of such".
DMSO, betel nut extract (brush, brush your teeth with...), curare, ricin, cobra-coral-pit viper venom, semi-drugs-semi-ex- plosives, etc.
Catalog $2.00.

K.O. SALES 3341 W Peoria #227 Phoenix, AR 85029

Rare ("un") chemicals and equipment.

WESTECH Box 593 Logan, UT 84321
Unusual chemicals, black powder, explosives, etc.

CAMOUFLAGE

As the ninja were often thought of as the invisible warriors one must assume they understood the magic of camouflage quite well.

They did...

From at least one standpoint the ninja of old had an easier job of becoming "invisible"; they did most of their work after night making camo a simple job of turning black.

Almost every ninja clothing piece, weapon, and skin covering concoction was, as Henry Ford once said, "in any color you want, so long as it's black."

This same idea still applies with only a few exceptions as we shall see.

When a traditional ninja needed daytime camo he usually employed natural substances such as branches and dirt to hide in.

At least with modern technology one certainly has more flexibility in choosing the correct blend of blending...

Before we get into the more traditional formats of camo let's look one of the newest arrivals on the scene. Most blending materials are designed to fit in with some type of foilage, either complete evergreen or some shading of brown-orange leaves.

The major exceptions to this are desert camo with its browns and yellows, night black coverings and pure white snow camo.

No one seems to have considered the idea of blending in with the actual tree, see, instead of with the various shades, shapes, and spikes of the many different trees, bushes, and enemy uniforms all mixed in most environments.

Trees, or at least most of them I have been on familiar terms with, do all have bark.

Get it?

Of course you do, you were smart enough to buy this book, right?

Designed with the bow hunter in mind (deer hunting season often falls about the same time the leaves do), this version can be employed all year round.

It is very good for position hunting where one spends much time in or about barked trees.

Sold by:

BOWING ENTERPRISES
Box 6076
Arlington, VA 22206

They carry every possible piece of gear except for underwear and ties; coveralls, jackets, pants, vests, shirts, butt pack, caps, and so on.

COV-U-ALL, INC.
1716 Main Unit 3
Venice, Ca 90291

Sells a number of two piece camo/orange/white outfits as well as cheap (inexpensive that is) one piece coveralls that are made from a tough fiber that will fold up small enough to be carried in a normal sized pocket allowing for instant access if a flurry of ducks suddenly attacks you in the middle of an open marsh and you are sans your fully automatic 10 guage and need to hide quickly.

They are also nice to toss into the old butt pack or vest pocket just in case.

Now for the piece de resistance, the suits are fully reversible with a completely different pattern on the other side, giving you two, two, two choices in one as they say in bubble gum...

Prices are great at $10 for the one piece coveralls. Colors run br-gr, br-wh, or straight white/orange non-reversible models.

We liked our test unit very much but found the sizes to run a bit on the large size so you may want to order down a trifle.

An interesting sidebar is the appearance of vinyl camo tape on the market. The tape is avaialble in a couple of widths and can be used to "sudden" camo any rifle, pistol, bow, small child, dog, and so on at short notice.

The vinyl construction leaves no sticky residue behind and can be unwrapped and even reused if necessary.

Made by:

KANE CO

5572 Brecksville rd
Cleveland OH 44131

We have already seen it being sold in a number of other catalogs.

CITY CAMO

In the days of old, when knights were bold...Ninja used to disguise themselves as farmers, showpeople, or simple wandering pilgrims living off spare change contributions.

This is hard to do in today's world, unless you live in San Francisco.

Okay, cop out time, following article reprinted from How To Get Anything On Anybody, because there really isn't much else to say...

Principles of Camouflage

Matching Background
a color or
pattern that
reflects light the
way
its surroundings
do.

Disruptive Coloration: Patterns that break up a silhouette; identification is difficult.

Counter-Shading:
Contrasts between shadowed
and unshadowed areas are
diminished by making the top darker
and the bottom lighter.

Netting: An object and its shadows are camouflaged when contours are modified by nets.

God's own camouflage in action.

Lee by tree and water hole; no camo.

Scott entering bush with camo on.

Scott beginning to break up natural lines and right angles.

Find the Scott in the bush...

COV-U-ALL, INC.
1716 Main st
Venice, CA 90291

Made from a new material called Tyvek, these suits fold up like paper, can be carried in a glove compartment, yet are tough and washable.

These are the cheapest suits on the market and come in one piece, or two piece models and even in winter-white.

CAMOUFLAGE JUMPSUITS

Camouflage - the added edge! Get the added edge needed to make every hunt a success with the Cov-U-All CAMOUFLAGE JUMPSUIT. Our water and wind resistant Jumpsuit, scientifically designed to never mildew or rot, slips over any clothing and folds up to pocket size. This zippered Jumpsuit weighs only ounces and fulfills all the requirements of the Federal Flammable Textile Act. When you're ready to hunt our Jumpsuit is ready to make you vanish into the brush! Examine the photos below. You'll see that the Brown-Green Reversible Jumpsuit is perfect for any type of hunting in Spring, Summer or Fall! Order Brown-White Reversible for Fall, Winter or Spring. Also available, as shown in the photo at right, are Artic Hunting Jumpsuits, with or without hoods; and Luminescent Orange Jumpsuits to protect you from careless hunters in the field.

TREEBARK CAMO which actually blends in with the bare-bark pattern of a tree rather than depending on foilage for cover.

First designed for bow hunters in a winter setting, it can be utilized in any area where large trees exist.

Our model has TREEBARK pants and a complete mask, but is using a normal style camo jacket. The entire TREEBARK line includes shirts, pants, masks, and jackets.

FUTURE SOLDIER

Our child star walks through the screen provided by an army surplus M 15 smoke gernade. Note the cover is thick enough for assault or retreat.

RECOGNITION

As the goal of any camouflage operation is either to remain hidden in the face of the enemy, or to flush out those who would endeavor to remain hidden; recognition comes into the spotlight.

There are a number of factors which prevent target recognition along with/besides pure camouflage.

These factors go hand in hand with camo and will make or break any attempt at covert operations.

Some of these factors are:

Movement: Avoid all unnecessary movement. If one is backdropped against an immobile background any movement will highlight the target at once.

As such a complete lack of movement in a street crowd situation will also point out a target like a rock in a flowing stream.

Gait and height from the ground will show up a man where an animal (or a man who had studied the local fauna) might well pass unnoticed.

Use all available cover in ANY SITUATION. Said cover will break up and blend in mankind with any background.

If possible try for travel in rain or other inclement weather to help hide movement.

Color: Besides using camo clothes one must realize that the quick flash of a watch, gunbarrel, ring or other uncovered toys is a sure sign of that-which-belongs-elsewhere...

Cover them, or use camo tape.

Sun glanced from white skin (actually the oil on the skin) really screams out "look over here", just like in those old Ronald Reagan cowboy movies.

Skin toning is best done with commercial camo creams but can be accomplished with charcoal, mud, burnt cork, carbon paper, or anything else that blends with the surroundings.

The other method of skin toning is break up the human shape by disruptive painting. In this style one cuts across eye sockets, noses, chins and other obvious features.

One other effective method to hide men or equipment is to use scim or camo netting to cover men or equipment; breaking up their obvious lines to airborne or even surface surveillance.

A final, effective method is to dig individual foxholes for important soldier hiding (remember we have backpack nuclear devices 250 times more powerful than good old Hiroshima) is still a very effective method of hiding (see Japan's habit of digging spider holes during WW II to hide behind the line sappers.) If the digging can be done at night and the material removed before daylight, the better.

If not, artificial netting or camo materials may well outdo the available natural brush for hiding the the project.

In war "games" I have participated in, some people (perhaps borderline fanatics) would hide under ice cold-winter streams for up to 1/2 of an hour, only to jump up to "stab" a warm enemy...

Position: Never hide next to a bush; always hide IN a bush (see the photos for the difference), never hide near a crowd, hide (yup, you got it,) IN a crowd. Always be in harmony with your envirnoment. Remember the nearer one is to the hunter the more obvious one is and vica versa.

In rural blending always, always, travel BELOW the skyline as not to become a silhouette against the sky. It is much more difficult to pick out a camouflaged person against a varying background than it is against a solid sky.

Shape: The human shape is quite recognizable when presented in "normal" format. If the image is purposely distored it becomes much more "invisible".

Again see the photos where Scott breaks up the lines of his body to conform with the local flora.

Gone...

Sound: Using sound wisely can make or break any camo op; if possible minimize all noise, if not, take care to BLEND IN with the normal background noise of the area.

Work to develop habits that mimic walking noises; attempt to walk on surfaces that are hard and do not cause give-away sounds. When walking near a creek, don't walk in the tell-tale mud, walk in the stream, use soft grass for a walk base when ever possible placing the feet down in an even manner with the weight evenly distributed on the edges or the entire foot.

Avoid dry twigs and sticks, when going through high grass use high steps so that the grass is not disturbed except where the actual placement occured.

American indians used to place the ball of the foot down on a solid-no noise surface, and then follow it with the edges of the foot and heel.

Never carry any keys or other noise makers on one's person.

Snow can be a real hazard as far noise is concerned, except with crusty snow where it is possible to poke a hole through the crust of the snow and then slip the rest of the foot through the noisy crust into the quiet interior.

If everything is dry and crackly, place a pair of heavy wool socks OVER one's shoes to quench the sound of heavy foot steps on/in almost every surface.

Try not to move too rapidly, watch where you are putting your footsteps, learn to constantly turn your head to watch, learn and listen in order to utilize all your senses.

If possible scout ahead and plan ahead to find blend vantage points along either a rural or civilized route.

Rather than redo an entire section of a book most of you already possess just for the stake of padding, read the section in How To Get Anything On Anybody on city tailing and surveillance to supplement this section.

--Observe
--Utilize
--Blend in
--Merge
--Keep down and quiet.

BODYFOOD

You are what you eat. If someone is serious about rapid strength and bodily development there are a couple of methods that can be used to cheat the normal timing of muscle producing tissue.

In the first place NO body building or up-strength program will work without 2 things; a weight lifting or other exercise program that will increase mass and build up tone in the part of the body you are interested in, and an adequate supply of high calorie/high protein food to use as muscle fodder.

No real advice on the exercise portion, there are a lot of good books and most gyms have one or more experts that can help set up what you want and how you want it.

If you are interested in one certain sport or martial art it is always a good procedure to ask the instructor for his training tips and incorporate them into your routine.

One thing we have noticed, however, is that machines (nautilus, universal, etc.) do make training more efficient in terms of time spent versus number of reps and different exercises.

Machines do not, no matter what the brochures say, help with balance or work on specific muscles and muscle groups like free weights do.

In my humble opinion you should mix the two systems for best results, if you only have access to one system or the other, I would (as would most body builders and martial artists) prefer free weights.

On the food end a serious effort requires something in the area of 6,000-8,000 calories of intake per day. This intake should ideally consist of a balanced, high protein diet with a low fat content.

This almost demands the use of a "weight-on" type of protein supplement to meet the necessary requirements. I find the ones made from milk and egg to be much easier on the taste buds and stomach than the soybean versions, but if you happen to like spooning out globs of brown-sticky cement like glue, and then eating it, do try the soybean supplements...

This program alone will work for anyone. Now for the cheating:

Anabolic steroids are drugs which increase the mass/size of the muscle cell. They have been used for years by body builders and many athletic types.

Perhaps you remember when the east german woman's swim team showed up for the olympics about 8 years ago, looking like something out of an Edgar Rice Borough's novel and winning most of the events.

Until they took the urine test...

These drugs do work and with a minimum of side effects. Why doesn't everyone use them? Several factors, including that many are not legal in the US (at least for humans), many events now require blood or urine tests which can show up the chemical helpers, there are some side effects to some drugs, some are difficult to get, and there is much misunderstanding about steroids.

This is not designed to be a complete course in a.s. use, but only to show the potential of these drugs and give a couple of reference points.

Some steroids can be gotten by a doctor's prescription. These are often injectables, meaning a number of semi-costly trips to the doctor's office (about twice a week on the average), and often a too light dosage as many doctors do not know what level of steroids will produce the best results as there are not a lot of good reference works on this program.

Steroids fall into two categories, oral and injectable. Orals are easier to take, can be done at home (as can injectables if gotten from a non-medical source) but tend to cause more possible side effects including liver trouble.

We put someone on a program of steroids/food/exercise for a couple of months and the results are recorded at the end of this article.

Our test case is NOT a scientific proof type test, nor are the dosages he used necessarily best for your body. Some experimentation with types of drugs and dosages is mandatory for best results.

Some possible side effects to watch for, and to switch to another drug if they appear are:

yellowing of the skin or liver trouble
too much water retention
joint pain

Again the injectables seem to cause less problems than the orals do. A further piece of advice on the orals is to place them under the tongue until they dissolve as to be taken directly into the blood stream rather than be partially destroyed by the stomach.

Our favorite orals are:

Dianabol- Probably the most widely used steroid. Quite effective at muscle mass upgrades. Can be gotten from a doctor or other sources including Mexico and Europe.

Anadrol- A very effective oral that is similar in results to Dianabol and can be used when a plateau is reached on dianabol weight gains. A bit morre expensive than dianabol and can be harder on the liver, watch for yellowing of eye whites and skin.

INJECTIBLES

Decadurabolin- (Deca) The old standby injectible. Good for body building, power lifting, and increasing strength. Runs about $20 a shot from doctors, $5-$10 on an inject yourself basis. Few side effects and has a generic form that is even cheaper.

Equipoise- A "new" drug being used by jocks the world over, this particular steroid is ony given to animals (horses and such) in the US. Few side effects and quite a good record in the weight lifting world, although a bit hard to come by on the black market and a trifle expensive. Tends to work on both muscle size and strength.

Another very interesting steroid/hormone that will see much press in the next few years is call Human Growth Hormone.

This unusual drug actually makes MORE muscle cells, unlike most steroids that only increase the size of available cells HGH increase the number of the cells.

Now used in Japan and Europe it is illegal in America, but pressure may change that in the near future.

Again, this is just a quick once over of this interesting field. If anyone is serious about anabolic steroids one should subscribe to the Underground Steroid Handbook and its bi-monthly updates (book $12 and $12 a year for the newsletters).

These people are THE authorities on this subject and will provide state of the art sources for many of the steroids as well as use and dosage.

> OEM Publishing
> 2801 B Ocean Park Blvd
> Suite 25
> Santa Monica Ca 90405

A final note; most stories about steroids are simply not true...Yes, some are made from animal hormones and for a while there was some problems as inferior steroids were on the market but these have pretty well been taken care of.

were on the market but these have pretty well been taken care of.

In fact, after meeting a number of our readers I would say these drugs are much less dangerous than those about half of your are already abusing...

TANFAST

If one wants to change one's appearance in a non-radical fashion and in fact, one that usually enhances one's looks as a side effect, consider getting tanned.

Quickly.

There are two ways to produce a natural looking tan without a trip to Hawaii; although Hawaii is a hell of a lot more fun than what I am about to describe...

The sun lamps developed in the last few years that produce both A and B type ultraviolet rays will produce a real, fairly natural tan within a couple of weeks if used 1/2 an hour a day.

Suntan parlours that charge 6 or 7 bucks a session will produce this effect.

There is another way.

The skin is tanned by two factors, one is the release of melanin (a dark pigment) in the skin, and the amount of a chemical called beta carotene contained in the fat cells directly below the skin.

This chemical is one of a family known as carotenoids and several are used as coloring agents in "all-natural" foods.

The yellow of a carrot is produced by one type of carotenoid. In fact, if you drank enough carrot juice, lots of carrot juice, your fat cells would take in this chemical and turn your skin a nice healthy shade, of yellow...

Another carotenoid called canthaxanthin, also called simply canthax, if ingested, will turn these fatty cells a healthy shade of bronze-red.

In effect, tanning you from the inside out.

If one consumes about 120 milligrams of canthax a day for two to three weeks, one will turn a dark tan.

This tan will also protect you from sunburn and some research shows it may actually reduce or remove the chance of skin cancer during exposure to ultraviolet rays.

After your tan is the shade you want, the dosage can be cut back to about half in order to maintain the color.

Once you stop taking the chemical the tan will gradually fade away in about 3 weeks.

A commercial brand of canthax called Orobronze is sold over the counter in Canada for just this purpose.

It has not been approved by the FDA in this county for this purpose , yet, at any rate, but can be found in some health food stores and in the back of health magazines as an "organic coloring agent."

It works.

HAND CONDITIONING

In the days of old when night were bold...Martial artists conditioned their hands to a degree that allowed them to fight folks dressed in battle armor with only bare hands (karate; empty hand).

This is not nearly as important today, you really don't see that many people wandering the bars and back alleys dressed in battle gear. Yet there is no denying the damage a steel-hardened hand can do to flesh and bone.

There are a number of drawbacks to severe hand conditioning; trying to much in too little time can easily break knuckles or even bones in the hand. There is some evidence to the fact that people with conditioned hands are more subject to arthritis than are normal people and severe conditioning can cause some loss of dexterity of the fingers.

The first danger is a real one, it is easy to become too involved with rushing things along, coupled with a certain numbness to pain that comes with conditioning, and injure the hands.

I have broken at least two knuckles that I know of over the last few years...They hurt...

Contrary to many movies, the side of the hand is not the place most utilized in fighting and does not need the same degree of hardness as do the knuckles, which take the bulk of the punishment.

There are two traditional knuckle hardening philosophies; in most karate the first two knuckles of each hand are hardened by hitting the makawara (a padded board with some built-in spring) and doing pushups on a hard surface while balanced on the first knuckles.

This treatment works and generally enlarges those knuckles until they can reach the size of eggs in a veteran fighter. Of course, one must be sure to strike ONLY with those two knuckles when power punching.

The chinese arts usually employ other methods which produce different results. Wing Tsun, probably the best known form of chinese boxing which incorporates hardening (Bruce Lee's orginial style) utilizes a method which works quite well.

In Wing Tsun the punches are thrown from the centerline of the body and strike, usually in the vertical position, with all knuckles striking the target at the same time.

To train this type of punch-hand a canvas bag is first filled with common beach sand. An ideal container is a bank money bag...

This bag is then attached to a smooth wall and struck straight on with alternating fists.

After a number of weeks of constant conditioning the hands will begin to harden and the sand will begin to feel soft (er). At this point the bag is emptied and filled with rice and the process is repeated.

When the rice becomes "soft" the bag is refilled with lead shot (as in shot gun shells) and then with ball bearings.

This conditioning can take years to complete properly. My instructor worked out on a 1 inch thick steel plate with a thin strip of rubber between it and the wall. This is necessary because there must be SOME give or wrists and elbows can break or form bone chips.

This system is probably adopted from some form of Hsing Yi where "iron palms" were created by the same sand upward progression. In this system open pails or boxes were filled with sand and struck by the flat palm, then rice and so on, up until the point where no one will shake hands with you.

It is also possible to purchase ready made punch bags filled with sand or shot. They work fine but start with the sand, not the shot!!

This type of conditioning tends to actually flatten the knuckles out to where your fist will become dead (no pun intended) level across the hitting surface.

I personally like this conditioning system, the trick is to remember to hit the damn thing on a regular basis. One way that works for me is to have the bag near the door and hit it 50 times EVERY TIME I go in or out the door.

This will either develop hard hands in a hurry or kill your social life completely.

It is necessary to do some sort of wrist conditioning with any hand hardening. Normal pushups are one way to accomplish this.

I have personally known two boxers who scored great punches to the opponent's face, only to end up in the next bed at the hospital with a snapped wrist because it couldn't take the increased pressure.

One method to accelerate hardening is to make a hand box. This is accomplished by pouring casting plaster or cement into a small box (say 4 by 4 inches) and as it begins to set press your fist into the material while holding it perfectly vertical and flat across the knuckles.

Do not dig the knuckles in, just press flat.

As the molds harden you can place each fist into its mirror mold and do pushups in this position.

The same molds can also be used with your hands in a back and forth twisting motion, grinding the knuckles into the plaster. Do this carefully, this causes a lack of blood to the knuckles and produces scar tissue...

Any of these systems can be slightly speeded up by soaking the hands in a super-saturated, hot, salt water solution to which a little vinegar has been added.

Of course there are methods to duplicate this conditioning with outside help. "Brass" knuckles are still sold as paper weights or key holders (although they are rarely made from brass any more). The problem here is that they look like brass knuckles, not key chains...

A better solution is loaded gloves. Usually known as sap gloves these are black leather gloves with 6 ounces of lead shot contained in a pouch over the knuckles or in the palm of the glove.

Sap gloves are very effective weapons and cannot be spotted unless you know what you are looking for. A hit from these gloves is a rough experience.

The bad news is many cops wear them and as such can easily spot them on someone else.

The best gloves we found are made by :

> Damascus Gloves
> Box 597
> Rutland VT 05701
> $40 a pair...

Their "Protector" gloves are made from deer skin and are very nice in their own right. The extra weight is hardly noticable and they can be worn as regular gloves, at least in the winter.

Damascus will sell only to "law enforcement agencies", this does include anyone writing on a security company letterhead.

Several firms, including The Sharper Image sell them at a higher price.

DAMASCUS GLOVES
63 Wales st
Rutland, VT 05701

Ask for the PROTECTOR model. These gloves are made from A-1 deerhide (how many acrylics died for that sweater?) and are great all around gloves. My pair has lasted two years...

The fact they each have 6 ounces of lead shot in them and will drop someone like a roundhouse from Mr. Ali, is only secondary...

Probably the best "hidden" quick-in weapon available as there is no access time.

How to MEASURE GLOVES

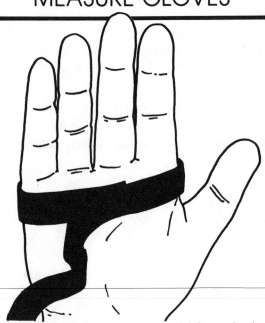

$38.00 Direct, more from other sources.

PROTECT YOUR KNUCKLES!

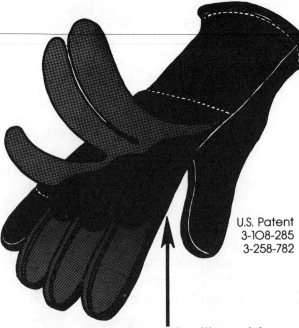

With a tape, measure right hand at widest part, over knuckles, with hands flat but not including thumb. Hold fingers loosely but touching. Put tape measure snug but not tight. If measurement falls between sizes, order the larger one.

U.S. Patent
3-108-285
3-258-782

A pouch with a minimum of six ounces of powdered lead is built into the back of each glove.

FOR MEN

If hand measures	order size
8" to 8½"	Small
9" to 9½"	Medium
10" to 10½"	Large
11" to 11½"	X-Large

FOR WOMEN

If hand measures	order size
6 5/8" to 7½"	Small
7" to 7 5/8"	Medium
8" to 9"	Large

DEFENSIVE AND OFFENSIVE DRIVING FOR VIP PROTECTION

At about 5:30 on the afternoon of September 5, 1977, Dr. Hanns Martin Schleyer, president of the Federation of the German Employers Associations, was on his way home to Cologne-Braunsfeld from the federation's office in Cologne proper. Escorting Schleeyer's Mercedes limousine were three West German police officers, traveling immediately behind Schleyer and his chauffeur, as they drove westward on Friedrich-Schmidt Strasse towards the Schleyer residence at number 10 Raschdorffstrasse.

As the Schleyer car turned right onto Vinconz-Statz Strasse and only yards away from Raschdorffstrasse, it was forced to an abrupt halt at what appeared to be an accident. Unable to react fast enough, the escort car collided with the rear of Schleyer's limousine.

Within seconds both cars were surrounded by five persons who in the confusion had emerged unchallenged from the left of the cars. Armed with an assortment of weapons, they opened fire killing the chauffeur and the three bodyguards. Unharmed, Schleyer was dragged from his car and forced into a white Volkswagon bus which then moved off at a high speed and disappeared in the heavy traffic on Junkersdorfor Strasse.

The Cologne police appeared at the scene hardly two minutes later to discover the incredible carnage. Showing evidence of multiple, point blank gunshot wounds, the bodies of the chauffeur and bodyguards were literally blown to pieces by the kidnappers' massive fire power. Forty-three days later, Schleyer was killed by the German Red Army Faction and his body was left in a greenAudi 100 with Bad Hamburg license plates in the Rue Charles Regency in Mulhouse.

About 10 months later on March 16, 1978 at about 9:05 a.m., Italy's leading senior statesman, Aldo Moro was ambushed and kidnapped by the Red Brigades. Beginning with the routine he had followed for years, Moro left his apartment to go to Mass at the nearby church of Santa Chiara. After Mass, he started off for parliament reading the morning papers. In his Fiat 130 were his chauffeur and bodyguard. Following in a white Alfa Romeo were three security guards. On the Via Mario Fani and just before reaching the intersection of Via Strasse, a white Fiat 128 suddenly overtook Moro's car and pulled to an abrupt stop at the intersection. Moro's chauffeur jammed his brakes and the security car following close behind couldn't stop quickly enough and bumped into Moro's car. The driver and front seat passenger of the Fiat 128 (which was bearing diplomat plates) jumped out as if to investigate the damage to their car. Then moving in from both sides, they drew pistols and killed both the chauffeur and bodyguard instantly. Another team of terrorists dressed in Alitalia Airlines flight crew uniforms moved in on the security car and opened fire killing the two policemen outright. The third policeman, who managed to roll out of the car on the other side, was killed by a sniper from a nearby rooftop. Moro was dragged out of his car and pushed into a waiting blue Fiat which quickly moved away. The whole action lasted barely 30 seconds. Moro was held as a hostage and on May 9, 1978 his body was found stuffed in the trunk of a stolen car in downtown Rome.

Both the above were well-planned and well-executed terrorist operations. Tactically, both kidnappings, more or less, followed the same scenario, though in different countries and by different terrorist groups. In the case of Moro's kidnapping, extra precautions were taken by the Red Brigades as evidenced by the snipers placed on the roof. Unfortunately, the Italian authorities had learned nothing from the Schleyer kidnapping. In both cases, overwhelming fire power was brought to bear at the point of attack and the areas were sealed off from possible outside interference while the assault was in progress. In both cases there was a total absence of a competent defense. The elements of surprise, predictability, escort procedure, special aids and general lack of preparedness, all ruled in total favor of the terrorists.

Throughout the Middle East, Western Europe and South America, groups of terrorists have made themselves famous by their successes or failures. Over the past 15 years or so, more than 300 politicians or businessmen have been kidnapped and large amounts of ransom running into millions of dollars paid out for them. Counter terrorism is basically divided into four functional tasks. They are (a) prevention (b) control (c) containment and (d) restoration. The threat is very real and counter measure programs are an essential part of today's security management programs. In the past, banks were the prime targets of terrorists, but due to the newly enacted Protection Acts, banks are now well protected with both armed guards and sophisticated electronic equipment. For the terrorists in need of funds to carry out their kidnappings for ransoms then became big business.

It has been found that most kidnappings take place not from a residence or office, but just as the potential target is leaving or entering one of these buildings or from the vehicle itself while the target is in transit. It has been estimated that an executive spends about 17 percent of his time in transit. The vehicle emerges as a terrorist target for the following reasons:

(a) It is often left with little protection in public areas and so becomes an easy target for an attack. (b) When it is in use, it will contain targets who are isolated from assistance and having virtually no protection other than the vehicle itself and whatever protective devices it may be modified with and who are most likely to be off guard due to the routine of their trips. (c) The use of the vehicle gives the terrorist a variety of locations and times to attack. (d) The number of persons in a vehicle is restricted and so allows an attack group to be larger. (e) Attacks on a vehicle can be simulated without the knowledge of the persons concerned. (f) The modifications made to a vehicle can be made out by an experienced person who can then build the counters to them. Marighella has listed various methods of action for terrorist attacks and the ones most vulnerable to a vehicle attack are: attack, ambush, sabotage, war of nerves, assassination and entry or break-in.

Hence, in this article, I will concentrate on VIP protection related to the vehicle and shall discuss it under three topics: the driver, vehicle tactics, and vehicle modifications.

The Driver

Protective driving is an integral part of executive protection. But one has to realize that no matter what is taught in the matter of driving tactics/strategies or however well the vehicle is armored/modified, it will all be useless if the driver fails to respond as he should when an attack takes place. Hence, the most important is the driver of the human element.

The driver and the other members of the protective team should realize that the driver is part and parcel of the team. The driver has to be first trained so that he gains confidence and skill in his own capabilities and that of the vehicle before he is trained in defensive, high speed and offensive driving. Throughout the training, it must be emphasized that priority is the safety and protection of the VIP and not the confrontation with or the capture of the terrorists. The whole concept of protection will be destroyed if the VIP is killed in a confrontation.

It should be realized that it will be detrimental to all if a driver gains more confidence than skill. A driver must learn the basics of car control or vehicle dynamics and he must realize that no force effects the vehicle, unless he himself exerts it. This he does in three ways: (1) by accelerating and braking; (2) by braking and changing direction; and (3) by moving the steering wheel. A skillful driver completes these maneuvers with precision and this precision only comes with practice. "Handling" a vehicle is the ability to keep the car in control when carrying out any sort of maneuver like cornering, evasive action, etc.

The driver should be taught the strengths and weaknesses and tactics of the terrorists and the counter measures to what a terrorist can use against him. Carlos Marigherlla's book--The Mini Manual of the Urban Guerilla describes certain tactics which are: surprise, better knowledge of the terrain, greater mobility and speed, and finally total command of the situation.

These four tactics were very prominent in the kidnappings of both Schleeyer and Moro. A driver has to be taught to recognize surveillance and any abnormal activity should be reported immediately. It must be stressed that it is better to suffer a little embarrassment in the event of reporting a false surveillance, than suffer the consequences of not reporting a suspicious surveillance. If a threat level is high, the driver can record his suspicions on a tape recorder or over the car radio, if it is equipped with one. Safe havens like police stations, military bases, fire stations, hospitals, etc., have to be mapped out and studied, as during a moment of stress the driver will not have time to ask for directions. A safe haven is absolutely essential in a danger zone. Hence, a driver's primary job will be to: (1) practice good vehicle and driving security so that the plans of a potential terrorist are thwarted, (2) to recognize surveillance and other suspicious occurrences and take appropriate action to eliminate the possibility of attack, (3) by recognizing that an attack is about to take place, or is beginning, and take specific defensive or offensive measures to thwart the attack and escape.

After the completion of his course in normal driving procedures and then in specifics in defensive and offensive driving, he should go through an intense course in motor mechanics. Then finally, he should be mentally tuned to go through a vehicle security check every time the vehicle is left unattended for over a specified period of time. A daily suggested check list can be as follows:

(a) Check for unauthorized entry into the car.
(b) Check hood and gas tank for evidence of entry.
(c) Check exhaust pipe for blockage or explosives.
(d) Check for any materials in the tire wells.
(e) Check garage doors after locking up, and the inside and outside of the garage doors before opening up.
(f) Check to see if all systems/modifications are in proper working order.
(g) Check the vehicle thoroughly especially after it returns from being serviced or repaired.

An intensive check list can be as follows:

(a) Check the car for any attached item like explosives, surveillance beepers and any other electronic item that is not supposed to be there.
(b) Check tires for correct pressure and the rims for cracks.
(c) Check all lighting and other normal car systems.
(d) The gas tank should never be less than half full as in a stress situation, the faster the car moves, the more gas it will consume.
(e) Check all wheel lug nuts to see if they are correctly tightened.
(f) Check all bolts and hoses. Spares can be carried as a precaution.
(g) Communications equipment and all weaponry should be in good working order and easily accessible.

Vehicle Tactics

As I have stressed before, the duty of the protection team is primarily the safety of the VIP they are protecting rather than the confrontation with, and capture of the terrorists. Hence, in this portion of the article, I will first concentrate on "prevention and avoidance" of a stress situation. Then I will touch on the "confronting and overcoming" of a stress situation, if it cannot be absolutely avoided. So, in vehicle tactics, you will read about driving exercises of a normal nature, then about high speed driving, precise maneuvers like the forward and reverse 180-degree turns, ramming and the countering of an attack from a moving car.

One has to again remember that the ability to practice safe driving methods and detect surveillance is of far greater importance than the ability to ram through a roadblock or perform a perfect bootleg turn. Many things can be done to minimize the chance of an attack or its severity, should it occur. The vehicle is a tremendously powerful weapon if it is used effectively. Before a driver goes into the specifics of defensive and offensive driving, he has to learn what his vehicle is capable of. To do this, he should go through various maneuvers on a "skid pan" so that he can get used to the vehicle's characteristics. A skid pan is a black-topped area with some oil on it which reduces the coefficient of friction. Ater continuous practice on a skid plan, a driver will come to know the "feel" of his vehicle. Weaving in and out of cones placed in a straight line at intervals of about 100 feet apart, at about 75 miles per hour, will again give the driver the car's maneuvering capabilities. In this excerise, braking should be done lightly for the purpose of stabilization. Quick steering action will be required, as well as a light and even acceleration. Backing up at relatively high speeds should also be practiced, though turning while backing up at a high speed should be avoided as far as possible. Throughout this part of his training, the driver should concentrate on achieving the stability and control of his vehicle. Other driving activities that can be practiced are the serpentine maneuver, evasive maneuver, controlled braking, skid control and off road recovery. All these maneuvers can be practiced on a dry surface before the practice begins on the skid pan.

Then the following considerations should be instilled into the driver's mind as he gains confidence to drive well under normal driving conditions.

(1) All mirrors should be properly adjusted for effective vision
(2) Seats and safety belts should be properly adjusted.
(3) Proper wheel control should be in effect at all times so
    that in a moment of stress, minimum time loss and
    maximum control can be achieved.
(4) Avoid being boxed in while driving, stopping for a light
    while parked. Always leave an "out."
(5) Avoid any unusual situation--even an accident. Play it safe.
(6) Doors and windows should always be kept locked.
    Documents can be handed out by lowering the window an
    inch or so through special slots meant for this purpose.
(7) Be wary of road detour signs, construction areas and
    police check points. There have been cases where
    terrorists have dressed in police uniforms.
(8) Always be surveillance conscious.
(9) Danger zones should be assessed and safe havens should
    be developed.

When the student driver is confident of normal driving, training should then start in defensive, high speed and offensive driving. Defensive driving is characterized as removing the vehicle from the scene of attack without confronting the terrorists or can be described as a combination of techniques to detect, avoid and if necessary, counter a potential terrorist attack. Offensive driving is the violet use of the vehicle against the terrorists in order to get out of a trap and escape. An example of this is ramming which will be discussed in detail later on in this article. But before we go into the details of defensive and offensive driving, It us discuss "high speed" driving as both defensive and especially offensive driving which have to be done at high speeds. In all the maneuvers, it should be noted that it is the combination of a good driver plus a good car which will result in a good maneuver. A good car should react quickly and accurately to accelerating, braking and steering and a good driver should be able to carry out these actions easily with a good car.

High-Speed Driving--The kinetic energy of a vehicle literally quadruples when speed doubles and this surge of power is terrifying, unless effectively controlled. The increase in kinetic energy not only multiplies the destructive force of the vehicle to the terrorist, but also to the passengers of the vehicle in which is the VIP is traveling. Secondly, the coefficient of friction between the road surface and tires is reduced with the increase in speed which will minimize the ability of the vehicle to remain effectively under control. Then due to increased speed, braking efficiency is reduced. Increased speed also has a tendency to reduce the driver's arc of vision and produces what is called "tunnel vision."

"Handling" of the car is the ability to stay in control while cornering or in any evasive maneuver. Every effort should be made to minimize the transfers of weight so that the vehicle will remain balanced and stable. Braking tends to lower the vehicle and when this happens the center of gravity is also lowered. Braking and the releasing of brakes should be done smoothly and are important factors when the vehicle is traveling at high speeds. Trying to turn at too great a speed and the improper control of weight transfer will make the vehicle spin out of control. If a vehicle is allowed to spin off its axis by more than 28 degrees, recovery is impossible and it will go out of control. When attempting to cover a great distance in a minimum amount of time, the speed at which the vehicle exits a turn is usually more important than the speed at which the vehicle actually negotiates the turn. The explanation is that the faster the vehicle exits the curve, the less time and space it will take to attain maximum speed. Here terminal velocity plays a great part And should be taken into consideration.

The braking efficiency of a vehicle is reduced at high speeds. If emergency braking needs to be done at high speeds, threshold braking should be used. This technique is done by applying braking pressure to that point just before the wheel stops to rotate and begins to slide.

Emergency evasive maneuvers work better if the vehicle maneuvering ability is used rather than its stopping ability. At 40 mph, one cannot stop a vehicle within a distance of 40 feet, but the vehicle can be swerved into the next lane within the same 40 feet. If a collision with another vehicle cannot be avoided, then one should strike the vehicle at either end so as to spin it, rather than impacting the vehicle's total weight. In the event of a tire blowout, the foot should be kept away from the brake and after removing the foot from the accelerator and firmly holding the steering wheel, one should let the speed ease before maneuvering the vehicle to the side of the road.

Offensive Driving Techniques--These techniques basically have three primary areas which are avoidance, detection and the countering of an attack. Avoidance entails the methods employed in avoiding becoming a target. Detection entails the recognition of surveillance and countering an attack is how one recognizes that an attack is about to begin, or has begun, and what methods are used to avoid the trap and escape.

Avoidance and detection are easy to understand, and so I will concentrate more on countering an attack from purely a defensive point of view. Once a driver sees that an attack is about to begin, he may utilize any one of a number of maneuvers taught to him, but I will concentrate on the "forward and reverse 180-degree turns." Normally, an assassination or kidnapping ismade by establishing a roadblock and when the victim's vehicle comes to a stop, the attack starts. If the driver of the VIP vehicle notices a suspicious roadblock, he can do the usual conventional turns like a quick stop, a fast reverse at an angle and finally, a turn into the direction from which he came or, if enough, full U turn without reversing. But in an emergency situation on a narrow road, the forward or reverse 180-degree turns may be employed. Both are precision turns and are carried out when the vehicle is in motion. Here the driver's timing of the vehicle's control comes into play. Forward 180-degree turns require better driver expertise than do reverse 180-degree turns. The speed necessary to carry out these maneuvers depends a lot on the vehicle and road surface.

To execute a forward 180-degree maneuver, the vehicle should be put into neutral gear, turning at the same time very quickly and sharply to the left/right and at the same instant applying the emergency brake very hard, which will cause the rear wheels to lock and stop rotating. In this type of maneuver, the locked wheels tend to lead. Just a fraction of a second before applying the emergency brakes, turn the steering wheel, which will cause the vehicle to begin rotating and the rear wheel to assume a leading position much quicker. At this point, the driver should release the emergency brake and while placing the car in low gear, should apply full throttle. This will prevent the engine from stalling. Also by the time the driver has completed all these actions one after the other, the vehicle would have rotated a full 180 degrees and will move in the direction from which it came. Such a turn, properly and efficiently executed, will take not more than three to five seconds to complete.

To execute a reverse 180-degree maneuver, the driver must bring the car to a dead stop, put it into reverse gear and begin backing, accelerating the entire time. When his speed reaches about 30 mph (while reversing), he should suddenly remove his foot from the accelerator and turn the steering wheel sharply. The vehicle will start to rotate and after it has rotated about 90 degrees, the driver should move into low gear and then should apply full power.

A reverse 180-degree turn requires less driver expertise and is less demanding on the vehicle then the forward turns. A great deal can also go wrong in the forward 180-degree turn than the reverse one. If the road is broad enough and time permits, an inverted "U" turn can be made on a quick stop then fast reverse at an angle and quick acceleration in the direction of original approach.

Car maintenance is generally a priority in executive protection, but more so when moments of stress are anticipated. When executing any of the above turns, the correct type of tire should be used--preferably a good quality radial tire with the tire pressure correctly maintained. An imbalance in tire pressure is extremely dangerous and the vehicle's maneuvering capability will be reduced.

If the attack comes on unexpectedly and a forward or reverse 180-degree turn cannot be executed and no other option is available but to confront the situation, then one has two options--to leave the road if possible and drive around the roadblock or, if this is not possible, then ram through the roadblock. If gunmen are seen on either side of the roadblock, then efforts should be made to get rid of the gunmen with the most dangerous weapons. When a vehicle blocking the road has to be forced out of the way, it must be kept in mind that one must strike the vehicle hard enough, yet protect one's own vehicle from being disabled by the force of the impact.

The guidelines for ramming are usually carried out as per the following procedure:

> (1) Slow the car down, as this will cause the nose of the car to drop and will also give the impression that one is about to stop.
> (2) Shift to low gear without being noticed.
> (3) Then pick a ramming point so that your front fender hits the terrorist vehicle over a wheel; preferably the rear wheel, but the end of the car which gives the most room for escape should be chosen.
> (4) Then accelerate hard, remaining fully depressed while ramming through and even after the break through has been achieved.
> (5) Once past the roadblock, try to break visual contact as quickly as possible to a safe haven.

Countering an attack from a moving vehicle--A common method of committing an assassination is for the terrorists to pull alongside the victim's car and then open fire. The terrorists usually will open fire when they are in the victim's car blind spot and will continue to fire until the angle does not allow them to fire any more. The attack will usually last 15 to 20 seconds and 15 to 100 rounds will be fired depending upon the type of weapons used. At times, two or three vehicles will be used, either as decoys, to slow one down or to box one in. At times, two people have been used on motorcycles for the assassination. The maneuverability of the motorcycle makes this team highly dangerous and the chances of the attackers getting away is also high. When an attack from a moving vehicle is anticipated, it would be better to resort to various maneuvers rather than to resort to high speed driving, unless, of course, there is no other option. Better vehicle control can be maintained at speeds lower than 75 mph. Swerving can prevent an attacker from drawing alongside and once an evasive action has resulted in the breaking of contact, speed should be resorted to in order to break visual contact as quickly as possible. If one is being attacked from a motorcycle, a quick swerve into them will neutralize the attackers effectively. The simplest counter would be the "panic stop" which will cause the attackers to overshoot and thus not enable them to use the angle of fire. A fast reverse 180-degree turn can then be used. Should the situation arise, driving over a curb which the terorrists may not expect can also be tried. Curbs can be driven over even at high speeds of 40 mph, but most important of all the curb will have to be mounted at between 30 degrees to 45 degrees. Driving over the curb at less than a 30-degree angle will result in the lost of control of the steering wheel and driving over the curb at more than a 45-degree angle may result in the blowout of a tire.

Drivers should eventually practice vehicle elimination which is forcing the attacking vehicle off the road or for it to go out of control; also, rear end ramming or causing the attacking vehicle to go into a spinout.

Vehicle Protection

As I said before, a driver has to be properly and thoroughly trained and the vehicle has to be able to perform in such a fashion that one does not get trapped in a spot where one can be stopped or attacked. Hence, the driver and the car are a compliment of one another. If an untrained driver is put behind the wheel of an armored/modified car, the car is worthless, just as a well-trained driver can't help it if he gets killed in an unarmored car.

An armored car is only as good as the material put into it. The reason for the protective gadgets that we fix in a vehicle is basically to break out of an ambush. Armoring a car is a science in itself as will be seen in the following paragraphs. A fine balance has to be maintained in protecting a vehicle. Adding unnecessary armor will burden the suspension and other delicate mechanisms and also have a negative effect on the vehicle's mobility. Not fixing enough of the appropriate armor will result in the risk of bullet penetration of the armor. So, enough is required, but not too much.

Vehicles usually come under two forms of attack. One is a hit-and-run sniping or blast of automatic fire from another moving vehicle. In these kinds of attacks, the VIP's car will at times, also be sandwiched between two other cars to prevent evasive action from being Taken. The second form of attack is one where the VIP's car is blocked at a roadblock or one-way street (as in the case of the Malaysian Police Commissioner in the 1970s whose car was sandwiched and he was shot dead inside the car), and a siege of attack takes place. So the car will basically have to be modified taking these two situations in consideration.

The "passive" sort of protection usually begins with the encapsulation of the passenger compartment with fiber and polycarbonate composites. Door panels and armored shields are installed. Installed behind the rear compartment seats are angled plates for bullet defection. Roofs are reinforced against grenade fragments and oblique fire and armor is added under the floor board to withstand land mine explosions. Bullet proof glass can be installed.

Armor--Before I go on, let me ask if when one is told that a vehicle is armored, if one then asks the important question, "To what level is the vehicle armored?" For the sake of the VIP, I would suggest that the minimum a car should be armored would be to stop 30-06 or 7.62mm rounds. When the threat first started, companies and individuals started to armor their vehicles they normally traveled in--i.e. their big limousines like Cadillac and Lincolns. Now of course, a low profile vehicle is used--one that fits with the vehicles commonly used in that country. One should remember that it has to blend in with the environment. Also, technological advances have done much to protect the vehicle better, but with lighter material than used in the past decade. Nowadays, depending upon the customer and need for protection, various combinations of fiberglass, ceramic armor, metal alloys, and soft armor are being used. Then there are also combinations of soda lime glass, silicone bonding layers, opaque armor, lexan and lexguard plastics. But again all of them have limitations depending upon the threat level of the situation and the protection level to which the armoring is required. Certain companies also cut the steel plating in such a way that the armor overlaps, thereby culminating weak areas (where the steel plates are joined). Steel blast shields can be installed on the floor of the vehicle in case grenades are rolled under the car. Cars which are armored will give you the protection only for which they are armored. Armored cars will stop pistol rounds and even can be made bombproof depending upon what one wants. The latest has been the armoring of the vehicle with a clear plastic cube of 1-1/4-inch thick General Electric Lexguard Laminate and which is reasonably bullet proof. It is technically called the Ballistic Cube 2000. Also other companies use the lightweight ballastic armor which is as effective as the heavier tungsten steel plates originally used. Then you have armor which is comprised of layerings of ceramic and plastic fitted together which gives reasonably good protection. Most attacks are carried out with small arms (concealable), but there have also been attacks where grenades and anti-tank rockets have been used as in the attack of General Krosen's car in Germany. One should think before one armors a car with Kevlar which is soft and can be made rigid for ballistic purposes. But it should never be used on doors and floors as water affects its ballistic quality.

Glass--With modern technology, bullet proof glass or transparent armor has become lighter and thinner and better. There are special plastic templates being made which are then laminated with a polycarbonate lining which prevents the sharding/spalling (fragmentation) of the glass if it is struck by a bullet. The mounting of the glass is an important factor. Here again overlapping is necessary as no one can tell when a bullet will strike the joining area. It would be better that all doors are framed with chrome steel over the windows as it offers greater ballistic protection. Windows can also be re-operated by installing compensator springs to offset the weight of the armored glass. One must keep in mind that heavy armor glass in a vehicle with a high center of gravity may cause the vehicle to turn over when taking a curve a high speed. So the additional weight will have to be compensated for when carrying out any sort of maneuver.

Gas Tanks--Gas tanks are also vulnerable and some companies fill the inside of the tank with foam. Thus, if the tank is punctured, the gas will leak out but won't catch fire and the tank will start to seal itself immediately. Gas tanks are also fitted with special materials that quench the flames if it does catch fire and will retard explosions. Some go even further to make the fuel tanks totally explosion-proof. Other companies strip the gas tank and fill it with expanded aluminum foil which holds the gasoline in a multitude of tiny cells where if it does catch fire, it will burn but not explode.

Tires--Tires range from a special bullet-resistant steel belt and sidewall radial for high speed driving to a roll-flat insert that will a low the car to be safely steered up to speeds of 50 mph, even if the tires are bullet-riddled. Others use a special plastic liner which absorbs the shock very well and also defrays the round. Tires basically should be protected with inserts which would give the vehicle a fast getaway capability for long distances. Tires are also one of the most important factors in a car when the car moves, stops or turns. Hence, tires will have to be designed so that a certain coefficient of friction is maintained between the car and the road. Armoring influences this coefficiency and adds weight to the tires which can ruin them, although certain modifications can avoid part of this problem. Tires have to be checked regularly for uneven wearing out and other forms of damage.

Depending upon the threat level, various other modifications can be made and gadgets added that will give better protection. Some of the "passive" systems are doors that can be fitted with electronically or manually operated dead bolt locks will will prevent access to the car. Extra-heavy duty springs shock absorbers, hydraulic systems and special stainless tubing for fuel line hoses can be installed. The strengthening of fore and aft bumpers should be seriously considered as in a ramming situation they will be an asset. The vehicle can also be equipped with a vast array of communications equipment ranging from multi-channeled citizen band radios to scramble-equipped telephones. The braking system will also have to be modified as the car will take a longer time to stop (with normal brakes) once it has gathered speed due to the weight of the armor. Hence, disc brakes are recommended for all four wheels and brake pads should be heavy-duty metallic ones. Three high-intensity lights may be inconspicuously mounted in the front of the vehicle--one facing straight ahead and the other two at a 30-degree to 45-degree angle, so that extended visibility may be obtained in case a problem occurs at night. A high-intensity rear light may also be fixed and used just before one goes into an evasive maneuver. In case the lights get shot out or damaged, the driver can be equipped with night vision goggles which can then be used.

The fun really starts though when the vehicle is equipped with "active" protection systems. The most common ones are soft gun ports whereby one can fire at the attackers from inside the car. These gun ports should be completely undetectable both from outside and inside. Weapon lockers and gun racks can be built into the back seats and on the floor boards but should not be obvious. Discreet ducts can be mounted within the side lamp mountings, which in a moment of stress, especially in mob situations, can spray CS or CN or other solutions of noxious chemicals. Some companies have their vehicles equipped with more vicious counter-attack systems like grenade launchers and hostile fire location systems. Oil slick emission units can be used to deter the attackers from following one's vehicle, or to lose an attacker on a turn or a curve. A powerful, but non-lethal electric shock system can be provided to instantly repel those intent on battering or overturning the vehicle (mob situation again).

The list of options, for both security and luxury can go on and on. It all depends on the threat level and how much the client (individual or company) is willing to spend. The attitude of, "Let's wait and see" is a stupid one to say the least and should never be condoned. If one waits too long then the situation may arise when one may not be able to see. Historically most kidnappings have taken place when the VIP's car has been brought to a stop and he has been physically removed as the vehicle was not adequately protected. Hence, in the long run, the "preventive" aspect is much much better than the "cure" aspect. All it takes is one mistake--like the one made by the American Military Advisor to El Salvador--Lt. Comdr. Albert Schaufellberg--he followed a routine and had his windows rolled down when he parked.

The above article was written by J.D.Aranha and first published in POLICE PRODUCT NEWS. It is hereby reprinted with the author's permission.

Nice job.

THE CARS

No, this is not a review of a rock group. Rather it is a semi-serious, semi-fantasy look at one tool all of us, from 007 downward employ at one time or another.

This section is based on several engineering projects completed by a mutual friend of ours who is a famous writer and really doesn't have any desire to see his name in print in this concept.

His lawyer tends to agree...

Most of these ideas, or systems, can work with or without the help of their counterparts, limiting your personal James Bond toy strictly to your budget and guts.

The actual stock vehicle is pretty much your choice, even Bond went from an Aston Martin to a Lotus. I will, however, comment ever so briefly on my own toys over the years, which include 5 Corvettes (too heavy), one XKE (never, never, buy an E-type unless you can afford two; one to drive, one to keep in the shop), one Ferrari (nice, too noticable for tailing, my dented fender cost more to replace than a new Pinto at the time), Jeep (wonderful if you never go over 65 and don't mind freezing your ass off), 4 (yes, 4) Lotus (Lotusi?).

Now I gotta admit the Lotus is a kick in the ass. It will out handle almost anything on the road, is fairly fast, and fun.

You had better live in or near a big city with at least one mechanic who has some idea why Colin Chapman, bless his corpse, did things in the way he did...

You better have a back up, around town car...

You better have a damn good attorney who enjoys going to traffic court.

The particular Elan I am now in possession of was "modified" by an ex-CIA agent to bring it up to formula 2, Gran Prix racing standards including a Cosworth engine...

Will take an AC cobra up to 130...

Three tickets in the first two weeks...

Enough bragging, start with anything you want. If you desire out-run-the-hiway patrol speed start buying hot rod magazines, I'm not going into the whole hot rod concept here...

Okay, my friend's 007 Special is a fairly fast car (American). His first cost efficient boost was to add an NOX injection system.

For about $300 you can double the horsepower of any car by shooting in pure NO2 (laughing gas). The oxygen boosts the power, the nitrogen cools it down.

It works, but only for a few seconds at a time! It also places double the strain on the rest of the drive train.

It is nice for those little escape bursts, however...

Option 2 was a good, superhet radar detector with a hidden location. Remember some states outlaw them and no cop likes them...

3. Was a simply installed metal compartment underneath and slightly ahead of the back bumper. One switch dropped two relays that dumped either a teflon/oil mixture or caltrops on the road behind him.

Yes, this works, causing the car chasing you to lose steering control, HOWEVER it will also do the same thing to the next set of innocent cars as well...

4. Electric operated smoke grenade which produced blinding smoke that seemed to come from the tail pipe.

5. Radar jammer. Yes, a former racing star sells these lovely devices which allow a driver to dial in the speed a K or X band radar gun will register.

Yes they are expensive and illegal.

One company sells plans if you wish to invest about $600 and a lot of work in building your own:

> PHILLIPS INSTRUMENTS
> 9513 SW Barbur #109
> Portland, OR 97219

One other possibility that has not been tried, to my knowledge, is to forget about dialing in speed and simply boost the available power of the commercially available transmitter circuit boards so they would overwhelm and/or burn out any radar unit receiving the signal.

Very illegal.

6. Bra made from material which does not reflect radar (used by the Air Force, available). Did not work well, let the gun register the car behind my friend's, which may have been going even faster, when wet did no good at all.

7. High powered radio wave transmissions which could interfere with electronic ignition or computer controlled fuel injection units.

Mixed success, did manage to stop several fuel injected cars, notably Cadillacs and Benz dead in the road. Caused several cop cars to misfire and lose speed.

8. Very high powered radio waves which caused the rubber holding the windshield glass in place to begin to melt.

A mean one, only in the experimental stage but some success...

9. Use of selection switches to alter outside lights as detailed in How To Get...

10. Not done, but being considered, revolving license plates. Note you better have the paper to back this up...

11. A good, non-crystal scanner that can and will monitor the state and local police frequencies no matter what locale you find yourself in..

A, B, C, METHOD OF TAILING

A time proven method of tailing a subject is to use a three man team which alters its positions according to a pre-arranged (and pre-practiced) system. This method is very, very difficult to detect as the subject is never given too long to make any team member. In this system the A man follows the subject. B follows dear old A and C parallels either A or B. When the parade reaches an intersection, C speeds up and crosses or turns ahead of the target. This allows C to keep him in view in case he enters a building or turns an unexpected direction.

As they turn the corner, A slows down, stops to look in a window, or turns into a shop while B speeds up to take A's place. After a decent interval A steps out, finds B's back and tails him.

In order to exchange B (who is now in A's original position) at the next corner, B crosses the intersection if the subject turns (or vice versa), C walks across the street and takes up a position behind the target. C is now in A's spot, B in C and A in B's.... Next corner A speeds up, passes subject who has turned the corner and pulls a quick "U" turn out of target's sight, walks back and parallels the subject (in C position), B (in ex-C position) crosses over and takes the position behind the target, C drops back and takes the rear ass position.

This method is a favorite of such notable people as the Drug Enforcement Agency and the FBI....

The person who occupies the B, or tail ass position has the dual function of watching out for the target's buddies who may also be tagging along (usually behind, but sometimes parallel) to spot a tail....

If such a hinderance is spotted B can often lose him by breaking off and taking the target's tail with him, only to ditch him at a convenient point.

DITCHING A TAIL

This is an art usually picked up from watching detective shows on television, or through osmosis.....However, it is a definite art....

ARRANGE TO STOP SUDDENLY; Drop something, pick it up and look around, watch the store windows to see who is behind you, turn a corner and stop there and watch for anyone following you.

RUN; Cross the street in the middle of rush hour drivers and turn around to see if anyone else is willing to risk his life to follow you. Quickly board a bus, wait until other people have boarded and leave through the back door. See if anyone else does likewise (note--a smart tail will not get off, but wait until the next stop then double back, or take the next bus assuming you're on it, don't be...) Run into a building and leave by another exit. Leave a hotel or restaurant, suddenly turn around and go back inside to see who is doing what. Reverse the direction of your travel one or more times and see who else is duplicating your unusual route. Get into large open areas where it is hard to tail or take the last taxi at a hotel....

AUTO TAILING

It is probably easier for an experienced person to tail someone in an auto than on foot. Inherently you can arrange to have several advantages. The first, and most important, is to have any and all autos in your team equipped with communications. CB walkie talkies will work in a crux.

Again, one auto can be used to tail, but two or three are far, far better. One can alter the appearance of an auto to some degree, although it is more difficult than it is to change a person.

To wit: Have dingle balls, or dice to quickly hang from your mirror; change the driver's identity by use of a wig or glasses; have one person lying down in the seat, then have him sit up (note you should always have at least two persons in each car so the driver can concentrate on driving, the spotter on spotting); change lanes and driving habits every so often.

Really well equipped tail cars will have a panel of switches added so one or more outside lights can be turned off. This system does wonders in night tailing, nothing stands out in a rear view mirror more than a one-eyed car, and when it is suddenly replaced with a normally lit two headlighted version, it is almost always assumed to be a different vehicle. The same trick will work with parking lights or tail lights.

In absence of a switch panel one can quickly pull over and disconnect a light. This is best done as the subject turns a corner and one of the other team cars is watching him....

Many surveillance assignments are botched or blown by one simple reason: failure to plan ahead. Not enough gas in the car, no appearance altering clothing, lack of maps, not enough communication between the team members....

LIE DETECTOR TESTING AND COUNTERMEASURES

As the more astute of you will remember Lee did a large section on polygraphs; "lie detectors" in his last book. The chapter was based on several studies including a CIA funded "cleaned" study wherein Lee managed to find the actual testers in spite of the screened CIA efforts, as well as several studies performed on our own.

At least one security magazine called our studies pure bullshit, others were not quite so blatant in their objections, but few came out and raved about our collective genius...

Your government has just spent, god knows how much of your hard earned tax money, to do a study very much like ours.

Guess how close we came...

In the first place any polygraph study is subject to various differing conditions including the expertise of the examiner, type of test, type of questions, countermeasures, etc.

A lie detector does NOT measure "lies", it records biological reactions to a fear, usually the fear of detection, but not truth or lies.

Lie detection exams are used for criminal case help, employment rating, and mass screening. There are several techniques employed in each of these situations which may also have a direct result on the findings.

The government study was consolidated by the Office of Technology Assessment (OTA) under the orders of the US Congress. They analyzed damn nearly every study conducted on, or about the lie detector.

First of all, many states have outlawed the use of this device as a pre-employment condition, a technique used by many corporations in the past.

On the other hand, the government has TRIPLED its use of polygraph exams over the past 9 years. The CIA and NSA are the two largest users (oddly enough, the FBI admits to not trusting the machine) but many other agencies also employ pre, or regular screening with the magic machine.

The dangers of this unit depend on whether you are more concerned with missing the guilty, or casting unfair doubt upon the innocent.

Out of the OTA's studies they found correct guilty detections ranged from 35-100%, a bit better than pure chance.

In voluntary testing, such as job screening, the percentages can run better. These numbers are also varied depending on the type of test used in each situation.

The army has already begun a 10 year program to improve the polygraph.

Other conditions that make or break a test can be whether the examiner is good, the setting of the test, if the subjects know it is a controlled test as opposed to a real life situation (controlled tests tend to be easier to beat), types of subjects and countermeasures employed.

Oddly enough, ethnic traits do have some effect, IQ seems to have a helpful edge on passing the test as the more intelligent subject may be able to anticipate the upcoming questions and act accordingly.

Also "low socialized subjects" tended to have less response to guilt reactions, while the upper end of the social scale would over react and cause false guilts.

One long term rumor that psychopathic types passed the tests as they felt less, or no guilt, for their actions seems to be totally false.

The fact that the machine was/is often used as a stage prop does have a major effect in the results. If a person is convinced that the unit will catch him; it probably will...

This is further borne out by the fact that the higher the possible punishment involved, the better chance of accuracy.

Before we get into countermeasures one must understand several things about the lie detector.

The basic theory behind guilt detection is fairly new and not yet developed or researched to its full capacity and the most widely accepted theory is that today's units measure mostly when the subject fears discovery.

There is still much research to be done in this field, and the fact that most courts will not accept poly findings, and many states and or firms no longer conduct such tests is probably good.

On the other hand, many agencies still regard a polygraph test denial to be an admission of at least some guilt.

You won't get the job or promotion...

COUNTERMEASURES

There are a number of active and passive countermeasures that seem to work with regard to the polygraph.

All of the ones presented in How To Get still hold true according to the OTA report except for one. They found the use of valium to not effect the test's outcome.

Remember Lee said it may or may not depending on the examiner as it tends to lower the entire response level rather than just the relevant responses.

They did not test, nor comment, on Elevil with which we still find positive results.

The OTA did suggest the drug meprobamate (sold as Miltown, a common tranquilizer) suppresses observable psychomotor responses while increasing the subject's ability to avoid lie detection.

Translated, the examiner thinks you're straight, the machine thinks you're honest...

In one test only 3 out of 11 guilty parties were even suspected of their deception after ingesting Miltown.

Another interesting drug is propranolol, a chemical which blocks beta responses. This resulted in a large number of inconclusives and passes while still fooling the human element as to drug use.

The different types of tests can make a real difference in countermeasure effectiveness. The type of sample test listed in Lee's last book, the CQT (control question test) does tend to stablize the overall responses making it a bit easier to come up with the correct results.

So...These downer type levelers can be somewhat offset by using an "upper" response on the control questions. Gripping the toes hard, especially on a taped thumb tack, thinking of thousands of black widow spiders crawling all over your vital organs, remembering the ex-wife, all can do an upward spike during a control question thus making the drugged essential responses appear within reason.

There are other, non-chemical, non-nail methods.

Simply coating the fingers with NEW SKIN or clear nail polish will help mess up any test but may be found out.

The following mental exercises can work depending on conditions, amount of practice and the subject involved.

If one understands the basic idea of the testing procedure it may be possible to shift, or disassociate oneself from the relevant questions by thinking of something else entirely, thereby not lying...

Practice with a biofeedback unit has also shown promise is controlling the body's involuntary responses to varying situations.

This does require much practice.

Several of these methods can be used alone, or in concert with each other to pass or invalidate a polygraph test. The best defense is still practice to see what works best for you.

It has also been suggested that the more people that believe that the polygraph is not valid, the more people that will make it exactly that.

PAPER LIE DETECTORS

Due to the generally unstable output of the polygraph machine a number of states have outlawed its use in employment screening applications.

This is important as a number of major corporations, from 7-11 and McDonalds all the way up to the super electronic firms did in fact use this device to decide which person would make an "honest" employee.

After the tougher laws were passed a new business sprung into existance, one could say, overnight. This is the paper lie detector...

In this idea the job applicant or employee is given a test ranging from 40-80 questions to fill out in conjunction with his regular flow of paper work. He is not advised as to the "true" nature of the test.

After the completion of the form the results are either called or mailed in to the issuing firm (which has charged the corporation at least $10 per test) whereupon each applicant is rate on a numerical scale as to his honesty.

Most of these firms justify their results against statistics gathered by comparing results with polygraphs of the same personnel.

A dubious starting point at best...

We took two such test for 20 applicants, some made up, some real, sliding the answers a degree or two in each test to figure out the scoring. Then a psychologist looked them over.

I came out a bad risk, our most honest employee came out average and our very most trust worthy friend who once drove a mile to return a dollar to a supermarket that had overcharged her came out the worst risk of all..

If you have to take one of these tests the following rules apply:

Up to half the questions will be control or filler questions that have no effect on your scoring at all.

The key questions all have the word "steal" (or substitute) in them. Questions like, "Just because a person has stolen once he will probably steal again", are expected to be a "Yes"!

On the other hand, any question that JUSTIFIES stealing in any way what so ever, "if everyone is stealing from work including the boss it is expected you will steal also" are a NO!

Or else...

In other words "Everyone steals sometimes from work, or it is any employee's duty to report any other employee he sees stealing " should be answered NO and YES.

In that order.

"Every employee steals something once", is a NO.

However, "Everyone at work could figure out a way to steal without being noticed", is a YES, because you have NOT justified stealing, but a NO looks like a trying to be "too clever" answer.

Obviously "someone who steals once is more likely to steal again" is a YES, while "Every person is tempted at times to steal", is a borderline NO.

"When I was a child I did steal small things"-NO Way Brother, nor have you ever been convicted of a crime.

Will most employees take a phony sick day from work? Now think my friend are you going to JUSTIFY STEALING?

No...

The remainder of the questions are coded to look like heavy duty, insightful psychological make-up questions about loving your mother as a child and whether other people talk about you behind your back and if you are unhappy at love/life are simply bullshit that is not graded in the score
anyway.

So remember that bad people do steal and take phony days off while good people know that they do, they, themselves WOULD NOT do the same thing even if the boss was running a bookie joint in the back room and asked them to help steal on their phony days off.

And, yes, they would snitch on other employees.

And yes, people who do steal continue to do so and you can blame them for it no matter what the JUSTIFICATION.

You'll get the job...

AUDIO ACQUISITION AND ELECTRONIC SURVEILLANCE

In this section we will look at some of the newer advances and sources in both acquisition and countermeasure technology as well as some additional ways to utilize existing equipment.

As Scott pointed out in the Big Brother Game, some of the best audio surveillance is conducted with some of the simplest equipment. Hardwiring, hidden VOX controlled tape recorders and direct coupled dropout relays are still the most reliable methods for collecting useable audio.

Two of the main problems associated with direct wire collection are noise and volume. In the first case one soon discovers a direct relationship between the length of any wiring and the amount of noise present on the final recording.

Wires, used in any circumstance, act as antennas and pick up electrical noise from a variety of sources. As the length of the wire increases the tendency to add noise also increases.

This is complicated by any natural generators of electrical noise in the area including certain lights, motors, radio transmitters, storms, ignitions and so forth.

Radio and television stations solve this problem by running balanced and shielded lines to all audio and video equipment. These rather expensive and complicated processes keep the lines completely free of spurious noise.

Until now there has been no real way to duplicate this sort of performance in surveillance applications where both access time and money may limit the complexity of the equipment in use.

VIKING is now marketing a unit that consists of a sub-miniature microphone and driver-power supply.

One installs the mic in the target area hooking it up to any unsed pair of wires (say the yellow and black pair in the typical 4 wire phone set-up) and then hooks the driver up to the same pair wherever the surveillance is to take place.

The unit has a number of advantages:

It is phantom powered. This means no power supply is necessary at the target end, but rather the power travels down the same wires, going in the opposite direction, as does the audio.

A nice touch as the unit can then powered virtually forever without needing any further premise access.

The unit is also nearly NOISE FREE. One gets the same quality of audio as with a shielded cable from an ordinary pair of copper wires.

This feature alone can make the difference between success and failure of many surveillance wires...

Lastly the unit will perform these feats for a distance of SEVERAL MILES using only the enclosed driver.

Power, low noise and distance, price about $300. The prototype unit we tested did exactly what the PR material said it would...

Defeating Ambience

Another problem in direct recording, especially when using a tape recorder or amplified sound focusing device (parabolic mic, "Hunter's Ears", etc.) is the fact that room ambience and small noises will tend to overcome the target signal drowning it out.

Anyone who has tried to record a lecture from the back of a room has experienced this problem, the signal is buried in the "grass" and very difficult, if not impossible to decipher.

Aftermarket processing can solve some of these problems, but no trick can put signal where there is none...

Another method is to use a compressor. This device, long employed in recording studios as well as for radio stations actually squeezes more signal onto the available tape (or carrier).

This compression has the effect of increasing the volume of the primary signal while actually lowering the effect of non-primary noises and room ambience.

We tested the 12BE compression preamp offered by VIKING and found it actually increased the usable range of any small tape recorder (especially when coupled with a sensitive condenser mic element) up to 2 or 3 times, depending on the situation.

This unit is a must when constructing any sort of briefcase recorder system.

It will make any recorder into a viable surveillance device.

Filters

In professional recording it is usually considered a breach of proper etiquette to filter any recording as it is being made. The master is normally recorded "flat" and then filtering is done before duplication or during the mixing process.

In surveillance recording, under normal circumstances, the per- petrater knows in advance exactly what he wants to record (normally the human voice) and may be faced with sounds outside this frequency range that interfere with the original recording.

Because of this possibility one of several types of filters can be employed:

A. Roll-off. This type simply stops, or "rolls off" any sounds below (or above) a certain, pre-set frequency. A very good choice where there may be low frequency interference such as traffic noises, wind blowing across the microphone or any "rumble".

B. Bandpass. This type of filter only lets a certain range of frequencies pass through it, preventing any frequency outside its response curve access.

Bandpass filters are often variable in response, allowing one to tailor fit a filter to any particular application, or simply set it for optimum response in the human voice range (say 500 Hz to 3,500 Hz-slightly better than a telephone line will pass).

In this second, preset mode, most low frequency hum as well as high frequency interference (such as music) will automatically be filtered from the final signal.

C. Notch. This filter is used to go into a frequency band and "notch" out one particular (or one narrow band) frequency.

Such units are very helpful if a certain, steady noise is affecting the recording. These filters can be used during the recording process if one has time to monitor and set up the correct filter (some are variable, some are pre-set), but are more often used after the recording is made to remove a certain noise.

D. Parametrics. This is a combination of filters that can be used in any of the above modes as well as be adjusted up and down in frequency response as well as in bandwidth.

Very handy units, they are usually fairly expensive and large for surveillance applications but are often found in local sound studios and can be very helpful in secondary processing.

MULTI-MODE AUDIO FILTER

This filter selects or rejects certain frequency components of signals you tune in. This allows it to reject undesired signals, such as noise and interference, while passing the desired signal, so long as the noise and signal are not on the same frequency. This frequency selection/rejection is optimized with 4 controls:

1. **Auxilary Notch Frequency** — The notch rejects a narrow band of frequencies.
2. **Function Select Switch (PK, NOTCH, LP, HP)** — PEAK (bandpass) passes a narrow band of frequencies, and rejects others — just the opposite of NOTCH. LOWPASS passes low frequencies, while rejecting high frequencies (e.g. hiss). HIGHPASS is the opposite of LOWPASS, it passes high frequencies, while rejecting low frequencies.
3. **Selectivity Control** — In PEAK, this control determines the filter bandwidth.
4. **The Frequency Control** — moves the peak, notch and lowpass frequencies from approximately 250 Hz to 2500 Hz. This spans the entire range of useful communications frequencies.

Applications: "Cleaning up" of audio signals from radio receivers or taperecorders. Removes such interference as heterodynes, whistles, buzzing noises, and other undesirable signals to bring out maximum intelligibility in the desired voice signal.

The AFI Filter is supplied with extensive applications information.

MODEL AP-1 AMPLIFIER

The AP-1 is ideal for monitoring the sounds picked up by Security Microphones Model A, B or C. This 2-watt full fidelity IC amplifier has a built-in 3 inch speaker and convenient headphone jacks, which enable you to listen to sounds with a high degree of accuracy. You can also easily record sounds for a permanent record by connecting a tape recorder to the line output. The AP-1 contains a built-in regulated power source which supplies proper voltage to the microphones at all times.

AUDIO PROCESSING

Three very useful aids in any audio collection operation. All will fit into a surveillance briefcase or can be utilized later in the lab.

Available at reasonable rates from VIKING INTERNATIONAL.

SUPER-LOGARITHMIC SPEECH PROCESSOR

The purpose of a speech-processing system is to provide the best possible intelligibility for voice recording. In our super-logarithmic speech processor this is accomplished by the use of three active filters to shape the voice frequency passband so that only the voice frequencies that add most to intelligibility are processed. Two of these active filers are placed before the input of the logarithmic amplifier, thus insuring a clean, noise-free signal at the amplifier input. The IC logarithmic amplifier has a 30 dB dynamic range and instantaneous attack and delay to provide a constant output regardless or input level variations.

The speech processor is installed between the microphone and the microphone input of any recorder.

THE ULTIMATE CONCEALMENT DEVICE

JUST WHISPER AND YOU CAN BE HEARD MILES AWAY!

Ear Mic is a revolutionary device combining a sub miniature transmitter and receiver housed in a hearing aid sized unit as small as a dime.

The bone conducting vibrations created in your ear canal when you speak are the means by which you can communicate hands-free and totally concealed. Range and speech clarity are excellent.

Ear Mic allows you to operate your field communication under severe environmental conditions, including extreme high noise levels, abnormal temperatures, vibration and shock.

Ear Mic works with any two-way radio equipped with external speaker microphone capability.

ADVANCED VIDEOTECH CO.
PO Box 122
Southampton, Pa 18966

MAGNUM DISTRIBUTION
943 Boblett st
Blaine, Wa 98230

A new toy that works with any two way radio that is equipped with an external mic/speaker output; one wears the earphone in-ear, as usual and then talks in a very quiet voice that is picked up through one's various bodily tubes and byways by the same EARPHONE!

This allows a hands free, super quiet, two-way conversation to transpire in any delicate situation. The entire unit can be hidden under a cap, helmet or long hair for greater security.

ADVANCED also carries some of the best walkie talkie's, booster, antennas, and cellular phones available.

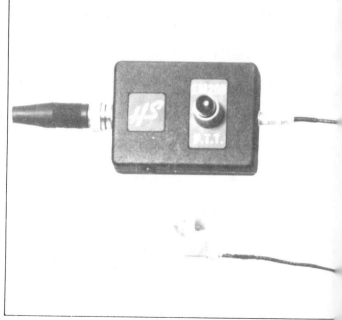

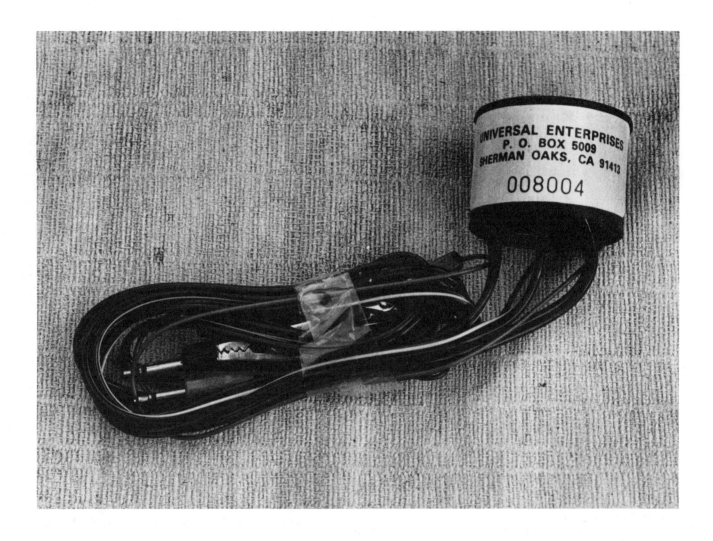

As this is being written Universal Enterprises is offering a loss leader drop out relay for $15.00.

It works.

Will they still honor this deal now? Send them $15.00, maybe public demand will force the issue...

TRM 1710
FM TRANSMITTER WITH CODED MODULATION

TRM 1711
FM CRYSTALLIZED TRANSMITTER WITH CODED MODULATION

Using wireless monitoring systems, you are never sure, if someone else is able to listen to the transmission, too. For that reason we have developed a wireless monitoring system, which guarantees monitoring without ˝eavesdroppers˝. The transmitter invertes automatically the signals sent, and an intelligible reception is only possible with the corresponding receiver TRM 2400 or TRM 2401 for the transmitter TRM 1711. This version is crystallized and therefore frequency stable.

We like to point out, that these systems are not professional scrambler. If you are in need of such systems please let us know, as they can be offered, too.

TECHNICAL SPECIFICATIONS:

Dimensions:	61 x 57 x 22 mm
Weight:	approx. 140 g incl. battery
Power supply:	1 x 9V battery
Running time:	30 hours
Transmitted frequency range:	TRM 1710 300 - 3000 Hz TRM 1711 300 - 3500 Hz
Frequency:	VHF range
Stability of the oscillator:	100 ppm

TRM 1720
FM DOUBLE MODULATED TRANSMITTER (SUB-CARRIER)

TRM 1720 is a sub-carrier transmitter, which consists of two units: the transmitter itself and a decoder, which has to be used together with the receiver. TRM 1720 was developed in order to secure the transmission against ˝eavesdroppers˝. On the side of the receiver, only the normal noise of radio interferences are heard, when the decoder is not used. As soon as the decoder is used with the receiver, the transmission is heard loud and clear without interferences. The range of TRM 1720 is between 150 - 500 meter, depending on the quality of the receiver.

TECHNICAL SPECIFICATION: TRANSMITTER:

Dimensions:	45 x 30 x 14 mm
Power supply:	6 V Lithium battery (2 CR - 1/3 N)
Running time:	50 hours
Aerial:	2 connections for a capacitive and inductive antenna
Frequency response:	300 - 4500 Hz

DECODER:

Dimensions:	168 x 90 x 30 mm
Power supply:	4 x 1,5 V Mignon Alkaline batteries
Running time:	25 - 200 hours (according to the loudness level)
Loudspeaker:	built-in
Jacks:	for headset or for recording

88

IMPROVING ON SURVEILLANCE DEVICES

In the last book Lee did a section on improving available devices, getting the most for your hard hustled dollar. We have found a few other improvements since then which we are proud to present for your perusal:

INFO UNLIMITED makes two high gain antennas; the HA1 helical and the HA2 high gain. Both will help extend the pickup range when installed on any receiver (and also make it more directional in pickup), if the HA2 is placed on the transmitter (bug) it will really add punch and range to the unit.

This is illegal, but by this point your whole set-up probably is, so...

Well worth the $25.00 for any mini-transmitter.

If you are purchasing any Starlight type NVD check to see if it has a thumb-screw type adapter to attach the eyepiece. If so, (and many do) measure the diameter of the holder and then check out the Edmund Scientific Industrial catalog for their selection of eyepieces, screens, and camera relays.

Much cheaper than buying from surveillance dealers...

A number of new active pre-amps for scanners and general receivers have hit the market since the last book (see photos) they are almost always worth the additional cost when trying to tune in the weak signal of a bug.

As a nice sidebar, many, especially the multi-band units, will help tune out the more powerful stations the receiver's AFC will try to focus in on.

Most of these pre-amps will fit nicely into a repeater or recorder briefcase...

Tubular 12.6 volt batteries, which can often be substituted for the called for 9 volt cell in bugs, thereby increasing output and range, are now widely available as they are utilized in some smoke detectors.

It has been shown that shielding a bug in a metal case, often even in aluminum foil, will make it "invisible" to non-linear ($15,000 "boomerang") detectors.

Of course, they will show up better to a common metal detector, but these are rarely used during a sweep, and also show nails, pipes, wires, etc.

After How To Get Lee received several dubious responses to his section advising the use of very expensive Lithium power cells rather than mercury batteries in transmitters whereever possible.

The following charts show the reason why...Remember Lithium do NOT shift voltage as they wear out.

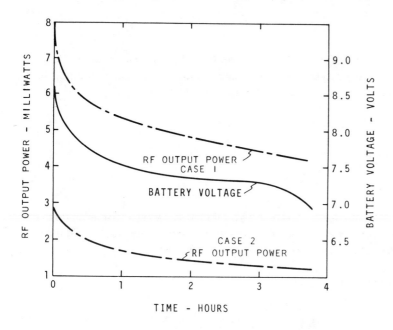

As shown in figure 9, the decay in transmitter output was approximately linear after the first few minutes of operation, and the half-power output level was not reached until after 8 hours of operation. A cell failure appears to have occurred at approximately 7 hours and 45 minutes into the test. The batteries were three 4.2-volt mercury batteries of the same type and manufacturer as those used in the test of transmitter #1. This would appear to be typical of the expected performance. Figure 10 shows the output spectrum with the strongest spurious radiation being the fourth harmonic (660 MHz), which is approximately 33 dB lower than the fundamental carrier frequency output, f_o.

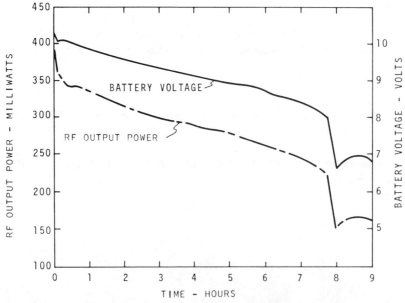

FIGURE 9.   Decay of output power and battery voltage

THE CASE OF THE AMAZING HUNTER'S EAR

A number of years ago some here unnamed individual came up with the idea of combining a small microphone, amplifier, and ear phones in a handy hand held case for the purpose of amplifing ambient sound.

It was felt this would be particularly advantageous to folks out looking for their dinner but who didn't want to drop by the neighborhood McDonalds...

A working prototype was constructed and deemed the Hunter's Ear with the idea of evening-up one of the few natural advantages mom nature gave to our animal friends.

A small ad was placed in a hunters type magazine and, one must suspect, hoards of electronic altered gun bearers took to the woods to aurally track down their helpless prey.

The first model lived in a plastic water pipe about 12 inches long with the mic element mounted at the front and the earphones connected at the back.
If the first unit made a rich man out of its inventor is not here important, the interesting fact is the sudden number of copies that appeared on the market.

Most kept the "ear" theme although some varied the prefix. Bionic ears, wonder ears, several hunter's ears, there were more ears available than at a corn stand...

Each ear maker tried to outdo the others and the devices gradually began to look more professional in nature, and some became more in ability. The pipe cases were replaced by flashlight cases and finally by molded plastic "ear" cases, the microphone elements got a bit more sensitive. Lee tested one of the earlier Hunter's Ears in HTGAOA with less than positive results.

Nevertheless, things do progress... After all the idea is a sound one; with the best engineering and components it should be possible to construct an aural version of a Starlight scope.

So how do the "second generation" ears rate?

Stay tuned...

EARS

We tested out two "bionic ears"; one from the Guardian Cane company, or VanSleek called the DOUBLE FARFOON and one HUNTER'S EAR from Viking.

Both were great fun in the bush of Africa, allowing the multitude of noises to be pin pointed and run from or id'ed...Depending on one's application.

The devices do help amplify the sound and give one an advantage, especially in still hunting, but are not quite as directional as they could be.

My other complaint was lack of an filtering devices to cut out wind noise or known sources of interference.

Viking is promising to change this...

The Farfoon can be equipped with a series of parabolic reflectors which increase the size of the unit but do make it many times more directional and more sensitive.

The heavy earphones are required to pick up the slightest noise, lighter weight "walkman" types allow better local pickup but can let the user miss some minor variations in the target noise.

Used at night, coupled with a night scope, these units can almost make one feel like he is taking part in a reshooting of the bionic man as entire hidden worlds come into play.

Over all we found the Viking to be a bit more sensitive and the Farfoon a bit more directional, although its amplification could be rasied with the optional reflector.

Neither unit is a Gibson parabolic, but neither unit costs like a Gibson para either...

For the money ($100-$175) they are a worthwhile addition to any outdoors kit or for simple scanning for you nosier types.

Both could use sudden noise overload protection (AGC), variable filtering and choice of mic elements.

Viking seems to be making some good progress in that direction.

Lee field testing the Hunter's Ear; ("I can hear something in there and it sounds big. I think maybe it's coming this way.") I suggested perhaps he should return to the jeep, as he was weighing all sides of this idea the subject stepped into view, making his mind up in what I believe to be record time for Lee.

A week later a woman was gored to death just about here by a Cape buffalo.

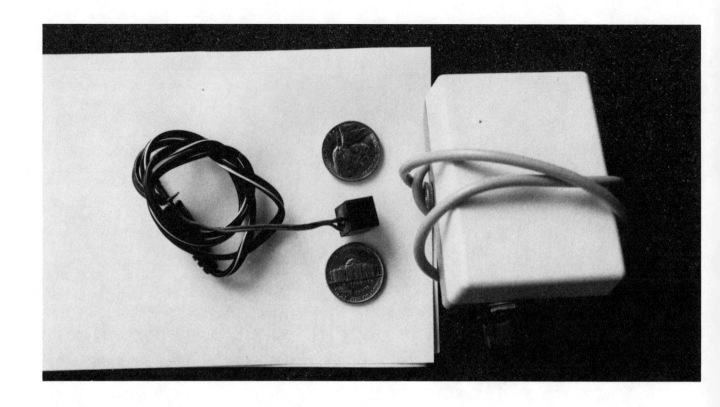

REMOTE SOUND ACQUISITION

VIKING ELECTRONICS' phantom powered, hum free amplifier that can transmit clear audio down a spare wire pair for a distance of 2 MILES!

Also a VIKING "Hunter's Ear" for those closer, but still dear sounds...

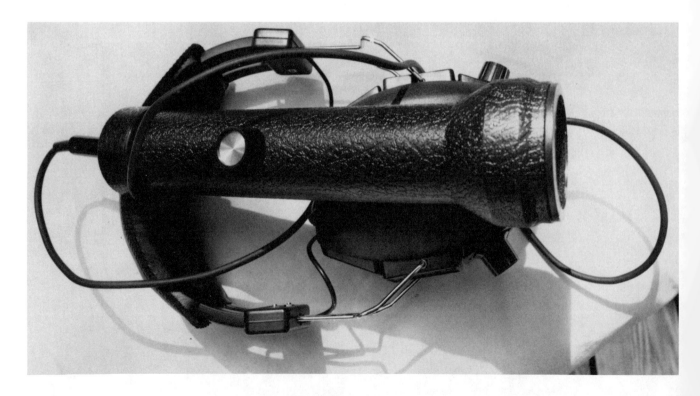

SURREPTITIOUS INFRARED AUDIO MONITORING

As the counter measure equipment field has made tremendous leaps forward in the last couple of years with directional receivers that pick up subcarrier transmissions as well as most type of coded or spread transmissions, coupled with more sensitive probes that shield out interference, the bugs themselves have made a few little technical pole vaults of their own.

One of the more interesting ideas is not to use a radio signal at all to transmit the modulation in question. Micro and Security sells three different micro to mini bugs that pick up room audio and then modulate invisible light (IR) beams to carry the transmissions 200-500 yards on a line of sight basis.

Of course the units must be mounted near a window or other open access area to project this beam to a special receiver without beam interruption.

The bug placement is not as difficult as it would first seem; behind a curtain, in a plant pot, behind a light shade and so on.

Besides the direct line-of-sight aspect the units have a moderate range at best, and tend to work better at night than during the daylight although they are operable during full sunlight.

Another interesting application of this IR modulation concept to couple it with a through-wall stethoscope so the entire unit can be attached the outside of a window or wall, pick up room audio and IR beam it to a waiting receiver.

While it is possible to detect an IR beam it requires a special viewer very few people, even professional sweepers utilize. The units also have the secondary advantage of no possible accidental discovery or unwanted interlopers picking up the signal.

A much less expensive route is to build (or buy one already assembled) one of the IR communicators sold by people like Info Unlimited, or Meredith and simply construct the transmitter as small as possible and use that for your IR bugging device.

Even if it is larger than the super German models it will still fit in a briefcase...

It is also probably possible to extend the useful range with the use of a telescopic lens on the receiver or perhaps even coupling an NVD unit to the receiver.

TRM 1810

IR MICROPHONE TRANSMITTER

TRM 1820

IR MICROPHONE TRANSMITTER LONG RANGE

We like to introduce to you the newest technology in the field of microelectronic. TRM 1810 as well as TRM 1820 are unique transmitter which make it possible to monitor conversations held in a room, by means of infrared light. The only condition which is necessary for the transmitter to work, is a window in the room to be monitored. Through this window the infrared-light will reach the outside where it is possible to pick it up with the help of a special developed receiver (TRM 2510). This unique process can not be received with a normal receiver and it is also not possible to detect it. An unwanted listening of a third person is therefore avoided. TRM 1810/1820 have to be installed near the window, in the curtains, plants or anywhere else, so that it is possible for the IR-light to reach the outside. TRM 1810 transmits all words clearly and distinctly up to a distance of 200 meters and TRM 1820, as a long range version, has a range of approx. 500 meters.

TECHNICAL SPECIFICATIONS FOR TRM 1810

Dimensions: 30 x 13 x 15 mm
Weight: approx. 15 g
Power supply: 2 x 1,5 V Varta
                V6 25PX
Running time: appr. 24 hours
Range: appr. 200 meters

TECHNICAL SPECIFICATIONS FOR TRM 1820

Dimensions: 44 x 30 x 17 mm
Weight: approx. 35 g
Power supply: 4 x 1,5 V Varta
                V6 25PX
Running time: appr. 12 hours
Range: appr. 500 meters

TRM 1830

IR STETHOSCOPE TRANSMITTER

TRM 1830 is the third product in our new line of transmitter which operate with infrared light instead of the commonly used frequency modulation. TRM 1830 has to be placed at the outside of the room which has to be monitored. With the help of a special adhensive kit, TRM 1830 has to be stuck to the window pane or the wall, and picks up all conversations held inside the room. Again a special receiver (TRM 2510) has to be used, securing, that no other party is able to pick up the transmission. With the receiver it is only possible to pick up the signal when there is line of sight between transmitter and receiver.

EXPERT BEATER BUG

Okay, you've just spent $40,000 on the latest "Bug Catcher Kit" from some not named firm in New York, got a heavy, heavy four days of training and you are ready to take on the bad guys of the world.

These two little gems, one room transmitter and one stethoscope (read outside of the wall) transmitter produce NO radio signals but transmit the audio over an invisible IR beam.

Let's see you find 'em...

"No sir, the room is perfectly clear, no radio signals in sight."

Right....

From our friends at MICRO SECURITY in Germany, see supplier's section.

LASERBUG?

As far as either of us knows, there are no commercial bugs that actually transmit their information on a beam of coherent light, although this would be the logical next step from the IR bugs.

However any of the laser tranceivers on the market could be used as a bugging device if placed so the beam would have a window to exit through and a straight line of sight to the receiver.

Size is the main disadvantage of most of the units available, however they are TRANSCEIVERS when all one wants for an eavesdropping operation is a transmitter.

One could take one of the kits available (Info Unlimited, Meredith) and just build the transmitter in one unit and a receiver in another, the size could be reduced considerably.

A more sensitive microphone should be substituted for greater pick up range.

IR lasers are better from the standpoint of the beam being "invisible" but they are more expensive and larger units. Few people would notice a visible laser beam if set near the window.

The court transcripts have been released.

CCS (Communication Control Systems) in New York is the largest supplier of electronic surveillance and countermeasure gear in the country. They are working off a federal bust by videotaping customers in their sales rooms, with their salespeople, attempting to purchase illegal gear or stating their intent to take such gear (like NVDs) out of the U.S. The owner, Ben Jamil, also owns The Counter Spy Shop at 1801 K Street, Washington, D.C. He has been an informant for the FBI since 1983. There is a strong possibility that at least one company we have listed is no longer in business due to his activities.

This firm has been busted several times and it would make sense that they are rolling over to work off some of the heat, as they are still in business.

If you find yourself in the position of being asked, either in person or through the mail, what use the equipment is to be put to, or any reference to wiretapping, bugging, etc., I would suggest you back off and break off all contact with that company.

LASER COMMUNICATIONS...

For years the CIA, among others, has employed a type of super "bug"; one that needed no access to the area to be monitored, worked from nearly a safe mile from the target, was portable and almost impossible to detect.

This device made the civilian marketplace about 5 years ago when it was offered, by a german electronics firm, for $25,000!!

Despite denials, it works...

It has some problems, i.e., outside noise, weather, interior covering noise, etc, but it does work.

The german device uses an infrared LASER tube to produce an invisible beam which is aimed at a target window and the reflecting beam picked up by a lens and fed to a demodulator.

As the persons in the target room speak, their voices actually set up vibrations on the glass of any window in the vicinity. These minute vibrations cause the beam of coherent light to vibrate (modulate) slightly in perfort accord.

When concentrated by a lens and electronically ciphered (demodulated) the target conversation can be heard.

The IR beam is invisible, making detection quite difficult. It also makes correct aiming/alignment difficult...

The commercial unit uses a visible LASER for aiming, and then switches to the invisible IR beam for monitoring purposes.

We have seen/used/built a similar unit for about $600...

PLEASE NOTE:

We are listing this unit for 2 reasons and 2 reasons only:

> 1. For your information so as to be watched for and countered.

2. For use as an experimental,one-way LASER COMMUNICATIONS DEVICE AND NOT TO BE UTILIZED AS AN ILLEGAL SURVEILLANCE DEVICE.

Any such use may well violate numerous federal and state laws and may well land the user in jail.

NOTE THE ABOVE WELL AND HEED IT!!

A few differences exist between our unit and the $25,000 german device; first and foremost, ours uses a VISIBLE LASER which places a red dot on the target window, and often through it onto a wall.

We are doing this for several reasons, it is about $2000 cheaper to use a visible LASER instead of an IR unit, although the substitution could be made.

During the daylight it is very difficult to see the faint dot on the corner of a window, although it is very bright at night.

It is much easier to aim and collect the returning beam with a visible unit.

You are not supposed to be using it for surveillance anyway, so who cares if a visible dot appears?

One should be aware that the red beam will "scatter" if it strikes a curtain leaving a very tell tale red glow that will at least alarm anyone within the target room.

One of the main problems in construction a one way communicator have been that the optically sensitive device (in our case a photo transistor) will react to any light falling upon it including our return beam.

To counter this effect we have used a special honeycomb light filter that only allows the BEAM FREQUENCY to pass through, stopping the stray non-coherent light.

The second problem is that outside noise, traffic, wind and such, also modulates the returning beam and tends to override the Inside conversation.

Luckily most of this interference lies in the lower end of the audio spectrum and can be filtered out with a low end cut off device that prevents the passage of anything below a certain frequency.

The honeycomb light filter has been around for a while albeit at a very expensive price. Some have now hit the surplus market and we found a very inexpensive source...

As our source also sells the best, cheap LASERS we could find, one can be certain that the filter actually does match the beam frequency exactly.

Realize that our unit is still experimental and requires a bit of adjustment to work perfectly but IT DOES WORK.

And for a hell of a lot less than $25,000...

At least two companies are working on a commercial version of this device; INFORMATION UNLIMITED, and one one other...

Under ideal conditions our unit will work from 1/4 to 1/2 of a mile from the target.

The main factor in good reception is that the angle between the transmitter and receiver is exactly 90 degrees. Note the drawing to see this is accomplished by maintaining a VERTICAL right angle rather than a horizontal one.

The return beam must be caught and focused into the filter/receiver unit. While this can usually be done optically please note:

ALTHOUGH WE ARE USING A FAIRLY LOW POWER HE-NEON LASER IT IS STILL POWERFUL ENOUGH TO BLIND ANYONE LOOKING DIRECTLY INTO THE UNIT ON A TEMPORARY OR PERHAPS PERMANENT BASIS.

Use care.

During the Vietnam "police action" we used a medium power LASER mounted on a helicopter gunship to flash a quick beam towards the site of any anti-aircraft fire with the idea of blinding the gun operator.

Operators of LASER surveillance devices have discovered that it is often possible to bounce the beam off of a reflective surface INSIDE the target room, such as a mirror or glass covered photograph, and produce better results than if just reflected from the window pane.

Needless to say they were usually using an invisible IR beam rather than our bright red dot.

Even the LASER itself is fun to play with...Dogs chase the bright red dot, neighbors jump out of bed and throw open the window when their curtains "catch fire", joggers fall down when (at night) a brilliant red UFO paces them, people dim their lights, well you get the idea...

Yes, I know that's a childish application of a high tech device, but it is still fun.

Once again I have to remind you this is NOT presented for use as a surveillance device and any such application, without consent of all parties involved is very likely against one or more laws.

LASER   EVESDROPPER

Light Beam Modulation

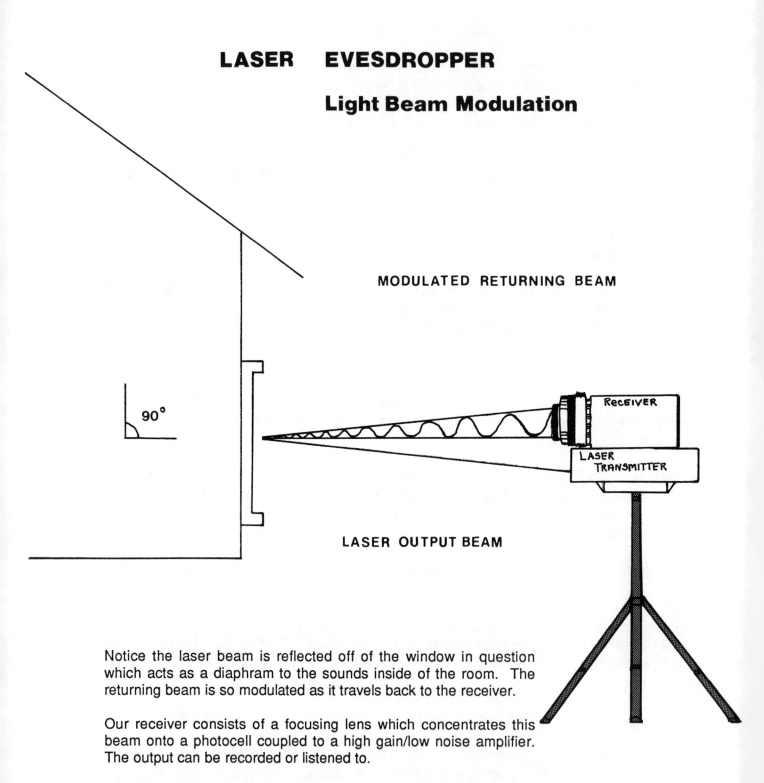

MODULATED   RETURNING BEAM

90°

RECEIVER

LASER
TRANSMITTER

LASER OUTPUT BEAM

Notice the laser beam is reflected off of the window in question which acts as a diaphram to the sounds inside of the room. The returning beam is so modulated as it travels back to the receiver.

Our receiver consists of a focusing lens which concentrates this beam onto a photocell coupled to a high gain/low noise amplifier. The output can be recorded or listened to.

The laser should be aimed at a 90 degree (or as close as possible) angle to the window so the return beam strikes the lens of the receiver. If properly set up this unit will operate at a distance of up to 1/2 of a mile depending on the power of the laser and the quality of the components used in the receiver.

MEREDITH LASER

A rather ungraphic view of the MEREDITH LASER we used to construct our answer to the $25,000 LASER bug.

This device will light up bedroom walls (at night) for nearly a mile...

Great fun, even if one doesn't use it for communications purposes.

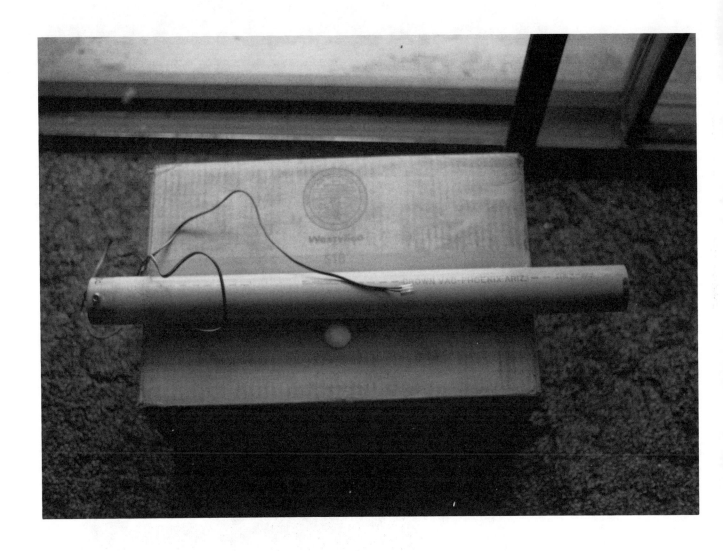

BETTER LIVING THROUGH MEREDITH ELECTRONICS

The LASER one-frequency filter that makes possible the one way communications device and, ah, the bug.

Bottom photo is the Starlight scope power supply and one of the three light amplification tubes for the kit.

HOW TO POWER YOUR HELIUM - NEON LASER

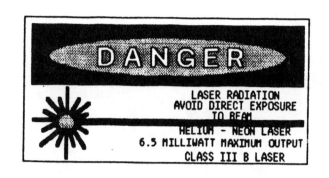

DANGER

LASER RADIATION
AVOID DIRECT EXPOSURE
TO BEAM
HELIUM - NEON LASER
6.5 MILLIWATT MAXIMUM OUTPUT
CLASS III B LASER

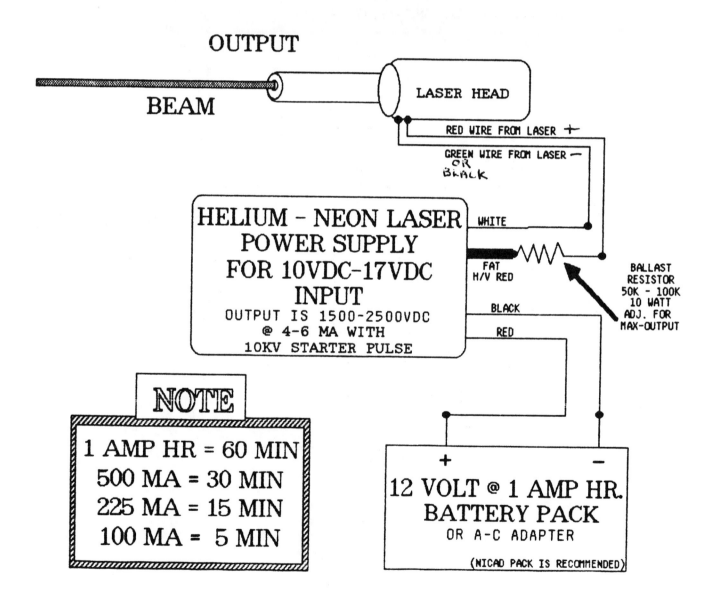

OUTPUT

BEAM

LASER HEAD

RED WIRE FROM LASER +

GREEN WIRE FROM LASER —
OR
BLACK

HELIUM - NEON LASER POWER SUPPLY FOR 10VDC-17VDC INPUT
OUTPUT IS 1500-2500VDC
@ 4-6 MA WITH
10KV STARTER PULSE

WHITE

FAT
H/V RED

BLACK

RED

BALLAST
RESISTOR
50K - 100K
10 WATT
ADJ. FOR
MAX-OUTPUT

NOTE

1 AMP HR = 60 MIN
500 MA = 30 MIN
225 MA = 15 MIN
100 MA = 5 MIN

12 VOLT @ 1 AMP HR. BATTERY PACK
+   —
OR A-C ADAPTER
(NICAD PACK IS RECOMMENDED)

Electronics for the one way LASER COMMUNICATOR.

Remember the light filter goes IN FRONT of the photo transistor, and a good notch or adjustable filter unit should be placed between the output and the earpones/recorder to knock off low frequency noise to which the unit is MOST SENSITIVE.

LIGHT BEAM RECEIVER AND AMPLIFIER

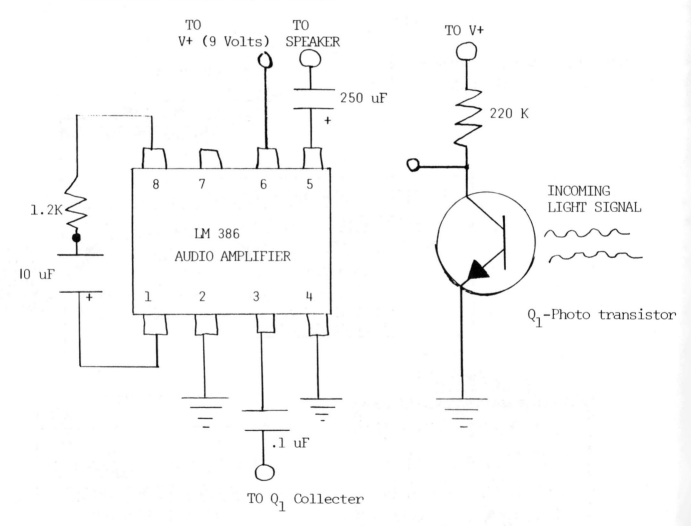

TO Q₁ Collecter

LASER ART

Scott shooting himself via the reflection (from a mirror) of the MEREDITH LASER. Plenty of beam for any modulation purpose.

Bottom shows the visible beam splatter on a curtain at night. It is a bit noticable...

SCANNERS IN SURVEILLANCE APPLICATIONS

Public service band scanners are fun, interesting and let one know if the police have a sudden interest in one's activities... Sometimes a nice thing to keep track of...

Previously they were not really good enough for surveillance applications because of their design. The units were controlled by crystals which were hard to find and keep on hand and they were designed to receive signals from at least 5 watt transmitters, not micro powered bugs.

New developments in the scanner area plus a whole slew of aftermarket add-ons have changed this situation.

Most scanners are now frequency synthesized so they are as stable as crystal units but DO NOT use crystals. This gives one instant access to a large number of frequencies at the touch of a button.

Preamps and Active Antennas

These add-on devices boost the strength of incoming signals much like adding a gain (yagi) antenna making it possible to receive weak signals without a long wire antenna. A number of different models are now on the market for under $100 from VIKING ALTERNATE TECH and the sources listed on the scanner helper (sounds like dinners my wife used to cook) page.

Filters

Notch and bandpass filters for rf that will knock out undesired signals, multipath and interference.

Sometimes coupled with an active antenna.

Converters

Scanners operate only in certain, pre-selected frequency ranges for two reasons; this is where the public service activity is and certain government agencies that shall here travel nameless, do not wish their activities to be monitored.

A converter will expand the useful range of any scanner by converting these out-of-band frequencies into the normal vhf or uhf ranges serviced by the scanner.

This allows monitoring of frequencies where some interesting activity takes place, as well as monitoring bugs placed in these fairly safe frequency areas.

Automatic Loggers

Working on a VOX (voice operated relay) principle these units start a recorder only when an audio signal is present, then stopping the recorder when conversation ceases.

They are wonderful units allowing unattended surveillance stations to be constructed as they will "condense" time down only to active periods.

When using a logger it is usually best to monitor a few channels at any give time (locking out the rest) as to tell who is talking and where they are located at any given time, however they can allow the use of multiple transmitters to monitor several rooms in a target area, each one set on a different frequency and record any audio as one conversation.

Use some of our mail order sources for the best prices on scanners and test every combination well in advance of actual use.

NEW TRICKS

A Look At Some New Tricks In Surveillance...

Two Ways

A cheap trick to help hide either two way conversations or a bugging operation is to purchase a receive crystal for a CB and then place it in the transmit slot.

This will knock the unit off frequency some 450 odd Hz...

SCANNERS

At first, both of us distrusted the use of scanners in any surveillance operation (except, of course to keep track of the various law enforcement agencies that might be involved), but with the advent of pre-amps, frequency expanders, VOX-relays scanner to recorder starters and gain antennas, the scanner has become a viable option as a bug receiver and/or relay station.

The new (er) frequency synthesized models are as accurate as the older crystal sets and much more useable. This has led to low prices on the crystal models as dealers are dumping stock; skip 'em...

SCANNER WORLD
10 New Scotland Ave
Albany, NY 12208

Has the best prices and widest variety we have located. Models from $85 up, real specs published and even a selection of two-way radios.

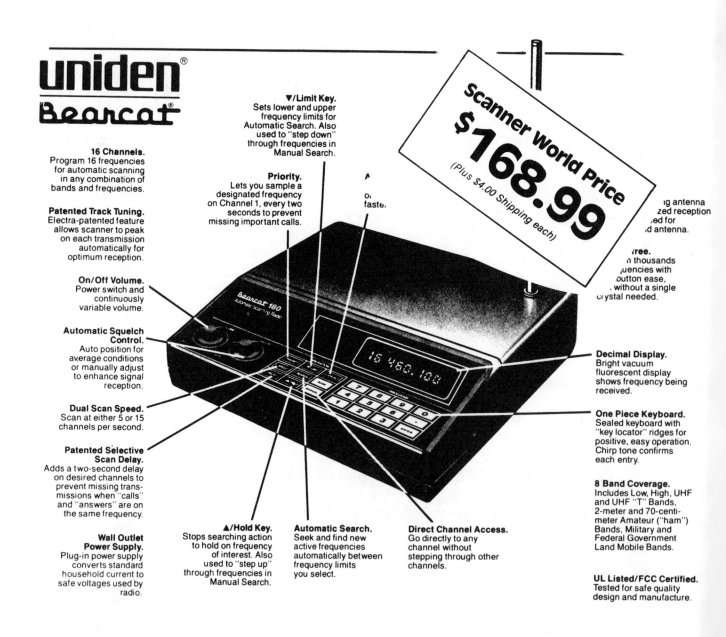

uniden®
Bearcat®

16 Channels.
Program 16 frequencies for automatic scanning in any combination of bands and frequencies.

Patented Track Tuning.
Electra-patented feature allows scanner to peak on each transmission automatically for optimum reception.

On/Off Volume.
Power switch and continuously variable volume.

Automatic Squelch Control.
Auto position for average conditions or manually adjust to enhance signal reception.

Dual Scan Speed.
Scan at either 5 or 15 channels per second.

Patented Selective Scan Delay.
Adds a two-second delay on desired channels to prevent missing transmissions when "calls" and "answers" are on the same frequency.

Wall Outlet Power Supply.
Plug-in power supply converts standard household current to safe voltages used by radio.

▼/Limit Key.
Sets lower and upper frequency limits for Automatic Search. Also used to "step down" through frequencies in Manual Search.

Priority.
Lets you sample a designated frequency on Channel 1, every two seconds to prevent missing important calls.

▲/Hold Key.
Stops searching action to hold on frequency of interest. Also used to "step up" through frequencies in Manual Search.

Automatic Search.
Seek and find new active frequencies automatically between frequency limits you select.

Direct Channel Access.
Go directly to any channel without stepping through other channels.

Decimal Display.
Bright vacuum fluorescent display shows frequency being received.

One Piece Keyboard.
Sealed keyboard with "key locator" ridges for positive, easy operation. Chirp tone confirms each entry.

8 Band Coverage.
Includes Low, High, UHF and UHF "T" Bands, 2-meter and 70-centimeter Amateur ("ham") Bands, Military and Federal Government Land Mobile Bands.

UL Listed/FCC Certified.
Tested for safe quality design and manufacture.

Scanner World Price **$168.99** (Plus $4.00 Shipping each)

SCANNER HELPERS

HAMTRONICS
65 Moul Rd
Hilton NY 14468

SPECTRONICS
1009 Garfield st
Oak Park, IL 60304

ALLCOMM
5717 NE 56th
Seattle, WA 98105

ARCOMM
24 Valley st
Lewistown, PA 17044

THE DOG HOUSE
P.O. Box 511
Fairfax, VA 22030

GROVE ENTERPRISES
Brasstown, NC 28902

AUTEK RESEARCH
Box 302
Odessa, FL 33556

BMI
65 East Palatine
Prospect Heights, IL 60667

HAMTRONICS offers a complete line of boosted antennas, band converters and filters, discount scanners, active antennas, ALLCOMM Multi-Mode filters, ARCOMM- antenna booster and pre-selector for up to four antennas, THE DOG HOUSE scanner signal meters, memory expanders, direction finders, GROVE- a complete discount scanner line plus boosters, filters, etc., BMI-NiteLogger, an automatic logger.

Nitelogger photo courtesy of *Popular Communications* magazine, 76 North Broadway, Hicksville, NY.

Also, several of our regular suppliers, including Viking and AT, offer units of interest.

HEAR THE NEW BANDS
ON YOUR SCANNER

Converts out-of-band signals to vhf or uhf scanner bands. Cables provided. Simply plug into scanner.

5 MODELS AVAILABLE:
806-894 MHz New Land Mobile Band
400-420 MHz Federal Government & FBI
240-270 MHz Navy/Air Force Satellites
135-144 MHz Weather Satellites
 72-76 MHz Industrial & Radio Control

ONLY $88 + $3 S & H

DIG OUT WEAK SIGNALS

Get **clearer distant reception** using **ACT–1 POWER ANTENNA** instead of scanner's built-in whip. This compact 21 – inch antenna has **integral preamplifier,** gives up to 15 dB gain (30 times as strong), plus all the advantages of a high antenna away from noise pickup. **Often outperforms** much larger indoor antennas! **Easy to install** on any vertical surface indoors or out. No mast required. **Covers all bands:** 30 – 900 MHz. Complete with 50 ft. cable, ready to plug into scanner.

**ACT–1 POWER ANTENNA
ONLY $79 + $3.40 S&H**

Model FL3

- Multi-Mode Audio Filter With Auto-Notch

SUPER SELECTIVITY!

The QF1-A's five filter modes help reje~ ~latter, hum, LF jammers and wh¹ for CW and TTY readers. The· ·ide. WORKS WITH ~ ·t into radios n~ 115VA~

The Best Active Antenna COSTS LESS!

The new ARCOMM AP4 active tuned antenna/preselector is the most versatile, best performing unit available. Ideal for use where outside antennas are not possible.

89⁹⁵

including FREE AC adapter

FEATURES:
- Tunes 540 KHz thru 32 MHz in four bands
- Improves RF selectivity and image re~~
- Accepts up to four exte~~
- Internal tel~

111

LAW ENFORCEMENT CODES

10-0	CAUTION	10-48	TRAFFIC STANDARD NEEDS REPAIRS
10-1	UNABLE TO COPY-CHANGE LOCATION	10-49	TRAFFIC LIGHT OUT AT
10-2	SIGNAL GOOD	10-50	ACCIDENT (F, PI, PD)
10-3	STOP TRANSMITTING	10-51	WRECKER NEEDED
10-4	ACKNOWLEDGEMENT (OK)	10-52	AMBULANCE NEEDED
10-5	RELAY	10-53	ROAD BLOCKED AT
10-6	BUSY-STAND BY UNLESS URGENT	10-54	LIVESTOCK ON HIGHWAY
10-7	OUT OF SERVICE	10-55	INTOXICATED DRIVER
10-8	IN SERVICE	10-56	INTOXICATED PEDESTRIAN
10-9	REPEAT	10-57	HIT & RUN (F, PI, PD)
10-10	FIGHT IN PROGRESS	10-58	DIRECT TRAFFIC
10-11	DOG CASE	10-59	CONVOY OR ESCORT
10-1	STAND BY (STOP)	10-60	SQUAD IN VICINITY
10-13	WEATHER-ROAD REPORT	10-61	PERSONNEL IN AREA
10-14	PROWLER REPORT	10-62	REPLY TO MESSAGE
10-15	CIVIL DISTURBANCE	10-63	PREPARE TO MAKE WRITTEN COPY
10-16	DOMESTIC PROBLEM	10-64	MESSAGE FOR LOCAL DELIVER5Y
10-17	MEET COMPLAINANT	10-65	NET MESSAGE ASSIGNMENT
10-18	COMPLETE ASSIGNMENT, QUICKLY	10-66	MESSAGE CALCELLATION
10-19	RETURN TO---------	10-67	CLEAR FOR NET MESSAGE
10-20	LOCATION	10-68	DISPATCH INFORMATION
10-21	CALL------BY PHONE	10-69	MESSAGE RECEIVED
10-22	DISREGARD	10-70	FIRE ALARM
10-23	ARRIVED AT SCENE	10-71	ADVICE NATURE OF FIRE
10-24	ASSIGNMENT COMPLETED	10-72	REPORT PROGRESS OF FIRE
10-25	REPORT IN PERSON (MEET)	10-73	SMOKE REPORT
10-26	DETAINING SUBJECT, EXPEDITE	10-74	NEGATIVE
		10-75	IN CONTACT WITH
10-27	(DRIVERS) LICENSE IN-FORMATION	10-76	ENROUTE
		10-77	ETA (ESTIMATED TIME OF ARRIVAL
10-28	VEHICLE REGISTRATION INFORMATION	10-78	NEED ASSISTANCE
10-29	CHECK RECORD FOR WANTED	10-79	NOTIFY CORONER
10-30	ILLEGAL USE OF RADIO	10-80	CHASE IN PROGRESS
10-31	CRIME IN PROGRESS	10-81	BREATHALYZER REPORT
10-32	MAN WITH A GUN	10-82	RESERVE LODGING
		10-83	WORK SCHOOL XING AT-----
		10-84	IF MEETING-----ADVICE T
		10-85	DELAYED TUE TO

10-33 EMERGENCY
10-34 RIOT
10-35 MAJOR CRIME ALERT
10-36 CORRECT TIME
10-37 (INVESTIGATE) SUSPI-
      CIOUS VEHICLE
10-38 STOPPING SUSPICIOUS
      VEHICLE
10-39 URGENT--USE LIGHT,
      SIREN
10-40 SILENT RUN-NO LIGHT
      SIREN
10-41 BEGINNING TOUR OF DUTY
10-42 ENDING TOUR OF DUTY
10-43 INFORMATION
10-44 REQUEST PERMISSION TO
      LEAVE PATROL----
      FOR------
10-45 ANIMAL CARCASS IN----
      LANE-----
10-46 ASSIST MOTORIST
10-47 EMERGENCY ROAD REPAIRS NEEDED

10-86 OFFICER/OPERATOR ON DUTY
10-87 PICKUP/DISTRIBUTE CHECKS
10-88 ADVISE PRESENT TELEPHONE #
      OF------
10-89 BOMB THREAT
10-90 BANK ALARM AT------
10-91 PICK UP PRISONER/SUBJECT
10-92 IMPROPERLY PARKED VEHICLE
10-93 BLOCKAGE
10-94 DRAG RACING
10-95 PRISIONER/SUBJECT IN CUSTODY
10-96 MENTAL SUBJECT
10-97 CHECK (TEST) SIGNAL
10-98 PRISON/JAIL BREAK
10-99 RECORDS INDICATE WANTED OR
      OR STOLEN

COMPUTER SECURITY METHODS

As many sources of information are now stored and processed on computers the idea of security becomes a paramount concern.

A complete look at both hardware and software protection and violation methods would (and does) fill several books. Here we are going to go into just a couple of ideas for both protection and interception of computer data.

Software

Most commercial software is "copy protected" so one person cannot buy a program and then duplicate it for all of his buddies mit out charge.

Most of these protection systems are simple and already considered outmoded. Every computer magazine carries ads for copy defeat programs that search for hidden files and different parameters and then copy the "protected" disc.

At one point, a few years ago, NSA came up with a code it announced was unbreakable as it was not based on any one key but used variables.

A teenage hacker claimed to have broken the code on his Apple. The National Security agency challenged him by giving him a coded document to unscramble.

The kid set up his Apple and turned it loose; for 12 hours it went through all the possible combinations and then printed out the message.

NSA was not happy...

Suppose you are putting valuable information onto a computer disc and want to protect it from prying eyes, what then?

What follows is an explanation of the most used privacy systems as well as a plug for the one we found that seemed to work very well.

The system we are pitching is made by Barry of EDEN PRESS, and yes he is sort of a friend BUT his system works. We had three of the top computer hackers around (including two which have written commercially available, popular programs) and they liked this system better than anything else they could find.

As usual we have no financial interest in this (or any other product) that we suggest.

Actually that's too bad, I could use the money, but too many books on surveillance and such are merely dressed up sales catalogs for some hardware supplier.

Not fair...

COMPARISONS AND VULNERABILITIES

HELLMAN-DIFFIE

This algorithm is the "Trapdoor-Knapsack" variety that has been widely touted as an "unbreakable" private/public key system. Adi Shamir formulated an attack upon this algorithm in 1982 which Leonard Adleman then extended into a high success rate implementation using the APPLE II personal computer. Hellman has acknowledged that this algorithm is now"....flat on its back..."

RIVEST-SHAMIR-ADLEMAN

The RSA algorithm is based upon extremely large prime numbers and the product of two or more such numbers. In its time, it was a very secure methodology owing to fundamental difficulties in factoring large primes. In 1984, however, factoring fifty digit primes proves to be "trivial" and eighty digit primes are within reasonable challenge.

Extending the impact of newer factoring methods, a family of processes developed within the past two years, one must realize that what was known about the RSA approach in 1981 requires radical rethinking. Active researchers now project such confidence that 125 digit---or perhaps even 200 or 300 digit---primes shall be routinely factorable in the immediate future.

DATA ENCRYPTION STANDARD

The 'DES', as managed by the National Bureau of Standards, is a microchip-based device lodged firmly in the public domain. FPIS Publications 46 and 74 provide extensive documentation and disclosures. The DES is an active 56-bit (plus 8-bit parity) algorithm which was declined by the National Security Agency. This leads one to conclude that NSA perceives sufficient implicit weakness that it is not suitable for U.S.cryptographic system useage. Hence, we could further conclude that at least NSA is confident of being able to penetrate a DES-based data file.

NICOLAI et al

One of the more visible wonts of NSA to keep private encryption systems off the public market lies in the legal battle waged by Carl Nicolai, William Raike, Carl Quale, and David Miller over one of their inventions, "Phasorphone". Their next product, "Cryptext", was an encryption device requiring an eighty-bit key that operates with Radio Shack's TRS-80 personal computer. The inventors simply encapsulated the circuitry of "Cryptest" and are treating it as a trade secret. Literature available on this product does not disclose the algorithm or its implementation architecture, but the eighty-bit key implies a "password/seed type of approach, much like the common denominator of the DES approach. While Messers Nicolai et al may not wish to acknowledge their algorithm as a DES look-alike or spinoff, the password/seed architecture seems to carry over in any event.

GAINES; KAHN

Helen Fouche Gaines wrote "Elementary Cryptanalysis" in 1939. This is, perhaps, the classic of open literature writings upon such a sensitive subject. This treatment of analog cryptographic methods encapsulates the body of knowledge of the subject through the post-WWI days. Because of self-inflicted wounds (i.e.: Gentlemen do not read other gentlemen's mail..." the U.S. technology during the post-WWI era took us into the early days of WWII essentially unchanged. Gaines' work, therefore, is particularly telling because it probably describes U.S. state of the art well into the 1940s.

David Kahn rocked the stodgy cryptographic community with his 1967 treatise, "The Codebreakers". While his stated intent was to trace the history of the subject, he actually makes incisive disclosure that eclipses Yardley's "Black Chamber" revelations. Kahn's discussion of the German system ENIGMA is particularly telling because it is widely believed that an Americanized variant served U.S. applications well into the late 1960s and may well persist today as a "backup" to the automated electronic data links now in use.

The significance of Gaines and Kahn, however, is that the kernel ideas are taken from behind the ultra-secret NSA veil and are discussed in the public domain. It may prove useful. therefore, that algorithms originally intended for mechanical implementations are considered anew in light of personal computers. Perhaps some remodeling will provide meaningful and advantageous products.

PRIVACODE TM

PRIVACODE has been developed purely from information available in the Gaines and Kahn realm, enhanced by current mathematical theory and practice, and implemented in the modern digital computer of the so-called Personal Computer variety. As a parenthetical aside, today's PC has more capability and capacity than did its vacuum tube grandfather, despite the "breadbox verus barn" size reductions.

Because PRIVACODE's architecture, modules and algorithms are undisclosed, a certain implicit security benefit is derived. But it is carefully emphasized that

PRIVACODE is being described as a privacy device and not a cryptographic system. This is because we remain convinced that the government's ire, focused through NSA's unbounded assets and unlimited analytical ability, can penetrate PRIVACODE the same as it may rend other systems.

Rather, PRIVACODE addresses constructive and needed applications in the business world. It accounts for the users' need for privacy at a high level of security by implementing proven algorithms that have withstood the test of analytic attack.

It is believed that the fundamental algorithms used in PRIVACODE have never been broken. They have been compromised through operator error and by physical capture of hardware. But even with those grevious adverse disclosures, the fundamental algorithms remain untouched and secure.

A BRIEF CRYPTANALYSIS PRIMER

Analytical and statistical methods aside, there are two fundamental methods by which any cryptographic scheme may be dissolved. The first is physical or operational errors that permit adverse possession of both a cleartext and an encrypted version of a file. The second is purely a sufficient volume of encrypted text such that statistical attacks proves feasible.

In the former situation, an analyst who can correlate the clear and encrypted versions of a file can determine the heart of the system--the keystream. Provided the analyst has knowledge of the algorithms and their implementations, he can use the keystream knowledge to compromise every file encrypted with that particular key. You lose not only the file under immediate attack, therefore, but you also stand to lose every file encrypted in that key. This gives rise to the idea of limited application of any particular key within a system, and to the practice of re-initializing after so many words have been encrypted, or after so many hours of on-line use has occurred.

In the latter case, pure "grist for the mill" is foreclosed upon by the solution derived in the initial case. Simply, it is a sound practice to reinitialize your keystream by some method, or to otherwise limit its continuous application. In so doing, the basis of statistical attack is sorely undermined. This is the precise reason why the "one time pad" is absolutely secure. The keystream is used once only and never is repeated. The solutions implicit in limiting application of a particular key are pertinent to limiting disclosure once an operational error has occurred as well as weakening statistical attack.

But, obviously, physical security and control of the cryptographic devices and related keying material transcend all other considerations. The military guards cryptographic materials by a combination of rigid physical security requirements, stringent clearance and access controls, and by meticulous accounting and procedural methods.

WHY IS PRIVACODE DIFFERENT?

We should treat the generic types rather than specific products in answering this question. Fundamentally, those methods which require a password to either access a stock algorithm, or to seed some mathematical keystream generator are implicitly vulnerable. But their vulnerability is the result of something other than the mathematical integrity of the algorithm. It is a basic issue of human nature.

Despite repeated precautions to the contrary, humans must select passwords they can remember. While this seems to profoundly state the obvious, it is the fundamental security flaw in DES and the hybrid systems. An Orange County psychologist purchased one of the more expensive and sophisticated DES-Hybrid systems on the market for protecting some of his more prominent client files. It took me a matter of several minutes to discern his password logic and then successfully attack his files. His method? He finally resorted to using the patient's last name as a password/seed because he simply couldn't synthesize and recall unrelated passwords.

Other users finally resort to writing passwords down somewhere, or in selecting one that never changes. The consequences are obvious in either case. Hence, I tend to dismiss password/seed systems on this basis alone without every entering the technical argument of whether the algorithm can be broken. My perspective is that of reading an encrypted file by the easiest method available and this means simply that you attack the human weakness if at all possible.

A passing, yet pertinent comment upon the HELLMAN-DIFFIE, RSA, and DES methodologies is that through either analytical or human factors, they are demonstrably weak. November, 1984's issue of OMNI Magazine treats the technical aspects of HELLMAN and RSA in sufficient authorative detail as to confirm what many have privately believed for some time.

The essential features of PRIVACODE which makes it different from the trapdoor, prime number, or DES approaches are critically implicit in its security. First, absolutely no disclosure of the algorithms or the architecture has been made except as rigidly controlled by the owner under stringent proprietary data agreements. Even then, fewer than five individuals have had a comprehensive access. Second, the fundamental algorithms, definitely cryptologic in origin, have been so markedly enhanced over their raw analog implementations that even threading from start to finish along that pathway is exceedingly difficult. Finally, the many modules in the PRIVACODE program interact in an incredibly complex manner such that knowledge of the algorithms would not compromise the process.

The unique features designed into PRIVACODE prevent buyers from attacking other user's files because each and every PRIVACODE disk has unique modules which will never be repeated in other disks. Further, the program undertakes to automatically prevent compromise by destroying input files when output files are created. This process is a total write-over and not simply a header delete.

Another unique feature of PRIVACODE is a user option that will make designated files "Hacker-proof". This is accomplished by selection of a module that will translate a file such that any retrieval attempt that is incorrect will result in a complete hashing of the file---not just header delete; complete hashing of the file, Hence, the hacker gets only one attempt. While this option is activated by a password/seed, one must realize that the basic security lies in PRIVACODE itself. And, as the point has already been made, PRIVACODE is not a password/seed system. Hence, fundamental security is not dependent upon the module activator.

From a manufacturing perspective, stringent security and quality control exists throughout. Only the purchaser has the index data necessary to replicating his disk, and the form of that data is useless to anybody but the manufacturer. Therefore, the purchaser is the only person who may order a replacement disk and the manufacturer has no idea of his identity in context of a particular disk until the purchaser opts to make that disclosure.

In summary, PRIVACODE is a high confidence privacy system intended for the professional and high technology marketplace wherein very sensitive and valuable data must be protected from competitors.

HIDING THAT VITAL PIECE OF INFORMATION: CODES...

With the exception of commerical radio, most communications (notably those from our readers) are meant to be entirely private.

While we have gone over some ways of protecting written communications from prying eyes, we have not shown how to protect the contents should they become "public" knowlege.

In How To Get Anything Lee got into the idea of physical deterrents to unauthorizied listening such as altering frequencies, and so on.

Now we are going to show a few examples of coding procedures that can be used on any radio, or most telephone conversations and some written communications.

Any code has several functions; first and foremost, hide the infromation from the enemy, make it appear that code was not even employed, and prevent the enemy from finding the location of the sending and receiving units.

There are few, no let me amend that, no unbreakable codes. The Germans felt their code machines during WW II were unbreakable, not knowing the Poles had smuggled a copy machine to the Allies and that so called "secure" communications were anything but that...

The same game goes on today with US/THEM, better machines, better computers, better spies...

The safest sinmple coding system for years is/was the book system. If both you and I have a copy of say, Penthouse Forum, for this month (it's always best to use intellectual materials) and no one else knows what written material we are refering to, no one can follow the conversation.

Sample: We are on the radio/phone planning a super secret software theft break-in.

Me: Hello silver spoons is that you? (prearranged code/answer)

You: Right on bro, how's the caddy hanging in there? (I'm receiving you okay, proceed).

M: P7-2-6

Y: P14-7-2

M: P2-6-9-9

Y: P7-3-3-3!

M: P15-8-4, P43-2-8, P6-4-5-6

Y: Over and out.

Okay, by looking up the page numbers (indicated by the "P") and then counting down the sentences from the top of the page, and then the words in that sentence, one arrives at the coded word.

Conversations are slow, but safe. Unless someone else knows the book you are using for the key it is a totally random situation.

It is not beyond the relm of possibility that the NSA has the personnel and equipment to computerize every book that is published, but it would be damn hard even using optical scanners instead of typists.

No one else could possibly attempt that task.

Okay, back to our conversation:

M: Police

Y: Car?

M: No motorcycle

Y: How many

M: Two on two bikes

Y: Bye...

Now this is just an example of the way this can be used but remember that it takes time to look up every word and find your answer.

This system is very good for interchanges where only a couple of chances exist and the keywords are already inked out for written exchanges.

An easier system for short codes is to construct a matrix of key words (see example) this means you can say 2-Charlie and your other half knows you mean "split".

He says 4-Alpha? Meaning, "pre-arranged meeting place 1"

2-Delta means, "no, number 2".

If the matrix is changed often it is very hard to break.

Most codes are much more effective if no one is aware that they are in use. Your partner need only be able to pick up on the key (matrix) words to hide the code.

Substitute more common words for the keys instead of the phonetic alphabet and mix them in with "hip" CB radio talk and it is almost impossible to tell a code is in effect, much less try and break it.

Another matrix system that contains pre-coded entire messages is also shown. In this random number set up any two numbers can be read off to create an intersection of a single number which then means a certain message.

If you are as worried about radio direction finding as you are about the actual message content there are a number of things you can do to help along your security.

Keep your messages very short. It takes some time to establish a location.

Change transmission sites often.

Use directional antennas if you can.

Change frequencies often.

Have a fallback system of communication if someone does not check in at a pre-arranged time. Phone booths are good bets.

If you know your enemy, choose a channel near him to prevent jamming.

If possible, record your message at a very slow speed on a good tape recorder and send it at the highest speed possible.

This shortens air time and sounds like garbled mush.

Invert the record/playback head (s) on both the transmitting and receiving recorders.

Use off frequency tranceivers (see last book).

Employ taped background noises that have nothing to do with your real location (trains, traffic, ships, bells, etc).

If possible record your enemy's transmissions, edit them to say other things, and re-broadcast them later on...

Use the lowest power signal that will still work for you.

Change id's often.

Use a coded warning and then lie.

No matter which side of the legal fence your intentions lay, remember scanners exist which will pick up every cop, FBI, and security radio signal out there.

Also many police forces are equipped with CB scanners that do the same thing as many criminals use CB for lookout situations.

Remember the possibility of using FM business channels and ham radio frequencies (this is illegal) instead of CB.

Let's break away and look at a couple of written code/ciphers, one of my favorites for short messages is to take a cardboard plate the same size of most messages your write, now cut out any number of square holes in the cardboard that would fit one word.

To use the magic mask one places it over a blank sheet of paper and writes in the cruical message, "Mom's will cut you out, hit man on way."

Around these scattered words one then writes a letter incorporating the real message. There must always be a close word involved so the other party knows when the real message is over and out.

The other person then places a duplicate mask over the letter and the real messasge is read.

One disadvantage to this system is the mask limits the size of the message.

It should be noted there are both codes and ciphers; the difference is that a cipher substitutes one (or more) numbers or letters for the intended letter.

A code uses a key which is understood in advance by both parties and allows words or messages to be understood when the key is applied.

A code is no more secure than its key.

A cipher is usually broken by comparing the frequency of use of letters in the language being utilized with the frequency of the symbols in coded message.

Computers make this a much easier job.

There is the story of the hacker who challenged the CIA/NSA's then "unbreakable" machine generated cipher with his APPLE computer.

Within 12 hours it had broken the "random" cipher and was typing out their messages.

They were not happy.

Most intelligence agencies use machines to make/read ciphers, but anyone can do a one time nearly "unbreakable" cipher.

Normally this is done on a pad so each cipher is used once and tossed out. Believe me, this makes decoding a bitch.

To do this type of pad cipher one assigns a number to each letter of the alphabet;

For ease let's go a-1, b-2, c-3, you get the idea...

Then a totally random number is generated, say 11789, now the correct numerical value of the intended letter is added:

11789+c=11792.

The receiver looks up the first number on his identical pad (11789) and subtracts from the given number to read "c".

Each letter requires a seperate random base so each pad page should contain enough random sets to send a complete message.

Random numbers can be just made up, copied from license numbers of the first 60 cars you see that day, taken from different pages and lines of any phone book, etc.

As long as it is random the creative process used makes no difference.

After the message is decoded the page is tossed out and the next page on the pad is employed for the next cipher.

Micro computers are made for encoding, and there are several good programs on the market to do just this, I am not going to take up the space to do a program here...

In the last book we discussed how to change a CB radio to an off frequency to avoid unwanted listeners. This system works but to really convert a CB or AM or even SSB tranceivers to frequencies that "do not exist" (the FCC sets distances between usable channels) by switching crystals or simple electronic modifications contact:

A.P. Systems
PO Box 263
Newport, RI 02840

For a $15.00 copy of their Bootleggers Bible. With this book and a good code nobody, but nobody, is going to understand your messages.

TELEPHONE USE

Some commerical scramblers will work within the limited bandwidth of a telephone system,some will not. Of course, any of the verbal ciphers or codes can be used over the phone but your chances of interception are just as high as on a radio, depending on who wants you...

Remember every overseas phone call, telex, Quip, etc is automatically intercepted by the NSA's computers and may or may not be recorded for later evaluation.

Also any portable phone (car, etc) must be assumed to be monitored, if not by us, by them.

After all, we have been recording the Russian's car to car conversations for years. One should assume they are returning the favor.

Now that scanning and monitoring are popular anyone can be listening.

Tacticom II Specifications

SKIPPING

Transmitter

Power Output	1-25 Watts (Selectable)
Modulation	16 F3 (FCC)
Spurious Suppression	40 dB

Receiver

Sensitivity	.3 Microvolts (20 dB SINAD) Normal or Skip Mode
Image Response	40 dB
Adjacent Channel Rejection	70 dB (EIA)
Audio Output	2 Watts (Distortion Less Than 5%)

Frequency-Agile Mode

Dwell Time	80 Milliseconds per channel
Audio Distortion	Less than 5%
Frequency Series	32 Internal Programs 64 Frequencies Each
Encode/Decode	DTMF

General

Frequency Range	135-175 MHz (any 3.2 MHz Band)
Temperature Range	−15°C to +50°C
Weight	3.5 lbs.
Power Requirement	12 Volts DC Negative Ground
Frequency Stability	± .0005%

There are two systems of radio transmission that hide a signal much better than any scrambler: spread spectrum and frequency hopping.

In the spread system the modulated carrier is spread over a wider bandwidth than normal. This means anyone listening with a "normal" receiver will hear only mild background noise.

In hopping two units are designed to skip to a certain number of different frequencies every second giving only a small burst of noise at each frequency.

This makes unwanted listeners almost nonexistent as "descrambling" must be done on a real time basis and it is almost impossible to trace the signal source or tape the message.

Now available in the US from VIKING.

Privacy Levels:
1. None
2. Basic
3. General or Industrial
4. Non-Tactical, Para-Military
5. Tactical
6. Strategic

OFTEN USED LOCAL CODES

1	ABANDONED MV	56	MUGGING
2	ACCIDENT	57	MURDER
3	AIRCRAFT COMPLAINT	58	MOTOR VEHICLE COMPLAINT
4	OK MESSAGE RECEIVED	59	NARCOTICS ACTIVITY
5	AIRCRAFT CRASH	60	NOISE COMPLAINT
6	ALARM DROP	61	NOTIFICATION
7	ASSAULT	62	OUT OF SERVICE
8	BANK TRANSFER	63	PARKING CONDITIONS
9	BICYCLES (STOLEN, RE-COVERED, ETC.)	64	PEACE OFFICER
		65	PERMITS
10	BOAT COMPLAINTS	66	PERSON WITH A GUN
11	BOAT IN TROUBLE	67	PERSON WITH A KNIFE
13	BOMBING OR EXPLOSION	68	PROWLER
14	BREAK (VEHICLES)	69	RAPE
15	BURGLARY IN PROGRESS	70	REPORT TO GARAGE
16	BURGLARY (BUS.-DWEL.)	71	REPORT FOR FUEL
17	BUSY STAND-BY UNLESS URGENT	72	REPORT TO HQ
		73	RECKLESS OPERATOR
18	CALL HQ	74	REQUEST DETECTIVE BUREAU
19	CARS MEET	76	REQUEST SUPERVISOR
20	CHECKS (FRADULENT)	77	REQUEST HOSTAGE NEG. SQUAD
21	CHECK TRAFFIC LIGHT	78	REQUEST WRECKER
22	CHILD ABUSE COMPLAINT	79	ROAD CONDITIONS
23	CHILDREN IN ROADWAY	80	SEX OFFENSE
24	CRIME PREVENTION UNIT	81	SHOOTING
26	DEAD BODY	82	SHOPLIFTING
27	DOGS AND ANIMALS	83	SIGNAL GOOD
28	DOMESTIC	84	SPECIAL INVESTIGATION
29	DISTURBANCE	85	SPEEDING CARS
30	DROWNING	86	SPECIAL OFFICER
31	DRUNK	87	STOLEN MV
32	DRUNK DRIVER	88	STOP TRANSMITTING
33	ELECTRICAL HAZARD	89	SUICIDE
34	ESCORT	90	SUSPICIOUS PERSON
35	FALLS	91	SUSPICIOUS VEHICLE
36	FIRE ALARM	92	TELEPHONE CALLS (HARASSING OR OBSCENE)
37	FIREWORK REPORT		
38	FLOODING CONDITIONS	93	THEFT FROM MV
39	GANG CAUSING DISTURBANCE	94	THREATENING
40	HELP WANTED BY POLICE-MAN	95	TRAFFIC CONDITIONS
		96	TRESPASSING
41	HIT & RUN	97	UNABLE TO COPY-CHANGE LOCATION
42	HOLD-UP GENERAL	98	VACANT HOUSE OR BUSINESS

43	HOLD-UP BANK	99	VEHICLE BLOCKING DRIVEWAY
44	HOSTAGE SITUATION	100	VANDALISM-MOTOR VEHICLE
45	IN SERVICE	101	VANDALISM-PROPERTY
46	INDECENT EXPOSURE	102	POLICE INFORMATION
47	JUVENILE COMPLAINT/GENERAL		
48	KIDNAPPING OR ABDUCTION CODE	1	LEAVE ROUTINE PATROL
49	LARCENY	2	CRIME IN PROGRESS-SILENT
50	LITTERING OR DUMPING	4	IMMEDIATELY LIGHTS AND SIREN
51	LOCATION	6	LIFE THREATENING
52	LOITERING		
53	MEAT COMPLAINANT		
54	MINI BIKE REPORT		
55	MISSING PERSON		
1	ROAD BLOCK	61	PACKAGE
2	COMPLAINT	62	PICK-UP PASSENGER
3	TEST CALL	63	HOLD OCCUPANTS
4	M.V. REGISTRATION INFO.	64	WATCH FOR & STOP VEHICLE
5	CHECK STOLEN CAR LIST	65	WATCH-DON'T STOP
6	COMBINE 4 & 5	66	PERSONAL ASSISTANCE
7	HIT & RUN	67	CONCEAL OFFICER
8	DRUNKEN DRIVER	68	STOP TRAFFIC
9	WANTED FOR M.V. VIOLATION	69	INDUSTRIAL EXPLOSION
10	ACCIDENT	70	LOCATION
11	ACCIDENT INJURIES	71	DIFFERS
12	BREACH OF PEACE	72	ESCAPE FROM JAIL
13	ROBBERY	73	TRY TO LOCATE
14	ON THE AIR	74	AIRPLANE CRASH
15	OFF THE AIR	75	BANK ESCORT
16	PHONE CALL	76	DIFFERS
17	ESCAPE FROM JAIL	77	PREARRANGED ORDERS
18	PHONE OFFICE FOR MESSAGE	78	UNTIMELY DEATH
19	RESERVOIR CHECK	79	RETURN TO STATION
20	NATURE OF COMPLAINT UN-KNOWN CAUTION	80	HI-JACKING
21	PHONE OFFICE-ADVISE	81	DIFFERS
22	MAIL TRUCK ESCORT	82	KIDNAPPING
23	STRIKE DUTY	83	LARCENY
24	ASSAULT	84	LASCIVIOUS CARRIAGE
25	PROWLER	85	LOTTERY TICKETS
26	MURDER	86	NON-SUPPORT
27	BREAKING & ENTERING	87	NARCOTICS
28	DROWNING	88	PROSTITUTION
29	LOCATION	89	RAPE
30	STOP CAR FOR INVESTIGA-TION	90	SODOMY
31	CHECK BANK OR POST OFFICE	91	SEDUCTION
32	REMOVE POLICE PLATES	92	TRESPASSING
33	CHECK RADIO TOWER	93	A.W.O.L. OR DESERTION
34	MILITARY CONVOY	94	MISDEMEANOR
35	ABDUCTION	95	FELONY
		96	STOLEN CAR
		97	STOLEN REGISTRATION PLATES
		98	MISSION PERSON

3X	EXPLOSIVES	99	EXTEND COURTESIES TO CAR
36	ADULTERY	100	HURRICANE
37	ARSON	101	RIOT
38	DESERTION	102	FIRE
39	BIGAMY	103	RAILROAD ACCIDENT
40	BLACKMAIL	104	BRIDGE COLLAPSE
41	BRIBERY	105	CONFIDENTIAL NOTICE-EMERGENCY
42	CARNAL KNOWLEDGE-FEMALE MINOR	106	REQUEST TO STATE POLICE
43	CHECK FRAUD	107	REQUEST PERMISSION
44	PERSON IS ARMED	108	TRAFFIC
45	COUNTERFEITING	109	ALERT SIGNAL (MOBILIZATION)
46	EMBEZZLEMENT	110	DIFFERS
47	FALSE PRETENSE	111	CD ACTIVITY
48	FORGERY	112	FOR USE BYEXECUTIVES
49	FORNICATION	113A	KEEP IN CODE
50	ANYMESSAGE?	113B	TALK FREE
51	ASSISTANCE-URGENT ARREST	114	DIFFERS
52	ASSISTANCE-URGENT INJURIES	115	TRANSPORTING A PRISIONER
53	ASSISTANCE-URGENT DIS-TURBANCE	118	MOTORIST ASSIST
54	ASSISTANCE-ROUTINE	119	BURGLAR ALARM
55	OFFICERS DOUBLING UP	120	REPEAT
56	BEFORE STOPPING CAR		
57	DRUNK		
58	WEATHER CONDITIONS		
59	STAY OFF THE AIR		
60	MESSENGER		

SECURE PHONES (?)

Suddenly the US government has become aware that the bad guys (no, in this case the Russians), may actually tapping some federal telephones in US.

No...

At any rate, the NSA has decided to install 500,000 (!) "secure" phones at such agencies as the CIA, Defense Department, various private contractors, and "others".

These secure phones would scramble conversations so only someone with another "secure" phone could unscramble them.

At present the US has only 1,000 secure phones that cost $30,000 each and are quite large and bulky.

Several contractors, AT&T, ITT, RCA, GTE, are all trying to bring the price down to a reasonable $2,000.

Of course one half million of these secure phones, built by the lowest bidder, would present no problem to their security as there is no way on earth any Russian could get his hands on one, much less understand the complex technology behind their design.

A hell of an idea, I say.

CORDLESS AND MOBILE PHONE DETAILS

Cordless and mobile phones offer all sorts of fun for the casual eavesdropper... Many people using either simply do not realize that the signal is transmitted over the air and can be received by anyone with the correct receiver.

Of course cordless phones have a very limited range, normally 1000 feet or less, a good receiver as well as a outside antenna, will allow reception several times that distance.

The older model cordless phone left the dial tone on at all times and had very few access frequencies. This meant anyone could drive down the street with a cordless handset and listen for a dial tone.

When a tone appeared one could dial out on that phone, leaving the toll charges for an unsuspecting customer.

The newer models use different frequencies and a coded access channel to solve this problem.

The newest cordless phones use these frequencies:

Channel	Base freq	Handset freq
1	46.61	49.67
2	46.63	49.845
3	46.67	49.86
4	46.71	49.77
5	46.73	49.875
6	46.77	49.83
7	46.83	49.89
8	46.87	49.93
9	46.93	49.99
10	46.97	49.97

Mobile Phones

Portable phones, either mobile or hand carried, have a much greater range than cordless models and are much easier to pick up.

131

The "old" style mobile had a limited number of channels and a set range. One dialed the mobile operator on a free channel and placed the call. If all local channels were busy (an often situation in big cities) the phone would automatically scan until a channel opened up, then would alert the user.

The new mobile phones are "celluar" meaning they go to a local receiver and/or repeater which is computer connected to other repeaters all across the country.

This system has a much larger set of access channels and can be dialed without human intervention. Any celluar system will dial any phone in the country, assuming your area is equipped with the system.

Prices on celluar phones, as of this writing, are about $1200 plus a monthly fee and call charges.

They will come down in both size and price in the near future, possibly bringing on the infamous Dick Tracy wrist phone...

Several court cases (the best in Kansas) have ruled that any intercepted and/or taped wireless phone conversation is a matter of PUBLIC RECORD and does NOT violate a person's civil rights nor fall under the anti-surveillance acts...

A good scanner coupled with an external antenna or booster can allow anyone to fulfill their peeping Tom (audio) fantasies.

UPDATED TELEPHONE TECHNIQUES

Please note that many of these items are based on the use of techniques listed in How To Get Anything On Anybody; we are not going to repeat the entire procedures in this book.

One of the major reason for changes is the "consumer" breakup of the Bell System. Now you are even encouraged to buy your own telephone, which is fine, unless you want to call someone in which case you need to buy one or more telephone poles and a lot of wire...

Well almost...

1. Phone stores no longer have anything to do with billing so CNA and DPAC operators WILL NOT give out information to anyone from a phone store.

This is gotten around by being "from" a public office in ANOTHER town. Operators will cooperate with these people.

2. Billing offices (located in the front of the white pages) will mail a copy of "your" bill (once you have the correct name) to any address (your "office" for instance) that you request it to be sent to.

3. Billing offices will give out the local DPAC number to a rep from an out-of-town public office or billing office.

4. Some CNA's cover more than one area code now so be sure to include the area code in your request.

5. With the new ESS systems some areas no longer have a three digit number for a computer readout of the number you are calling on. Ask a friendly installer about your area.

On the latest ESS systems your number automatically appears on the board of the operator whenever you call "O". She will sometimes give it to you if you are "John, from repair, can you call me back on this line?" When she does answer and ask what line she shows you on...

6. CNA now includes unlisted numbers in its memory bank and will give up to three billing names for any number requested.

7. If CNA does not come up with a listing for a certain number you can call the local billing office as a Public Office employee FROM OUT OF THE AREA and request a name because "CNA has no listing and I have a customer who is disputing the call on his bill."

8. If DPAC has no listing, one can ask for the number for the local test board. Repeat the story you gave before with the addition that DPAC has no listing.

The test board will have the info on ALL installed phones including lines that were attached that very day.

9. Another method that still works is to simply get a number on YOUR bill and then call the billing office to dispute the call. They will do the above steps for you and give the billing name.

10. The best way to get an address is to utilize the correct billing name you just got your filthy hands on, call the billing office and ask for a new copy of "your" last bill to be mailed to this address...

The bill will contain the billing address.

11. Some local telcos, South Central Bell for instance, have tossed in the towel to those nasty people using CNA for their own devious uses; if you call the operator and ask for a listing on any number she will give you the billing name AND ADDRESS for a $0.40 charge...

Hopefully this practice will spread...

12. Several courts have upheld the installation of a pen register (not a tap, only records the number dialed and length of call) as "public information" that does not require a warrant.

13. The enclosed CNA list is current AT THIS WRITING. The numbers will be changed for security purposes in the not too distant future. Use one or more of the "special sources" we have listed for updates.

14. Bell is gradually updating their entire network to CCIS #5 and then to #7 (this refers to the operating software for the ESS computers).

When, and if, they get #7 installed a few interesting options may be offered including...Call restriction, where the CO will automatically intercept and stop any calls from any calling number you request.

And...Call trace, wherein one can dial a coded number and find out the number of the party one just talked to AFTER THE CALL IS COMPLETED.

This is possible because the CO computer receives all calls (in ESS) and then "dials" your phone. The call is not put through until (see the article on phone phreaking) the called party actually lifts the handset.

This system allows TSPS operators, among others, to see the calling number BEFORE the call actually put through.

Several arrests have been made because someone phoned a threat into the local police department and were told to "please call back on 911 because I can't put you through on this line."

911 automatically displays the calling party's number...

The call trace option is already in effect in Austin Texas (why, you ask, I haven't any idea) and is aimed at people who are receiving threating or obscene phone calls.

This pilot program is a slightly modified version wherein the id of the caller will be revealed to the cops (for a customer charge of $5) but NOT to the caller. This may change.

Other options include a selective ringing feature where any of three numbers will produce its own particular ring ($0.25 per call, $0.10 per day), selective call forwarding and selective call rejection.

The Austin experiment will last one year and may decide the fate of #7 for the rest of the country.

If actually implanted a number of interesting investigative and hacker options are bound to show their little heads.

Stay tuned to this channel for further information.

PS. For more information on the great Austin Experiment one can call 512-499-8010.

Reach out and touch someone...

15. A phone surveillance trick one of us left out of the last book is to connect the speaker in a speaker phone across the spare pair (usually yellow and black) in a phone line.

The speaker will act as a low budget microphone and transmit any sounds down the wires. A good audio amplifier can be hooked up to the pair in another office or B box, or anywhere down the hard line and will faithfully pass on all conversations...

If you have a speaker phone set-up CHECK THIS MODIFICATION OUT!!

It is utilized more than anyone would think...

TAPPED OUT

A number of years ago, in the days of hippies and yippies, a group of phone phreaks formed an informal network headquartered in New York.

They published a newsletter entitled YIPL which featured such things as how to build toll cheating blue boxes, inside telco phone numbers, and in general how to use Ma Bell in ways she was never designed to be used in.

Later they changed the name to TAP (Technological American Party) and continued to print circuits for blue/black/red boxes give out confidential telco information. They even held parties where everyone wore a mask to help confuse the various FBI and telco security people who attended.

Some of the members pulled pranks, like the time Adam tied up all the phone lines coming into Santa Monica except the one they controlled and then told every caller that got through during the next hour that Santa Monica had just suffered a nuclear melt down and was destroyed.

Things began to go downhill after Captain Crunch went to jail for the second time and many other phreaks were busted on fraud-by-wire charges.

The newsletter began to come every few months, if at all. Then two of the founders, Al Bell, and Tom Edison had a falling out and one split with the mailing list pretty much destroying TAP.

Also most phone companies began using new computerized systems that blue boxes would not work on.

Many of us admired the somewhat crude, but very useful information provided by TAP.

Good news...

A new publication entitled "2600" has just appeared. 2600 is much more professional in layout and the info is up to date. They aim a bit more at computer users, but have already published access codes and numbers to major credit organizations, found a new box that allows free calls under some circumstances, FBI computer files and other enlightening bits of information.

At $10.00 a year ($1.00 for back issues) this is one of the best deals we have run into.

The following pages are copied directly from the best phone newsletter ever. Period.

2600
Box 752
Middle Island, NY 11953
$12.00 per year.

THE THEORY OF 'BLUE BOXING'
their history, how they're used, their future

After most neophyte phreaks overcome their fascination with Metrocodes and WATS extenders, they will usually seek to explore other avenues in the vast phone network. Often, they will come across references such as 'simply dial KP + 2130801050 + ST for the Alliance teleconferencing system in LA.' Numbers such as the one above were intended to be used with a blue box; this article will explain the fundamental principles of the fine art of blue boxing.

Genesis
In the begining, all long distance calls were connected manually by operators who passed on the called number verbally to other operators in series. This is because pulse (aka rotary) digits are created by causing breaks in the DC current. Since long distance calls require routing through various switching equipment and AC voice amplifiers, pulse dialing cannot be used to send the destination number to the end local office (CO).

Eventually, the demand for faster and more efficient long distance (LD) service caused Bell to make a multi-billion dollar decision. They had to create a signaling system that could be used on the LD network. Basically, they had two options: (1) to send all the signaling and supervisory information (ie, ON and OFF HOOK) over separate data links. This type of signaling is referred to as out-of-band signaling, or (2) to send all the signaling information along with the conversation using tones to represent digits. This type of signaling is referred to as in-band signaling. Being the cheap bastards that they naturally are, Bell chose the latter (and cheaper) method—in-band signaling. They eventually regretted this, though (heh, heh)...

In-Band Signaling Principles
When a subscriber dials a telephone number, whether in rotary or touchtone (aka DTFM), the equipment in the CO interprets the digits and looks for a convenient trunk line to send the call on its way. In the case of a local call, it will probably be sent via an inter-office trunk; otherwise, it will be sent to a toll office (class 4 or higher) to be processed.

When trunks are not being used there is a 2600 Hz tone on the line; thus to find a free trunk, the CO equipment simply checks for the presence of 2600 Hz. If it doesn't find a free trunk the customer will receive a re-order signal (120 IPM busy signal) or the 'all circuits are busy...' message. If it does find a free trunk, it 'seizes' it—removing the 2600 Hz. It then sends the called number or a special routing code to the other end or toll office.

The tones it uses to send this information are called multi-frequency (MF) tones. An MF tone consists of two tones from a set of six master tones which are combined to produce 12 separate tones. You can sometimes hear these tones in the background when you make a call, but they are usually filtered out so your delicate ears cannot hear them. These are *not* the same as touchtones. To notify the equipment at the far end of the trunk that it is about to receive routing information, the originating end first sends a Key Pulse (KP) tone. At the end of sending the digits, the originating end then sends a STart (ST) tone. Thus to call 914-359-1517, the equipment would send KP + 9143591517 + ST in MF tones. When the customer hangs up, 2600 Hz is once again sent to signify a disconnect to the distant end.

History
In the November 1960 issue of the Bell System Technical Journal, an article entitled 'Signaling Systems for Control of Telephone Switching' was published. This journal, which was sent to most university libraries, happened to contain the actual MF tones used in signaling. They appeared as follows:

DIGIT	TONES
1	700 + 900 HZ
2	700 + 1100 HZ
3	900 + 1100 HZ
4	700 + 1300 HZ
5	900 + 1300 HZ
6	1100 + 1300 HZ
7	700 + 1500 HZ
8	900 + 1500 HZ
9	1100 + 1500 HZ
0	1300 + 1500 HZ
KP	1100 + 1700 HZ
ST	1500 + 1700 HZ
11 (*)	700 + 1700 HZ
12 (*)	900 + 1700 HZ
KP2 (*)	1300 + 1700 HZ

(*) Used only on CCITT SYSTEM 5 for special international calling.

Bell caught wind of blue boxing in 1961, when it caught a Washington State College student using one. They originally found out about blue boxes through police raids and informants. In 1964, Bell Labs came up with scanning equipment, which recorded all suspicious calls, to detect blue box usage. These units were installed in CO's where major toll fraud existed. AT&T security would then listen to the tapes to see if any toll fraud was actually committed. Over 200 convictions resulted from the project. Surprisingly enough, blue boxing is not solely limited to the electronics enthusiast; AT&T has caught businessmen, film stars, college students, doctors, lawyers, high school students, and even a millionaire financier (Bernard Cornfield) using the device. AT&T also said that nearly half of those that they catch are businessmen.

To use a blue box, one would usually make a free call to any 800 number or distant directory assistance (NPA-555-1212). This, of course, is legitimate. When the call is answered, one would then swiftly press the button that would send 2600 Hz down the line. This has the effect of making the distant CO equipment think that the call was terminated, and it leaves the trunk hanging. Now, the user has about 10 seconds to enter in the telephone number he wished to dial—in MF, that is. The CO equipment merely assumes that this came from another office and it will happily process the call. Since there are no records (except on toll fraud detection devices!) of these MF tones, the user is not billed for the call. When the user hangs up, the CO equipment simply records that he hung up on a free call.

Detection
Bell has had 20 years to work on detection devices; therefore, in this day and age, they are rather well refined. Basically, the detection device will look for the presence of 2600 Hz where it does not belong. It then records the calling number and all activity after the 2600 Hz. If you happen to be at a fortress fone, though, and you make the call short, your chances of getting caught are significantly reduced. Incidentally, there have been rumors of certain test numbers that hook into trunks thus avoiding the need for 2600 Hz and detection!

Another way that Bell catches boxers is to examine the CAMA (Centralized Automatic Message Accounting) tapes. When you make a call, your number, the called number, and time of day are all recorded. The same thing happens when you hang up. This tape is then processed for billing purposes. Normally, all free calls are ignored. But Bell can program the billing equipment to make note of lengthy calls to directory assistance. They can then put a pen register (aka DNR) on the line or an actual full-blown tap. This detection can be avoided by making short-haul (aka local) calls to box off of.

It is interesting to note that NPA + 555-1212 originally did not return answer supervision. Thus the calls were not recorded on the AMA/CAMA tapes. AT&T changed this though for 'traffic studies!'

CCIS
Besides detection devices, Bell has begun to gradually redesign the network using out-of-band signaling. This is known as Common Channel Inter-office Signaling (CCIS). Since this signaling method sends all the signaling information over separate data lines, blue boxing is impossible under it.

While being implemented gradually, this multi-billion dollar project is still strangling the fine art of blue boxing. Of course until the project is totally complete, boxing will still be possible. It will become progressively harder to find places to box off of, though. In areas with CCIS, one must find a directory assistance offfice that doesn't have CCIS yet. Area codes in Canada and predominantly rural states are the best bets. WATS numbers terminating in non-CCIS cities are also good prospects.

Pink Noise
Another way that may help to avoid detection is to add some 'pink noise' to the 2600 Hz tone.

Since 2600 Hz tones can be simulated in speech, the detection equipment must be careful not to misinterpret speech as a disconnect signal. Thus a virtually pure 2600 Hz tone is required for disconnect.

Keeping this in mind, the 2600 Hz detection equipment is also probably looking for pure 2600 Hz or else it would be triggered every time someone hit that note (highest E on a piano =2637 Hz). This is also the reason that the 2600 Hz tone must be sent rapidly; sometimes, it won't work when the operator is saying 'Hello, hello.' It is feasible to send some 'pink noise' along with the 2600 Hz. Most of this energy should be above 3000 Hz. The pink noise won't make it into the toll network (where we want our pure 2600 Hz to hit), but it should make it past the local CO and thus the fraud detectors.

VITAL INGREDIENTS
SWITCHING CENTERS AND OPERATORS

Every switching office in North America (the NPA system) is assigned an office name and class. There are five classes of offices numbered 1 through 5. Your CO is most likely a class 5 or end office. All Long-Distance (Toll) calls are switched by a toll office which can be a class 4, 3, 2, or 1 office. There is also a 4X office called an intermediate point. The 4X office is a digital one that can have an unattended exchange attached to it (known as a Remote Switching Unit—RSU).

The following chart will list the office number, name, and how many of those offices existed in North America in 1981.

Class	Name	Abb.	# Existing
1	Regional Center	RC	12
2	Sectional Center	SC	67
3	Primary Center	PC	230
4	Toll Center	TC	1,300
4P	Toll Point	TP	
4X	Intermediate Point	IP	
5	End Office	EO	19,000
R	RSU	RSU	

When connecting a call from one party to another, the switching equipment usually tries to find the shortest route between the Class 5 end office of the caller and the Class 5 end office of the called party. If no inter-office trunks exist between the two parties, it will then move up to the next highest office for servicing (Class 4). If the Class 4 office cannot handle the call by sending it to another Class 4 or 5 office, it will be sent to the next office in the hierarchy (3). The switching equipment first uses the high-usage interoffice trunk groups. If they are busy it goes to the final trunk groups on the next highest level. If the call cannot be connected then, you will probably get a reorder [120 IPM (Interruptions Per Minute) signal—also known as a fast busy]. At this time, the guys at Network Operations are probably going berserk trying to avoid the dreaded Network Dreadlock (as seen on TV!).

It is also interesting to note that 9 connections in tandem is called ring-around-the-rosy and it has never occurred in telephone history. This would cause an endless loop connection (an interesting way to really screw up the Network).

The 10 regional centers in the United States and the 2 in Canada are all interconnected. They form the foundation of the entire telephone network. Since there are only 12 of them, they are listed below:

Class 1 Regional Office Location	NPA
Dallas 4 ESS	214
Wayne, PA	215
Denver 4T	303
Regina No. 2 SP1-4W [Canada]	306
St. Louis 4T	314
Rockdale, GA	404
Pittsburgh 4E	412
Montreal No. 1 4AETS [Canada]	504
Norwich, NY	607
San Bernardino, CA	714
Norway, IL	815
White Plains 4T, NY	914

In the Network, there are three major types of switching equipment. They are known as: Step, Crossbar, and ESS. Check past and future issues of *2600* for complete details on how these systems work.

Operators

Another vital ingredient of the Network is the telephone operator. There are many different kinds. What follows is a discussion of some of the more common ones.

• **TSPS Operator.** The TSPS [Traffic Service Position System (as opposed to This Shitty Phone Service)] Operator is probably the bitch (or bastard for the phemale liberationists) that most of us are used to having to deal with.

Here are her responsibilities:

1) Obtaining billing information for Calling Card or 3rd number calls.

2) Identifying called customer on person-to-person calls.

3) Obtaining acceptance of charges on collect calls.

4) Identifying calling numbers. This only happens when the calling number is not automatically recorded by CAMA (Centralized Automatic Message Accounting) and forwarded from the local office. This could be caused by equipment failures (ANIF—Automatic Number Identification Failure) or if the office is not equipped for CAMA (ONI—Operator Number Identification).

(I once had an equipment failure happen to me and the TSPS operator came on and said, "What number are you calling *from?*" Out of curiosity, I gave her the number to my CO, she thanked me, and then I was connected to a conversation that appeared to be between a frameman and his wife. Then it started ringing the party I originally wanted to call and everyone phreaked out (excuse the pun). I immediately dropped this dual line conference!)

You shouldn't mess with the TSPS operator since she *knows* where you are calling from. Your number will show up on a 10-digit LED read-out (ANI board). She also knows whether or not you are at a fortress fone and she can trace calls quite readily. Out of all of the operators, she is one of the *most dangerous!*

• **INWARD Operator.** This operator assists your local TSPS ("0") operator in connecting calls. She will never question a call as long as the call is within *her service area.* She can only be reached via other operators or by a Blue Box. From a BB, you would dial KP+NPA+121+ST for the INWARD operator that will help you connect any calls within that NPA only.

• **DIRECTORY ASSISTANCE Operator.** This is the operator that you are connected to when you dial 411 or NPA-555-1212. She does not readily know where you are calling from. She does not have access to unlisted numbers, but she does know if an unlisted number exists for a certain listing.

There is also a directory assistance for deaf people who use Teletypewriters (TTY's). If your modem can transfer BAUDOT (45.5 baud—the Apple Cat can), then you can call him/her up and have an interesting conversation. The number is 800-855-1155. They use the standard Telex abbreviations such as GA for Go Ahead. They tend to be nicer and will talk longer than your regular operators. Also, they are more likely to be persuaded to give more information through the process of "social engineering".

Unfortunately, they don't have access to much. I once bullshitted with one of these operators and I found out that there are two such DA offices that handle TTY. One is in Philadelphia and the other is in California. They have approximately seven operators each. Most of the TTY operators seem to think their job is boring. They also feel they are underpaid. They actually call up a regular DA # to process your request—no fancy computers here! (Other operators have access to their own DA by dialing KP+NPA+131+ST (MF).

The TTY directory assistance, by the way, is still a free call, unlike normal DA. One might be able to avoid being charged for DA calls by using a computer and modem at 45.5 baud.

• **CN/A Operator.** CN/A operators do exactly the opposite of what directory assistance operators are for. You give them the number, they give you the name and address (Customer Name/Address). In my experiences, these operators know more than the DA operators do and they are more susceptible to "social engineering." It is possible to bullshit a CN/A operator for the NON-PUB DA # (i.e., you give them the name and they give you the unlisted number). This is due to the fact that they assume you are a fellow company employee. The divestiture, though, has resulted in the break-up of a few NON-PUB #'s and policy changes in CN/A.

• **INTERCEPT Operator.** The intercept operator is the one that you are connected to when there are not enough recordings available or the area is not set up to tell you that the number has been disconnected or changed. They usually say, "What number did you dial?" This is considered to be the lowest operator lifeform since they have no power whatsoever and usually know very little.

• **OTHER Operators.** And then there are the: Mobile, Ship-to-Shore, Conference, Marine, Verify, "Leave Word and Call Back," Route and Rate (KP+800+141+1212+ST—new number as a result of the break-up), and other special operators who have one purpose or another in the Network.

Problems with an Operator? Ask to speak to their supervisor...or better yet, the Group Chief (who is the highest ranking official in any office), the equivalent of the Madame in a whorehouse (if you will excuse the analogy).

Some CO's, by the way, have bugs in them that allow you to use a 1 or a 0 as the 4th digit when dialing. (This tends to happen mostly in crossbars and it doesn't work consistently.) This enables a caller to call special operators and other internal telco numbers without having to use a blue box. For example, 415-121-1111 would get you a San Francisco-Oakland INWARD Operator.

CNA NUMBERS

AREA CODE	CNA-CODED	AREA CODE	CNA-CODED
201	2,016,767,070	518	5,184,718,111
202	2,023,437,106	601	6,019,618,149
203	2,037,896,815	602	3,032,938,777
205	2,059,887,000	603	6,177,875,300
206	2,063,825,124	605	4,025,802,155
207	2,077,875,300	606	5,025,832,861
208	3,032,938,777	607	5,184,718,111
209	4,155,432,811	608	6,082,526,932
212	5,184,718,111	609	2,016,767,070
213	8,185,017,251	612	4,025,802,255
214	2,144,647,400	614	6,144,640,123
215	4,126,335,600	615	6,153,735,791
216	6,144,640,123	616	3,132,238,690
217	2,175,255,800	617	6,177,875,300
218	4,025,802,255	618	2,175,255,800
219	3,172,654,834	619	8,185,017,251
301	3,013,431,401	701	4,025,802,255
302	4,126,335,600	702	4,155,432,861
303	3,032,938,777	703	8,043,448,040
304	3,043,448,041	704	9,127,840,440
305	9,127,840,440	707	4,155,436,374
307	3,032,938,777	712	4,025,803,255
308	4,025,802,255	713	7,138,617,194
309	2,175,255,800	714	8,185,017,251
312	3,127,969,600	715	6,082,526,932
313	3,132,238,690	716	5,184,718,111
314	3,143,448,041	717	4,126,335,600
315	5,184,718,111	801	3,032,938,777
316	8,162,752,781	802	6,177,875,300
317	3,172,654,834	803	9,127,840,440
318	5,042,455,330	804	8,043,448,404
319	4,025,802,255	805	4,155,432,861
401	6,177,875,300	806	5,128,282,501
402	4,025,802,255	808	5,184,718,111
405	4,052,366,121	809	5,184,718,111
406	3,032,938,777	812	3,172,654,834
408	4,155,436,374	813	8,132,287,871
412	4,126,335,600	814	4,126,335,600
413	6,177,875,300	815	2,175,255,800
414	6,082,526,932	816	8,162,752,782
415	4,155,436,374	817	2,144,647,400
417	3,143,448,041	818	8,185,017,251
419	6,144,640,123	901	6,153,735,791
501	4,052,366,121	902	9,024,214,110
502	5,025,832,861	904	9,127,840,440

503	2,063,825,124	906	3,132,238,690
504	5,042,455,330	912	9,127,840,440
505	3,032,938,777	913	8,162,752,782
507	4,025,802,255	914	5,184,718,111
509	2,063,825,124	915	5,128,282,501
512	5,128,282,501	916	4,155,432,861
513	6,144,640,123	919	9,127,840,440
515	4,025,802,255		
516	5,184,718,111		
517	3,132,238,690		

ACRONYM LIST

Sometimes just knowing what to say is half the battle...

/ABHC	-AVERAGE BUSY HOUR CALLS
/ABV	-ATTENDANT BUSY VERIFICATION
/ACD	-AUTOMATIC CALL DISTRIBUTING SYSTEM
ACS	-ADVANCED COMMUNICATION SYSTEM
ACTS	-AUTOMATIC COIN TELEPHONE SERVICE
/ACU	-ALARM CONTROL UNIT
/ADCI	-AUTOMATIC DISPLAY CALL INDICATOR
ADP	-ADVANCED DATA PROCESSING
ADS	-AUTOMATIC VOICE SYSTEM
/ADX	-ASYMMETRIC DATA EXCHANGE
/AFADS	-AUTOMATIC FORCE ADJUSTMENT DATA SYSTEM
AIC	-Automatic Intercept Center
/AIOD	-Automatic Identification Outward Dialing
AIS	-Automatic Intercept System
/AMA	-Automatic Message Accounting
/AMARC	-Automatic Message Accounting Recording Center
/AMPS	-Advanced Mobile Telephone Service
/ANC	-All Number Calling
/ANF	-Automatic Number Forwarding
ANI	-Automatic Number Identification
/AP	-All Points
/ARPANET	-Advanced Research Projects Agency Network
/ARQ	-Automatic Repeat Request
/AIA	-Automatic Trouble Analysis
/ATM	-Automatic Teller Machine
/ATR	-Alternate Trunk Routing
ATT	-American Telephone and Telegraph
/ATTIS	-American Telephone and Telegraph Information Systems
/AUTOVON	-Automatic Voice Network
/AUTODIN	-Automatic Digital Network
/BCP	-Byte Controlled /protocals
/BDT	-Billing Data Transmitter
/BELCORE	-Bell Communications Research
/BHC	-peak Busy Hour Calls
BICS	-Building Industry Consulting Services
BIOC	-Break Into Other Computers
/BIS	-Business Information System

/BOC	-Bell Operating Company
/BORSCHT	-Battery, Overvoltage, Ringing, Supervision, Coding, Hybrid, and Testing Info
BOS	-Business Office Supervisor
/BPOC	-Bell Point of Contact
/BSC	-/BinarySychronous Communication
/BSI	-Business Service Instructor
/BSP	-Bell System Practices
BTL	-Bell Telephone Laboratories
/CAMA	-Centralized Automatic Message Accounting
CBS	-CrossBar Switching
/CC	-Country Code (or Calling Card)
/CCCF	-Central Cross Connect Field
/CCI	-Computer Carrier /Interupt
/CCIS	-Common Channel Interoffice Signaling
/CCITT	-International Telephone and Telegraph Consultive Committee (in French)
/CCS	-/Centa (100) Call Seconds per hour
/CCSA	-Common Control Switching Management
/CDA	-Call Data Accumulator
/CDO	Community Dial Office
/CEVI	-/CommonEquipment Voltage Indicator
CF	-Coin First /payphone
CICS	-Customer Information Control System
/CLR	-Combined Line and Recording
/CLRC	-Circuit Layout Record Card
/CMD	-Centralized Message Distribution
CMS	-Circuit Maintenance System
/CN/A	-Customer Name/Address
CO	-Central Office
/COAM	-Company Operated and Maintained network
COER	-Central Office Equipment Report
COMAS	-Central Office Maintenance and Administration System
COS	-Class of Service
COSMIC	-Common System Main Interconnection frame
COSMOS	-Computer System for /Mainframe Operations
/CPO	-Customer Premises Equipment
/CREG	-Concentrated Range Extention with Gain
/CSACS	-Centralized Status, Alarm and Control System
/CSDC	-Circuit Switched Digital Capability
/CSL	-Coin Supervising Link
/CSMA	-Carrier Sense Multiple Access
/CSO	-Central Services Organization
/CSP	-Control Switching Point
CSS	-Customer Switching System
/CUG	-Closed User Group
/CUVI	-Common Unit Voltage Indicator
DA	- Directory Assistance (C-/computerized ,/M-Microfilm)
/DACS	-Digital Access Cross Connect System
/DAV	-Digital Over Voice
DAVID	-Digital Over Video
/DCE	-Data Communications Equipment

```
/DCTS          -Dimension Custom Telephone Service
/DDD           -Direct Distance Dialing
/DDS           -/Dataphone Digital Service
/DDX           -Distributed Data Exchange
/DIAD          -(magnetic) Drum Information
                Assembler/Dispatcher
/DIAS          -Defense Automatic Integrated System
DID            -Direct /Inwart Dialing
/DIS           -Distributed Information Service
/DIV           -Data in Voice
/DLL           -/DialLong Line Equipment
/DNHR          -Dynamic Non-/Hierarchial Routing
/DNR           -Dialed Number Recorder
/DNIC          -Data Network Identification Code
/DOC           -Dynamic Overload Control
/DP            -Dial Pulse
/DRE           -Directional Reservation Equipment
/DSA           -Dial System Assistance
DSS            -Direct Station Selection (or Digital Switching
                System)
DIE            -Data Terminating Equipment
/DTF           -Dial Tone First /Payphone
DIG            -Direct Trunk Group
/DTMF          -Dual Tone Multi Frequency
/DTS           -Domestic Transmission System
/DUV           -Data Under Voice
/DV            -Destination /Vocoder
/DVX           -Digital Voice Exchange
/EADASS        -Engineering and Administrative Data Acquisition
                System
EAS            -Extended Area Service(or Engineering /Admin.
                System)
/EBCDIC        -/Extended Binary Coded Decimal Interchange Code
/ECASS         -Electronically Controlled Automatic Switching
                System
/ECDO          -Electronic Community Dial Office
/ECO           -Electronic Central Office
/ECS           -Electronic Communications System
/EDTCC         -/ElectronicData Transmission Central
                Communications
/EFT           -Electronic Funds Transfer
/EMN           -End Marked Network
EMS            -Electronic Message System
/EO            -End Office
/EOTT          -End Office Toll Trunking
/ESAC          -Electronic System Assistance Center
/ESAD          -Equal Access Service Date
/ESB           -Emergency Service Bureau (911 exchange)
ESS            -Electronic Switching System
/ESSEX         -/Experimental Solid State Exchange
/ETFD          -Electronic Toll Fraud Device
ETS            -Electronic Translation System
/EVX           -Electronic Voice Exchange
/FACD          -Foreign Area Customer Dialing
```

```
FAN                    -Full Access Network
FAT                    -Foreign Area Translation
/FDM                   -Frequency Division Multiplexing
/FFS                   -Freeze Frame Systems
/FRU                   -Field Replacable Units
/FSP                   -Frequency Shift Pulsing
/FTG                   -Final Trunk Group
FTS                    -Federal Telephone System
/FX                    -Foreign Exchange
/GTE                   -General Telephone Electronics
/HACD                  -Home Area Customer Dialing
/HDLC                  -High Level Data Link Control
/HNPA                  -Home Numbering Plan Area
/HOBIS                 -Hotel Billing Information System
/HUTG                  -High Usage Trunk Group
/IDD                   -International Direct Distance Dialing
/IDF                   -Intermediate Distributing Frame
IIS                    -Integrated Information System
/INWATS                -Inward Wide /AreaTelephone Service
/INAD                  -Initialization and Administration System
/IOCC                  -International Overseas Completion Center
/IOD                   -Identified Outward Dialing
/IP                    -Intermediate Point
/ISC                   -/InternationalSwitching Center
ISIS                   -/InternationalSwitched Interface System
/ITG                   -International Telecommunications Union
JIM                    -Job Information Memorandum
/KDCI                  -Key Display Call Indicator
/KP                    -Key Pulse
/KSU                   -Key Service Unit
/KTS                   -Key Telephone System
/KTU                   -Key Telephone Unit
LAN                    -Local Area Network
/LCC                   -Lost /CallsCleared
/LCD                   -Lost Calls Delayed
/LCH                   -Lost Calls Held
/LDD                   -Local Digital Distribution
/LDM                   -Limited Distance Modem
/LDS                   -Long Distance Service
/LDX                   -Long Distance Extender
/LIU                   -Line Interface Unit
/LL                    -Long Lines
/LLN                   -Line Link Network
/LLP                   -Line Link Pulsing
/LMOS                  -Line /Maintenace Operations System
LSS                    -Loop Switching System
/MAAP                  -Maintenance and Administration Panel
/MCC                   -Master /ControlConsole
/MCI                   -Microwave Communications Incorporated
/MDAS                  -Magnetic Drum Auxiliary Sender
/MDF                   -Main Distributing Frame
/MF                    -Multi-Frequency
/MFT                   -Metallic Facility Frame
/MILNET                -Military Network
```

```
/MTBF        -Mean Time Between Failure
/MTR         -Magnetic Tape Recording
/MTSO        -Mobile Telephone Switching Office
/NBO         -Network Build Out
/NCA         -Network Control Analysis
/NOTIS       -Network Operator Trouble Information System
/NPA         -Number Plan Area
/NPDA        -Network Problem Determination Application
/NPDN        -/Nordic Public Data Network
/NSN         -No /SuchNumber
/OCI         -Out of /CityIndicator
ODD          -Operator Distance Dialing
/DIS         -Office Information System
/OIU         -Office Interface Unit
/ONI         -Operator Number Identification
OR           -Originating Register
/OSI         -Open System Interconnection
OSS          -Operation Support System
/OUTWATS     -Outward Wide Area Telephone Service
OW           -Order Wire
/PABX        -Private /AutomaticBranchExchange
PAM          -Pulse Amplification Modulation
PATROL       -Program for Administrative Traffic Reports on
               Line
/PBX         -Privat Branch Exchange
/PC          -Primary Center
/PCI         -Panel Call Indicator
/PCM         -Pulse Code Modulation
/PLTV        -Phone Line Television
/POS         -Point of Sale
POTS         -Plain Old Telephone Service
PP           -Primary Point (or dial Post Pay /payphone)
/PPCS        -Person to Person,Collect, Special
PPM          _Pulse Position Modulation
/PPN         -Project Programmer Number
/PSDS        -Public Switched Digital Service
/PSW         -Public Switching Network
/PTT         -European Postal, Telephone and Telegraph
               Authorities
/PVPR        -Packet Voice between Packet Radio
/PWM         -Pulse Width Modulation
/QRSS        -Quasi-Random Signal Source
/RACEP       -Random Access and Correlation for Extended
               Performance
/RASC        -Residence Account Service Center
/RC          -Regional Center
/RCC         -Radio Common Carrier
RET          -Real Enough Time
/RJE         -Remote Job Entry
/RMATS       -Remote Maintenance Administration and Traffic
               System
/ROTL        -Remote Office Test Line
ROTS         -Rotary OutTrunks Selectors
/RP          -Revertive Pulse
```

```
/ROS            -Rate Quote System
/RR             -Route Relay
/RRO            -Rate and Route Operator
RSS             -Remote Switching System
/RSU            -Remote Switching Unit
/RT             -Real Time
/RTA            -Remote Trunk Arrangement
/RTAC           -Regional Technical Assistance Center
/RU             -Receive Unit
/SA             -Service Assistant
/SAC            -Special Area Code
/SAMA           -Step-by-step Automatic Message Accounting
/SARTS          -Switched Access Remote Test System
/SBS            -Skyline Business Systems
SC              -Sectional Center
SCAN            -Switched Circuit Automatic Network
/SCC            -Switching Control Center (or Specialized Common
                 Carriers /or Satellite Communications
                 Controller)
/SCOTS          -/Surveilance and Control of Transmission
                  Systems
/SCPC           -Single Channel Per Carrier
/SDCU           -Satellite Delay Compensation Unit
/SDDS           -Switched Digital Data Service
/SOLC           -/Sychronous Data Link Control
/SDM            -Space Division Multiplexing
/SDX            -Satellite Date Exchange
/SF             -Single Frequency
/SLN            -Service Link Network
/SNA            -Systems Network Architecture
/SOTUS          -Sequentially Operated /Teletypewriter Universal
                 Selector
SPADE           -Simple Channel Per Carrier Assignment By Demand
                 Equipment

/SPC            -Stored Program Control
/SRCC           -Simplex Remote /Connunication Central
/SSB             -Simple Side Band
/SSTOMA         -Spacecraft Switched Time /Div. Multiple Access
                 (/theoretical)
/STP            -Space-Time-Space Switching Architecture
/SV              -Source /Vecoder
/SXS             -Step-by-step Switching Equipment
/TAC             -Technical Assistance Center
/TACAS           -/TAC Access Control System
TAP              -Technological American Party (or Tech. Assist.
                  Program)
/TASC           -Telecommunications Alarm Surveillance and
                 /ControlSystem
/TASI           -Time Assignment Speech Interpolation
/TC             -Toll Center (or TeleConferencing)
/TCE            -Telephone /CompanyEngineered
/TCT            -Test and Code /TreatmentFrame
/TDD            -/Telecommunicatiosn Device for the Deaf
```

```
/TDM          -Tandem (or Time Division Multiplexing)
/TDMA/DA      -Time Division Multiple Access/Demand Assignment
/TDRS         -Traffic Recording System
TEARS         -Traffic Engineering for Automatic Route
                Selection
TELCO         -Telephone Company
/TELSAM       -Telephone Service Attitude Measurement
/TG           -Trunk Guard
/TGUE         -Trunk Group Usage Equipment
/TLN          -Trunk Link Network
/TLP          -Test Level Point
/TM           -Terminal Management
/TMS          -Time Multiplexed Switch
/TN           -/Telenorm
/TNDS         -Total Network Data System
/TNOP         -Total Network Operations Plan
/TOC          -Trunk Operating Center
/TORC         -Traffic Overload Reroute Control
/TP           -Toll Point
/TPU          -Trunk Processing Unit
TS            -Time Sharing
/TSI          -Time Slot Interchange
/TSPS         -Traffic Service Position System
TTY           -/Teletypewriter
/TU           -Transmit Unit
/TUR          -Traffic /UsageRecorder
TWX           -/Teletypewriter Network
/UNICOM       -/Universl Integrated Communications System
/USOC         -Uniform Service Order Code
/USP          -Usage /Senstive Pricing
/UT           -Universal Trunk
/VAC          -Value Added Carrier
VAN           -Value Added Network
/VF /BSY      -Verify Busy
/VMS          -Voice Message Exchange
/VMX          -Voice Storage Service
VSS           -Voice Storage Service
/WATS         -Wide Area Telephone Service
/WC           -Wire Center
/WO           -Work Order
WORD          -Work Order Record and Details
/XBAR         -Crossbar Switching Equipment
/YIPL         -Youth International Party Line
```

CORDLESS TELEPHONES

Any cordless telephone equipment conversation is anything but private. In a recent court case, the judge allowed tape recordings of a cordless telephone conversation to be used as evidence in a drug case. A cordless telephone user was dealing in illegal drugs and didn't realize that his communications were being intercepted by a curious neighbor. What he thought was a private conversation was actually going out all over the neighborhood to every scanner listener for miles around. Be aware that a cordless call is anything but secure, and possibly not "protected" by Section 605 of The Communications Act of 1934.

It's easy to monitor cordless telephone conversations; take a shortwave receiver or a scanner radio and tune in.

A shortwave receiver is necessary for picking up the base transponder side of the cordless telephone conversation. The outgoing frequencies for the base transponders feed into the AC power lines, giving extremely good reception up to a couple miles away. The frequencies to concentrate on with your shortwave set in the standard AM or FM mode (if available on your receiver): 1.705, 1.735, 765, and 1.825 MHz.

These frequencies are also shared by other "carrier current" devices, such as intercoms and local paging systems. Besides hearing the base transponder portion of cordless phone calls, you can sometimes pick up some other interesting signals just above the AM broadcast band.

Your shortwave antenna system for maximum reception to this band will be a long wire running the length of your house. The longer the wire, the greater the reception at 1700 kHz. It may take some fine-tuning with your band spread knob to pull out each individual conversation. With less selective receivers simply tuning to frequencies around 1.7MHz should lead to interesting discoveries!

The ultimate range of the carrier current transmissions should be approximately one block from the transmitting station, although many monitors report reception over several miles! A little, hand held, shortwave receiver will permit you to walk around the block and hear many different phone calls.

The handset of the cordless telephone device operates in the 49 MHz region, utilizing narrow band FM. It is necessary to employ the use of a scanner radio to pick up the handset side of the conversation. The following frequencies may be programmed into your scanner to pick up the present cordless telephone conversations: 49.830, 49.845, 49.860, 49.875, and 49.890 MHz.

The range of the handset will be only a couple houses away. A good outside VHF low-band or 6 meter band ham antenna will be necessary to pick up any handsets more than this distance. Since the cordless phone handsets are limited to a maximum output power not to exceed 10,000 microvolts per meter at 3 meters, we are dealing with extremely low signal levels.

Some handsets also retransmit out the base side of the conversation--and if this is the case, you will hear both sides of the telephone call. Some handsets have more sophisticated circuitry that masks the calling side of the conversation from being retransmitted out on the cordless side. This means you will only hear one side of the conversation on 49MHz. Many of the 1700 kHz band pedestals also carry both sides of the conversation.

Some major manufacturers made cordless telephones that operate exclusively at 49 MHz; they're "49/49" MHz cordless phones. These devices use two frequencies out of the five in the 49 MHz band. If you and your scanner are agile enough, you should be able to switch back and forth between the two 49MHz channels to hear both sides of the conversation. The range of these units is slightly greater than that of conventional cordless handsets, so you might be able to pick up someone up to a block away.

Cordless telephone users who have extended their range by using outside antennas will give much greater signal levels for eavesdropping. Their antennas will look similar to low-band, ground-plane antennas.

NEW FREQUENCIES

New cordless telephone sets manufactured after October, 1984, operate on frequency pairs in both the 46MHz and 49MHz bands. Since these two frequencies are independent of the AC power lines, many cordless telephone owners will employ outside antennas for greater range. This means that reception will be a great deal easier--especially the base transponder on the 46 MHz band. The following frequencies are assigned to base transponders and should provide you with a minimum of two blocks of range if an outside antenna is employed:

46.61 MHz	46.77MHz	46.63 MHz	46.83 MHz	46.67 MHz
46.87 MHz	46.71 MHz	46.93 MHz	46.73 MHz	46.97 MHz

The Federal Communications Commission has allocated these frequencies on a temporary basis to aid in relieving the current congestion on cordless telephone frequencies.

Most of the new cordless base transponders will repeat out both the handset as well as the telephone line side of the conversation on the base frequencies--you will hear both sides of the conversation. A good outside, 50MHz, low-band antenna will help pull in these frequencies loud and clear .

The associated handset channels for the newer cordless telephones will be transmitting on the following frequencies:

49.670 MHz   49.830 MHZ   49.845 MHZ   49.890 MHZ   49.860 MHz
49.930 MHZ   49.770 MHz   49.990 MHz   49.875 MHz   49.970 MHz

Since few handsets will ever employ an outside, permanent-type antenna, chances are the range to these portable handsets will be far less than the range to a base transponder with an outside antenna.

CONFIDENTIAL?

There is still great debate as to whether or not cordless telephone conversations are indeed protected by Section 605 of The Communications Act that classifies certain radio transmissions as "secret. It would be to your advantage not to divulge to anyone what you hear on your shortwave receiver or scanner set. Remember, someone might be listening in on your conversation, too, and I am certain that you wouldn't care to hear about it from a neighbor.

PART 15 DEVICES

Cordless telephones fall under the Part 15 category as defined by the Federal Communications Commission rules and regulations. To better understand cordless telephone regulations, here's an excerpt of the rules:

15.117--A low power communication device may be operated on one or more frequencies without any type of modulation provided it complies with certain frequency and power output requirements.

Frequency tolerance of the carrier will be greater than plus or minus .01 percent.

Emission type will be confined within a 20 khz band centered on the carrier frequencies.

The emission of RF energy on the carrier frequency shall not exceed 10,000 microvolts/meter measured at 3 meters distant. That's why they don't go very far.

The out-of-band emissions, including harmonics, shall not exceed 500 microvolts per meter measured at 3 meters.

The device shall be completely self-contained. The antenna permanently attached to the enclosure containing the device (probably excluding the addition of an external antenna to make transponders illegal).

Ultimately, cordless telephones will switch to the 900 MHz band--but that is still years away. For now there's plenty of activity at the 46 MHz and 49 MHz band. You will find that activity at the 1.7 MHz band will taper off because ultimately these frequencies will turn into commercial broadcasting channels.

NEW CAR PHONE TECHNOLOGY

Two manufacturers plan to bring out a cellular phone with a list price of about $1,000 within a year.

Good mobile phone service is available in cities that may not have the sophisticated cellular telephone systems. Almost every city in the country is served by radio common carrier mobile telephones, AT&T VHF and UHF telephone systems, as well as trunked radio telephone systems.

While not as sophisticated as cellular telephone systems, the radio common carrier (RCC) and the telephone company systems use individual channels for phone calls, retrieving messages, and basically staying in touch with modern, full-duplex telephone sets. VHF and UHF telephone systems use mountain top sites that give you several hundred miles of roaming. In cities where usage is low, there is usually a vacant channel to place a phone call on. In larger cities, your equipment will find a channel and tell you that a dial tone is available.

Common carriers provide cellular telephone service with the cells on the 870-880 MHz band, and mobiles in the 825-835 Mhz band.

If you listen to the mobile phone channels, you'll hear a tone on unused channels. Here's a listing of mobile telephone channels used by telephone companies in major cities:

Albuquerque: 152.510, 152.570, 152.630, 152.750, 152.810.

Atlanta: 152.510, 152.540, 152.600, 152.630, 152.660, 152.690, 152.750, 152.810.

Baltimore: 152.510, 152.630, 152.750, 152.810, 4554.400, 454.500.

Boston: 152.510, 152.540, 152.600, 152.660, 152.780, 454.524, 454.475, 454.500, 454.525, 454.550, 454,600.

Chicago: 152.510, 152.570, 152.630, 152.690, 152.720, 152.750, 152.780, 152.180, 454.375, 454.400, 454.425, 454.450, 454.475, 454.500, 454.525, 454.550, 454.575, 454.600, 454.625, 454.650.

Cincinnati: 35.42, 152.510, 152.630, 152.750.

Cleveland: 152.510, 152.630, 152.690, 152.750, 454.400.

Dallas: 152.510, 152.630, 1522.690, 152.750, 152.810, 454.400, 454.475, 454.550, 454.600, 454.625, 454.650.

Denver: 152.510, 152.540, 152.600, 152.630, 152.690, 152.750, 152.780, 152.810, 454.375, 454.400, 454.425, 454.450, 454.475, 454.500, 454.525, 454.550, 454.575, 454.600, 454.625, 454.650.

Detroit: 152.570, 152.600, 152.630, 152.690, 152.730, 454.375, 454.475, 454.525, 454.575, 454.625.

Houston: 152.510, 152.630, 152.720, 152.750, 454.400, 454.425, 454.450, 4544.475, 454.500, 454.550, 454.600, 454.650.

Indianapolis: 152.510, 152.540, 152.630, 152.690, 152.750, 152.810, 454.375, 454.400, 454.425, 454.475, 454.500, 454.525, 454.550, 454.600.

Kansas City: 152.510, 152.540, 152.630, 152.690, 152.750, 152.780, 454.375, 454.425, 454.450, 454.475, 454.550, 454.650.

Las Vegas: 152.510, 152.540, 152.570, 152.600, 152.630, 152.660, 152.690, 152.720, 152.750, 152.780, 454.375, 454.425, 454.450, 454.475, 454.525, 454.500, 454.575, 454.600, 454.625, 454.650.

Los Angeles: 35.38, 35.46, 152.510, 152.570, 152.630, 152.690, 152.720, 152.780, 152.810, 454.400, 454.450, 454.500, 454.550, 454.575, 454.625.

Miami: 152.510, 152.570, 152.600, 152.630, 152.660, 152.720, 152.750, 152.780, 454.375, 454.400, 454,425, 454.450, 454.500, 454.550, 454.600.

Milwaukee: 152.510, 152.570, 152.600, 152.630, 152.720, 152.780, 454.400, 454.475, 454.600.

Minneapolis/St. Paul: 152.570, 152.600, 152.630, 152.690, 152.750, 152.780, 152.810.

Nashville: 152.510, 152.570, 152.630, 152.690, 152.780, 152.810, 454.375, 454.450, 454.475, 454.525, 454.600, 454.625.

Newark, NJ; 152.540, 152.750, 152.810, 454.425, 454.475, 454.575.

New Orleans: 152,510, 152.630, 152.690, 152.810.

New York City: 35.50, 35.66, 152.510, 152.570, 152.630, 152.690, 152.720, 152.780, 454.375, 454.450, 454.525, 454.550, 454.625, 454.650.

Oklahoma City: 152.510, 152.540, 152.630, 152.660, 152.720, 152.750, 152.580, 152.810, 454.375, 454.400, 454.425, 454.475, 454.500, 454.600, 454.650.

Philadelphia: 35.50, 152.510, 152.540, 152.630, 152.690, 152.750, 152.810, 454.400, 454.425, 454.475, 454.500, 454.550, 454.575, 454.600, 454.650.

Phoenix: 151.510, 152.540, 152.570, 152.600, 152.630, 152.660, 152.720, 152.750, 152.780, 152.810.

Pittsburgh: 35.42, 35.66, 152..510, 152.630, 152.690, 152.750, 454.375, 454.400, 454.425, 454.475.

St. Louis: 152.510, 152.570, 152.630, 152.660, 152.690, 152.750, 454.375, 454.400, 454.425, 454.450, 454.550.

Salt Lake City: 152.510, 152.570, 152.630, 152.690, 152.750, 152.810.

San Diego: 35.38, 35.46, 152.510, 152.570, 152.630, 152.690, 152.810, 454.550.

San Francisco: 152.510, 152.540, 154.630, 454.550.

Seattle: 152.510, 152.540, 152.630, 152.660, 152.690, 454.375, 454.450, 454.500.

Washington: 152.510, 152.600, 152.630, 152.690, 152.720, 152.750, 152.780, 152.810, 454.375, 454.425, 454.475, 454.525, 454.550, 454.575, 454.625, 454.650.

NEW COUNTERMEASURES

There are some new ideas, techniques and equipment on the market for ES countermeasures as well as some refinement of older ideas we would like to present here.

Use these techniques in conjunction with those ideas in both the previous books.

Squealers

It is possible to make a number of bugs, both hardwire and transmitters give themselves up, so to speak by using a little known technique.

Take a common, garden variety audio frequency generator, connect it to a tweeter that is capable of emiting ultra high frequency (the specs should be listed) usually through a fairly powerful audio amplifier.

The alternative to this is to use on of the premade "pain field generators" that already emit high energy ultrasonic waves.

If a generator I used sweep it from 15KHz to 40Khz while flooding the room in question with the output; this will cause many microphones to audibly "squeal" thus pinpointing their location.

Spectrum Analysis

This is the only real method of transmitter detection that works with any sort of reliability. There are a number of spectrum analyzers on the countersurveillance market that are designed for this work however a good (read Tektronix) spec analyzer will work very well for our purposes.

The Tek is not cheap,say $8,000 for a used unit so what is the advantage to employing it over the surveillance models?

It is possible to RENT spectrum analyzers from commercial electronic suppliers in most big cities. These are usually rented by consulting engineers or radio/television engineers for a look at their signal.

Many larger radio and television stations will own their own units and may rent them out for a day or two if you can convince the chief engineer that you know what you are doing and will return the unit...

In order to use the Tek for our use a complementary preamplifier is plugged into the left hand compartment of the frame (most units already are so equipped) a small amplifier or even a tape recorder can be plugged directly into the VERT SIG OUTPUT on the rear of the mainframe. This will allow one to listen to the signal in question.

The spectrum analyzer is an AM receiver but will also pick up FM signals by means of slope detection, displaying both.

To begin the search set the unit to the ZERO SPAN mode so its display becomes that of an oscilloscope and it will tune continuously from about 10 KHz to 1 GHz...

An antenna must be hooked up to the Tek to make it function. There are several specialized types of antennas we will cover, but for general searching a simple whip type is a good bet.

It is very simple to make this on one's own; simply cut a piece of stiff wire to a 1/4 wavelength (see the last book) of the frequency to be search (88-108 MHz is about 30 inches, the lower the frequency the longer the antenna) and hook it up as shown.

The first thing to do is to become familiar with the operation of the unit as well as what various signals "read" like.

Remember that every rf source will produce some signal and with a little practice the operator can tell what frequency the signal is located on, how strong it is (by height of the "spike") and even what kind of transmitter is making the signal.

Once a signal is isolated it can then be id'ed by listening in on the vertical output.

Remember most signals on the scope will belong to commercial radio and television stations and then public service, aircraft and marine transmitters.

Surveillance transmitters normally have several characteristics that an experienced operator can easily spot, although the more professional units will be harder to spot.

The first give-away is low power coupled with a "dirty" signal. This will show up as a central carrier with odd and even harmonics, each lower in power, on both sides of the original carrier.

The resulting display will consist of a center, higher spike double bordered by harmonic shorter spikes.

The FCC does not allow such harmonics in commercial transmitters and any dirty unit must be checked out.

One should always place a source of audio in the area to be searched. If alerting the listener is a problem, simply turn on a radio, if it is not use some thing with a signal that varies on a regular basis such as a metronome which can make a signal easier to spot. Another trick is to make a sudden LOUD noise, many small transmitters will shift off frequency when over modulated. This appears on the display as a "chirp"; a blunt, tall spike with dull edges, almost like a tall mushroom cloud.

A good practice is to take at least three readings (with a whip antenna) in a triangle shaped pattern of, say 10 yards apart within the target area.

Powerful radio and other commercial signals will not vary much in strength as they are saturating the area to begin with, small local bugs WILL show variations and one can make a rough guess as to direction and range from the unit.

Bugs with filtered outputs, or pulse modulation can be harder to find as they are more professional in output and have to be carefully analyzed. Often a direction sensitive antenna can be helpful in isolating such units.

It should also be remembered that a professional may "hide" his small transmiiter just next to a more powerful signal in an attempt to hide it.

As a spectrum analyzer operator has the advantage of more sensitive equipment and probably range, he should be able to locate any transmitter that a receiver could pick up; HOWEVER it is wise to spread the display at each powerful signal and look carefully for low spikes hidden at either edge of the main carrier.

It also possible to hide a signal in a frequency range with lots of noise, possibly from nearby electrical equipment. A wise bugger may even plant something that makes spurious noise in order to hide the signal.

Any area of wideband noise should be spread out and carefully examined as the analyzer will still be more sensitive than the surveillance receiver will be.

Pulsed bugs are much harder to locate as they are only on for a short period of time and then off. Since the Tek sweeps it would be possible to miss the bug by being on its frequency during an "off" period.

To counter this possibility Use the storage mode on the analyzer with maximum bandwidth setting. Use a fast sweep speed.

If a curious signal is spotted continue to use the storage mode and narrow the bandwidth to find the unit.

Direction Finding

If one hooks a dipole antenna (shown) up to the Tek it is possible to rotate it until the signal peaks (this will mean the antenna is directly in front of the widest portion of the antenna), or continue rotating the antenna until the signal dis- appears, or "nulls".

At this condition the transmitter is directly along the axis or the dipole, in other words it is pointing directly at the transmitter.

Of course it can still be in one of two directions.

To counter this move your unit and take another reading, now draw a line along the first axis in both directions and do the same with the second reading.

Where the lines intersect is the transmitting site...

Ultrasonic Snooping

Many devices, including tape recorders, some transmitters, video cameras, ultrasonic and rf flooding techniques, emit low frequency radio waves and or ultrasonic sound.

A good condenser mic that will pick up at least 35 kHz can be hooked up to a special, low frequency spectrum analyzer will show up any of the ultrasonic tell-tale emissions.

In addition our combination low and high frequency antenna will pick up low frequency radio waves that will show up on the low frequency spec analyzer or some radio receivers.

Television cameras, and monitors emit a 15,750 kHz radio signal (a flyback horizontal signal) that will show up quite clearly.

Tape recorders emit both electrical noise from the motors (usually AM) plus a bias frequency of 28 to 90 kHz.

This technique will also show up low frequency transmitters.

TDR

A time domain reflectometry test is the hot "new" set up in detecting telephone bugs. The unit bounces pulses down a line and then displays the reflections of any splices, taps, unusual areas etc.

Tektronix also makes a TRD for use in radio/tv work that can be easily adapted to surveillance work by running the phone line through 600 ohm balancing transformer (available at any electronics store) and trying one wire to the ground and one to the center (coax) connection, and then reversing the connections.

Light

Several manufacturers make photo detection devices that will show up an IR bug or LASER bug. One can also check with any of our night vision equipment that is IR sensitive for beams.

If you are unsure where to rent Tektronix equipment it is possible to call them (in Beaverton, Ore) and ask for suggestions of someone in your area that might rent the equipment.

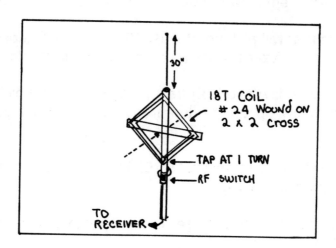

TSU 3000

Over the years a number of companies and private engineers have attempted to design a perfect "anti-tap" device for securing conversations on any public phone system.

Most have had two outstanding characteristics in common:

     A. They failed.
     B. They were expensive.

Now we have a new entry into the field the TSU-3000 from Research Electronics, Inc. that attempts to beat both the above restrictions.

Does it accomplish this ideal?

First off, REI is not a new entry into the field. They were previously called Security Research International and based in Florida where they designed some very nice counter-surveillance gear both for their own clients and to wholesale to several other suppliers in the field.

Their prices were always low to moderate (for this weird field) and their devices usually did about what they were supposed to do...

Now?

The TSU 3000 is not a new breakthrough in anti-technology; however it is a combination of just about every workable anti-tap theory under one roof.
The device installs between any phone and the telco line. Firstly it isolates the telephone electronically from the line. This means, in effect, your phone and ringer are no longer connected to the telephone line but to the TSU 3000 instead.

The first thing one may note is that the phone ringer no longer works but a pleasant electronic tone from the unit is substituted whenever ringing voltage (AC) comes down the line.

With a twist of the proper control the 3000 will actually allow the operator to listen down the line while the phone is still in an off-hook condition.

Should any audio (other than random static, or minor cross-talk) be present you got a problem...

This isolating effect also protects the phone from several sophisticated bugging attacks including infinity transmitters, voltage controlled devices, remote control (rf or spike voltage jolts) turn on, and rf flooding.

A nice touch, right off the bat.

Now the unit has two other basic advantages; the first is the use of a sensitive voltage spreader that you adjust to the characteristics of your particular line.

This is not a new concept, but one that does work. By increasing the operational voltage of the line while reducing the current drop-out relays (telephone secretary, recorder turn-on, self record units) will NOT sense an off hook condition even when the phone is in use, thereby failing in their function of remote start and record turn on of mini-recorders.

This type of attack is by far the most common bugging attempt from mad spouses all the way up through $200 an hour private detective "consultants".

This is true because the devices are cheap (I believe $14.95 is the cheapest we list in the suppliers section), easy to obtain (Radio Shack even sells one), and do work quite well.

Remember, the simpler the technique, the better chance of success.

At any rate we tried 5 (count them), 5 different types of drop out relays on the junction box outside our cell (Editor's note: Lee and Scott were, well, sort of, not exactly kept, but "given" a very nice cabin to work out of until the book was completely finished due to some slight variations in working schedule (s), they were never actually locked in and the gentleman outside the door was strictly a bodyguard), and, after we had "fine tuned" the voltage pot, NOT ONE DROP OUT RELAY TURNED ON DURING ANY CALL.

Not bad.

The next protection "device" is a variable noise flooding generator. The operator can adjust this feature, while watching a LED bar graph, from minor interference to complete flood.

When pressed into operation this feature jams the line full of white (actually, in this case I would suspect "pink" noise; random static-noise centered in the human speech frequency range).

Should this noise remain on the line your intended receiver would not hear much of the conversation. It does not work out this way because the phone company central office (CO) works at filtering out any weird noise on the line.

162

In this case, it does a remarkable job.

The operator's manual suggest a bar graph setting of 8 (out of a possible 10) for most conversations.

While this is possible I found that I had trouble hearing the person on the other end of any long distance call. Note they could hear me fine (two commented it simply sounded like the normal noise of any long distance call since the break up of Ma Bell, even on local calls), but the noise feedback into my ear piece was very noticable.

On the plus side I could make myself heard quite nicely and it would well be worth asking the other party to talk loudly, or even shout, should the conversation be one I did not wish recorded for security purposes.

When I adjusted the noise level down from 8 to 2 1/2 in steps, my reception improved considerably although not in a linear fashion.

That is to say the noise level would seem about the same for several steps and then decrease abruptly.

This af flooding should, if done correctly, prevent most other common types of phone attack including simple lineman's set attachment anywhere down the line to good serial or parallel radio transmitters installed anywhere down the line.

It should even stop inductive coupling, a very hard to combat approach of line tapping.

RESULTS:

We installed a direct transformer tap to the nearest box as well as an inductive amplifier on the line and then recorded several calls.

Perfect.

Then we switched in the flood (modulation) effect of the TSU 3000 and it was bye-bye recording.

With the unit turned up to 80% (8 on the bar graph) the static/noise was overwhelming with not trace of conversation available to the naked ear.

This effect seemed to stay in place down to on or about 5 on the graph at which time a few random words would sort of aurally appear mixed in with the static.

With the bar graph on 2 (the makers lowest rating of "still works") several words at a time could be picked out on a careful replay.

What does this sort out to?

About the best deal on the market for anti-tap measures, although not a perfect answer.

There will be some noise on the line making low level conversations difficult to hear (although use of a microwave system such as Sprint seemed to have no effect on the line noise or masking qualities of the unit), some adjustment of the unit is necessary (this is minor, anyone can do it) and it will, of course, not stop the conversation from being recorded or tapped at the other end of the line...

But.

For the money this unit will knock out 99% of any tapping attempts on the users end of things (before the CO) at a price better than many of the single shot anti-tap phones on the market.

Could this be duplicated without buying the unit?

Sure, but the engineering and building hassle would seem to make this a no-win situation. Any one of the unit's effects can be done with the proper construction, but to duplicate the whole idea and make it all work together as one happy family, would be very difficult.

The only tap we found effective at all with the modulation turned up, was to place a direct or inductive tap in the phone unit itself prior to going into the 3000.

This is difficult because of access and ease of detection (read the other books dammit) and not really a heavy threat, and it still picked up considerable noise.

The bad temptation is to run the modulation index at too low of a level which would allow a really anal tapper to get enough audio to filter down to meaningful conversation.

Any conversation worth masking should be worth a bit of noise in your receiver.

The other obvious problem is that the device, like other maskers, is not FCC approved for hook up to any pulic phone system in the US as it puts unwanted noise on the line.

There is a slim possibility of enough noise alerting the local phone company to some problem and coming over to find none other than your non-approved device hooked up to the line, although this has never happened to our knowledge.

The unit also has easy access on the rear panel for connecting a digital VOM for line checks or tracing down a "problem".

I would advise purchase of this unit, use of the voltage regulator and isolation factor at all times and throwing in heavy flooding when a sensitive conversation was taking place.

Type of operation should prevent most attempts and throw any successful attempt into confusion during those times you don't want to reach out and touch the wrong party.

The Telecom Security Unit (TSU3000) has been developed by Research Electronics, Inc., in order to provide a "realistic approach" to the problem of telephone communication security.

Eavesdropping devices which utilize high effective impedances, capacitive or inductive coupling are for the most part indetectable by conventional methods. Telephone analyzers, which require expert technical knowledge, will completely miss these devices unless accompanied by sophisticated "Time Domain Reflectometry." Expensive, time-consuming sweeps and the infiltrations of outside technical individuals can be avoided with the new TSU-3000.

The Telecom Security Unit was developed by Research Electronics, Inc., based on military countermeasure technology with a unique blend of R.E.I. experience and design. The TSU-3000 utilizes your existing telephone while the interconnected security unit is hidden out of sight.

One of the few devices that actually does prevent most types of telephone tapping. Not a scrambler but quite simply the combination of the best anti-tap technology available all in one package. It may have slight negative qualities, but for the price there really is nothing else on the market that will touch it.

A very nice design job; see the text for a more complete look at the TSU-3000.

R.E.I. also makes several nice transmitter locators, courrier briecases, noise generators and so on. The are a born again version of another company (Security Research International) that has been in the field for many years.

WDM-1

A Quick Fix To An Annoying Problem...

ADAMS AND ASSOCIATES
BOX 93124 #D13
Pasadena, Ca 91109

This is a very workable solution to about 98% of all wiretap problems.

No, it is not a TSU-3000; but it is a part of that device...

Technically this is a voltage spreader coupled with a volt meter. This allows one to check both on hook and off hook voltages for any unusual activity and then gradually adjust the input voltage of the phone so it will do two things:

1. Still Ring.
2. Not activate drop out relays (tele-starters, auto-recorders, and many other Madison ave type names).

This, right off the bat, stops most spouse-business partner-private detective type spying as well as many police type jobs. It will also prevent some pen registers from turning on...

This means you can, for very little money, prevent any sort of automatic turn-on device from operating on your phone line.

The device does work, we gave it our certified messy housekeeping test and seal of approval.

One beauty of this idea is that one only uses it for sensitive calls, letting the tap operate on all "normal" calls so the bad guys think their unit is working..

A real deal.

EXOTIC BRIEFCASE
CONSTRUCTION

The briefcase has always been the snake boot of the businessman. The fancier the case, ergo the more important the person attached to the handle.

Never mind the contents are often lunch or running shoes...

Cases run from dead snake hide to gold polished aluminum. Some have locks, some have handcuffs, some have personalized lettering.

In the last few years the age of specialization has reached the case. They are no longer briefcases; they are courier cases, attache containers with built in invisible shields, weapons, counter weapons, recorders, transmitters, and countersurveillance devices.

Let's take a look at some of LAW ENFORCEMENT ASSOCIATES' offerings:

> Courier case with dye gas and alarm if opened by unauthorized persons-$1300.
>
> Attache with alarm and handle that tosses several thousand volts of non-lethal electric current into folks who shouldn't be fooling with it.-$1,000.
>
> Attache with built mic and hidden switch. Will hide a mini recorder in the lid and tape whatever you wish...-$400.
>
> Case with built in bug and recorder detector that will let you know if someone else is using the above case...-$1200
>
> Undercover back-up system; comes with a body worn mini transmitter that broadcasts to a crystal controlled receiver and recorder built into the case. Can be left to run all by itself with its carrier sensing switch. Comes with every accessory possible.-$4000.
>
> Portable repeater. Automatic receiver-transmitter that takes in weak signals kicks them up to 15 watts in your choice of channels and re-broadcasts the signal to a distant location.

Works on rechargeable supply, AC, or car DC.-$8000.

OUR MAGIC ANSWERS

Remember these examples are just from one company, there are others, but LEA is fairly representative from both type and price standpoints.

As in our weapons systems, these suggestions and combinations are not God's word, etched in stone. Substitute as you feel the urge...

1. The first necessity is a good case of some sort. For most applications I prefer a Halliburton because of the good workmanship, positive locking, changeable combo lock and good looks.

Other cases may be as good or better, but for the money, the big H shouts importance and respect.

Halliburtons also come lined with thick foam that can be cut to fit any internal components.

They even include a paring knife...

2. A very interesting idea that will be more expensive and probably not available from this company as we go to press, but will still be around, DAK INC. sells, for $11 (that is not a misprint) at this time a two piece miniature transmitter-receiver combination. One goes into the case, the other in your pocket.

Once activated, the receiver sets off an alarm if the case is moved more than 12-15 feet from the receiver.

Very handy in airports, planes or anyplace one might forget the case. Also prevents theft quite nicely...

3. The next item I personally like is a bullet proof liner under the bottom foam. There are a number of ways to accomplish this from simple Kelvar fabric cut to fit, to custom made attache liners.

As the case is flat and not flexible it is easier to provide heavier protection than it is in a wearable vest.

Several companies make liners, others make clip boards (for police use) that work just as well. Edmund sells a liner for $120 which will stop .357's, .45's, 9mm's etc.

DANEGELD sells Kelvar fabric plus armor steel plates. These plates come in 6" x 10" and 10" x 12" sizes and have a layer of Kelvar laminated to the front to stop splatter.

They will stop .308, and .223 rifle rounds not to mention other, lesser calibers.

The plates sell for $35 and $60 depending on size.

The most diverse collection is offered by WILLIAM DONOVAN CO. They feature both liners and light weight clip boards in three protection levels.

Level A stops .22 thru .45 auto from a 5 inch barrel.
Level B stops 9mm (4 inch barrel) thru .38 sp 6" barrel.
Level C stops .357 mag 158 grain, 6" barrel...

Sizes range from 8" x 10" to 12" x 18" and you even get a choice of colors. Prices in the $30-$70 range...

It is hard to stress just how important one of these protection devices can be in any sudden crisis situation.

Besides bullets you get protection from knives and striking weapons.

4. Audio compressor VIKING ELECTRONICS. For a more complete explanation of why this route is superior to many of the commercial sound collection units on the market please read the section on audio acquisition.

5. VIKING mini electret mic with 15 feet of cord. This is a very sensitive unit which can be used directly in the case or can be extended outside the case for other applications.

6. Transmitter. Here we are concerned with a series of factors depending on which version of the case one wishes to construct so I am suggesting three models, ALTERNATIVE TECHNOLOGY's crystal controlled unit for extreme stability and small size, INFO UNLIMITED's 1 mile range model for more power and yet still very small and affordable, and lastly a 1 watt heavy duty, larger transmitter.

7. Receiver, a sensitive front end receiver either crystal controlled to your x-mitter or even a good scanner.

8. AT's wide band pre-amp (under $50) for scanners or small receivers.

9. VOX. Either from Viking or AT or ES; note that I prefer a separate VOX rather than a built in voice operated recorder.

10. Good recorder, size and tape time are your limiting factors here. I still like the Viking long play models for any sort of extended play service, although for a briefcase you can also consider one of the new switchable speed units out.

11. Mercury switch.

12. Electronic contact mic from MICRO ELECTRONICS in Germany is my first choice, second probably FARGO COMPANY in San Francisco.

13. Fisheye micro lens and camera attachment from ES or LEA.

14. Camera with motor drive and remote switch. Any good mini 35 such as the OM we used for this project will suffice as long as it has a fully automatic lens/speed adjusting system.

15. High gain amplifier from WYNN ELECTRONICS, second choice electronic stethoscope from ES (about $60 and $100 in order, see How To Get).

16. Electronic shocking device from IU.

17. Alarm buzzer or completed movement alarm from ES.

18. Burglar Mist from:

> WORLD SOURCES
> 313 Blount Rd
> Lutz FL 33549

This wonderful little plastic box is a manually operated, pressurized unit which emits 4 ounces of CN stun gas. Enough tear gas to fill 16,000 square feet.

19. Silenced high standard .22 with electrically operated BMF activator attached to its trigger.

20. Various bugs, lock picks, and other devices that will get you arrested.

21. Various optical enhancements depending on your need and wallet size; could include TASCO credit card sized binoculars $90 from SHARPER IMAGE, folks like that, ES spy scope monocular ($25), variable power spotting scope ($30 range) IR scope, NVD, mini camera such as the Minox EC a fully electronic spy camera designed for copying documents on a min-8 mm film cartridge, or taking photos completely unobserved, or just one of the new sub mini-Pentax's, etc.

NINJA 1990 MAKES THE CASE...

Just for the fun of it let's begin with the worst possible case; pun intended. This is for information only, ONLY! Should you get caught with this little device you never heard of me, this book, this publishing company, any of my friends, the TV show 60

Minutes, well you get it.

This is illegal it about seven ways I can think off right off hand without even calling up my paranoid attorney who no longer returns my phone calls anyway.

Suppose, just suppose, some real no good type took a foam padded briefcase, like a Halliburton and then drilled a small, say .22 thousands of an inch, hole in the side.

This hole could even be covered up with a decal, airline tag, black rubber plug, etc.

No suppose this same despicable type mounted a high standard .22 semi-automatic pistol with our SWD silencer attached to it within the layers of foam rubber gluing, or otherwise perfectly aligning the exit hole in the silencer with the hole in the case.

This would be done through a solid rubber wipe.

If the BMF activator and motor/speed control was clamped onto the trigger and a hidden push button switch secreted under the handle or latch of the case WITH A SAFETY!!!! (an easy one is to run two mini jacks so they short out the switch when a wire is inserted between them, the wire must then be physically removed for the switch to function) and the button was pushed the gun would instantly empty its clip into the target with zero noise as the foam/case contains (uh, I mean, if I had ever really tried this very illegal idea I feel sure, sure of this) even the little bolt and escaping gas noise.

Probably good for about 5 years in prison.

2. Normal Superspy Recorder case. Stock in trade, I mean you've, just to have one even to just flash at cocktail parties, if nothing else.

Use a lockable case, drill a small hole, usually under the latch, for a mini condenser mic. Cut out a containing space in hard foam or fiberboard to contain a mini recorder, Viking compressor, and VOX.

This is usually covered with a false bottom or at least a foam pad giving the impression that there is nothing below the pad.

The recorder can be plugged into the VOX (and into the compressor) so that it will turn on at any sound and record the ensuing noise.

Alternatives are to use a mecury switch so that the recorder/compressor will turn on when the case is laid on its side, or even a hidden normal on/off switch.

The recorder should be shielded in lead foil or a custom made heavy metal case to defeat recorder detectors that look for the DC field generated by the recorder's motor.

Even a metal case like a Halliburton will help somewhat in this respect, but both will set off regular metal detectors and will not stand up to a visual take-apart search.

This type of case is normally "left behind" after interviews to be recovered later after the mistake is noticed, or simply to record sensitive conversations.

With the new "if one party agrees" laws this may even be legal if you are part of the conversation in question.

Entire setup (minus case) maybe $300.

REMEMBER EACH OF THESE CASES CAN/SHOULD HAVE BULLETPROOF LINERS, MOVEMENT ALARMS, AND OR DEFENSE MECHANISMS.

4.   Now let's take the same good recorder, hidden and shielded and add some tricks. The first is to drill a hole in the back of the case (you have, of course chosen a dark colored case) and mounted the rubber coated contact mic element from the Micro Electronics through the case so it extends just so slightly past the back case wall.

Now if the case is pressed up against a wall so the rubber vibration cement rests against a wall it will pick up and amplify noises from the next room.

Feed this into a compressor and recorder and you have a real interesting combination.

Want to see what the last job applicant, or last deal maker had to offer before you go into the fire. Just position yourself correctly in the reception room...

Sort of 5. In the same or in another case construct a coil of thin, varnished wire around four pegs glued into the bottom of the case.

The correct winding will take some experimentation, but you've got nothing better to do, right?

Solder both ends into a mini-plug and put it into a super amp like the Wynn or ES, in the same jack where the normal small phone induction coil would connect.

Run the results into a recorder.

If done correctly this coil equipped case can be placed near a telephone, or even a phone wire and will pick up and record BOTH sides of any conversation.

Great for those business meetings where the man covers the mouthpiece and says, "excuse me a moment".

All three of these recording tricks can be combined into one false floor case with a three way switch to choose what to record.

6. A motorized camera can be connected by fiber optics (ES, LEA) to a mini-fisheye lens which has been connected to a drilled out hole hidden by latch, handle or clever placement of initials in order to photograph any and everything in the vicinity.

Can be timed to snap off, or best connected to a hidden push button switch to allow whatever photos one wishes to take.

Use an automatic light meter, bury the camera under files and papers, smile a lot.

Great for plant tours, stake outs, interviews. Can be coupled with any of the audio recording tricks.

Can even be used with a min-video camera if you do not plan on opening the case for any reason.

7. Future tech. Just thought I'd toss this in. Computers operate on a certain frequency connected with their clock rate.

Some experiments have already been conducted on picking up the bits and bytes by radio...This means one could gain access to ANY running program without any direct connection to the machine in qestion.

No problem with security codes, access lines and so on...

Coming soon to a theater near you...

The *CEB4000A Anti-Theft Briefcase* is priced at $1,295 including a one-year warranty against defects in workmanship and electronic components. A catalog of *ASP's* electronic countermeasure and security offerings through *SRI* is available for $2.00.

Sales Offices At:
P.O. BOX 18595
SECTION 1512
ATLANTA, GA 30326
U.S.A.

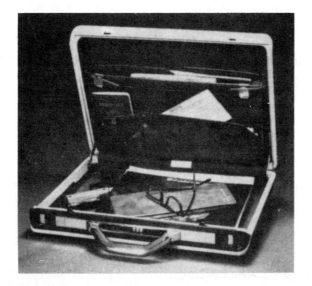

COURIER CASE WITH DYE-GAS

Couriers can assume a very low profile with this conventional looking executive briefcase. Looks like millions of other attaches, yet contains a special access alarm device, which if bypassed, triggers a very loud alarm and generates a large volume of non-toxic orange/red dye which completely stains the contents of the case. There is no need for a telltale handcuff and chain like conventional courier cases. An exclusive pull-ring trigger is virtually invisible, yet offers instantaneous protection.

UNDERCOVER BACK-UP SYSTEM

The Undercover Back-Up System is a completely self-contained transmitter/receiver/recorder kit, ingeniously packaged in a rugged utility carrying case, with all the supplies needed for successful operations. The kit features a body transmitter that generates up to one-watt power output. Transmitters are crystal-controlled and are about the same size and weight of a cigarette pack, and may be worn or carried anywhere on the body. They are supplied with an ultra-sensitive external microphone which positively connects with a locking collar, eliminating the possibility of accidental disconnection. A short rubber duck and flexible wire antenna are supplied with each transmitter. Transmitters are powered by standard alkaline batteries which can provide one-hour of duty at one-watt transmission output. The six-channel, crystal-controlled receiver is built into the carrying case and permits operation on its internal rechargeable batteries, AC, or vehicle power supply. The receiver features exceptionally high sensitivity, illuminated carrier/modulation/over-modulation indicators and carrier activated tape recorder switch, for remote control of the tape recorder during unattended operation. Two receiver antennas are supplied: a magnetic mount high gain, low-profile whip for vehicle rooftop applications, and a short wire whip antenna for base operation. Operates in a frequency range of 150-220MHz, with up to six-switch-selectable channels. The cassette tape recorder can be operated at standard or long play, permitting you to record up to six hours of audio per cassette side, with extraordinary fidelity. Packs neatly in one rugged carrying case, along with miscellaneous patch cords, power cords, cassette tape, rechargeable batteries and operating instructions.

A BRIEF LOOK AT CASES

A look at some commerical super cases available from suppliers we have covered.

Prices start at a few hundred bucks and quickly work up to nearly $10,000.

By following our crystal clear instructions one can duplicate any of these for much, much less cash outlay and customize it to your exact needs.

PORTABLE REPEATER

A portable repeater can be used in areas where original radio signals are too weak to be received. The repeater is actually an automatic, self-contained radio receiver-transmitter which receives an incoming signal from a remote transmitter and re-transmits the original broadcast over a greater range. The Portable Repeater is a fifteen-watts power output unit. It is powered by internal rechargeable batteries and also operates on AC or from a vehicle 12VDC power source. This unit offers a multi-channel capability and operates in a 150-174MHz frequency range. Because of its compact size and its ability to operate from a variety of power sources, the Portable Repeater can provide dependable service whether located in a building, in rural areas, or in the trunk of a car. Each unit is supplied with a magnetic mount whip antenna and push-to-talk microphone in the event you wish to use your Portable Repeater for standard transceiver applications. Other specialized accessories are available on request.

Portable Repeater   No. 6917-150

THE WILLIAM J. DONOVAN CO.

P. O. Box 5215 • Hamden, Connecticut 06518

DEFEATS
(Cartridge & Barrel Length)

LEVEL A   .22 LRHV (6″); .380 APMC (4″);
             .38 SP., 158 gr. (6″); .45 Auto MC (5″)

LEVEL B   All of above; 9mm MC, 124 gr. (4″);
             .22 MAG JHP (6″); .38+P, all gr. loads.

LEVEL C   .357 MAG, 110 & 125 gr. (4″); .357 MAG,
             158 gr. (6″); 9mm, all gr. loads (4″);
             9mm Canadian NATO & German GECO, (4″).

Protection in a briefcase!

In case liner or clip board form, a ballistic armor panel concealed in a portfolio, briefcase or just a paper bag, affords low cost protection for the business or police executive, courier of valuables and others.

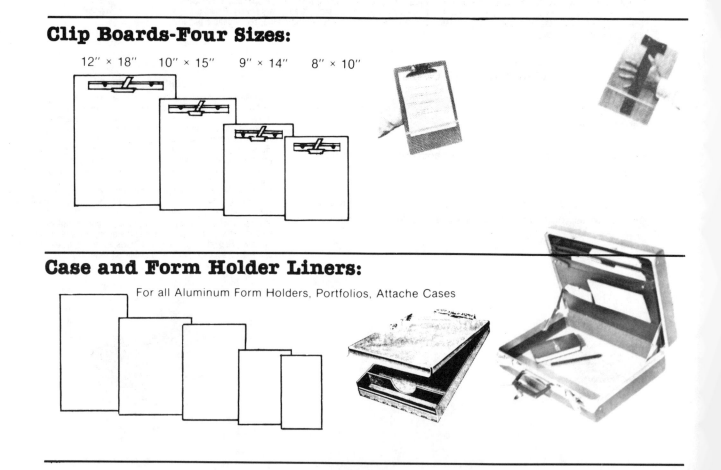

Clip Boards-Four Sizes:

12″ × 18″   10″ × 15″   9″ × 14″   8″ × 10″

Case and Form Holder Liners:

For all Aluminum Form Holders, Portfolios, Attache Cases

OPTICAL SURVEILLANCE CASE

Everything the well dressed snoop needs for photo fun with friends:

UNVERISAL Starlight scope with both eyepiece and lens adapter
Electronic Minox C camera for unobserved or close copy work
Lens cleaning kit
Low light monocular
Monopod
Vise clamp for securing camera to auto window or other flat object
35 mm automatic/manual camera
Homemade shutter release with fifty foot trip cord
NOT SHOWN:

Briefcase alarm system
Monocular to camera adapter
Fiber optics and lens adapter for thru-hole/under door viewing
Extra film, batteries for everything

This set-up will allow surveillance photography in all light conditions except complete darkness (in which case one would susbstitute the MEREDITH IR scope, light source, strobe and Fresnel lens for the Starlight scope) and under every possible condition.

ULTIMATE ENTRY AND AUDIO SURVEILLANCE CASE

Another entry in our do-it-yourself briefcase contest (winner won an all expenses paid week being grilled by the FBI at an undisclosed location-bring bathing suit), this case will :

A. Stop most bullets.
B. Shock and scare any potiential thief.
C. Get one into nearly anywhere.
D. Allow placement of almost any sort of electronic surveillance device (s).

Contents include:

Kelvar and plate lining, alarm system and/or gas, audio compressor and long line, hum free amplifier-mic from VIKING INTERNATIONAL, FEDCORP electronic pick, regular picks and lockaid pick gun, device to tear most lock cylinders from doorways, pengun, two through wall listening devices, three room bugs, two phone taps, one in-wall outlet bug, recorder, jacks, wire, tools, line matching transformer, and earphones for listening in (active) to phone lines, wire, induction coupled phone tap for either active or passive tapping, VOX recorder starter, Minox C camera, batteries and African Wildlife Society patch.

You never know.

You can't beat this seat-up for $6,000 ANYWHERE. Our cost about (please don't write me, we do NOt sell these) about $2,000...

BOOSTER STATION WITH SURPRISE

Our trusty case modified into a relay station by adding a receiver, VOX recorder, and powerful transmitter to re-broadcast the signal from a weak bug.

The case is locked and then a $30 Night Watch buzzer alarm is rigged to give warning of any opening while a $30 Burglar Mist unit is screwed down to flood the area with CS stun gas if the case is opened fully without first reaching inside to disable the device.

Also contains a black widow spider (upper right), perhaps it is trained to guard....I don't know....

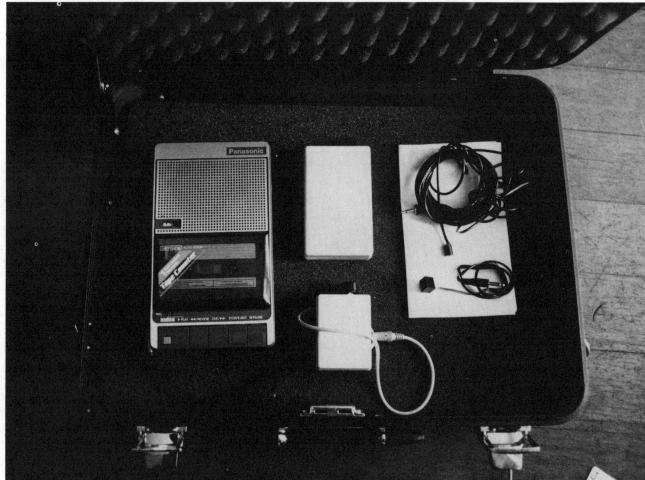

Capri is expanding their line with a number of pre-assembled units and kits that fit our collective needs almost to a "T".

This SR-6 Scan Record is the missing link between a pre-amped scanner and a cassette recorder. Once the senisitiivity is set it will only turn on the recorder when the scanner is locked into a voice. There is an adjustable 1-2 second delay to keep the machine running after the transmission ceases as to seperate messages.

This unit allows you to track several different agents or every room in a house with your magic briefcase. It will also work with any non-scanner receiver with a squelch control. A real nice little unit.

Only $37.00.

GENERAL OPTICAL SURVEILLANCE

Remember when we were all kids and ordered those amazing things from the back of Superman comics? You know, the x-ray glasses that let you see through people's clothes (odd thing was, they only worked thru girl's clothes), and well as the device which would let you see "clearly through any wall?"

This little Fulton's Folly consisted of a ball point pen holder with a small drill bit which screwed into the holder which then sort of allowed one to drill through a thin wooden wall.

When this was accomplished (how the noise and saw dust was hidden was never actually explained), a mini-fisheye lens like the security lenses installed in apartment house doors, was shoved through the hole.

Can't imagine who read Superman comics and bought these things, or why... Although there was this cute 16 year old who lived next door to me, well that's another story.

Anyway you can get a supertech version of this toy that really works from several sources including our old friends at ES ($300).

Using fiber optics, those mini tubes that transmit light in a coherent fashion along with a 7 times magnifying eye piece this 17 inch gooseneck sheathing will pass through a 3/8 inch opening.

This would, in theory, of course, allow one to peer under some doors, through some keyholes, and in many adjoining rooms such as hotel rooms, apartments, and duplexes the wall electrical sockets are built in one hole with plates simply attached to either side.

If one plate is removed the remaining space may be big enough to take advantage of the optic device.

Coupled with a through wall type listening device this would produce a regular technicolor film.

GOING FOR THE DISTANCE

A few updates from the How To Get area; ES carries what is billed as the "world's most powerful binoculars", a 35 x 50 setup with a 73' field of vision at 1,000 yards.

This means a couple of things; first of all they will not focus down to less than 150 feet and you will need a tripod for stability.

A very handy mini-tripod is included in the $160 price tag that will support the unit on a table or dashboard or attach directly to a car window.
A separate "C" type clamp is available to grip any binoculars and then screw into a tripod for $14 also from ES.

For really long range viewing a telescope can sometimes be employed. Most scopes are simply not suited for land observation, having been designed with the sky in mind.

Even with a reversal device to flip the image right side up they just don't make it.

A couple of exceptions are the D31,611 (who else, ES) a 32 power w/15mm eyepiece. A screw on eyepiece will boost it up to an amazing 150 power.

Field of view is 73 feet at 1,000 yards and a camera can be connected with an optional adapter.

Under $300.

For $189 they also offer a 25 power spotting scope which comes with the correct adapter for any 35 mm camera.

OPTICAL SCANNERS

In How To Get Anything On Anybody Mr. Lapin devoted a chapter to "scanning", i.e., audio spying without a particular target in mind.

A fishing expedition...

Optical scanning can be as much or more fun. And possibly just as illegal.

First of all, select a good location. High density areas such as apartment buildings are always fun. Other possibilities are empty areas where any activity may be interesting.

Daylight scanning should begin from a proper vantage point, often a car. A pair of good 8-10 power binoculars are used to general scan, or isolate interesting targets.

My favorites are Bushnell Sportviews. They feature 10 power, clear optics with a very nice feature called "InstaFocus" that allows one finger, rocker bar focus adjustment.

A notebook should be maintained on any location so any interesting activity patterns will stick out when reviewed over a number of days.

When a possible is located it may be necessary to change vantage points for maximum exposure. Once well established the binoculars are swapped for a variable power spotting scope (usually employed in hunting or target practice) is set up for a closer look.

In bright light long camera lenses can be used to capture those happy moments forever.

Night hour scanning is done in much the same fashion. For general, outdoor to outdoor, or outdoor to indoor (say, through a window for instance) a laser boost may be used along with your trusty NVD to spot those oh so interesting little scenes that might otherwise slip by without notice...

Once a far off action is noticed it may again be necessary to shift one's vantage point to utilize the NVD sans laser, or at least just with an IR filtered flashlight.

With our UNIVERSAL TECH model it is also then possible to then photograph the IA (interesting action) or even record it on video tape.

Why? Well, several reasons come to mind; morbid curiosity, suspect location, suspect tailing, casing a joint (as James Cagney might have put it), blackmail (I had a friend who used this idea for just that purpose and made quite a nest egg. I still go see him on visiting days...) or just to get into the practice of surveillance and tailing.

Besides, let's be honest for moment folks, everybody has an intense desire to know what the hell goes on next door or in that expensive penthouse across the street...

Optical surveillance can also be coupled with its audio counterpart for a synergistic relationship. If a "possible" is spotted with optical aids, it is much easier to approach the target to install audio helpers.

Besdies, your trusty notebook will give you a movement pattern of the target, allowing you to plan your approach in relative safety.

What can be spotted with optical scanning? Well if you are young enough to have your juices still flowing in the right direction you might start your practice sessions at the local lover's lane.

Go home to your old lady afterwards and I guarantee a sudden re-interest in your marriage...

Any major apartment complex is a cornucopia of domestic squabbles, drug dealers, affairs, fights, and other real life monopoly games.

Sometimes it is both fun and instructional, as they say on public television, to simply choose one target and optically record his day, if nothing else this will prove your life isn't as dull as it seems.

Another interesting experiment is to rent a room overlooking one of the seedier parts of any major city and spend your evening watching Hill Street Blues in real life.

Just for the hell of it we did this on 42nd in New York and Ellis street in San Francisco.

Mean streets...

One thing this type of individual scanning does teach one is the ability to spot persons or activities which seem out of place, or out of sync.

Depending on what you are searching for this talent can be very useful.

SWAROVSKI AMERICA LTD.
1 Kenney Dr
Cranston, R.I. 02920

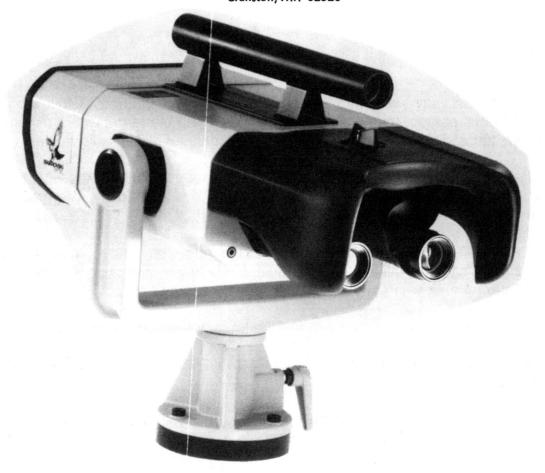

A complete line of optical devices, many of which lend themselves to surveillance uses. Binoculars, monoculars, telescopes and very, very accurate rifle scopes.

Most of their line is aimed at high-objective, low light viewing and includes fully coated lenses, correct objective and pupil lens sizes and precise mechanical construction.

The twin telescope shown offers a 30 x 75 magnification, finder scope, and case. One can also get tripods, treepods, clamps and rubber eye cups to complete the package.

They are not cheap, but are used the world over for high quality surveillance missions.

REMOTE OPTICAL SURVEILLANCE

In the distant past, say two years ago, the only practical method of following a vehicle, or even a person, from a safe distance was to tag the target with a minature radio transmitter and then attempt to remain out of sight, but still in radio range.

This system required one or more follow vehicles equipped with an expensive radio receiver and ranging system. The better systems would actually interpret the transmitted beeps into a rough idea of distance and direction.

This system has a number of major faults; the range indication is never too accurate, reflected signals can give false direction readings, the target may suddenly go out of range or enter an area where the weak signal simply cannot escape.

It is also a very expensive arrangement and the transmitters are prone to loss.

Some brilliant fellow has now come up with a replacement for the radio tag; the optical tag...

In order to use a long range optical tag one purchases a small device which contains one or more LED's that emit light in in a non-visual wavelength, usually 850 nm.

The units strobe for maximum visibility.

What good is a non-visible signal? NVD's will "see" this wavelength quite well. In fact, they pick it up to such a degree that the flashes can be seen for 2 or 3 miles, can be spotted in deep foliage, through clothes, and even through a cardboard box.

The flashes will show up under 10 feet of water.

One such flasher, dubbed the FIREFLY, measures one inch long, sports 3 LED's and clips directly onto a 9 volt battery. One battery will power the Firefly for several days. A magnet can be glued to the unit allowing instant application to any steel surface.

Such as a car bumper.

Non-flashing models can be used to provide a light source for total darkness starlight scope viewing.

While testing this concept we came up with a number of useful ideas:

Vehicle tailing
Tagged person tailing
Package tagging
Covert signaling
Trail marking
Tagging of friendly personnel in a combat situation
Identification of friendly cars, boats and aircraft
Marking of a house
Marking of a landing zone

We even know of one group that uses the device to invisibly mark a halo (high altitude low opening) drop location for dropping off certain packages they don't want the general public noticing...

The Firefly is sold by:

AEROSPACE LOGISTICS
11601 Pendleton st
Sun Valley, Ca 91352

A similar unit which is powered by two penlight cells is made by:

B.E. MEYERS & CO
Marymoor Business Campus
17525 N.E. 67 court
Redmond, Washington 98052

The markers sell for under $150, of course you must also have access to a starlight scope in order to use the flasher.

This does help limit use to low light or nighttime conditions, but any NVD with the ability to limit incoming light can be stopped down to daytime conditions.

We found this idea to be the easiest way to follow and/or find a subject vehicle in all conditions. The ability to remain several miles behind and still follow the target makes getting burned next to impossible.

As the viewer is completely portable is is easy to switch cars or tailers in a matter of seconds, something which is impossible with conventional radio tailing.

A most unusual story which was related to me by a "usually reliable source", it seems that a small group of normally honest folks had this one little illegal chore to preform.

This whole scene took place in a small town with under 10 police cars. It was a simple task to clamp a flasher beacon on the underside of each car and equip a lookout with a night scope.

Fairly foolproof...

Another friend once suggested placing a beacon on the car used by his girlfriend's husband...

The problem with this concept is someone has to keep watch for the marker. Kind of takes the spontaneity out of romance.

One New York company which shall go nameless, sells the units (for a lot more money) as a kidnap recovery device. The idea being to clip the unit onto the potential victim's belt so he could quickly be spotted while being hustle off into a crowd.

There might be some validity to this idea, but it would be limited at best. A kidnapper would have to be rather stupid not to search and spot the flasher and once the victim was placed inside a vehicle or building the flash is gone, gone, gone...

A better suggestion might be to attach it to a briefcase, or valuable cargo, or even to the bumper of an executive's car that might be employed in an ambush or kidnap attempt.

The Firefly comes in three models, one of which remains on the entire time, rather than flashing. This is being used by such groups as SWAT teams.

Snipers equipped with NVD's are placed in position and then each SWAT team member is issued a constant marker beacon. The bad guys show up by simple lack of same...

A nice idea that helps prevent friendly deaths.

These units are also used in war game situations if one side is smart enough to equip key personnel with beacons making the "enemy" easier to spot.

Some police type departments are also placing the beacons on tracker and attack dogs. This allows the dog's controller (the only person who can call him off an attack) to follow the animal at a much closer distance through all types of terrain.

In turn this allows enforcement units to reach the scene much quicker thereby calling off the attack before too much harm is done, not losing valuable dogs, and shortening the time to reach the target (as runners and lost people rarely take the most direct route).

Even the use of the NVD helps with the chase/search.

The units can also keep tabs on human search teams.

Even the availability of the unit on an officer's belt can suddenly ease the tension of a building search or hostage situation.

Practice with the units is necessary, but their amazing effect will shock you...

BRIGHT LIGHTS

Both the FIREFLY and the MEYERS infrared marking units shown side by side. Note the three LEDS on top of the FIREFLY and the single on the face of the MEYERS unit.

There is very little difference in price or brightness, both work very, very well. The FIREFLY is a bit more compact and the MEYERS seems to last a tad longer on its two internal penlight cells.

As you can see from our Starlight scope photos, both units are as bright as a small star when viewed correctly, yet only a faint, faint, red glow (you must hold the unit near your eye to see it at all) is visible under non-NVD viewed conditions.

These are great, devices that work for many different applications.

B.E. MEYERS CO
17525 NE 67 ct
Redmond, WA 98052

AEROSPACE LOGISTICS
11601 Pendleton st.
Sun Valley Ca 91352
FIREFLY

METROREPS
147 W 83rd st
NY NY 10024
FIREFLY

NIGHT MARKINGS

Looking thru the UNIVERSAL Starlight scope at both types of sub-miniature IR marking beacons. First shot is 300 yards, second is THROUGH A BLACK SWAT JACKET.

Talk about an effective target device...

SURVEILLANCE CAMERA TRICKS

The art of surveillance photography has come a long way, baby, in the last few years. See the section on IR photography for instance...

Cameras can be used in very creative situations; it has been a long rumored, rumor, that a camera, hidden behind the clock at the Las Vegas airport makes a permanent record of everyone who drops in to the friendly city.

Whether it is true, is really not the point, but it is amazing how many people the FBI finds in Vegas only days after they pull some high money crime...

If you want to hide a camera, an interesting place to put one is behind the grill material of a speaker. If you look through various grill cloths that are audio transparent you will find some act almost like a one way mirror.

This means one can hide a camera behind the cloth in either a real or a fake speaker box and get some outstanding photos.

The camera can be tripped by almost any means; a simple mechanical weight switch placed below a chair or bed cushion (yeah, I know, my mind is in the gutter these days after being locked in a hotel room with a man who has nothing except trying to escape out the bathroom window and pick up as many women in possible in as short of time as possible and somehow convince all of them to be in this room, well, skip the details, you get the idea) plugged into the manual shutter release area of the camera, a trip wire, a timer, or even a radio control set up.

One can either make up, or purchase 16mm film cameras, or 35mm stills, that are set up on a timer to snap one exposure every so often.

Fiber optics (as shown) can be used to shoot through pin to keyhole sized openings, real one way mirrors can be used as they are easily available from police suppliers ans Edmund Scientific.

Besides the low light photography detailed herein many IR scopes and Starlight type scopes, including the ones we have plugged can be hooked up directly to most video cameras and VTR's (or VCR's, if you prefer). If yours does not include this option

EDMUND SCIENTIFIC sells, in their optional, industrial catalog, many such conversion devices.

The video method has many advantages, the foremost being the zero time element involved. No costly or time consuming developing process in required, the "photographer" can see the prints as they are shot, or right afterwards.

The tape can be converted to film if necessary by any good local video house, the tape can be reused and the entire process gives several hours of recording time.

It is often easier to look at an electronic monitor and adjust a scope-camera arrangement then it is to look through the small eyepiece of the scope or of the camera.

A READY MADE SURVEILLANCE CAMERA SYSTEM; THE CONTAX

A fairly recent addition to the American 35mm camera market, the CONTAX system is a ready made surveillance set up.

The camera really is a system; the back, lenses, drives and control systems are separate and can be combined in a number of ways for different effects.

The back can be motorized, combined with a bulk load holding 250 shots, made to automatically record the date and time of each shot directly on the film and uses a completely ELECTRONIC shutter method.

This is great because a number of devices can then be added that operate on an electronic instead of a mechanical basis.

Two of these items are remote control transmitter-receiver units that let one run the camera from a distance.

As the phone company says, the next thing to being there...

One system uses a crystal controlled radio system that will fire individual frames, or run through the entire roll at 3 shots per second, from a distance of 1,000 feet...

The transmitter can control up to three separate cameras.

Another remote system used an infrared beam to trigger the electronic shutter. This is a straight line system with a distance limitation of 60 feet but can be bounced around corners with the help of windows, mirrors or other reflective surfaces.

So we have a camera that is small, electronic, motorized, takes a huge variety of lenses including fiber optics or pinhole models, can be bulkloaded, and fired remotely with full auto exposure...

Where would one use this system?

How about in a briefcase, behind a speaker grill, in a bedroom, etc?

The CONTAX is available from larger camera dealers.

CONTACT! CONTAX...

Remote Control System
❶ Infrared Controller S Set·Receiver
❷ Infrared Controller S Set·Transmitter
❸ Cable Switch L
❹ Radio Controller Set·Receiver
❺ Radio Controller Set·Transmitter

You know, it seems like the general public is getting more and more surveillance minded all the time. Every day a new product appears on the market that just screams "use me, use me", unlike most women I have dated, but that's another story...

As discussed in the text, the CONTAX is actually a modular system that the "camera" is just one component thereof.

The entire 35mm layout can be configured to fit any need from a 250 single shot telephoto surveillance set up, to a radio or infrared trigger remote unit that automatically records date and time of each shot on the film itself and accepts long life, external batteries plus damn near any lens you can dream up.

As their own literature puts it, "great for remote wildlife photography".

Yeah, I know some great wildlife I would like to record with this little gem...

Too bad the no-fault divorce laws have been passed...

MOBILE SURVEILLANCE VAN

The ideal mobile observance post is one that is totally at ease with the surroundings yet large enough to contain a variety of audio and video surveillance equipment to meet any contingency.

It is a real plus, as anyone who has ever passed away what seems like major portion's of one's life on a stakeout can tell you, to also have available the bare necessities of life such as a toilet, food stocks, room to move around in and so on.

A major drawback to any dream stakeout vehicle is the most obvious one; cash...

Equiping a full surveillance post, whether it is mobile or fixed, is a very costly operation even for a major police force.

Luckily American ingenuity has come to the rescue. Let me introduce you to:

SURVEILLANCE VAN CORP OF AMERICA
41-23 Bell Blvd
Bayside, NY 11361
718-428-5100

Has constructed a number of efficient, full spectrum surveillance vans which they will rent out on a job-by-job basis.

This approach helps cash flow by requiring no major construction expense, allows the rental to be billed to the customer or the job, and doesn't waste capital by sitting idle between assignments.

Even is one is considering construction of any surveillance post a look at what SVCOA offers is helpful in planning a comparable unit.

From the outside the van appears to be a delivery truck with no unusual markings. It is designed to used at distances as close as fifty feet from the target without arousing suspicion.

A solid partion separates the driver's compartment from the goodies in the back, allowing even close inspection.

Visual surveillance is accomplished by a hidden periscope which rotates 360 degrees by means of four reversible gear motors and uses first surface mirrors for definition.

The output is viewed on a b and w electronic monitor and the operator is able to operate all camera functions, including a 10 to 1 zoom lens as well as focus via a console control board.

A video recorder bleeds off the video feed recording everything needed along with a time code for later editing and identification.

An instant printer can produce a hard copy of any scene, on the spot, in 15 seconds. It is also possible to key the recorder on and let the van perform a days worth of recording by itself. This recording can be viewed in about one hour using the recorder's fast forward mode.

The audio system consists of a synthesized high performance receiver for monitoring "covert transmitting devices", an automatic scanner to cover most frequencies, four sensitive microphones which are hidden under the vehicle itself and gather sound within a 50 foot radius of his post.

A VOX recorder will automatically record up to 50 hours worth of the various audio sources.

The van is insulated for temperature and sound containment and comes with life support facilities which include a color television, chemical toilet, AC and DC power converters, refrigerator, fresh air and air conditioning systems and a fire extinguisher.

Night vision equipment can be installed on the video system.

All in all, the vans are equipped slightly better than my apartment and sound like more fun to be in...

A NEW DIMENSION IN AUDIO
AND VIDEO SURVEILLANCE

SURVEILLANCE VAN CORP OF AMERICA
41-23 Bell Blvd.
Bayside, NY 11361

Look out Hertz...

HIGH AND LOW TECHNOLOGY IN THE ART OF SURVEILLANCE

For a look at both ends of the modern spectrum consider these two facts:

1. The FBI is photographing the insides and outsides of all major federal buildings and airports and god knows what else, for storage in their new Surrogate Traveler computer which can display sequential photos of any building in its memory at the press of a button.

This technology will be used to combat terrorists, hijackers, kidknappers, and so on...

2. The US District Court for the District of New Jersey has ruled that any seizure of evidence from a trash can, garbage dump or wastepaper basket is constitutional WITHOUT a warrant because the owner has given up his right to a reasonable expectation of privacy.

Anytime anything is set out for collection it is public matter...

Dig away.

LEGALITIES OF VISUAL SURVEILLANCE

The fourth amendment of the constitution of the United States reads, "The right of the people to be secure in their persons, houses, papers, and effects, against unreasonable searches and seizures, shall not be violated, and no Warrants shall issue, but built upon probable cause, supported by Oath or affirmation, and particularly, describing the place to be searched, and the persons or things to be seized."

This amendment protects people against unreasonable searches (which may be applied to surveillance) by government agents (cops to FBI).

An interesting note is it does NOT include the same protection from CIVILIAN searches!

An offical must ask himself if his actions could be violating the target's "reasonable expectation of privacy".

If a person is sitting in his home/auto/etc with no drapes and a light backlighting him, he does NOT have a "reasonable right to privacy" if the subject is viewed through a keyhole/with a starlight scope/with an IR viewer he probably IS having his rights violated (without a proper warrant of course).

Now note if a private citizen INCLUDING private investigators and private security personnel is using the scope (s) etc, THIS AMENDMENT DOES NOT APPLY!!

If the citizen was acting under orders of an offical agent he will be considered as an "agent" of the agent.

So to speak.

This would invalidate the surveillance/search...

Now, do understand that states cannot make a law that is any more towards the liberal side than the federal counterpart (in this case the constitution) but they CAN make stricter laws...

A wise person checks this out.

There are going to be some very interesting court cases regarding this ...

MAGIC MIRRORS

One of the simplest and most oft employed methods of covert surveillance is the use of one way mirrors.

These special mirrors are front surface reflecting devices that will function as a "normal" mirror from the front while acting as a transparent window when viewed from the rear.

This effect depends upon a light difference between the target room, which must be normally or even brightly lite, while the viewing room must be several times darker.

These mirrors can be purchased from magic suppliers or a number of police suppliers. They can come pre-etched with some sort of design (often country western, for some strange reason) to be placed on the wall of any waiting, interrogation, or suspect room.

If one is on the viewing side of the mirror many strange and wonderful things can be observed with no one the wiser.

If one is on the other end of any such mirror and suspects surveillance and/or photographc recording at work there are a couple of methods to tell if this is indeed true.

1. Approach the mirror and hold a common pencil, or other thin sharp object up to the mirror in question. If the looking glass is a normal variety the pencil lead and its reflection will seem to be separated by about 1/4 of an inch.

If it is a front surface, see-thru model the points will actually appear to touch...

2. Approach the mirror and suddenly shine a bright directional light (such as our STREAMLIGHT) at the glass. If it is indeed a two way trick, you will see the shocked faces of the audience and/or video equipment in fine detail...

Of course, one can simply arrange to cover the mirror if any suspicions exist, although this will alert the enemy and they may get a bit more serious in their next effort.

PEEKING

Long known as the capitol of china, just kidding...It's late tonight and I've got cabin fever in this fucking hotel room and the fucking publishers still have a guard outside the door and room service here consists of a coke from the machine down the hall...

I know I shouldn't take it out on you...

Here's another little trick that belongs in the back of a comic book with the x-ray glasses and free stamps from every country in the world.

Except this one works.

Fiber optics, those skinny little glass tubes (as one techie friend of mine puts it; electronic spaghetti) that transmit light in a coherent fashion from one end of the tube to the other.

With the correct lens and bundling a fiber optic tube can transfer a clear picture from one end of the bundle to the other. This opens up applications such as viewing inside the human body prior to surgery, viewing the working interiors of mechanical devices or...

Our friends at EDMUND SCIENTIFIC sell several versions of fiber viewers from simple viewers to complicated versions with built in light sources.

We borrowed one of the cheaper models (see photo) a viewer with eyepiece and fish eye gathering lens that retails for under $200.

What good is a fairly short fiber viewer?

Let's face it, everybody is a bit of a peeping Tom, and no real offense intended, most of you readers lean a bit more in that direction than the average man-on-the-street...

The ES viewer will slip under doors, through keyholes, around corners, into window sills, through small peepholes etc. It will provide a small, but accurate view of what is going on at the opposite end of the bundle.

This super periscope lets one see things hereforeto not available. It can be used for photographs, but is not designed to fit over a camera lens as were some of the more expensive models we experimented with.

For the money it can be used in a variety of situations that would be potentially dangerous or at least difficult without modern magic.

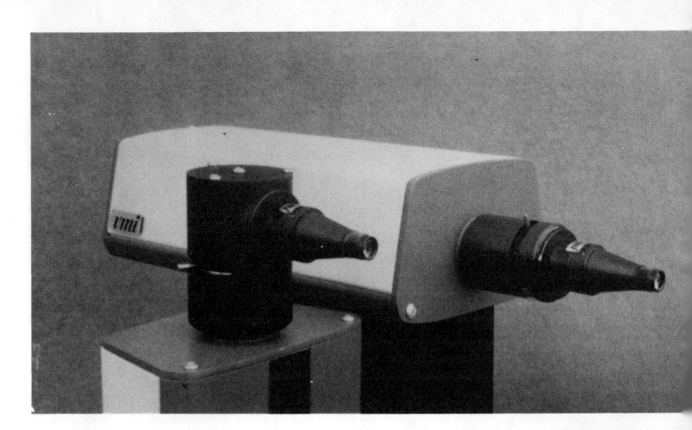

PINHOLES

VISUAL METHODS' (supplier's section) neat fiber optics camera lens that goes thru a half inch hole, is fast and provides perfect photos.

Also one of their video fiber lenses that allows taping of almost any scene.

NIGHT VISION DEVICES

This is a very brief recap of those wonderful units that let you see in the dark. Hopefully you have read one of our other books, or someone else's that has covered these in detail.

If not, do so...

There are two main types of NVD's; light amplifiers and infrared viewers. The first type actually takes available light, such as starlight, and amplifies it up to 70,000 times.

This allows passive viewing in very, very low light conditions. The first generation units, utilized in Viet Nam, used three separate tubes to couple and amplify the ambient light.

Later units (second generation) have only one view tube that has three built in stages for the same, or better, amplification.

Second generation units are usually better in comparison.

IR units were used in WW II and dubbed sniperscopes. These devices need a separate source of aimed light in the infrared wavelengths.

This light is invisible to the naked eye, but the viewer receives and coverts it to the visible spectrum. Of course, anyone else with an IR viewer can also see this light source.

However IR viewers do work in absolute darkness while starlight types need some light to function.

Both types are fairly delicate instruments and should be handled as such. Starlights will "bloom" (or smear) if aimed at a light source (2nd gen units less) and direct aiming at a bright source can damage the tube forever.

It is a good idea to keep lens caps in place when the unit is idle.

This is the dear old AN/PVS-3 1st generation Starlight scope tested and then employed in Vietnam. It consists of three tubes in series, power supply, rubber eyepiece, diopter and field focus rings, fiberglass belt carrying case, 3X magnification, and complete mounts for the M16/AR15 rifle...

It is not fair to compare this unit with today's more advanced 2nd generation, mini-scopes BUT for the $1450 price tag this is simply the cheapest Starlight scope on the market (fully assembled) and it does work.

This scope is from STANO COMPONENTS and was lent to us by Alan for our trip to Africa (see te text). I used this scope almost every night and had a ball with it.

Under the proper conditions it will do almost anything a second generation unit will do except it is a bit dimmer and does not come with a camera relay.

On the other hand, it does mount on a rifle...

KENYA

Kenya; the name conjours up a mixed flow of images even today, three weeks from my return. A totally different culture, violence and beauty.thrown together within a savana melting pot.

California-like landscape with a daylight zoo parade of zebra, wildebeast, topi and cats. Natural camouflage in life or death interaction as brown fur blends with wilting bush.

Night brings on a totally different world; as alien as midnight in Times Square. The friendly spotted/striped fauna has become instantly extinct, leaving only an undefined, unseen world of noises you would run from in any civilized arena.

Yet each groan, screech, or crunch sounds exactly at home in this suddenly hostile environment. Friends are friends no more.

Why Kenya? Why us?

Simply because it's the real thing. The thought occured to us that in order to test devices made for use in one type of jungle or another we really should go to a real jungle.

And there are damn few of those left.

So here I am, crouched behind some sort of weird tree who may have helped Michael Caine in the movie Zulu, or perhaps may have been around for the original battle...

It is getting dim out, light is failing and the shadows are getting longer. Some baboons are playing behind me oblivious to my spear (yes, dammit, a spear, unlicensed gun ownership can bring up to life in jail...), much less my starlight scope.

I am posing for a photo, Lee's idea, "the old and the new", technology greets the Masai Mari...

Somewhere behind me lurks a cape buffalo, probably the most dangerous animal in all of Africa, likely to charge without any warning, hopefully still munching away happily in his grass delicatessen unaware, or at least uncaring of my presence.

Please lord, let him be hungry, not angry...

I am about to try out a first generation NVD (starlight scope) on loan from the guys at STANO corporation. While landing in Nigeria I hastily scraped off the US government label as well as stashed the offical US warning that this device was/is not allowed out of the USA for any reason.

Much less into an area where rebels are still coming across the border daily to take potshots at any handy target.

Including tourists...

Wonder what I could get for the scope on the black market here? Let's see, I would only owe STANO...

--An interesting sidebar here is that when I left San Francisco they put my Haliburton case containing camera, lens, flashlight and STANO scope through the x-ray machine.

The female security guard looked at the machine, gasped, pulled back and called for the local on-duty police to come over while she made me open the case.

This is it; good idea goes bad, hello San Quentin, goodbye Kenya, how will my mother take this, how can I say that I never saw the label about not removing device from "US borders".

I was forced to open the case whereupon the guard reached in and said, I lie not, "ah hah, what have we here?". She reached in and with a flourish brought out my flashlight...

"What is this?" She demanded, handing it over to the cops.

Swear to god, I stuttered, "ah, ah, ah, a flashlight..."

"And how do I know that?" She was waving the device about in the air over the x-ray machine.

"Well,", I quickly responded, "you could turn it on."

As this novel idea struck her one of the cops did just that, waving the bright beam about the airport walls.

"It doesn't open," was the next problem.

"Please don't do that," I was reaching for the flashlight, "it is rechargable, run it through again and look at the batteries, but don't try and unscrew it."

Cops glare. Security guard glares. Flashlight handed back with a severe look and a warning about smuggling devices through security.

The starlight scope w/warnings lies so exposed in the gray foam...

And these people are guarding us against terrorists?

At any rate as the light falls I begin edging through the bush towards a waterhole some 100 yards distant. Every night noise seems to be beaming at me through a 100 watt amplifier, and I normally love hunting.

The question here is who is hunting whom?

Suddenly Lee stage whispers "what's that animal".

I turn and can still sort of see his outstretched arm aiming towards the bush in front of me.

Please, no buffalo tonight, I'll never eat at McDonalds again...

The scope is turned on, a quiet high frequency oscillation fills my hearing. I depress the soft rubber eyepiece to reveal the dull green glow of the scope and see nothing.

The lens cap is on.

After a quick rotation of the rubber end cap (containing a selection of different sized openings to adjust for ambient light conditions), produces a sudden surge of viewing...

The animal in question, nearly invisible to my normal sighted cohorts in crime jumps into my eye almost on top of me.

A silver-backed jackel sniffs a wayward breeze, catches my unwashed scent (we only had cold water showers in camp) and scurries off into the bush.

I edge onward and inward.

The moon goes behind a cloud and my screen goes all-green. At this point I reach around the front of the device and pull off the rubber lens cap exposing the entire collection lens to the semi-moonlight/starlight.

I can see again.

Suddenly another noise and an over-amped safari buddy shines my lovely Streamlight, super-powerful flashlight into the bush ahead of me.

The STANO scope blooms out into bright white/green flash, blocking out everything else...

As I start to yell, Lee grabs him and the light disappears, leaving the bush again visible. I adjust the focus ring and the waterhole snaps into view.

After a few moments of waiting a slight non-breeze noise occurs just off to my left.

A quick lift of the wrist, not so easy when lying in amassed vegetation that contained a black mambo earlier in the day, and the waterhole snaps back into view.

A beautiful zebra walks into my viewscreen. Graceful and wary, it is approaching the waterhole with a determined, perhaps thirsty air...

An amazing sight, not visible to anyone else when;

BEHIND IT IS A CAT.

Slouching, creeping at a speed faster than I can run, a spotted, sinkly beast is stalking my favorite zebra and then a quick leap and a snort/scream...

100 yards behind me I can hear my fellow criminals trying to control their excitement and wonderment; what was it? What happened? Why couldn't we see it?

A feeling of ultimate power washes over me as I stroll (with the help of the scope) back into camp like a harbinger for Atilla the Hun, sure of my technological superiority...

Yes officer, I saw it all...

Before I reach my band of semi-chicken buddies Lee hisses and points behind me.

I turn and can see bush and shadow, not much else. I raise my hand and in a prearranged signal the flashlight again turns on.

This time with a Streamlight infrared filter snapped down over the focused lens.

I too snap down the IR filter over my scope and the local habitat once again become very visible, highlighted by a powerful, invisible beam of IR light my scope picks up and amplifies many times.

A small mongoose is working his way down towards the waterhole, hoping for a sanke, any snake for a midnight snack.

I wish he was looking for cape buffalo...

This particular scope that has let me view the world in a totally new light, if you'll excuse the pun, is a 1st generation AN/PVS-3 on loan from STANO.

This may sound familiar to some of you...It was the main scope used during the 'Nam "police action", usually on the top of an M-16.

And, in fact, if it is a memory, it may be a mixed one. Let's look at the negative first; it is a first generation unit, this means there are three tubes stacked end to end inside this case instead of one as in a second generation unit.

It also means the light amount control is more mechanical than electronic, the unit will "bloom" if exposed to a bright light while in operation, and it is hardly a sub-miniature unit.

The AN/PVS-3 checks in at 3 pounds (which still makes it about the lightest of the military scopes.

It utilizes an 18mm intensifier tube (some newer units have a larger tube).

Now for the good; the thing WORKS! Remember this was a top secret device no civilan could buy for ANY reason just a couple of years ago.

It is quite rugged (built to those lovely battleship grade military specs our armed forces are so proud of) the on/off switch is in a convenient location, there is a rubber eye cup that must be depressed (with your eye) that hides even the smallest glow from the view screen.

The scope is packaged in the original package which includes mounts for M-14/AR-15 (and their automatic counterparts) should you want to do more than just look at animals attacking animals with it, instructions, IR filter, hardshell-belt looped carrying case and the afore mentioned rubber lens cap with several different sized apertures for adjusting to ambient light conditions and which can be removed in a hurry to allow full lens collection under starlight conditions.

And for the second good news; IT'S CHEAP! That is, cheap in context, no NVD is "cheap" per se, look at the prices listed for the 2nd generation units we are covering.

At the time we borrowed the unit STANO was selling it for $1450. This is not a used unit, it is a surplus unit, one of the group the government has decided to sell off in lot quantities.

STANO chooses the best tubes from an NOS (new old stock) lot and assembles these units.

STANO (and the government) lists the range of the unit as 400-600 meters.

Yes and no.

With a fair moon and the cap off, object recognition of a human size figure is probably possible at 400-600 yards.

Notice I said recognition of an OBJECT. This does not mean you tell what the object IS, much less hit it with a .223 bullet...

On the other hand, have you ever tried to hit a man sized object with an M-16 at 600 yards in full daylight?

It is safe to say the North Viets didn't suffer too bad from 600 yard M-16 kills...

If the available light falls to cloudy starlight-no moon, your range will quickly fall to 25 or so yards...

The scope is straight forward to use; first you focus your eye to the view screen with a diopter ring then a field focus ring is gripped with your thumb and forefinger for quick ranging.

Under changing light conditions I saw/watched/identified mongeese, leopard, hyena, jackel, zebra, lion, topi, gazelle, Masi warriors, irate friends, excited lodge managers (I don't know, the man was obviously on drugs-he kept yelling about guests being eaten and lawyers) and various other flora and fauna.

What was a good trip was made into a great trip with the addition of this unit. The few ex-white hunter-guide types we ran into were green (without the scope) with envy. One told me he had seen only one other NVD in Africa in his life and was dying to use it.

He saw rhino, hippo and wanted to buy the unit...

I should note this unit comes with a 3X non-removable eyepiece. I liked this magnification, if helped with "aiming" yet was not powerful enough to cause much light loss as higher powered scopes will, by design, cause.

For those of you trying to go to war on mom's allowance, there is an even cheaper route.

MEREDITH INSTRUMENTS (see suppliers section) sells the necessary pieces to actually assemble your own first generation NVD.

Tubes, lens, eyepiece and power supply will only set you back $650. You must assemble the unit and SUPPLY YOUR OWN CASE and there is no warranty on your work.

The device will work just like the one we took to Africa because the tubes are furnished to Meredith by Alan of STANO corp...

TOURIST TRAVEL KIT

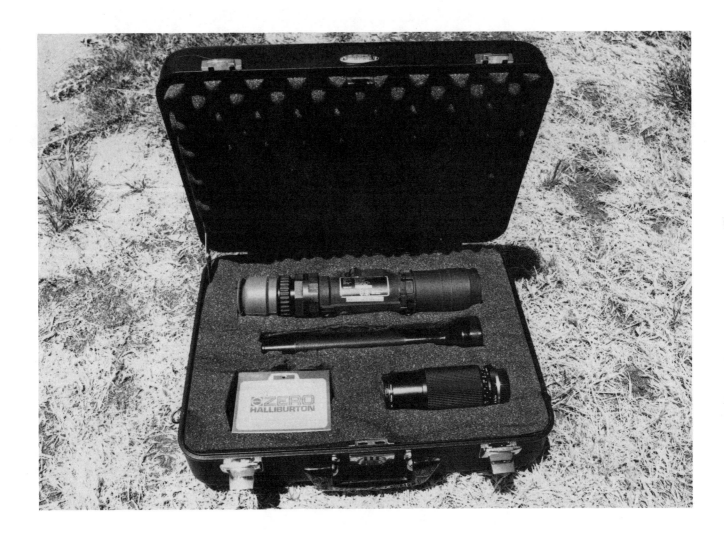

Halliburton with STANO NVD installed above Streamlight flashlight (with IR cap in place), zoom camera lens and label where the camera that took this photo would have gone.

Got us through every security check necessary except in San Francisco where they felt the flashlight posed a real danger during a hijack attempt...

If you look closely you can almost read the US sticker that forbids the NVD to be taken anywhere outside the USA...

A rather poor shot of Scott and friend. In his defense he claims a bad stomach, and has not had a shower in several days (man was it dusty!) and is rather in a hurry to get into the bush and take up a post near his favorite waterhole before dusk falls completely.

Still it is a real comment on today's world when you have a man with a Masai spear and a Starlight scope mixed together and it seems natural.

MISCELLANEOUS MEMORIES

1. Lee attempting to take back something he has just said in Swahili that obviously did not mean "I like your clothes."

That man can be so charming...

2. High level accommodations paid for by our publisher; ("You'll love it, all the stewardess' stay there").

ULTIMATE STARLIGHT SCOPE

After two years of testing and using NVD's (well, not every minute of course) we came up with a number of universal complaints about our test units.

These included:

 Heavy, bulky, large
 Cheap controls, switches and cases
 Lack of versatile in lenses and viewing options
 Not bright enough
 EXPENSIVE!

Have we got a deal for you. Finally a unit turned up that did away with most of our bitches...

UNIVERSAL TECHNOLOGIES Box 38169 Dallas, TX 75238

Makes one of the most compact NVD's we came across. They use top grade aluminum for the case, the best controls available, furnish the most options at a stock price, and supply the unit directly to customers at one of the cheapest prices around for a second generation unit.

One of the nicest features of the UT unit is the fact that it is built around a "universal" concept...

Get it?

The front end contains a standard lens mount so different focal length lenses can be attached as the situation warrants. The buyer even gets a choice of 135 or 200mm stock lenses.

Other choices may be added by the user (higher powers cut down on light transmission).

The rear end utilizes a removable eye piece that is focused (diopter focus) by each user.

This eye piece is one of the biggest and brightest we tested.

If the eye piece is removed a 3 inch "screen" can be substituted. This large lens acts as a view screen letting more than one person view the target at the same time.

A great innovation, this... True to the laws of physics it is a bit dimmer than the individual eye piece as the same light is now being spread over a larger surface, but the unit is so good this makes little difference.

A tiny bit of the green glow also escapes when this system is employed, making it possible, at least in theory, for a concerned sniper to sight down and use the glow as a target.

The individual eye piece has a rubber cup that prevents this errant light escape.

The rear lenses are changed with a simple 1/4 turn of a thumb screw.

If you don't want to share the secrets of the night with your current date, or paid audience, the view screen lens can be exchanged for one of several adapters.

UT carries adapters for attaching the unit to any popular SLR camera allowing crystal clear photographs to be produced.

Not good enough?

Okay, they also supply adapters to hook up with most any video camera so you can record real home movies...

Just think if Allen Funt had access to one of these...

Operation:

The UT scope uses two AA penlight cells and is turned on with a combination on/off and gain control.

The front lens has the usual F stop settings for control of incoming light levels plus a focus ring.

The back end has the above mentioned diopter focus ring.

We found it best to leave the F stop control set on wide open (2.8 in the 135 mm lens, 3.8 in the 200), turn the unit on and barely crack open the electronic gain.

The F stop control can be closed up in brighter conditions.

Then the diopter ring is focused by the operator for a clear shot of the view screen.

The unit is then pointed at the target and the focus quickly adjusted. At this point the gain can be increased for the brightest image one can stand without a headache appearing on the scene.

How good is it?

Bloody amazing, as our British cousins would say...

In starlight one soon forgets the idea of a nightscope and begins to feel one is looking through a pair of low power field glasses with a coat of light green paint over the eyepiece.

In daylight.

Looking at the larger view screen is akin to watching a small tv set.

In daylight.

Range varies with conditions, but in starlight I was able to peer into a forest taken right out of some grusome fairy tale (we're talking black here) and pick out a person at well over 100 yards...

I was able to read an auto license plate under small moon conditions at 200 yards...

If mounted on an accurate rifle I would take bets of hitting a man sized target at 200-300 (or more) yards.

Focus is perfect. Light is great. The picture is crystal clear.

The damn thing is scary. Especially if you consider that many government bureaus including various drug enforcement agencies have already purchased a number of these units.

Price?

"Retails" for about $4600. Direct price (to police, offical agencies, and our readers) at this time about $2600...

I have already seen this unit advertised in other catalogs for 5 grand...

And it's probably worth it.

Even at our White Flower Day sale, no salesman will call, direct to the public, once in a lifetime, K-Tel price, the scope comes with one lens, eyepiece, hardshell, foam lined carrying case, your choice of camera adapter, removable handle, instructions, and a lens cleaning kit.

A nice touch...

To sum this experience up; this is the most versatile, best priced unit we could find. It is equal to the state-of-the-art second generation units (simply stated, the best available) at a cheaper price.

It will make a voyeur out of anyone. Why take that special girl to the movies when you can watch the neighbors?

Seriously, one of the few real deals available in the field of optical surveillance. Use it or lose it...

All photographs and night camo test in this book were done with this unit.

What do I really, really think of the UT NVD?

I bought our test sample at the same price available to you....

THE UNIVERSAL TECHNOLOGIES STARLIGHT SCOPE SYSTEM

The best NVD scope we could find; 2nd generation, AGC, adjustable gain both electronic and manual, switchable front and rear lens, relay for any 35 mm camera or video tape recorder, eyepiece plus large projection screen (has a 25 mm tube), handle, lockable, padded case...

Many narcotic agencies have already purchased them, other government groups are lining up, already showing up in other catalogs for twice the price.

Uses the best non OEM parts available, about $2500...

It is bloody amazing how many people one can impress by letting them look through this projection screen into what seems like total darkness.

The definition is better than television and it will stun anyone...

This is a not too photogenic shot of the UT NVD with the large eyepiece installed instead of the single viewer.

LITTON is one of the two or three actual manufacturers of NVD tubes (other people buy the tubes and put together their 'own' scopes) so it would figure, in a strange sort of fashion, that LITTON stuff is pretty top of the line all the way down...

AEROLOG INDUSTRIES, INC.
17029 Devonshire st. Suite 151
Northridge, Ca 91325

Seems to sell LITTON goodies at LITTON prices; a most unusual animal indeed...No 1,000% markup, see?

The M-931 ranging scope shown is a good example. This 2+ (depending on whose PR one believes) scope is one of the very smallest around, can be relayed to a camera, video camera, rifle and so on.

Besides the "usual" starlight vision this scope gives a three digit, LED readout of the range to the primary target...

Great for those night golf games, or mortar shoots...

They also stock a nice LITTON modual NVD (like our UNIVERSAL), goggles (checking in at $6,350-less than almost anyone except UNIVERSAL), the beautiful LITTON riflescope and other things that go bump in the night.

Well worth keeping track of.

UNIVERSAL's low priced binoculars (Starlight 2nd generation) and MICRO SECURITY's IR receiving and demodulating unit for their IR bugs.

Technical Specifications TRM 2500: Housing: camera-housing, Range: 200 meters, Wavelength: 930 nm, Power Supply: 9 V battery, Weight: approx. 1,5 kg

To guarantee a perfect receipt of the signals transmitted by our infrared transmitters TRM 1810 and TRM 1820, we have two specially developed, receivers in our program. Both receivers pick-up the infrared-waves sent by the transmitters, convert them into electrical signals and make them audible through a built-in amplifier. TRM 2500 is fitted with a socket for headphones, which makes it possible to listen direct to the conversation transmitted. Additionally to that, TRM 2510 has a recording unit in form of a cassette recorder, built into an attache case, which makes an immediate recording possible. Both receivers are built into a housing of a single lens reflex camera and are therefore perfectly concealed.

LITTON RIFLE SCOPE

In the entire field of starlight type NVDs there are only a couple of actual OEM makers of the heart of the beast; the photo tube.

Litton is the best known in this limited field, they sell both tubes that amplify light as well as the complete NVD package. This practice has led some critics to claim that Litton sells the seconds and keeps the best tubes for themselves.

We have not found this to be true. We tried out a Litton M-845 rifle nightscope and found it to be quite identical in operation and at the same level of efficiency as our UT model.

Leading one to believe the UT version uses a Litton tube...You see, only a couple of companies actually make the second generation micro-channel tubes, Litton being the best known.

The main differences between the two units is that the M-845 is designed to be mounted on a rifle and comes with a choice of mounts to fit everything from an AR-15 (M-16) to a "Steyr-Diamler Puch AUG with NATO dovetail", should you ever receive one as a Christmas gift...

The Litton also places a bright red dot as an aiming point in the middle of the scope. There is both an elevation and azimuth (windage) adjustment which re-positions the aim dot to adjust for combat conditions.

The lens is fixed at 1.55 magnification and the focus is fixed starting at 25 meters and stretching to infinity.

This device is the brightest, smallest, and lightest nitesite we have seen and has several nice features such as a built-in battery condition indicator.

We turned several of our more stable testers loose on both the UT general scope and the M-845 and here is a general look at the results:

Litton has a daylight filter which snaps on allowing for day sighting, UT does not. The litton lens cap is waterproof and clips onto the scope. We lost the lens cap to the UT the second day.

The red aim dot was simply TOO large to focus at a distant target as it covered a major portion of the vital organ areas.

We really missed being able to switch front end lenses as was possible on the UT to adapt to conditions.

 Ditto with the back end, even though the M-845 was NOT made for anything but shooting bad sorts in the dark it was so nice to use the wide screen on the UT, or photograph the intended target.

The UT was able to focus down to about 6 feet making it possible to use at short ranges or indoors.

Both very rugged and well made.

Larger intensifier tube in the UT easier to use.

In general, two the of the best scopes in the world today. The UT seems better for all around use, and can be adapted for short range weapon work, but does not compete with the Litton as a pure rifle night sight.

IRT-1000 INFRARED AIMING LIGHT

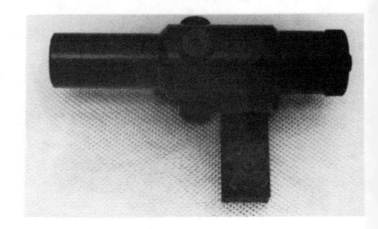

Rapid accurate, night time aiming without sighting down the barrel is possible with the IRT-1000 and a night vision device. With this added dimension of flexibility, fire can quickly and accurately hit a defined target under low light level conditions. Aiming beam is invisible to the naked eye but visible through a night vision device such as the F 4934 Night Vision Goggle.

An infrared aiming beam that will light up a target several hudred feet distant for a night sniping operation from FAIRINGTON TECHNOLOGIES. Price is about $1400 HOWEVER the shooter MUST wear a pair of Starlight scope binoculars on some sort of IR strap-on viewer to be able to use the sight, advancing the cost a great deal...

Below is the best rifle sight now available, the LITTON M-845 2nd generation Starlight scope with red aiming dot. This scope uses the best LITTON tube (as does our UNIVERSAL) which gives one the feeling of looking through dim binoculars in daytime...

This unit has a range of several hundred yards and is effective EXCEPT the red aim dot is a bit too large for most targets and detracts from the accuracy otherwise possible. Hopefully this will be corrected.. In the neighborhood of $6,000...

IMPROVING THE PERFORMANCE
OF YOUR NVD

There is a way to increase the effective range as well as improve the resolution of any starlight type night scope. This nifty trick combines both infrared and starlight technology.

As starlight scopes are sensitive to most bands of infrared light it is possible to boost the available light by use of an IR source.

To be successful the source must be powerful and somewhat focused. There is a commerical version called the DARK INVADER which uses an NVD with an IR spot illuminator mounted on top of the scope.

Made by:

> OMICRON INTERNATIONAL
> 17525 N.E. 67 court
> Redmond Wa 98052

This unit retails for $4,000 w/o the IR booster and $4500 complete.

We took our trusty STREAMLITE flashlight and attatched the available rubber lens cap with a built-in infrared glass filter.

The flashlight now put out only IR light (and some heat). It became impossible to see any output from the unit with the naked eye.

When the powerful Streamlite is aimed at a target and the result viewed through an NVD it becomes possible to extend the usable range of the scope to a great degree.

At shorter ranges it becomes possible to read house numbers or identify people where only the outline would have visible with a non-boosted NVD.

This also makes it possible to use a starlight device in total darkness.

Another good light source can be made by putting a filter sold by MEREDITH over a Q-BEAM flashlight. Q's are made in both 100,000, 200,000 and 300,000 candle power sizes and the filter fits right over the lens.

Now take some black silicone compound and seal the edges to prevent visible light leak.

Q-Beams can be found on sale for $15-$20, this will give you a powerful IR booster for about $30.00...

For those of you that always fly first class and won't leave home if the Ferrari Boxer won't run that day, FAIRINGTON TECHNOLOGIES has your booster.

Their Set Beam is a portable, handheld light source which produces 6,000,000 candle power.

That's right, 6 MILLION!

This unit is ideal for blinding 747 pilots as they fly over your home or spotting deer at night to poach with your 20 mm cannon.

It will run up to 90 munutes on rather large batteries and the price is a mere $6,000.

The good news is that they will toss in a free IR filter.

Other sources sell IR filters for smaller flashlights (Info Unlimited for one) but most smaller lights are not powerful enough to provide useful boost except in a dark room.

Always use glass filters, plastic are not efficient and tend to melt from the heat.

LASER BOOSTERS

If you need to see even further than a boosted NVD will allow, there is one additional option.

An IR diode laser can be used as the new light source. A good laser will throw a spot hundreds or even thousands of yards to light up a target.

The laser is a bit expensive (best prices from Info Un and Meredith), will run down the battery pack in about 45 minutes of use and will provide a direct line back to the viewer if anyone else has an IR converter.

Either of these assists can also be mounted on a rifle to greatly better the range and accuracy of any night sighting system.

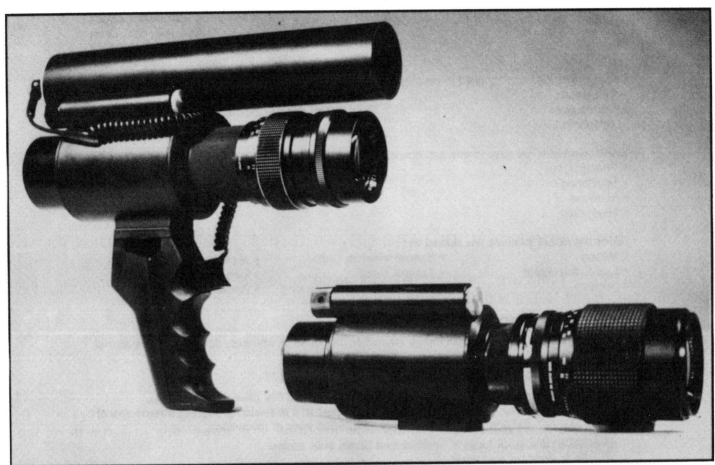

MODEL #3010
WITH GRIP

DARK INVADER™

MODEL #3000
STANDARD

SUPER TECH

The OMICRON Dark Invader system with and without IR spot light source. Prices about $5,000 and $4,000 in that ordor.

Below-FAIRINGTON TECHNOLOGIES standard Starlight scope with relays.   About $4,000

CHEAPSHOTS;

Easy ways of improving day and night optical surveilance

Besides the improve the available light angle there are a few methods that can help along many NVD's and/or daylight vision devices.

The first is to add a focus lever ring for instant focusing. This $25 gadget slips over the focus ring of any 35mm camera and allows almost instant field focusing of any camera whether attached to a telescope or IR/NVD type device.

Anyone who has ever tried to take a quick shot of a drug transaction, goodbye kiss or man firing a gun, knows just exactly how important it is to be able to focus in on the subject in a split second.

This EDMUND SCIENTIFIC device accomplishes this quite nicely.

ES also sells a $4.00 rubber eyepiece that will slip over many nightscopes and eliminate the small amount of light that escapes from the viewer as well as cut down on the ambient light letting the device be used in higher light levels.

Now we come to the ES selection of adapters; they offer a variety of focusing mounts and adjustable slide tube adapters, that coupled with the correct camera store available screw rings will matchup most any 35mm camera to most telescopes and to most modern (second generation) NVD's.

This little trick (they range in price from $8-$50) can save you several hundred bucks from "police suppliers".

Note these devices are not generally available in the regular ES catalog but one must request the professional/industrial catalog.

STARMAKER-BUILDING YOUR OWN STARLIGHT SCOPE

It is possible, a mentioned previously, to actually construct one's own Starlight NVD unit.

This procedure will save a fair chunk of cash and can be accomplished by anyone with a knowledge of kit building and soldering.

Note this is a first generation unit that uses coupled tubes left over from that fun police action in Asia...

Normally three tubes are coupled to each other by mechanical placement and powered by a high voltage power supply.

Three tested and glued tubes can be purchased from MEREDITH for $450, a power supply for $25 that includes a data sheet.

A few bucks more buys the front end and eyepiece lenses and you can even purchase a containing tube from them if you can not come up with one on your own.

The hobbyist can supply the case (usually a simple PCV pipe) and a couple of 12 volt rechargable batteries (also available from Meredith), as well as a few hours or more or less honest labor.

I realize that is a difficult concept for some of our readers, but it really isn't that difficult...

This package will give a workable NVD configured to the builder's specifications for just over $500...

Not bad.

Since writing the above MEREDITH now offers the entire package including rechargable power supply and lenses for under $650.

This will give you a first generation unit for $700-$2000 less than the available commercial units.

STARHIDING

Now that we have seen the impact of a second generation Starlight type scope in both war and peace, it is natural to raise the other side of the coin; how does one ESCAPE the magic eye?

The army, as one might expect, is also a trifle concerned with this very question. Their answer was to design a new type of tiger stripe camo cloth which would blend in with the surroundings under starlight conditions, thusly helping conceal anyone wearing a uniform made from this pattern.

Does it work?

As an astute reader can surmise from our photographs with the UNIVERSAL unit, the device amplifies all ambient light in direct proportion to the original source. This means the background tends to light up as does the lighter portions of ANY camo cloth.

In our tests (also verified by a popular magazine) the new starlight "invisible" cloth shows up to a GREATER DEGREE THAN DOES NORMAL CAMO CLOTH WHEN VIEWED THRU A GOOD NVD!

One can also see that normal camo cloth does not blend in with anything when Starlight viewed...

What about black cloth?

Look at the photo of our model with the FIREFLY IR beacon device in her vest pocket. Note the surrounding shadow area is highlighted so effectively that the black stands out almost as well as in daylight conditions.

If the night is completely (or as nearly so that a Starlight can still function) and one is lying in total blackness, there is some blending effect but not nearly enough to stake one's life on if the Starlight is mounted on the barrel of a rifle...

In effect, we found that NO single, or cross blending of colors and patterns would allow hiding from a Starlight (or from an IR viewer under those conditions).

Not good news for the person on the wrong end of a scope.

Still there is some defense possible against either unit. First of all it is necessary to realize, or suspect that such a unit is being employed against one before trying to hide.

Remember that a strong light source will overload any photo sensitive tube, many commercial television cameras have had their tubes spotted or destroyed by a quick, accidental, direct shot of the sun.

Pointing any Starlight scope at a bright light source will cause the tube to "bloom" wiping out all viewing area. On first generation units this bloom can become painful to the eye itself and may kill the tube by quite literally destroying part of the photo sensitive surface.

Second generation units employ an auto gain control circuit that is designed to catch blooming and cut off the tube before it transmits the bright spot to the user's eye.

Even so, these units will bloom when exposed to light and will continue to show bloom traces for some time after the light is removed.

It is also possible to destroy or at least mark the tube of a second generation unit by pointing it at a strong light source.

So it becomes a simple matter to simply stand in front of a bright light in order to blind the NVD.

Uh, yes, that's true, except the sniper can then simply lower his device to see you in full relief and commence with said shooting operation under normal conditions...

The alternative is to employ an infrared source of considerable power which falls within the sensitive range of both Starlight and IR viewing devices.

Such a source will bloom the entire tube not only making target identification impossible as well as masking the exact location of the IR source.

However it is not inconceivable that someone could simply spray the entire area with automatic fire thereby hitting the source and the target out of sheer saturation.

For this reason it is best to assume a defensive position a bit away from and below the IR source.

Use the most powerful source available, the 300,000 candle power Q beam making an ideal blinding unit. If you are far enough away from the viewer, the minor red glow from the IR filter will not show up to the naked eye.

This technique is especially effective if the NVD is being employed simply to observe or spy upon one rather than actually take one out of action.

If there is any reason to suspect such surveillance on your place of residence, no matter how temporary, it would not hurt anything to do a four sided IR blinding curtain.

LASERS

In a top secret project that was put into effect in the last portion of the Nam "police action" medium powered LASERS were pod mounted on the outside of copters and low flying planes.

These coherent light units were hooked up to a photocell flash detector and computer. When enemy anti aircraft guns (or rockets) were fired at the plane the computer instantly noted then direction of the flash and shot back a quick burst of LASER light at the target.

This had the effect of blinding the enemy gunner, sometimes on a permanent basis...

Such blinding LASERS are now carried in both Russian and American tanks to blind oncoming armor and troops.

Note the effciency factor; a medium powered LASER doesn't require too much power, doesn't have to kill or punch holes through armor, but can render an entire company useless in seconds.

If a LASER, either one that falls within the visible or the IR bandwidth was to be pointed at a NVD, it would, in all probability ruin the device and possibly harm the operator.

The only problem is the beam must hit the unit exactly on target.

Again, there are a couple of options:

1. Use your own Starlight scope to guide the beam of an IR LASER into the enemy's unit.

2. Employ a lens in front of the LASER to diffuse the beam to cover a larger spot, but still be concentrated enough to blind the other unit. This modification will allow less than perfect aiming.

3. Use a visible LASER and guide it by eye or with a simple binocular set up into the enemy's unit. This will probably work because the beam from your weapon will not show up brightly until it is aimed into the lens, and too late to avoid.

4. Employ a Fresnel concentrated IR strobe unit (as shown elsewhere in this sterling publication) in several different directions as rapidly as possible.

This should have the effect of knocking out he viewer and viewee for several seconds at least. Enough time to escape...

DAY AND NIGHT CAMO

A look at several varieties of camo cloth, woodland green tiger stripe, etc, to see how they blend in with typical North American foilage.

Three of the same samples shot thru the UNIVERSAL Starlight scope under very dim moon conditions.

Not good...

CHEAP IR VIEWER

For those of you who spent every cent of your hard (our reader's?) earned money on this very book and want to obtain the very bottom line, moneywise, in IR viewers we present the following plans.

This unit is based on an RCA 6032 viewer which will pick up radiation in the 500-1200 millimicron range and convert it to visible light.

Once the source radiation is picked up by the 6032 tube it is electronically focused, as in a common television CRT by a variable focus ring and then imaged on a viewing tube.

Basically the circuit we are presenting provides the necessary power supply voltage to allow the tube to operate at maximum effiency. One should note this voltage is about 12,000 volts!

Enough to give the builder a real surprise; or give his next of kin an even better surprise.

Be forwarned.

The power supply consists of a switching oscillator and a rectifier to smooth out the current.

A final voltage divider circuit supplies the high focusing voltage to the RCA tube.

Building the unit is fairly easy if one remembers several important steps:

   A. The tube is glass and fragile.

   B. Producing a sharp image requires exactly the correct voltage and may require some experimentation from tube to tube. The controlling resistors should be chained together so some variance can be induced. A good starting resistance is 2000 MEGOHMS for r-9 and 190 MEGS for R-8 ALTHOUGH THIS MAY HAVE TO BE ADJUSTED!!

Either a PC board or a wire-to-wire circuit can be used but, due to the voltages involved use god construction pratcies including keeping all joints clean and non-cold, using as short of leads as possible for ALL connections, locking all components in place with epoxy, friendly plastic or wax, using silcon or high voltage putty for any and all heat sinking.

Mount everything except the transsitor T-2 and the high voltage side of the transformer.

Once this is accomplished, check with a VOM across the battery leads for an open circuit (after depressing S1).   Then put a 6 volt battery on line and check for about 175 volts on D-7's anode.

If all is go, mount the rest of the circuit.

When connected mount 6 volts on line again and adjust R-6 for maximum sparking (or maximum current draw).

It is now time to solder connections to the image tube. BE CAREFUL!

This is a fragile, vaccum tube with a coating that can be damaged by too much heat. Use short solder times with a solder station (not a wood burning iron!) and heat sinks.

If you heat the glass it will implode making a nice sound and ruining your project..

Solder R-9 between the focus ring and the fluorescent ring. Then, carefully, solder several short pieces of wire to the ring around the objective tube and any point on the focus ring.

Connect your version of R-8 across these wires and the high voltage wires from the power supply.

This should leave the wire from the junction of D-9-C4 connected to the R-8 end which leads to the bljective tube witht he other lead connected to the board ground and the R-9 eyepiece end of the RCA tube.

When you and your god have made peace and you feel everything is A-OK, give the circuit some power and watch for the glow of the phosphor screen.

Good.

Now shut down the power and lay (glue, tape) a piece of window screen across the end of the tube. Turn it back on and the image of the screen should appear.

Now start varying the value of R-8 to make this image a clear as possible. You should find that you are right on the money or within 10-15 percent of the best possible picture.

When the image is as sharp as it will get, solder the resistors in a chain and move onward and upward...

Next turn out the room lights and turn on the toy. Note any areas where sparks or high voltage discharges seem to appear. These areas should be covered with high voltage putty.

Oops, after you turn the power off, of course.

Did'nt loose any readers there, did we?

Good.

Now the toy must be mounted in a casing. Most people employ PCV piping, available at your friendly hardware store.

A focus lens must be mounted at the front of the unit (power can vary with your application, or a general mount can be used to allow lens switching for specific jobs) and a view lens at the rear.

2 and three-eights inch tubing is ideal for most lenses. Use screws to secure hold the above lens tubing inside the general PCV outer tubing.

Normally the case will look like out drawing; the optics in the tubes above, the power supply and battery in the handle.

The design is not critical, just make certain the optic tube is light tight, so only the reflected image light appears on the screen.

A common trick is to mount one's light source (a flashlight with an IR filter) on top of the unit (as shown) so the device is always aimed correctly, however a seperate, more powerful Q-beam source can be utilized.

The tube, board, entire kit or unit can be purchased from good old Info Unlimited for $2.50 to $200, depending on how much work one wishes to put out...

PARTS;

R-1	10,000 ohms
R-2	1,000
R-2	4700
R-4,R-5	100
R-6	100,000 pot
R-7	2200
R-8	200 Megs
R-9	2000 Megs
C-1	10 uf 25 volts electrolytic
C-2	1 UF 400 volts el
C-3	1 uf 25
C-4	.001 uf 15 kv ceramic

Q1,Q2	2N2222 NPN
D1,D2	1N4002
D3-D-8	1N4007
SCR1	C107D
B1	9 VOLT NIC-CAD
S1	SPST pushbutton
T1	12-400 volts swithcing transformer
T2	11 kV pulse trans 400 volt primary

RCA 6032 imaging tube, PCV tubing, lenses, cbattery clip, flashlight, IR filter, tape, wire, etc.

All available from electronics suppliers or Info Un..

This unit works very nicely for the money but not up to the Meredith (more expensive) standard.

SUPER CHEAP

NIGHT EYE
BASIC SYSTEM

All new "NIGHT EYE" device allows you to **see in total darkness**. Lightweight, self-contained & range adjustable up to over 100 meters, low cost & equal in performance to those costing 3 to 4 times as much. Options available.

SD5 .....PLANS .....$10.00   SD5K .....KIT/PLANS $99.50
SD50 ....ASSEMBLED BASIC UNIT $169.50

The saying you get what you pay for may or may not apply here in more than one way...

The top unit is from INFORMATION UNLIMITED and looks like a great deal for the money, while it will not compete with the $500 MEREDITH unit it costs considerably less. Problem was that IU was having tube delivery problems and was backed up on orders. This may have changed by now.

Below is ETCO ELECTRONIC's answer to the super cheap IR viewer. Again specs may have changed by now and ETCO was also experiencing delivery problems.

The INFO UN unit does come to us with a good reputation from someone we trust...

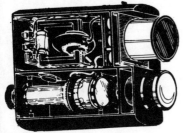

This IR source/viewer has been sold for several years now. At one time it was the best, and only, cheap unit available, this is no longer the situation and we find several units in the same and lower price ranges to actually outperform this particular unit.

Top sold by UNIVERSAL ELECTRONICS AND SECURITY ($550), bottom by FAIRINGTON TECHNOLOGIES ($1500).

SUPER INFRARED SCOPE

As amazing as a Starlight scope is, there are several disadvantages when compared to a more conventional infrared viewer.

The first, and most notable for many of us on fixed incomes, or who haven't be trickled on by the infamous "trickle down" effect, is price.

At an average of $5,000-$6,000 the Starlight NVD is not cheap.

The second, and possible fatally disadvantage, is that there must be some light to be amplified by the tubes. On a totally dark night, or inside a building where light does not penetrate, any light amplification device has no input to process.

Of course an IR light source can be used with a Starlight scope to help fill in as a light source, but one has now just added onto the package price while not actually using the device's real potential.

On the other hand, most IR scopes on the market are simply overpriced toys. Some use plastic eye pieces or (god forbid) even plastic front lenses along with second or surplus IR tubes.

18 mm is the average tube size and the images produced, even with a powerful light source, are often blurred beyond recognition.

A couple of these devices require bulky battery packs to be worn on the belt with wires running to the unit itself.

We tested a number of IR viewers and found none to actually compare in any way, shape or form with a top flight Starlight scope.

Except one...

MEREDITH INSTRUMENTS has put together a 25 mm IR viewer that is professionally constructed and self contained. Our test unit measured about 10 inches INCLUDING battery power supply and a 1.4, 12.5 (wide angle) to 75 mm (telescopic) professional quality tv lens.

The unit will focus down to about 1.5 feet and out to infinity at a twist of the built in focus ring.

A simple on-off switch operates the unit, a rubber eyepiece couples the user to the tube-screen without allowing outside light to interfere, while stopping any chance of the faint tube light giving the user's position away to a potential enemy.

Made from blackened, light weight aluminium, the unit is quite shock proof and the professional tube/lens/eyepiece will give the same OR BETTER resolution as a top Starlight unit.

This device is small enough to be called pocket sized yet accurate enough (including cross hairs) for any IR use one can come up with.

Note this does not include a light source. Herein lies a number of user choices. We used our trusty 20,000 candle power Stream light with a snap on IR filter for our experiments.

In total darkness this set up was good enough to pick out a man at about 75-100 yards, recognize him at 35-50 yards, and count his teeth at any lesser distance.

MEREDITH also sells IR glass filters with rubber holders for Q-beam lights. These lantern type spotlights are cheap (anywhere from $29.95 up) and come in 100,000-200,000-300,000 candle power.

One simply takes the cheap glass filer and attaches it to the Q-beam with the rubber holder and then fills in the edge gaps with black silicone from any hardware store.

This provides a cheap source of IR light that is totally invisible to the naked eye from a distance of more than a few feet.

Two hard and fast rules; the 300,000 candle power model tends to get too hot and will crack the glass, never, never, use a plastic lens for your light source as they tend to lose a lot of light in the conversion and will melt on any powerful (i.e., hot) source.

Any of the IR beacon units we tested worked AS WELL on this scope as they did on the more expensive Starlight models.

The amazing definition of this scope does not photograph well as the unit is not designed to be coupled to a camera and any shots must be made while holding the light source, holding the scope and holding the camera (count your number of hands) while trying to focus on the small eyepiece screen.

Price?

$600 at this writing and a steal at that level. NONE of the other units within thousands of dollars could touch this device for ease of operation, range and clarity.

What a beautiful unit, buy at this level before the other dealers start tripling the price...

INFRARED SCOPE USER'S IMPRESSIONS

After living with the MEREDITH IR scope a number of impressions come to mind:

The scope is a joy to work with, focusing is crisp and clear and the zoom telescopic feature adds much to the overall advantages of this unit.

Every light source (or most) give off a mass of different light frequencies some of which fall into the IR range, so the unit can actually be used sans source if enough available IR is floating around.

This is usually not the case as you will find the naked eye does better with ambient light than the scope does. One exception to this was a man smoking a cigarette. I could see more facial features with the scope than without.

The most bothersome feature is actually a non-feature; trying to hold a light source while focusing and using the scope takes about 3 hands. This problem was solved by the use of assistant, or by taping the source and scope together.

On the other hand this very feature allowed the substitution of any light source necessary for the project at hand.

The scope works just about as well with any of the IR marker beacons at thousands of dollars less than a Starlight model.

The 20,000 candle power Streamlight is perfect for close work and/or inside work, but the higher power Q-Beams are required to utilize the scope to its fullest potential.

The scope is perfect for inside work, you can focus in on virtually every item in a large room with no tell tale visible light to give one's presence away...

It is also great for completely checking out any area one is about to enter.

The unit is made right; it is rugged and light weight and works better than the units we tried that cost 2-3 times as much.

THE OPPOSITE ENDS OF THE NIGHT VISION GAME

The MEREDITH IR viewer (around $600) that works like magic and the PENTAX Nocta IR viewer-camera set up for taking photos up to 150 feet in complete darkness.

Around $6,000...

INFRARED UPDATE

After using several IR viewers and sources, and just before we went to press we talked to MEREDITH INSTRUMENTS again and discovered several new factors:

The owner (Dennis) has now update "our" best buy in IR viewers with a new eyepiece giving up to 40% better resolution coupled with a new front end lens letting in about 15% more light.

Note this is a non-zoom, 50 mm front end.

The power supply has been reduced in size and is rechargable, giving about one full evening's viewing on a charge. The entire unit is now easily pocket size including the small external power supply and batteries.

It can still be quipped with a zoom lens if one wishes, including a higher powered zoom than our test version which makes it great for long distance, private detective type surveillance operations.

The fixed lens gives a wider field of view and focuses down to a shorter distance making it ideal for inside of closer work.

Price? Still in the $550-$650 range...

Dennis will also design and provide a camera adapter for the rear end for a few books more making this instrument even more versatile.

With these updates the device is equal to, or better than (in terms of resolution, distance depending on the IR source) to our Starlight scopes.

This unit is far better than the $1600 range units we tried...Mention us to him (no, we don't get any kickback) for the best deal...

He also now sells 5 and 1/4 inch glass IR filers that fit over any (INCLUDING THE 300,000 CANDLE POWER Q-BEAMS!) for about $25...

From Kodak similar filters will run you $150...

MEREDITH has also updated their Starlight scopes where a PBS-39 Hyper Mini scope (still first generation) comes completely assembled and includes a recharagable power supply (their addition) for about $1395 at this writing.

A complete 1st generation kit can be had, INCLUDING CASE!, for about $650.

This means one can actually spend a couple of hours assembling the 3 tubes and supply/recharagable batteries and end up with a true Starlight scope for about $650.

Pretty amazing when you realize the history and potential of these devices...

For money versus performance MEREDITH wins in the night vision game all the way around.

Now do note most of these items are aimed at surveillance/viewing NOT the gun mount market, MEREDITH prefers to leave this to others...

INFRARED PHOTOGRAPHY

There are several systems that allow photography in total darkness. This can be accomplished on subjects or even on documents with the proper equipment.

One of the things to be in mind is that to photograph anything one must first SEE what is about to be "shot".

One can actually accomplish IR photography on a shoe string budget...

To take an infrared photograph for next to nothing (assuming one has access to a 35mm camera) simply attach a strobe unit to the camera and purchase a Kodak gelatin Wratten filter number 87.

This gelatin filter passes only the IR portion of any visible light source, containing the rest of the bandwidth from view. Place this filter over the entire front of the strobe unit and tape all the edges with black electrican's tape.

Notice when you use the strobe it appears that no light is actually visible. Only invisible IR wavelengths are passing the filter.

The camera must now be loaded with Kodak High Speed Infrared film; a job which is easier said than done..

This film is sensitive to light only in the 700-900 millimicron band. This means that visible light will NOT expose the film, however it does mean that the film canister WILL NOT stop the IR light from exposing the film.

Once the canister is removed from its protective covering ANY light will contaminate the film AT ONCE through the canister-cover.

One cannot change the film in the normal manner; it must be inserted in the camera in TOTAL DARKNESS.

This is best accomplished in a changing bag, if one does not have access to a professional bag one can fake it by using a thick canvas bag, or even placing the camera and film under the covers of a bed IN TOTAL DARKNESS.

Unless you are used to using a changing bag, practice inserting "normal" film into the camera several times before attempting the IR switch.

It is very easy to not quite lock the film tab into the film advance roller.

Ask Scott...

Our one roll of IR film that we carefully carried to Africa after arguing with a number of customs and security officals (one should NEVER take a roll of IR or other high speed film through an airport x-ray machine, they WILL fog such film, especially if they are a bit out of adjustment) and shot with a powerful IR source at a dark waterhole full of things making strange noises at our unwanted interviews, came out TOTALLY BLANK BECAUSE SOMEONE WHO SHALL GO NAMELESS CHANGED IT UNDER THE COVERS IN THE TENT AND BLEW IT!!!

Any photographs taken at risk of life and limb should at least come out...

When using IR film a couple of adjustments have to be made:

Firstly, the lens must be focused out from the film by 25% of the focal length of the lens employed.

This is easier than it sounds because most 35 mm cameras have IR markings already figured out on the lens. These are usually done in orange ink and are marked along with the normal focus settings.

For exposure settings certain variables come into play; first of all use the most powerful strobe you can come up with for a power source, now take a complete set of photos at a known distance with this film and strobe.

RUN THROUGH THE ENTIRE ROLL USING EVERY EXPOSURE POSSIBLE.

Have the film developed (takes a special process) and choose the best exposure.

Now take these figures; distance to subject (let's say 25 feet) and multiply the exposure (let's guess f3) times this to give a factor of 75...

In the future take your factor of 75 and DIVIDE it by the distance to the subject to get the correct exposure (use the nearest figure and bracket your shots).

Again this technique requires you to know WHERE the subject is and WHEN to shoot.

Of course it is possible to set the camera's exposure time to one or two seconds and loose off a flash ot two while looking thru the SLR view finder to get a quick, IR look at the territory...

It is also possible to take IR photos without an IR light source by placing an IR screw-in filter in front of the lens so only IR light passes onto the film plane.

This means a conventional light source can be utilized, or even ambient light to take IR photos.

This situation rarely arises in surveillance work as the main advantage of IR photography is to be able to take completely un-detected photographs in total darkness rather than take IR shots in normal light conditions.

The main use for this type of photography is in the scientific fields, although it can help in detection of forged documents and other investigative applications.

A better, and more expensive method is to order one of MEREDITH'S IR viewers with a camera adapter on the eye piece section.

This will, along with the proper IR light source, let you view in total darkness and then take a photo, with the correct exposure, when the time is right.

Another, even more expensive method is to purchase a a special camera that is already set up to IR photograpy standards.

Does such an animal exist?

No.

Just kidding.

Pentax sells a camera already normalized for dark surveillance and photography. This amazing unit comes with a 300 mm telephoto lens (f3.3), an image converter tube and two pre-mounted and pre-focused IR light sources.

One source is a constant source for viewing, the other is a strobe type source for photographic use.

This allows both thru camera viewing as well as a perfect shot at a permanent record.

It works.

Yes, it is very expensive...

Things To Remember

1. For B&W IR photography a blue green filter is required over the light source and an opaque infrared filter is needed over the lens.

Filters for blue-green excitation:

9780 Corning glass color filter, C.S.

No. 4-76 3966 Corning glass color filter C.S. No. H.R. 1-59 molded and tempered for heat absorption.

Opaque filter:

Kodak wratten filter No. 87

2. Infrared film should be kept under 55 degrees F, preferably well under...Unexposed film should be stored in the fridge or freezer and brought out at least 2 hours prior to use.

3. It is possible to photograph human subjects in total darkness without their knowledge or consent by setting up a trip wire or release on a cash drawer, valuable animal etc.

This is best done by taking the same photos, minus the subject, while marking exposures and focus distances and presetting the camera for best results.

Additional flash (slave units) can be triggered by trigger circuits utilizing infrared detectors.

Some units may give a dull glow that will be visible if the subject is looking directly at the light source. This can be fixed by using indirect lighting and aiming the source (s) at light toned walls or reflectors.

4. If a commercial filter is not available a piece of glass or gel of No. 87 or 87C wratten filter material can be rubber banded or taped to the front of a strobe unit.

Exposures should be decided by experimentation but most strobes will give guide numbers in the 200-300 range. Some glow will be emitted by 87 filter material while 87C will stop all visible light but also needs 2 1/2 more stops of exposure.

5. IR photography will sometime work wonders with altered documents or redone art works. It will show up watermarks on stamps and sometimes "see" right through ink that has blacked out a valuable piece of information.

THERMAL VIEWERS

I lied.

There is a third type of night vision device; the thermal viewer.

This unit converts heat to visible light. Since every object radiates some heat a good TV will show up the environment on par with an IR unit, highlighting the warmer objects within the field of view, such as human bodies.

Even a standard IR unit will show some thermal content bands, but only those of high heat radiation such as auto engines. A thermal unit will show up most objects in a nighttime scenerio.

Thermal viewers will also "see" through smoke and foilage. Fog dissipates IR energy however, and they are not effective under that condition.

Passive IR (thermal) units have no depth perception ability and are easily fooled by decoy IR sources.

On going research leads me to predict fourth generation scopes that will combine both light amplification and thermal viewing.

Even with their built-in limitations todays TV's are ideal for locating bodies in thick cover or aiming things at vehicles, aircraft, or missile launchers...

IN THE DARK BRIGHTLY

This section may seem a bit on the unimportant side, I mean a flashlight is a flashlight, right?

Well...

Up until the last few years this was true. One could buy multi- cell models, cute models, recharageable models, pastel models, and so on but they all worked about the same.

No more my child. First of all came the invention, or application of the Krypton gas filled flashlight bulb. This was a real step upward as the high pressure inert gas allows the filament to burn much hotter and much longer (up to 25 hours).

The best known supplier of krypton bulbs is:

CARLEY LAMPS INC
1502 W 2228 st
Torrance, Ca 90501

Their bulbs feature a hard glass shell, focused lens to aim the available light, shock mounted filaments, spacers and bases to fit almost every flashlight.

Now for the interesting part, CARLEY's are actually matched to the type of battery and voltage used. Three different series work with 1-7 cells of either carbon, alkaline, ni-cad, or even lithium.

Although any bulb can be used with any type of power supply, life
will be shortened.

How good are the new bulbs?
Up to 300% more usable light from any flashlight
Up to 400% more range
Up to 400% more bulb life

FLASHLIGHTS

As the lamps have beccome future tech, so have the flashlights. TEKNA offers a complete series of lights from a sub-mini one (lithium) cell, krypton bulbed penlight up to mini-strobes (same electronics) to a minature 12 volt, 8 battery unit that will fit in a shirt pocket and gives off 18,000 candle power!!!

Tekna lights use a Lexan lens that is both tough and acts as a switch so you must turn the O-ring, lens assembly to operate the flashlight.

This makes the light waterproof (uh, that is, waterproof to 2,000 feet) and damn near indestructable.

I shot a .22 LR rifle at the lexan lens from 30 feet.

It bounced off...Tekna's are avaliable from many dealers including EARLY WINTERS.

Now for my pride and joy. We wanted the best possible flashlight for our trip to Africa and so we begged:

>STREAMLIGHT INC
>1030 W Germantown Pike
>Norristown Pa 19403

for a test model of their SL-20.

To their credit they sent the toy 2nd day UPS so we would get it in time. It turned out to be the most popular item we took along except for the starlight scope.

The SL-20 is their mid-priced light. It is a sealed unit with a knurled handle for easy gripping even in wet situations. Instead of the usual big air/filament bulb it uses a quartz halogen sealed beam head coupled to a stick of five rechargable nicad batteries all housed in a tough aluminum case.

I do mean tough, many police have started using this light as a non-club, club, without damamging the flashlight. Although the same cannot always be said of the criminal...

I came close to trying out this baton feature on a very curious and very ugly hyena. It might have been a first for STREAMLIGHT advertising...

Streamlights feature a computer focused beam control system that really works. We tried several other makes of about the same output and could see far more of the target than with the competitor's models.

Streamlight says their engineering makes the SL-20 up to 7 times brighter than conventional flashlights of the same voltage.

They're right...

I photographed a pair of glowing, beautiful eyes at a distance (measured in the daylight with an armed backup) of over 1/4 of a mile!!!

I owe Lee one for this as we had just heard some very interesting noises with our Hunter's Ear at 11 pm and I thought it would be a great test to track down the noise using the sound amplifier only.

Lee suggested using the streamlight first.

What pretty eyes; what a large cat...

Lee assures me he would have given me credit for the portion of the book I had already worked on and donated some of the profits to my favorite charity had I continued the experiment...

The SL-20 comes with two rechargers (one stock, additional one about $15) that will recharge it from 110 AC or from a 12 volt car battery.

This latter option was invaluable as we could drive across country and be assured of a charged light as dusk descended.

A fully charged SL will give about 1 and 1/2 hours of light.

We bounced this flashlight over roads used in the worst (best?) rough road race in the world; the Kenya rally, at about the same speeds (if only I had thought to record some of Lee's screams I would be set for life), dropped it off a major cliff when a rather mean hippo took a sudden dislike to my presence (would he have objected to Joan Embry and Johnny Carson? By the way, Joan was in our camp, nice lady...)

Back in the states I taped the Streamlight onto the barrel of AR-15 and discovered I could blind and then shoot just about anyone.

Couple this with a IR filter and a NVD and you have THE POWER.

Oh yes, for a few bucks more the Streamlight comes with a snap-on rubber lens cap that contains a built-in IR filter which allows NO visible light to escape and extends the range of an NVD considerably.

Yes, this little gem sells for just under $100 but man is it worth it.

What does a gram of coke cost these days?

Of course the Streamlight has numerous non-sexy uses around the house....

One can also purchase a larger version of the Stream; the SL-35 which emits

35,000 candle power for those times when you aren't satisfied with just seeing a leopard, but would rather blind the poor creature for the rest of the night.

These rugged, powerpacks are ideal for checking out that bump in the night that awakens you from a deep sleep. Most lesser powered beams would allow the bad guy to actually use the light as an aimpoint and blow it and yu away.

The SLs are so bloody bright they tend to blind rather than act as a target.

if all else fails hit the sucker over the head with it...

OUTRAGEOUS

Designed for the purists among us who would use a .500 double rifle on a whitetail deer, a couple of super lights exist.

The first, and probably the most practical is the Streamlight 1 MILLION. You can guess where from sprang the name...

A totally handheld unit the #1 operates from rechargable batteries or from car electrical systems.

One million candle power; think about it, this will throw a beam 1 mile and can be seen for 35 miles! It will show accurate colors up to 500 yards.

Why would any sane person need this unit?

For one thing it comes with an infrared filter...Get the idea? It is possible to extend the workable range of either an IR viewer or an NVD to great distances with no one being the wiser.

A great search and rescue (or kill) device, well worth the $700...

Now the very, very, ultimate light delight is the Set Beam by FAIRINGTON TECHNOLOGIES. Weighing in in the blue corner at 6 pounds this remotely controlled searchlight runs off a car, boat, aircraft or rechargable battery to hurdle out a focused beam of 6 million candlepower.

What possible use could you have for a light that would let Helen Keller see fine print 1/2 a mile away?

Well the first thing that comes to mind is when you are driving along at night and some dumb son-of-a-bitch refuses to lower his bright beams causing spot blindness and confusion.

I dare say if his rudeness was returned in kind with either of these focused beams it would be the last time he did not dim.

Assuming, of course, he lived...

Just kidding.

Both super power beams are great for identification of objects through fog, smoke or darkness. They are often used in helicopters for pinpointing ground vehicles.

In addition both have IR filters that operate in the wavelengths observed by NVDs (400-1,000 nm) extending the range of any NVD to a fantastic extent.

Any of these powerful lights can be adapted to IR use by adding a filter and sealing the edge light leaks. Then they can be hand held or taped to an IR viewer or NVD to give total darkness capability, extended range and resolution, act as a weapon sight, or illuminate a dark room/alley where the bad guy may be hiding.

All without giving away your position.

They can also be rigged up as a perimeter alarm/guard system with the use of mirrors and low light tv cameras or motion sensors.

Again, if you can afford second generation (third gen units are simply smaller in size) NVDs we do suggest their purchase due to the simpler construction, automatic gain control, anti-blooming feature and lighter weight.

On the other hand, if you can't spring for a 2nd generation unit, the first units, such as our STANO loaner, still open a whole new world to the casual viewer.

Look how well we did in Viet Nam with these very scopes.

You're right, forget I said that.

If money is a real problem and you are a bit handy with your hands buy the components from MEREDITH for a starlight scope, MEREDITH, INFO UNLIMITED, or F&P ENTERPRISES for IR viewers and build your own.

IN THE DARK AIDS (VISIBLE)

As we have already covered in the help-along your NVD unit section there are a number of ways of improving night light sources.

The first is the use of the krypton bulb with the correct battery set. This will transform a cheap penlight into a useable white light source. A nice idea, but the Tekna lights which are already set-up is cheap enough not to bother with upgrading your favorite mini-source.

One step above the Tekna, for those of you who want the very best, is the Black Star. This totally hand made Krypton/Lithium flashlight checks in about the size of a min-Tekna, say 4 inches, and is constructed from onyx (very black) areospace aluminum.

The index ring and momentary contact switch are brass to prevent rust or contact oxidation.

Both the power pack and the light are modular and replaceable. At $17 a very nice addition to a "tool kit" or key ring.

Made by our old friends at ARMAMENT SYSTEMS PRODUCTS, up to their usual caliber of workmanship and innovation.

Now as to our Streamlight loaner; I can not say enough about this light, it proved invaluable in Africa time and time again. We had the SL-20, the mid sized unit with five sealed ni-cads and a quartz-halogen sealed beam "bulb".

The unit will recharge in excess of 1,000 times before the battery pack needs replacement. It can be gotten with either (or both) rechargers that run from 110 AC, or 12 volts DC.

We found this second feature to be convenient as we could charge the light while bouncing over what passes for roads in Kenya, and be assured of a workable source when it came time to pitch camp.

The recharger fits over the on-off switch (a strong, well placed unit) requiring the light to be in a more or less horizontal position during the charging.

Our SL-20 proved so durable and powerful we gave the ordering address to several different suitably impressed fellow travelers.

The unit is also heavy enough to be used as a baton type weapon, a fact many police have been thankful for over the years.

Neither of us actually hit any large animals, but the fact that the beam was powerful enough to blind damn near anything/body was a comfort more than once.

The focused beam actually seems to amplify the usable light.

Streamlights have a knurled grip which does aid in slippery (or nervous) conditions and a holster can be purchased.

For under $100 it is a backup you will use again and again.

Streamlight also makes a 1 MILLION candle-power hand held search light. This model uses a xexon bulb and a 12 volt power supply. It will throw a narrow, focused beam of bright white light one mile...

It can be used as a signal for 35 miles in clear conditions, and will even allow true color viewing at 500 yards...

Price? In the $700 range...

Next to the total overkill, 6 million Set Beam, (at $6,000) this is the most powerful, hand held light on earth...

The Streamlight 1 million is also available in a "B" model which puts out light in the 980 nanometer range. Invisible to the naked eye, but will transform any IR type decoder into a device the gods of old would have been jealous of...

If you really stop and think can't you come up with at least one scene that would be interesting to see from a half mile or so away in total darkness?

Set Beam

- High peak candle power — nearly 6,000,000 candela.
- Hand held size — less than 4" across, about 6 lb. in weight.
- Electronically controlled variable beam opening.
- Sealed for free on water use.
- Military specification to withstand hostile environmental conditions, shock and vibrations.
- Special optics to eliminate blinding side lobs reflection. Great viewing contrast.
- Used with any car, boat or aircraft battery.
- Modular design. Readily replaceable subsystems for easy maintenance.

1. REMOTE CONTROL UNIT
2. SEARCHLIGHT
3. POWER SUPPLY UNIT
4. I.R. FILTER

FARINGTON TECHNOLOGIES, INC.
PO Box 475
Windham NH 03087

The ultimate flashlight; 6,000,000 candles will light up your neighbor several miles away, even from a helicopter.

Comes with electronic remote control, flasher, IR filter, back and carrying pack, tripod adapter, adjustable beam and recharageable pack for 30-90 minutes of portable operation.

Amazing.

WORKING UP A JACKET ON ANYBODY

One of the most common things a private eye is asked to do is to work up a dossier "jacket" on a particular subject. The reasons for this may vary from mad spouses to possible industrial espionage.

Ninja were known for turning battles around, regardless of desperate odds by their amazing spy network.

As Tom Wolfe said, " information is power."

Actually he said, "you can never go home again,", Scott said the other one, but more people know who Wolfe is...

Ninja would often collect their data by posing as peasants, actors, beggars ("got any spare change?"), farmers and so on. In today's specialized society intermingling is no longer quite as effective and in the days of Samuari and roses.

Technology helps solve this problem.

For the sake a arguement we are going to assume you have no friends, or at least none you can turn your back on for more than a minute or two...So our surveillance will be conducted in solitary.

This means it must be done in the same manner porcupines fuck...

Very carefully.

Assuming you have his residence or business address and/or phone number began there. If you do not, go spend $30 and read How To Get to find out this little first step.

Now set up optical surveillance on area in question within the time frame which will be of the most interest. This will probably be done in an active manner; meaning you sit there reading Playboy (our readers do NOT read Hustler) with your trusty binoculars and spotting scope waiting for some sign of action.

When night creeps in on little fog feet set up the NVD, using a booster source if necessary.

Always keep a notebook of ANY activity, running down license numbers of visitor's vehicles.

Run a credit check on your subject and/or visitors. See last book.

Establish a mail cover. Now this can simply be meeting the mailman by pure coincidence as he deliver's "your" mail, duplicating the box key, setting up a covert forwarding address and then returning the mail, etc.

A quick cover is one where one simply records the outside info, a more detailed look requires mechanical or chemical help as described elsewhere.

If you wish to take a chance on the next 5 years of your life you can break in, photograph all documents and bug the apartment and phone.

If you still have hopes of some sort of interesting life not viewed from behind iron bars, you might attempt to set up a parabolic mic, say in a nearby tree, aimed at a window in the target's house.

Now to help guard against those little accidents where you come to collect the tapes and the entire LA SWAT team is waiting for your appearance, several people, including INFORMATION UNLIMITED sells a vox controlled transmitter which will only switch on when the noise exceeds your preset threshold and then broadcast to a receiver stashed somewhere else.

This set up; saves tape, and is hard to find as it only operates when necessary, and is difficult to spot if the dish is camo'ed. It is also quite directional and selective.

Now you (we; one) come to the problem of following the target when he decides to jump into the Ferrari or onto the NOX injected, blown honda and disappear off to some clandestine meet.

From practical tests I can assure you the nightsite market beacon is a god send. Instead of cursing red lights, trying to find a weak radio signal, and then discovering you've been following the multi-path bounce back from a cement wall as with a very expensive radio direction finder, you can hang back well into traffic (or even on a deserted road) as not to arouse suspicion and NEVER lose your target.

It is also possible to throw a dimmer lens over the front of the NVD and use it during the daytime although the range is somewhat cut down.

If you have the luxury of more than one tail car this method works even better, none of the standard tricks of putting out lights, changing plates, adding mud, parking, quick turn arounds, will work with the marker system.

Each tailer can always find the target with the minimum of hassle and from a fair distance.

Any of the normal ABC, or progressive methods will work even better with this innovation.

Now couple this with the information gathering methods detailed in the last book and you should be able to find out everything from a person's sexual preferences to what his boss eats for breakfast.

Some additional suggestions not covered in How To, and suggested by an expert in the field:

If the target is a business check of the Certificates of Incorporation in a secretary of state's office can reveal all sorts of stuff including:

names of directors
names of officers
general partners etc.

One can often contact these people for additional information.

If the company is traded publicly traded the Securities and Exchange Commission is a storehouse of background data.

Another trick is to get a copy of the annual report of the company in question and note the name of some gadget used in the same department where your man works.

Now one can write the person enclosing a questionaire (because your survey company has been retained by the manufacturer of the machine) to get a profile on famous scientists that use the exciting machine...

Most will feel flattered at such a suggestion and fill out the sheet giving you whatever information you need.

Another trick is to "become" a registered investment counselor.

How?

Simple, register...

There are no tests, no background or educational requirements, no qualifications. Now that you are an expert and registered with the government, you can offer "expert" advice, before only available to certain large investors, to your lucky target, or rather, friend, if he just fills out this questionaire...

If you are writing a "stock" letter from Acme Lost Children Finders, write the body of the letter in one type face and then change daisy wheels or type fonts so it appears you have attempted to match a computer generated letter when you type in the target's name and address.

This will look like it is just a common, everyday, run of the mill, computer letter that deserved no special treatment...

CIVIL TRACKING UPDATES

The following articles are accompanying and updated techniques to go along with the ideas presented in How To Get Anything On Anybody.

In some case ONLY the changes are presented, in others the entire idea may be covered. Even if you don't have any special reason for trying to track down someone at the moment, there is a good chance you will in the future.

Many of these sources can be used for building a complete dossier on a person (or a business) and constructing an entire background which can be used for a multiple of purposes.

1. Some firms now compile weekly lists of new homeowners. Insurance salespeople buy these lists as do other businesses for direct mail campaigns. Remember that every new person moving into an area could have someone trying to find them back at their previous residence. They often contact direct mail list brokers.

2. TRAFFIC RECORDS; This index will tell the traffic ticket number. It is in alphabetical order according to name. After obtaining the ticket number, the clerk gets the ticket for you. The ticket shows: full name, date of birth, current address, physical description, the time, date, and location the violation took place, officer's name, tag number, and the name and address of the person whom the tag is registered to if different from the violator, year, make, model as well as color of the vehicle.

3. STATE AUTO LICENSE DEPARTMENTS; If one gets a license number most states will provide one with the name, address, date of birth, serial number, year, make and model of the vehicle. Some states will also record the driver's license number and insurance company and policy number. Some will give you the data by telephone. Some will want a form and fee first.

4. DRIVER'S LICENSE FILES; These records can be accessed if you have the driver's license number. However, the driver's license number can be dug up in all kinds of records. These records will show all violations, the county where the ticket was issued, full name, birth date, date of driver's test, address and some will show the vehicle owned and insurance company. The records will also state any accidents, file numbers and any investigation agency that may have investigated the accident. These records can be ordered by mail.

5. TITLE DEPARTMENTS; Title departments have records similar to State License

Departments. These records are accessed by the serial number of the vehicle. They will show if there is a lien on the vehicle and quote the name of the lien-holder.

6. To buy auto license lists:

R. L. Polk Co.
6400 Monroe Blvd.
Taylor, Michigan 48180

7. If one writes to this address, the military will find your subject for you if he is on active duty. The request should include:

1. Name
2. Service Serial Number
3. Last Known Address
4. Date of Birth
5. Social Security Number (if available)

Make a $2.00 check payable to the Treasurer of the United States:

A. Army (Officer Personnel on Active Duty)
The Adjutant General
Department of the Army
Attention: AGPF-FC
Washington, D.C. 20310

B. Army Personnel on Active Duty
Commanding Officer U.S. Army Administration Center
Attention: AGPF-VI
Fort Benjamin Harrison, In. 46216

C. Army (Enlisted and Officer Personnel not on Active Duty)
Commanding Officer
U.S. Army Administration Center
9700 Page Boulevard
St. Louis, Mo. 63132
D. Air Force
Directorate of Administrative Services
Department of the Air Force
Attention: Military Personnel Records Division
Randolph Air Force Base, Texas 78148

E. Navy

Chief of Naval Personnel
Department of the Navy
Washington, D.C. 30270

F. Marine Corps
Commandant of the Marine Corps (Code MSRB-10)
Washington, D.C. 2059

G. Coast Guard (Enlisted Personnel)
Commandant (PO)
U.S.Coast Guard
1300 East Street, N,W,
Washington, D.C. 20591

8. VOTER REGISTRATION RECORDS; A good record to check in skip investigation. Even though the subject's name might not be registered, a son, daughter, or spouse might be. Such records will show name, address, date of registration, and political party.

9. AUTO REGISTRATION RECORDS; Shows the name, address, date of birth, year, make, model, serial number of vehicle. The subjects date of birth is important in a skip trace because the tag number has to be renewed. Some offices will index by both name and license number. Others will index only by license number.

10. GENERAL INDEXING RECORDS; These records contain many records on the target filed at the court house. They are likely to be in with real property records. They will include: IRS tax wars, liens between two parties, assumed names and final judgements from all civil and criminal courts.

11. Social Security has a department that will forward a letter to lost relatives, neighbors, friends, etc. They will not give you the address but will forward your messages. The address to contact is: Social Security Location Services, 6401 Security Blvd., Baltimore Maryland, 21234.

12. CASUALTY INDEX; This idea was begun by the Hooper Holms Company, Morristown, New Jersey. This contains more than six million individuals and lists their insurance history. This contains all policies an individual has ever applied for. The purpose of this data is to find insurance frauds.

13. CREDIT INDEX; Here is another computer list begun by the Hooper Holms Company. They gather only negative credit history thus drastically reducing the mass of records.

14. AUTO LICENSE INFORMATION

ALABAMA	FLORIDA
Motor Vehicles & License	Dept. of Hwy. Safety & Motor Division Vehicles

P.O. Bos 104
3030 E. Blvd.
Montgomery, Ala. 36130

Kirkman Building
Tallahassee, Fla. 32301

ARKANSAS
Motor Vehicles Division
P. O. Box 1272
Little Rock, Ark. 72203

GEORGIA
Dept. of Revenue
Motor Vehicle Division
Trinity Washington Bldg.
Atlanta, Ga. 30334

ALASKA
Div. of Motor Vehicles
P. O. Box 960
Anchorage, Alaska 99510

ARIZONA
Arizona Motor Vehicle Div.
P. O. Box 2100
Phoenix, Arizona 85001

CALIFORNIA
Dept. Of Motor Vehicles
P.O. Box 11231
Sacramento, CA 95813

COLORADO
Dept. of Revenue
Motor Vehicles
140 W. 6th Ave.
Denver, Colorado 80204

HAWAII
KAUAI
Director of Finance
County of Kauai
Lihue, HI 06766

HAWAII
Director of Finance
County of Hawaii
25 Apuni Street
Hilo, HI 96720

MAUI
Director of Finance
County of Maui
Wailuku, Maui 96793

OAHU
Director of Finance
County of Honolulu
1455 S Bertainia
Honolulu, HI 96814

CONNECTICUT
Motor Vehicles
60 State Street
Wetherfield, CT 06109

IDAHO
Motor Vehicles Division
Dept. of Law Enforcement
P.O. Box 34
Boise, ID 83731

DELAWARE
Motor Vehicles
P. O. Box 698
Dover, DE 19901

ILLINOIS
Sec. of State
2701 S. Dirksen Parkway
Springfield, IL 62756

DISTRICT OF COLUMBIA
Bureau of Motor Vehicles

INDIANA
Bureau of Motor Vehicles

301 C. Street N.W.
Washington, D.C. 20001

IOWA
Dept. of Transportation
Office of Vehicle Registr.
Lucas Building
Des Moines, IA 50319

KANSAS
Div. of Vehicles
State Office Bldg.
Topeka, Kansas 66626

KENTUCKY
Dept. of Justice
Bureau of State Police
State Office Building
Frankfort, KY 40601

LOUISIANA
Dept. of Public Safety
Vehicles Regulations Div.
P. O. Box 6619
Baton Rouge, LA 70896

MAINE
Motor Vehicle Division
1 Child Street
Augusta, Maine 04333

MARYLAND
Motor Vehicles
6601 Richie Hwy. N.E.
Glen Burnie, MD

MASSACHUSETTS
Registry of Motor Vehicles
100 Nashua Street
Boston, MA 02114

MICHIGAN
Dept. of State
Bureau of Vehicle Services
7064 Crowner Street

Room 314 State Office Bldg.
Indianapolis, IN 46204

MISSISSIPPI
Motor Vehicles Office
P. O. Box 1140
Jackson, MS 65101

MISSOURI
Dept. of Revenue
Motor Vehicles & Driver Bureau
Jefferson City, MO 65101

MONTANA
Dept. of Justice
Registrars Bureau
Motor Vehicle
Deer Lodge, MT 59722

NEBRASKA
Adm of Titles
Dept. of Motor Vehicles
Capital Building
Lincoln NE 68509

NEVADA
Dept. of Motor Vehicles
555 Wright Way
Carson City, NV 89711

NEW HAMPSHIRE
Motor Vehicles Division
85 Loudon
Concord, NH 03301

NEW JERSEY
Division of Motor Vehicles
Bureau of Office Services
25 South Montgomery Street
Trenton, N.J. 08666

NEW MEXICO
Motor Vehicles Division
Manual Jujan Building
Santa Fe, NM 97503

Lansing, MI 48918

MINNESOTA
Driver & Vehicle Services
Transportation Bldg.
St. Paul, MN 55155

NORTH CAROLINA
Div. of Motor Vehicles
100 New Bern Ave.
Raleigh, N.C. 227611

NORTH DAKOTA
Motor Vehicles Dept.
State Office Building
ninth and Boulevard
Bismark, N.D. 58505

OHIO
Bureau of Motor Vehicles
P.O. Box 16520
Columbus, OH 43216

OKLAHOMA
OK Tax Commission
Motor Vehicles Division
2501 N. Lincoln Blvd.

OREGON
Motor Vehicles Division
1905 Lana Ave. N.E.
Salem OR 97314

PENNSYLVANIA
Dept. of Transportation
Motor Vehicles Bureau
Harrisburg, PA 17122

RHODE ISLAND
Registry of Motor Vehicles
State Office Building
Providence, R.I. 02093

SOUTH CAROLINA

NEW YORK
Motor Vehicles
Registration Records Section
Empire State Plaza
Albany, N.Y. 12228

TENNESSEE
Motor Vehicles Div.
Information Unit
Jackson Building
Nashville, TN 37242

TEXAS
Dept. of Highways
Motor Vehicles Division
40th and Jackson
Austin, Texas 78779

UTAH
Motor Vehicles Dept.
1095 Motor Ave.
Salt Lake City, UT 84116

VERMONT
Dept. Of Motor Vehicles
Montpelier, VT 05603
Oklahoma City, OK 73194

VIRGINIA
Div. of Motor Vehicles
Box 27412
Richmond, VA 23269

WASHINGTON
Dept. of Licensing
P.O. Box 9909
Olympia, WA 98504

WEST VIRGINIA
Division of Motor Vehicles
1800 Washington Street, East
Charleston, W.V. 25305

WISCONSIN

Dept. of Hwy Public
Dept. of Transportation
P.O. Box 7909
Columbia, S.C. 29216

Vehicles Files Transportation
Motor Vehicles Division
P.O. Box 1498
Madison, WI 53707

15. TITLE TRACE SOURCES

We are including only changes from HOW TO GET ANYTHING ON ANYBODY;

ARIZONA; Title, registration, tag. State of Arizona, Department of Transportation, Motor Vehicle--Record Division, 1801 West Jefferson Ave., Phoenix, Arizona 85007.

CALIFORNIA; Title, registration, tag. State of California, Department of Motor Vehicles, P.O. Box 2747, Sacramento, California 9995812.

FLORIDA; Title, registration, tag. State of Georgia, Motor Vehicle Unit, Department of Revenue, Atlanta, Georgia.

HAWAII; (808) 955-8221.

ILLINOIS; State of Illinois, Secretary of State, Sixth Floor, Centennial Building, Springfield, Illinois 62756.

LOUISIANA; (504) 925-6353, 925-6268. Title, registration, tag. $4.00. State of Louisiana, Department of Public Safety, Vehicle Registration Bureau, P.O. Box 66196, Baton Rouge, LA 70896.

MICHIGAN; Title, registration, tag. State of Michigan, Department of Public Safety, Driver and Vehicle Services, Lansing, MI 48918.

MISSISSIPPI; Title, registration, tag. State of Mississippi, Department Motor Vehicle Comptroller, Title Division, P. O. Box 1383, Jackson, MS 39205.

MISSOURI; Title, registration, tag. No fee. State of Missouri, Department of Revenus, Motor Vehicles Bureau, P.O. Box 100, Jefferson City, MO 65701.

MONTANA; Title, registration, tag. No fee. State of Montana, Registrrrar's Bureau, 925 Main Street, Deer Lodge, MT 58722.

NEBRASKA; No fee. State of Nebraska, Department of Motor Vehicles, 301 Centennial Mall, Lincoln, NE 68509.

NEW HAMPSHIRE; Title, registration, tag. State of New Hampshire, Department of Public Safety, Division of Motor Vehicles, John O. Morton Building, Concord, N.H.

UTAH; No fee. State of Utah, State Tax Commission, Motor Vehicle Division, State Fair Grounds, 1905 Motor Avenue, Salt Lake City, UT 84416.

WISCONSIN; Title, registration, tag. No fee. State of Wisconsin, Department of Transportation, Division of Motor Vehicles, Bureau of Registration and Licensing, Hill Farm State Office Building, Madison, WI 53702.

WYOMING;   Title, registration, tag. State of Wyoming, Department of Revenue & Taxation, Motor Vehicle Division, 2200 Carey Avenue, Cheyenne, WY 82002.

SPECIAL SOURCES, GENERAL PURPOSE

A look at some very helpful sources that just don't fall into any particular category.

1.   THE INTERNATIONAL ASSOCIATION OF CREDIT CARD INVESTIGATORS
1620 Grant Ave
Novato, Ca 94947

The international headquarters for this organization. They are sort of a liason between credit card issuers and law enforcement organizations.

A very professional newsletter is issued to members detailing new frauds, anti-fraud techniques and devices and other news of interest to anyone who deals with plastic money.

They have branches all over the country (and some overseas), give seminars (average attendance 300) and provide data to both the enforcement people as well as the credit card companies themselves.

As of this writing, membership IS LIMITED TO FULL TIME EMPLOYEES OF CREDIT CARD COMPANIES OR LAW ENFORCEMENT PERSONNEL.

They DO NOT let private detectives nor security people into membership as of this writing.

According to the executive director, Mr. Drummond, this policy may be subject to change in the future.

2.   NATIONAL ASSOCIATION OF PRIVATE INVESTIGATORS
2320 North Lincoln Ave
Suite 111
Altadena, Ca 91001
Tone access number # 818-577-0005

A PI that also operates a free (to other investigators) nationwide computer referral service that allows one to access the exact sources one needs; polygraph operators, PI's, electronic surveillance, writing analysis, security, credit card fraud people, process servers, lawyers etc.

If you have a background and a specialty he will also include you free in the listings...

The data is very specific and covers all background information as well as hourly charges etc.

Also provides low cost phone company data including CNA updates for a set fee (I believe about $12) per year.

3.   TELEPHONE AREAS SERVICED BY BELL AND INDEPENDENT CO'S
        NTIA Report 82-97
        US Department of Commerece
        National Telecommunications and Info Administration
        Office of Policy Analysis and Development
        Boulder, CO 80303

A report, including maps of which company services whom and what within the amazing, albeit broken, AT&T system. Invaluable to anyone using CNA or DPAC type, ah, jokes...

4. If you are tracing anyone without luck and suspect your target may have ever used the services of a bail bondsman (and who hasn't?), simply call up a few bail bondsman in the city where the target has resided. Tell the guy your target has listed him as a reference, and that you too are a bail bondsman, and ask what offense your target was bailed out for, where he is living etc.

Most "brothers" will be more than happy to help.

5. Newspaper morgues. In-house libraries of any news makers from the past...Usually limited to reporters working for the paper itself, but a good con job as a reporter from another town and/or buying some underpaid reporter a couple of drinks will get one access to a pile of information.

6. Banks: In How To Get we explained how to get information from a bank once YOU KNOW WHICH BANK TO CONTACT. Now to find out this juicy tidbit is to place a call to the target himself and claim to be from the local electric company.

Explain this is a courtesy call before you (they) turn off service to the target's house.

This will elicit a response to the effect of "you son of a bitch, I paid you in full on the last bill".

"You did? Well it's probably those damn computers again (implying they screw up on a regular basis), what bank was the check written on and what was the check number if you know it? If not, just give me the bank and the branch and I'll have this matter taken care of personally."

And you will...

7. More Banks. Two other useful ideas are simply to mail the lucky target a check (one can even use a certified check, but it takes a little longer to access) and a polite note on "your" business letterhead apologizing for the overcharge and issuing a refund check.

When it is cashed, as it will be, simply look at the bank and account number of the person who deposited it...

Another method is to sue, in small claims court, the target for anything. $50 for his dog eating your strawberry plants and then subpoena his bank records.

The county clerk will gladly issue the subpoena...

8. Credit Bureaus. These are still good sources and the methods we mentioned still stand EXCEPT many, many computer hackers now have passwords for TRW and access it freely. It may be cheaper to use a friendly hacker than to bribe a member or join.

Also realize many credit bureaus do not cross state lines with their information so be certain to try every state your target may have operated in...

9. Driver's License. Same methods work, see our list of updated addresses; HOWEVER another clever trick for those of your who don't have the word processor up and running yet, is to call the state headquarters for said license and simply claim to be the owner of said...you are following all semi-legal language, aren't you?

Good.

Anyway, you are John Doe and you demand to know why you just received a notice of suspension on your driver's license.

The underpaid, bored clerk on the other end will want to know your full name and date of birth.

Of course you have this by now...

The clerk will run a computer check and announce your license is not being suspended...

You will cleverly respond with the fact that they probably are suspending yours instead of some godless child molester who has run over six people what address do they show you at...

With luck you will get a response....

Be sure to always thank underpaid, helpful clerks, it builds good karma and clears the path for the rest of us...

And, as my dear departed grandfather used to say, be thankful it is them instead of you...

10. Dead Licenses. Most states belong to an organization known as the Driver's License Compact and trade information on bad folks, people with drunk records and so on.

Texas, in their spirit of "fuck you" (they don't subscribe their banks to the Fed either, no bank numbers on the checks, no guarantee) will not trade any information.

If no trace can be found any where else, try Texas, a number of skips have figured this scam out.

11. Special Sources, more...The ones quoted in How To are still good, add:

> DATA RESEARCH, INC.
> 3600 American River Drive
> Sacramento, Ca 95825
> 800-824-8806

for getting driver's license info and some other background facts.

12. Mail. Sometimes this works, sometimes it just don't...To get a post box owner's address go to the box window and demand to know why "your" box hasn't been closed, like you asked last month, and the mail forwarded?

Of course there will be no such record.

Well maybe the mail is being sent to the wrong address 'cause you sure as hell ain't getting it and it ain't in the box. What address do they have you at?

A smart clerk will ask for id; a lazy one won't...

SPECIAL AUDIO SOURCES

> DOV INDUSTRIES, INC.
> 41-23-Bell Blvd
> Bayside, New York 11361

A sister company to the SURVEILLANCE VAN CORP OF AMERICA, they specialize in design, and custom design of surveillance equipment. Free consultation for your needs, in both audio and visual surveillance.

Special sources come and special sources go, some are open to anyone, some are closed to almost everyone, but most offer services that are difficult to obtain anywhere else.

NATIONAL ASSOCIATION OF LEGAL INVESTIGATORS
303 N Shamrock
East Alton, Ill 62024

A closed society strictly for licensed investigators that spend most of their efforts doing investigations for attorneys, either for the DA or for the plaintiff.

They publish a newsletter which is professionally done and offers a number of tips on accident and general investigation procedures. They also publish a directory of members for people requiring their special services.

$35 a year dues but they WILL check out all applicants as to truthfulness of application...

FINGERPRINTS; FINDING, HIDING, AND TRANSFERING

The last few years have brought about amazing advances in fingerprint technology. True, most have been in the line of finding and identification, but where there is any technological advance there is usually a counter advance not far behind...

First let's look at an interesting super method for bringing out those bothersome latent prints that just don't show up with the usual methods of print gathering.

This technique really works and is good for investigators, cops, or, well, or anybody who likes to gaze into swirls and ridges.

In the past any light coating of oil, say gun oil for instance, has pretty well destroyed any prints that may have been on the surface in question. If the oil didn't remove the prints, mixing any commercial latent print powder onto/into the oil resulted in an artistic mess which bore no resemblance to anything any crime lab or court wanted to see.

It is also interesting to note most city police forces simply do not have the time or manpower to even attempt to take prints after anything less than an out and out murder and will usually only do so to placate an irate homeowner rather than for any chance of a matchup.

It is possible to now do a superior print job without the help of any offical agency or lab.

The idea behind this process is that a chemical group known as cyanoacrylates will react with the amino acids found in latent prints. This process must take place in a sealed area and for a set period of time.

Left to its own resources this process can take up to six months to actually develop visible prints.

Luckily a couple of catalysts have been found to speed up this reaction time.

Where does one secure a reliable cyanoacrylate? Any form of "Super Glue" or "Crazy Glue" is usually a cyanoacrylate. If in doubt check the label.

The easiest way to utilize this process seems to be to take a large glass jar designed for use as a terrarium or to use a glass fish aquarium.

Inside the container place a light bulb (plugged into a socket with the wire running out the top) of 100 watt rating. Now run a picture-hanging type wire across the top of the aq/ter and line the bottom third of the container with reflective (aluminum) foil.

A final non-flammable holder must be fashioned out of wire in order to suspend a small metal cup about 4-5 inches above the light bulb.

Into this mini cup place 2 drops of glue for every gallon capacity of your tank (a five gallon tank would take 10 drops).

Now hang (no pun intended) the evidence from the top wire into the tank.

Seal the edges of the tank with fiber tape (or duct/gaffers tape) and turn on the light. In a few minutes the tank will fill with white fumes indicating the start of the process.

Any prints will be completely developed within 45 minutes. The ridges will appear as white lines which can then be treated with any commercial fingerprint powder and lifted with tape.

It is a good idea to include a oven type thermometer to gauge temperature. The process seems to work well at or about the 200 degree (F) mark.

It may be necessary to reposition the bulb or use a dimmer switch to maintain this range.

When you open the tank do not breathe the fumes, let it all clear before attempting to remove the prints.

This process has brought out prints on everything from glass and metal to cotton sheets! Sometimes a flashlight will help highlight the white prints.

Another method is to skip the heat (light bulb) and substitute cotton pads you have soaked in a solution of 30 grams of sodium hydroxide per quart of pure water.

Once the pads (say 2 inch squares) have dried the glue can be added directly to them and the process repeated without the use of the light bulb.

Time required is about the same as the other method.

One advantage to this system is one can dry the pads and then use them on short notice inside a plastic bag or jar at short notice and in non-lab situations.

It is also possible to purchase commercial pads/cyanoacrylate systems from:

Dura-Print Box 210116 San Francisco, Ca 94121

Price is in the $200 area for 150 tests.

AUTOMATIC RECOGNIZATION AND STORAGE

The FBI alone receives about 22,000 fingerprint cards daily, each accompanied by a request to identify. They keep a full time staff of 500 people to classify the cards so they can be fed into the computer for possible matchups.

The process of entering a fingerprint into a computer is an analog to digital conversion that requires quite a bit of computing power. This fact limited it to the FBI and other unlimited funds agencies until your friendly micro-computer appeared on the scene with its amazing speed and number crunching ability.

Normally an electromechanical process is required that lets the computer "see" the print much like a high resolution camera would. The digital resolution of a print can be as much as 1000 by 1000 elements within a one inch area.

After the computer "views" the print an algorithm method converts the print to a computer sentence (a numerical storage method consisting of a series of 1's and 0's).

The agency then usually assigns a Personal Idenification Number (PIN) to the print. The PIN number can, of course, be cross referenced with any number of other files or data banks.

The price for this entire process, hardware, software, conversion device, is slowly but surely dropping into the $2000 price range, thus letting almost anybody with a bit of cash have a lot of fun.

The modern computer's ability to match prints is nothing short of phenomenal, even so by its very requirements it creates certain problems that did not exist when the system was entirely manual in operation.

The sophisticated electronic equipment is very critical of the quality of the print it is required to "read". This means a high quantity of cards are rejected every day because of either poor technique in the orginial technique or because of poor printing stock.

While this creates some advantages for persons wishing to NOT have prints recognized for some reason or another, which we will get into a bit later, the FBI is gradually attempting to solve this problem by asking departments to switch over to inkless printing.

In this method a ceramic pad that has been saturated with a chemical is employed. The operator, who needs no special training, has the "victim" roll his finger over the pad where it becomes coated with this chemical and then rolled lightly over a coated card where a permanent black print appears.

The pad is reusable forever and the developer can be applied to any kind of paper stock thus allowing a high quality print on good paper that the machine can read almost every time.

Government agencies, security departments and police departments are being advised to switch over to this inkless method.

As a further inducement it is cost comparable to the present system and less messy to boot.

Another joy of future technology.

FINGERPRINTS; MESSING UP, OF :

The time worn method of wearing gloves is still the best way to insure that one does not leave one's spoor where one does not wish to leave one's spoor.

Cheap plastic surgical gloves can be purchased at any good pharmacy for a mere pittance which allow one to feel almost everything and yet still leave no visible prints.

Leather driving gloves are another good bet.

Wiping of prints still works, in most cases, as does a quick spray with WD-40 (destroys the surface tension of fingerprint oils on any prints you might have missed).

However, new LASER print detection technology will bring out almost any latent print on almost any non-friendly print surface including cloth...

At the moment this wonder laser is priced in the $20,000 range; thereby out of current reach for smaller police departments, or at least usually employed only in heavy cases in the departments that foot the heavy bill involved.

Don't bet your life on this however...

So, be safe, not sorry.

If you know you have to be fingerprinted for a certain task, say getting a driver's license for instance, it is possible to take a product sold in drug stores called New Skin (used as a skin covering or "make a bandage", this was actually the first plastic ever invented).

New Skin can be used to block out, repeat or just mess up parts of a fingerprint. Of course, if an astute technician looks at the print he will notice some thing amiss.

When was the last time you had an astute technician when applying for a driver's license?

FINGERPRINTS; TRANSFERING OF.

It is, and has been, for some time, possible to transfer fingerprints, i.e. is to leave prints of someone who was not actually on the scene.

One method to do this is to buy a commercial product known as Aqua-Seal at skin diving shops. This product is a repair sealer for neoprene wet suits and is available wherever fine wet suit repairers are sold.

A light coating of this sealer can be brushed on any finger and allowed to dry. Then repeat the process until an even coating is spread over the finger in question.

As the final coat becomes tacky (about 5 minutes on the average) place someone else's finger carefully on the coating.

Remove and let dry.

If performed correctly a nice imprint of the other print will be left in place of yours.

This print will now appear in dust, stains, or perhaps most importantly in ink.

Make you take a fingerprint record for a driver's license? Have to leave prints for any, ah, minor court appearance in which you may have just, just slightly altered you name?

Want prints of someone who was a thousand miles from a certain scene to appear on the scene?

Just dozens of fun uses...

RESEARCH BY THE NUMBERS

Many detectives, private and otherwise, have picked up on a trick long employed by writers....

When a famous spy novelist wants to know how many elephants Mr. Hun took over the Alps, or how long Cassanova's third leg was, to make his next Great American Novel strickly realistic, he does not take up a suite at the New York library on a monthly basis, he hires a research specialist.

Some "specialists" are simply college students with time on their hands, some are professional firms that have access to many data bases across the world and know how to go about getting any fact, petty, pretty or otherwise...

Some of these researchers can actually come up with more information than a good detective simply because they know how and where to look..

Some detectives simply use their services and then double the charge to you, Mr. customer....

Let's look at on of the best in the business:

INFORMATION ON DEMAND
PO Box 9550
Berkeley, Ca 94709
800-227-0750 (in Cal 415-644-4500)

For 15 years has been digging up the goods on virtually ever subject one can come up with for almost any customer one can....

How do they work?

For pay...On a $75 an hour basis IOD will come up with any information that you require including:

Competitor Info
Credit Reports
Bibliographies
Industry Surveys
Legal Material
Marketing Material

{atent Services
Technology reviews
and on...

In a few days they can usually tell you what you want to know, or how much it will cost...IOD uses private researchers, libraries, worldwide data bases and anything else it takes.

They will work with a set "stop fee" in advance in case things look like they are getting out of hand or advise you as costs rise.

The only stipulation is they will access ANY public data base or talk to anyone who WILL talk to them.

They will not employ underhanded methods to dig out info from sources that wish to remain "unsources".

On the other hand that's why you bought this book right?

If the info you need is easily available, even in a private data base or another country this is a quick, cost effecient method of access.

Other such sources are available through public and private (including college) libraries, although one sometimes has to press a bit to get them to dig for you.

PASSPORTS

Let's skip right over to the biggie; passport forgery. No document in the world allows so much access to many things; with a visa it let's one cross international borders with relative ease, it is positive id for cashing checks or just chatting with the police...

Passports are designed to be difficult to forge because of the importance placed upon them. In spite of this, passport forgery is increasing at the rate of 12% a year...

The average passport is checked for 60 seconds whenever a person arrives at any international passport or immigration area. This does not constitute enough time for a through search.

Note this is the average, any information on any computer, such as the "Watchdog" can demand a further search...

Most governments issue three types of passports; regular, offical (or service) and diplomatic. Anyone traveling on non-government business should receive a regular passport.

Official passports are issued to lower government officials as well as senior elected representatives.

Diplomatic passports are for officials with a high government status such as ambassadors and consular personnel.

However some countries will issue diplos to lower officials, senior business personnel or even students studying overseas...

Governments can and do also issue passports to non-citizens. These are usually for residents of countries being "protected" by the host country and are known as a laissez-passer or alien passport.

All passports usually consist of 32 pages that are stitched and glued to a cover. The paper is special and usually printed with a visible background and may also contain an "invisible", or ultraviolet design.

It is also possible to imprint the second design as a watermark.

"Fugitive ink" is usually employed; if any water or stress is applied this ink will run badly.

285

The inside first cover is usually imprinted with some message of safe conduct, the inside back cover will be printed with warnings about that passport.

Reasons for false passports vary from people with criminal records wishing to enter/leave the country, people bringing in some exciting souvenir(s) that the government does not approve of, so they do not wish to appear to have come from a country that sells such items...

Any well dressed man or woman, coming from a country that is NOT on the DEA's hot sheet has an excellent chance of passing through customs without even a minor search.

Profiles have been computer prepared of possible smugglers and, although the courts have ruled them illegal, are still used by customs to spot potential trouble makers.

These profiles include country of origin and destination, weight of luggage carried upon departure compared with return weight, if payed in cash (a big * on the giant computer in the sky), dress code, hair length, snakeskin boots, etc...

Forgery

A number of methods are employed in passport fakery:

Get a real blank passport and fill it in with whatever you wish.

Get a real valid passport and print copies IF YOU HAVE ACCESS TO THAT TYPE OF TECHNOLOGY.

Do the paper trip; get a phony birth certificate and apply for a real passport.

Some people attempt to remove the photo and signature on a real passport and replace them with their own. This is usually done on passports that do not laminate the photo area.

On US and other laminated versions one can carefully use a razor to cut through the laminate around the photo and signature. The photo emulsion layer is then peeled back and soaked off.

Now the criminal inserts the new materials and sets the original laminate back into place. A clear layer of laminate is then applied over the entire area. This has worked quite a number of times over the years.

Another popular idea is to take out entire pages and substitute them from one passport to another. This is a bit easier than it used to be as many countries no longer perforate every page with the passport number.

One can cut the binding stitches, leaving them in the passport and then reuse (usually glue) the original bindings back into place with the new pages.

Some people will dunk the entire document in acetone for a moment or use a steam iron on the inside covers to expose the binding stitches. The original covers can then be wrapped around any new inside...

Typed areas can sometimes be changed by using a super sharp razor to lift off the original typing, or by using sticky tape or IBM lift-off typewriter tape and then retyping over the original area.

This method will usually show up when exposed to UV light...

The watermark on these pages provides a nice method of exposing falsies. Fake watermarks can be printed in pale ink but will flouresce under a UV check light showing the forgery.

A better method is to a page is coated with ink that matches the original color of the document except for the area in which the watermark will appear.

Now the forger uses a slightly darker color of ink is used to "shade" the watermark in on the paper while another sheet of opaque paper is shaded with blank areas for the new watermark and the two pieces are glued together it gives the impression of a real watermark AS LONG AS THE MARKS ALIGN PERFECTLY.

In this procedure the paper used should be half as thick as the normal page so the glued thickness will seem normal.

An even better method is to use three sheets, printing the mark on the middle sheet so it does not have to match anything...

In 1980 an international group met and suggested all countries adopt machine coded and readable passports. If and when adopted this will allow a computer to read the coded imprint in a second or two while the customs official visually compares you to the photo and signature.

Expect it soon.

Another cheery fact is that the army and the treasury departments are now, even as we speak, testing a device which provides identity verification by electronically scanning a subject's hand and comparing it with stored computer data.

This scan compares finger length, curvature and thickness of the webbing between fingers.

ID TRICKS

INTERESTING I.D. NOTES from Barry Reid, author and publisher of the two classic books on "alternate identification", THE PAPER TRIP I and THE PAPER TRIP II. (Available from Eden Press, P. O. Box 8410, Fountain Valley, CA 92728. Prices are $12.95 and $14.95, respectively.)

The job of creating a new identity complete with government- -issued documents is not terribly difficult, but should always be accompanied by knowledge not usually found in bookstores and libraries. There are many details and techniques a person should be aware of before he proceeds. The purpose of my books, THE PAPER TRIP I and THE PAPER TRIP II, has always been to present conveniently this kind of information.

After numerous revisions, however, I still receive letters asking for more details on changing identity. While the books continue to speak for themselves, I will cover here some of the areas which have produced the most questions. Please don't regard these observations as some kind of quick summary or overview of the books themselves, however. Rather, they should be considered more detailed explanations of some of the "problem area" found in paper tripping.

BIRTH CERTIFICATES

We can no longer regard the use of a deceased infant's birth certificate as very secure due to the possibility of someone else's having already used it, or using it in the future. Using a name for which the birth and death occurred in the same county was never advisable, since an investigator who suspected such a practice would naturally look first in the county of birth to locate a possible death certificate. Names for which birth and death occurred in different states can be considered reasonably safe since there is still no interstate cross-referencing of birth and death certificates. For that matter, there is almost no intrastate cross-referencing, either, since most states do not wish to fund such projects. Only some of the most populous counties have made such efforts. To find out if that has happened in your county, simply call the Vital Records Clerk and inquire. Finally, even when such projects have been started, they have extended their stamping "DECEASED" on birth certificates to only a few years back.

The only way using a deceased infant's birth certificate could result in a bust would be for someone to use it when applying for a U.S. passport. If someone else had already obtained a passport with that birth certificate, the Passport Office will definitely be aware of it, and will instruct the F.B.I. and postal inspectors to apprehend the applicant when delivery is made. The person who first used the birth certificate will naturally come under suspicion, too.

Probably the best foundation for a new identity is to adopt a new name out of thin air. Begin using it and apply for a new state ID in that name. In no state does a person HAVE to go to court to change his name legally. Open use without intent to defraud is basis enough for a name change to be legal. Women don't go to court to have their drivers licenses changed to their husband's surname when they marry, they simply request a new drivers license in a new name. Men, likewise, can achieve the same thing without going to court to obtain a "judgement" or "declaration" of legal change of name. People just have to insist on it. If a person DOES obtain court-sanctioned change of name, there will be absolutely no resistance later on when changing other ID and records to the new name. The common law gives us the right to call ourselves by whatever name we choose, so long as we do so without intent to defraud or deceive others.

A minor will almost always have to present some form of proof of age/birth before being issued a drivers license or state ID card. A person who still LOOKS like a minor may be required to do the same. A person who is not obviously still a minor is almost never required to produce a birth certificate, and usually any other form of ID is sufficient. Most states rely on the "penalty of perjury" statement they require applicants to sign before being issued drivers licenses or ID cards. This means that the state takes your word that all the information you supply is true and correct to the best of your knowledge; no proof of age or identity is actually required. It's always easier, however, in dealing with bureaucrats, if someone already has some documentation with the new name on it, such as mail, receipts, library card, business card, out-of-state ID, voter registration, or even some form of mail-order ID card. In the best Paper Trip tradition, "Give them the paper they want, and you'll get the paper you want".

A person can disappear very efficiently and effectively from a particular state's files by first securing a new identity in another state. A Californian, say, who goes to Oregon can obtain an Oregon State ID card or drivers license (either of which are issued "on the spot" thanks to the Polaroid process), can return to California and present the new ID to secure new California ID in the Oregon name. California will not be aware that the person was once someone else; the assumption will be that an Oregonian has simply moved to California (there's a twist!),and that the name he presents is the name he was born with.

Some states make a practice of confiscating out-of-state ID when it is presented to obtain new ID. A person can always call the agency first to see if this is the case. If so, the out-of-state ID can simply be kept in one's pocket. It will be enough to SAY that one has, or had, out-of-state ID, but that it's become lost, misplaced, etc. If the ID number can be , a telephone/computer inquiry can settle the matter in minutes. The out-of-state ID will be preserved for possible future use, and the new state ID will then be issued.

SOCIAL SECURITY

A question often asked is how to convince a Social Security clerk that a person who is obviously now an adult has never obtained a Social Security number (SSN) until now. Because the SSN has become a de facto universal identifier, it is seemingly "inconceivable" that a person could have been living without one. But there really ARE some possible answers!

He might explain that he is working for the first time, and needs the SSN for his employer's W-2 form. If a person has never needed to pay taxes, he would never have needed one. He could have been institutionalized (prison, mental hospital), a student studying abroad, someone living off a generous inheritance, a missionary serving his church, or simply living in a self-supporting ("survivalist") way in the country or woods. He might allude to having been a hustler for cash, even a professional criminal, but now realizes it is time to "join society and pay taxes". A person with a believable explanation, despite his age, can still get a new SSN. It always facilitates matters, however, if he can show documentation which indicates he's been that person for some time.

People should remember that almost all requests for their SSN are not required--or authorized--by law. Just because an insurance company, a doctor's office, hospital, or other agency asks for it, doesn't mean they are legally entitled to do so. People who object to this practice will often make up spurious numbers, or refuse to provide their SSN, demanding instead that the particular agency prove by regulation established by law that they are entitled to use the SSN. (Real "experts" will demand the section citation of the Privacy Act of 1974 which exempts the agency and thus allows it to obtain SSN's. The mere mention of a specific piece of legislation is enough to make some bureaucrats back off. Try it sometime!

The SSN has become the most important identifier in computer files, along with names and /birthdates. Individuals who alter these three elements in their records when they fill out new forms are actually creating lots of instant electronic privacy for themselves. To prove the point, a person could make up a totally fictitious name, with presumed /birthdate and SSN, and begin using it in harmless, unofficial ways. It will be a quiet pleasure observing how fast it becomes a "real person" solicited daily by a growing volume of mail offering anything from free photography to new credit cards...

FINGERPRINTS

The thumbprint now taken by many states on their applications for drivers licenses is an absolutely worthless practice from the law-enforcement standpoint. It works from the psychological viewpoint, however, because people THINK, or fear, that it can trip them up, and that its real purpose is to catch fugitives, imposters, etc. (With over 40 million Americans having arrest records and the fingerprint documentation to prove it, the "fear" component is very real!) First, a /thumbprint alone is not enough to identify someone from the F.B.I.'s system of classifying prints. They consider /thumbprints essentially worthless, and do not accept the state-generated variety for classification. What do the states themselves do with them? NOTHING, either ! They are simply filed with the applications. They serve as a form of "psychological deterrence" to those who might otherwise make light of their applications for drivers license or ID card.

People who genuinely object to the practice, however, make sure that the state will receive an absolutely worthless print by using a couple tricks. They will already have made their thumb's surface oily or greasy, and when the thumb is placed on the paper for printing, they will press harder than the clerk does and also make a slight twisting movement. This produces a very smudged print, indeed. Since few clerks are trained in proper fingerprinting technique, they will not notice that the print is now a useless smudge and proceed to file it with the application. People who object to their /thumbprints being taken when they cash checks use similar methods to guarantee a zero trail.

Thanks to modern chemistry, it is now possible to cover prints and/or leave different ones intentionally. Several different methods are explained in THE PAPER TRIP I, but one goes like this:

A product called "New Skin", sold in all drug stores along with /bandaids, etc., can be sprayed or brushed onto clean fingerprint surfaces. It will "tack up" in about 10-15 seconds, and prints from the opposite hand, or toes, can be rolled into the tacky surface. Even if the person's real fingerprints are already on file with the F.B.I., a new classification will automatically result because of the way identifying characteristics are counted. The new classification will not reveal the original prints, since the new prints are not only reversed, but can be made out of natural order (first finger rolled onto third finger, etc., etc.) A person who intentionally wants to leave prints of a misleading nature will make tiny needly holes in the "New Skin" prints so that the natural oils can emerge. The new print will stay on the finger for at lease a day.

Perhaps the ultimate advice on fingerprints is to avoid situations and circumstances in which they are taken or required. If a person can't do this, however, it's good to know that fingerprints CAN be altered convincingly.

One more trick: It's quite easy to create a full set of "lay-away" prints for future use. "New Skin" can be sprayed onto fingers and toes that have been coated witha very light oil. Once the "New Skin" has dried it can be lifted and peeled off with tweezers. The new "skins" can be glued later onto clean finger surfaces with Super Glue. All the resulting prints will be reverses of the originals when glued into place, with no chance of being classified the same as the originals. The marvels of modern chemistry!

PASSPORTS

Only 14% of Americans ever own a passport. Those who do obtain one and use it for its usual purposes should realize that the Customs people are now compiling computerized records based on each border-crossing "transaction". These records will soon be interfaced with IRS records, Justice Department records, and any other agency's "wanted" list that seeks out foreign travelers simply because something is "suspected" of them. The end result will be a very active form of surveillance of U.S. citizens who exercize their rights to travel.

It is never advisable to apply for a U.S. passport under a false name. People who think they HAVE to do this are not thinking through their real needs. What they actually want to do is travel and return to the U.S. What they usually don't consider is that they can do this without having or using a U.S. passport in the first place. There are several ways of accomplishing this:

1. It is perfectly legal to "walk across" the borders into Mexico and Canada with no ID at all. This may not be advisable, but it can be done. It's best to carry at least a drivers license or state ID card. Customs agents can tell as soon as you speak whether or not you were born in the U.S. If there's ever any doubt, regular, state-issued ID does the trick.

2. Once across the border you can make arrangements for foreign travel. You can THEN use your legal U.S. passport for visas, if necessary. You will not have to worry about a Customs agent's viewing your 37 Colombian visas the next time you return to the U.S., since you will be walking back in--as a "weekend tourist", or perhaps as a guest on board someone's boat returning with the Sunday afternoon regatta from Bermuda.

3. Once out of the country, some people make arrangements to buy or obtain foreign passports. (Foreign trade officials and attorneys often have "cousins" who can be most accomodating...) They then travel on the foreign passport as non-U.S. citizens.

4. Travelers who use these methods take extra cautions to protect their ID once they return to the U.S. They will rent a safe deposit box in the foreign border city, or have a foreign attorney guard the documents for them. They know it would never be advisable to cross back into the U.S. with "other" documents in their possession.

5. Americans can enter and return freely--without a passport--from Mexico, Canada, Jamaica, Cayman Islands, Bermuda, Bahamas and most of the other Caribbean countries. Once in these countries, it is often possible to cross into still other countries depending on prevailing legal conditions. A very helpful book along these lines is INTERNATIONIAL INVESTING ($9.95 from Eden Press), by Doug Casey. Despite the title, the details of foreign passports, expiration, extradition, and just plain "moving around" are well defined. It's the only book of its kind.

CONCLUSION; If your use of a U.S. passport would be likely to cause unwanted interest in your activities, consider not using one at all. Americans are not sophisticated travelers, as a rule, and don't know that much of the rest of the world regards "flags of convenience" a normal operating procedure. In other words, they realize people sometimes need to "make arrangements". It should follow from this that, once abroad, it may not be necessary to have a passport at all: some ID from your temporary "home" country can be enough to get you across still more borders. And, just for the record, folks, the Paper Trip works overseas, too!

MAIL ORDER ID CARDS

A recent federal law has greatly affected the suppliers of ID by mail. If a card carries a person's birth date or age, it must also have on both the face and back of the card, in not less than 12-point type, the legend 'NOT A GOVERNMENT DOCUMENT'. The makers of these cards do NOT have to apply this legend if the card does not carry a birth date or age.

At Eden Press we offer ID cards with a signature box over the space where birth date would normally appear. The resulting card looks very professional, and does not have to carry the above legend. Of course, we still make "birth date" cards, if ordered. At only $6 per card, they can make great back-up ID.

For a complete list of books from Eden Press, send for their free Book Catalog. Address is P.O. BOX 8410, Fountain Valley, CA 92728.

BLENDING IN ON PAPER: ID'S

Every society demands certain paper verification of its members. If you ain't got no card, you ain't...

We in the US sometimes forget how easy we have it in this area. No internal passports, loose laws about having to carry id, very little attempt to follow one's movements by computer tracing a person's paperwork.

It does get a little more tense when you leave/enter the country, but once you are here, you are here...

Most other countries are so much more strict in their paper tracking it surprises Americans the first time they run into this situation.

Years ago a man named Barry Reid "invented" a system of finding the names of people that had died at a young age and then asking for a copy of their birth certificate and using this document to add to other id and "become" the person.

It worked.

The show 60 Minutes went through the process on the air with Barry to show how easy it was.

Congress got pissed off, formed a committee (what else?), spent a fortune and produced a huge book about defeating this method of being swapping.

Barry put out his next book explaining how to get around their book...

Anyway, most birth and death certificates are now cross referenced so this is NOT a hot idea any more.

At least in the US.

Canada is not quite up to our level yet and most other countries do not even try to match the two papers up.

There are also cases of court houses in small towns burning down and losing all birth/death records... These claims must be taken at face value...
The rough piece is the social security card. Getting a fake one is easy, but a real one under a new name is hard. Why haven't you had to work in the last 26 years?

If we do ever have an "internal passport" it will be based on the SS number.
Still there are a number of ways of changing one's name and proving papers. Some will give you a complete set of fake ids that will pass trial up to a certain level.

The trick is knowing that level...

Other methods will give you "real" id in someone else's name.

Why go into this at all? Remember the ninja specialized in "fitting in" for espionage purposes and information gathering. Many of you may find, at one time or another, this ability to become a chameleon very useful.

It is not even necessarily illegal IF NOT USED FOR FRAUD. Again, cop out, however, this is up to you to find out.

In no particular order let's look at several ideas:

FAKES

A whole industry has sprung up around the sales of documents that look offical, but really are not. Most of these firms simply take a photo, supplied by you, and information, also supplied by you from a mailer and using the standard Poloroid card making machine, ship out an id card.

These cards often attempt to stay within the fine teeth of the law by not claiming to be any specific id, although they may have the name of a state imprinted in bright red letters at the top of the card, they never actually claim to be an offical state id.

Furthermore they will say something like "all information herein certified true per original application".

Meaning they typed what you sent in correctly...

These firms come and these firms go, depending on market and government harassment. There are several directories of them on the market and I will list a few at the end of this section.

Other companies provide id that looks damn, damn, close to the real thing including government driving permits, international driver's licenses, gun dealer permits, company id, student id, etc.

Is this legal?

I'm not sure. However the best I have ever seen is/are produced by:

RICH Suite 148
828 Royal st.
New Orleans, LA 70116

He has done several of the above for me and they are real, real good...

Of course enclose an SASE and a buck or so for a catalog on any of these.

PASSPORTS

A passport is the ultimate id, good anywhere. Passports ARE entered into computers when you enter/leave most countries.

Some airlines will help provide info to various government agencies. They automatically let the gov know where you've been and for how long, making it much easier to decide upon how complete the enterance search should be, where to look for bank accounts, etc.

Getting a "different" passport can be tricky, the government really doesn't want people to know exactly how much checking they do before issuing this document.

Of course, one little computer entry means instant arrest if you are wanted for any reason and attempt to flee these hallowed shores.

Or come back to them.

The fact that some people really, really would like a new passport has opened several capitalistic outlets.

One legit country has decided to bolster its income by simply selling citizenship.

Costra Rica, will, for a small fee, make you a real live citizen of a NEIGHBORING COUNTRY. Of course they require support documents, but these can be a bit, ah, less demanding than the US would require.

One must travel to the neighboring country to get fingerprinted and pay the final fee upon issuance.

The fee? $15,000, I think a diplomatic passport can be arranged for a slightly higher, small fee.

If interested:

El Punto Costarricense S.A.
PO Box 90

Paseo Estudiantes Costa Rica

One person who has got to be thought of as one of the world's real entrepreneurs, has formed his own country.

Really.

After searching maps, charts, legal documents and hiring an airplane, he found an area of the world that no country had claimed as its own.

A free space on the old monopoly board.

The founder, one Ralph I (formerly Otto Hubner) there upon named his country the Principality of Castellania.

It was founded in 1974 and issues stamps, marries people, graduates interested parties from the University of Castellania, and even issues press passes.

The offical language is german and they do issue passports which are officially recognized by about 10 countries and by another 100 "de facto".

This is possible even in the US as they are registered as some sort of agency like the Red Cross (which can issue sort of passports).

They have an office in the US, which is lucky because Castellania is under water during high tide, making doing business there a rather tricky proposition.

Their fees are a bit more in line, however, becoming a passported citizen is only $145.00.

Info is $3.00, passport application $5.00. I do not believe the US honors this passport at this time.

> Principality of Castellania
> PO Box 40201
> Pasadena, Ca 91104

It would be interesting for someone to take a trip to South America or Africa, where countries are changing names every few days anyway, and see if your passport would be honored...

Not interesting enough to go to jail for, however.

In 1948 the United Nations passed a Universal Declaration of Human Rights which was to be respected by all member nations. This article, 13, 11, was designed to let certain organizations, such as the Red Cross to issue passports to displaced persons.

Many refugees from WW II and even Nam have entered the US and other countries on one of these passports.

An organization known as the World Service Authority issues passports and birth certificates to anyone under this still standing UN declaration.

They have issued 50,000 such passports already. Many of these documents have gotten people into countries where they could apply for citizenship.

This is NOT a US nor UN document. It does NOT guarantee a visa or entry anywhere although, many countries, including the US have recognized these passports.

Some nations may grant visa rights on the passport, some may do it on a case by case basis, some border guards may wave you through, some may not allow entry, some consulates may act the same way.

However, for the $230 fee it is an offical document that helps establish human rights in much of the world.

> CRITICAL
> Apdo. 311-1002 PE.
> San Jose, Costa Rica

You do have to fill out an application which includes a fingerprint and photos.

MONEY AND JOBS

Opening bank accounts in "safe" nations, like the Cayman Islands and Switzerland is risky. The Swiss will often help the US government if they feel a legal reason exists and the Cayman's seem to be crashng down around our ears right now...

At the very least a mail cover will provide reason for warrants or other action.

An interesting alternative is provided by:

> THREE R'S Ltd
> Box 242
> Station M
> Toronto, Canada MGS 4T3

For a $50 fee they will open and maintain a bank account in any name you so desire (plus a minimum $50 deposit), in NY or Canada.

For $30 they will become your last employer and provide job references.

Good ones, one must presume...

DO IT YOURSELF

It is also possible to make your own id's by taking a piece of white cardboard about 3' long and 2' high and using press-on transfer lettering, or having an artist friend carefully print the logo and necessary support information in the correct size on the board, and then leaving a place for your FULL SIZE head shot photo to go, shoot it yourself.

It is also possible to take a photo of a real id of any sort, and have it blown up to this size by a "poster photo store" and then cut out the original personal photo leaving a head sized blank space.

In either case the party in question mounts the board/blow up on a wall at head level, stands before it and has a friend take a photo, usually with a poloroid, of the entire affair.

This will produce a one piece id with no obvious alteration.

Some people prefer to do the id at one time, the head shot at another, and then glue the two pieces together.

Use an SLR camera and have the photographer adjust the distance to place everything in the proper size.

PAPER

There comes a time in every man's life when he must destroy some written record, be it a list of friendly bettors on the local horse track, a number code master sheet, or simply a list of phone numbers the FBI or one's wife has taken a sudden interest in.

Luckily a couple of instant-sure fire techniques do exist. As in astrology each method represents a earth, water or fire sign.

Earth: Bury it.

A small joke, there is no earth in this particular idea...

Water: Most novelty and/or magician supply stores stock a type of water soluble paper.

This stock can be written on with pencil, pen, blood, whatever, and will retain the scratchings forever.

Except, if one places the sheet in water it dissolves IMMEDIATELY, if not sooner.

One can even type on this type of paper, and the quick loss factor could well save one's hyde...

Fire can be used if sheets of paper are soaked in a solution of potassium nitrate and then allowed to dry. The sheets will function as normal paper until a flame is touched to any part of the paper.

When this occurs the paper will burn completely in a fraction of a second, leaving almost no ashes.

Used by bookies for years this is known as flash paper, and is also available from magic supply stores.

MAIL COVERS

Another interesting privacy invasion is the establishment of a mail cover.

This beast is simply an arangement whereby the interested party (usually an officer of some sort or national security type) views the OUTSIDE of every peice of mail addressed to you and records the available information.

This may not seem too threatening at first. What can be dangerous about simply reading the outside of an envelope?

Plenty.

In tthe past this practice has traced down wanted people, given the IRS free access to any bank account one may have, anywhere, revealed illegal deposits in foreign (read Swiss) banks, allowed grounds for warrants to arrest the addressee or at least open his mail, and so on.

Mail covers are governed by a very different set of laws than are mail opening warrants. As you would suspect they are much easier to establish both within and without the law than are other types of surveillance.

There are numerous methods of setting up a private mail cover ranging from the simple version of physically intercepting the target's mail, copying down the information and putting in back where it belongs, to filing a change of address forwarding the target mail to a mail drop you have set up with a false id, opening and reading, or just recording cover information and then sending it on in a new envelope with forged writing, to making friends withsomeone in the post office...

The enclosed page is copied from the book that is the last word on this subject;

THE POSTAL MAIL COVER
Alternative Technologies Information Service
61 Gatchell st.
Buffalo, NY 14212
$10.00 or
from us (CEP) same price....

This book explains the techniques of covert covers, mail reading, and using the laws to stop same from happening to you.

POSTAL COVERS
PUBLIC RECORDS

An index of all public records is kept at USPS headquarters library, 475 L'Enfant Plaza, West, SW, WASHINGTON, DC 20260 .

Everything about you including your own address is a record and disclosure must comply with the DMM, ASM and federal regulations concerning disclosure.

YOUR ADDRESS CAN ONLY BE DISCLOSED TO THE PUBLIC FOR THE FOLLOWING REASONS:

1. If you file a change of address, your old and new address are public knowledge available for a small fee ($1.00).

2. If you use a bulk mail permit or imprint the permit information is public information available for a small fee.

3. If you use a P.O. Box for business purposes or if it can be proved that one advertises using a Box as the address, the information on the Form 1093, "Application for Post Office Box or Caller Number" becomes FREE public information. proof of advertising is simply that the requestor show an ad or circular with the Box listed on it. ANYBODY could go to a typesetter and have a bogus circular drawn up and then walk into the Post Office and demand access based on 352.44. There is no requirement that the requester identify oneself and it appears that a record need not be kept of such a disclosure.

4. A.P.O. Box holder's's address and other information for Form 1093 can also be disclosed for the following reasons:

   a. To ANY government agency upon written certification that the information is required for performance of its duties. (All they have to do is sign a statement they need the information for routine use. However, if they are lying--they have violated the F.O.I.A. or Privacy Act. The requesting agency will be in trouble and the USPS will have covered themselves.)

NOTE! Agencies are only allowed to request information necessary and relevant to the performance of a duty specified BY LAW. The disclosure records leave a paper trail back to the agency requesting. 1. Appeals may obtain the records released and 2. Further F.O.I.A. inquiries of the requesting agencies employees' papers and records may find that the information was requested ILLEGALLY not for routine use.)

b. To a person empowered by law to serve legal process upon WRITTEN CERTIFICATION that the INFORMATION IS REQUIRED TO EFFECT SERVICE.

This I believe is a possible violation of the 4th Amendment and the Privacy Act. What if the information required to effect service doesn't pertain to the person to be served a subpoena or summons, but a relative or friend? Besides, most offices don't require written certification. They may 1) give it to a person who identifies oneself as a process server over the phone. Sometimes they simply give the information out to one who presents himself or shows a business card. A real hardass will ask to see the court papers. But it appears that NOBODY ever requires prior written certification. The rule simply isn't enforced hardly anywhere. (Hang 'em out to dry).

c. In with a subpoena or court order.

d. To a law enforcement agency after PRIOR ORAL APPROVAL made by a Postal Inspector that it involves a criminal investigation.

ANALYSIS; Note that in all probability all of these written certification requirements ARE NEVER MET. The employees are usually ignorant of the DMM ASM regulations and will give out information to any government agency that requests it even over the phone! Process services can often also get information over the phone by identifying themselves or simply walking in with a business card. Violation of these requirements is a violation of the ASM and the Privacy Act and the employee involved is liable for administrative discipline, civil litigation and possible criminal prosecution.

5. The mailing address of a person a court wants to locate for jury service can be given out as public information upon prior written request by the court.

6. If the location of a residence or a place of business is known to a Postal Service employee, whether as a result of official duties or otherwise, the employee may, BUT NEED NOT, disclose the location or give directions to it. No fee is charged for such information. If you take delivery of mail, anybody who wants to find you may very well find you through the post office simply by asking. Think about it. If you want to know where somebody who has a box lives, don't ask for the box information. Simply walk in and ask the folks at the desk if they know where the person lives. He's/she's an old buddy you haven't seen in a long time and you forgot the address, but they live in the area. Make up a good story. Most people have their P. O. Box close to where they live. If one has a phone number, but no address the general area can be located by the first 3 numbers by calling the operator. Next one goes to the local post office and asks at the desk.

I have covered the basic rules of disclosure of business, residence and P.O. Boxes. As you can see you have almost no privacy, but with regard to boxes one can hang a postmaster of employee out to dry legally if one wants regarding disclusures of Box information (PS Form 1093) in many instances.

There is a lot of other information available concerning the disclosing of information pursuant to F.O.I.A. and Privacy Act requests. These are too enormous for this report. You can obtain them by looking up the appropriate sections listed above in the ASM at your local post office.

The above article was copied, word for word, from POSTAL MAIL COVERS, by P. Adams and is available from ALTERNATIVE TECHNOLOGIES or from US (CEP).

I cannot over-emphasize the importance of this publication for anyone who receives mail with the express permission of the US postal service...

MAGIC MAIL

In How To Get Anything Lee showed how the average snoop could actually use a chemical (liquid Freon) to read through envelopes by making the paper transparent for about 30 seconds...

We are now going to go that extra step we are known for and tell you an even better trick.

Or at least an update on this trick; the best, quick acting see-thru chemical we found is:

FREON TF
Chemtronics
Hauppauge, NY 11788

Sold in most electronic supply stores for the cleaning of contacts, circuit boards, etc., for a couple of bucks, this 97% pure Freon TF will turn any envelope as clear as glass for about 30 seconds, allowing the contents to be read, and then dry without leaving any trace.

Another Chemtronics product; DPL, also will render paper totally transparent. This effect lasts for several minutes BUT will not dry up completely unless a very thin layer is sprayed on the package in question and mild heat is applied to speed the drying process.

If too heavy of a spray is used it will simply not dry up, but remain transparent forever and ever...

If you want to try this approach practice in the safety of your own home first...

Another trick for actually opening mail without leaving a trace is to inject carbon tetrachloride (common chemical, used for typewriter key cleaning) under the flap of an envelope.

This will dissolves the glue quite nicely thank you, allowing the flap to be opened, the letter read and then the flap is re-glued back with none the wiser.

Best believe beloved, federal, state, county and private agents are using this version of mother nature's gifts every day.

SEE NO EVIL, HEAR NO EVIL

CHEMTRONICS electronic degreaser that let's one view thru any envelope for a good 30 seconds and then goes away without any footprints.

Available from any good electronics dealer.

POLAROID's ultrasonic ranging system that let's anyone play bat and "see" in the dark.

Accurate, versatile distance measurement in air or other gases.

Polaroid's Ultrasonic Ranging System, which provides automatic focusing in thousands of SX-70 Sonar cameras, is finding increased use in a wide range of commercial, scientific and industrial applications. Here's what makes the system unique:

Accuracy. Detects and measures the presence and distance of objects within a range of 0.26m to 10.7m (0.9' to 35').

Sensitivity. Senses objects as sound-absorbing as foam-rubber, and as small as a flower stem.

Compactness. The system represents a vast improvement over conventional sonar devices in terms of size as well as precision. It weighs just 26gm (0.95oz) and measures a sleek 9.3cm x 4.7cm x 2.4cm (3.7" x 1.8" x 0.9")

THIS AD SAYS IT ALL.

Buy a unit for those of you who want to read through mail (a "postal mail cover!"), or wrap your valuables in lead foil if you are on the other end of the idea...

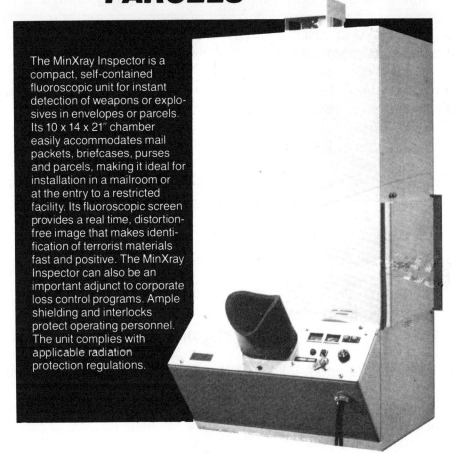 

NO PEEK

Now that we have shown you how to read mail which is probably none of your business with the help of chemical tricks you may begin to wonder if someone else (most likely a legal agency) is doing the same nasty thing to you...

Maybe. And they have the advantage of offical sanction, including post office help, if they are doing it with a warrant. This is NOT to infer they always do it with a warrant...

How to combat this invasion of privacy? A couple of ways, starting with the easiest and working up to the more difficult.

To combat the see-through chemical treatment simply wrap your inner letter in a non-paper lining, i.e., aluminum foil or poster board.

To prevent the use of fluoroscope or even x-ray devices lead foil must be employed.

Now one must suspect if one of these electronic see-through devices shows a lead barrier chances are very good that the letter or package may then be opened to see what the problem is.

Can one protect the package from curious voyeurs?

No.

However one can establish if a sealed container has been violated.

Which is almost as good...(Just for the sake of conversation if you receive an illegal shipment in the mail, drugs, surveillance equipment, bodily parts of an ex-wife, you are NOT in trouble until you open the package and then DO NOT turn it in to the "proper" authorities.)

Under present laws there is no way to prove you knew what you were receiving until you see it and then retain possession.

The first and easiest method is to place Scotch tape over the sealed edges INCLUDING THE CORNERS ON AN ENVELOPE, and then write something in your handwriting across all the tape. With this method any break in the tape will be hard to reseal without notice.

The next method is almost foolproof, albeit a trifle more involved. To accomplish this, purchase some sealing wax of several different colors.

This is usually available at "better" office supply stores.

Think back, this is what they used in days of old, knights of round tables and such, for the exact same purpose. The king, duke, or other noble type sealed his royal decrees with wax and then pressed his personal seal into the wax, making it hard to open and reseal without distorting the seal.

Today's technology does make it possible to do this...

So? Simple, melt and combine at least 2 different colors of wax and let the resulting art deco swirl drip onto the seal and corners of the letter/package in question.

Now take an instant color photograph of the color scheme and INCLUDE IT in the middle of the letter or in a separate letter.

It is very, very, hard to duplicate a random color swirl pattern after steaming or melting it in order to open the correspondence. Of course, one should also sign the photo with a certain color ink to prevent substitution of wax and photo...

The last method is new and quite secure. Born from the need to seal evidence collected by law enforcement agencies so nobody (remember the French Connection?) could borrow or alter said evidence without leaving a trace, this product can also be utilized for postal protection purposes.

Called Tamper Guard and sold by Becton Dickinson, 1720 Hurd dr, Irving, TX. 75062, this super sticky plastic tape has a number of advantages.

It is made from a tough tear resistant plastic dyed red. The dye is such that almost any solvent (used to loosen the glue) causes a bleed in the tape.

If someone attempts to peel the tape off it will rip several layers of paper. The edges are serrated to reveal any tampering attempt.

We have tested this product and if you encircle a package sticking the tape to tape it is damn near impossible to remove or alter without leaving an obvious trace.

This product comes printed with such phrases as; "confidential, to be opened only by addressee, secret, do not remove this seal," or,"security seal."

A large, 108 foot roll (you just can't need more than that) runs only $13.50.

Sticks to paper, cardboard, metal, plastic, and so on.

LEGAL ALTERNATIVES TO CARRYING
AN ILLEGAL GUN

In the sunshine state (California in this case) it is a felony to possess a set of nunchacku, it is a misdemeanor to carry a loaded, concealed pistol...

However, in some states, such as New York, one can pull a life sentence for carrying a pistol.

Oh Ms. Justice how you do differ from time to time and place to place...

Many of the weapons we have discussed are "arm's length" weapons; good against a knife or similar device, but what in hell can equal a gun in stopping/killing power and still be legal?

Modern technology rears its ugly head once again.

By combining different fields and sciences it is possible to equate the power of a gun; after all guns are some 500 years old, its about time we came up with something else...

For years the CIA has been rumored to have a totally electric pistol that shoots poisoned darts for close in, instant kills.

This has not been offically verified (or deined) but many people have experimented with the idea of a constant electromagnetic barrel that would pull a steel "bullet" down the barrel as the electronic field shifted position, finally spitting the projectile out the end with consdiderable force.

Most efforts to duplicate this effect have failed.

Is that how the CIA dart gun works?

THE BLINDING LIGHT

Ninja of old used any advantage in a contest to gain a second or two, this time was used to run or strike.

The ninja had several methods of blinding the opponent at close range. Often small blow guns filled with eye irritant would be suddenly shot into the enemy's face.

This could be something as simple as pepper (which is still used today in a number of "tear gas" guns) or could be a complicated smoke screen/irritant combination.

Other favorites were to empty an egg, fill the hollow shell with the chemical and then add a wax plug to keep it all together. A couple of eggs tossed in the right direction could gain quite a bit of time and confusion.

And could mean death for the enemy, or escape for the ninja.

It still can.

We will go into chemical and electrical stun/stop ideas elsewhere but there is one totally harmless device one the market that will give anyone that little, necessary edge...

The unit is sold as a "laser-like stun device which will "bleach the retina of the eye for a short time giving the user a chance to escape (or attack).

The idea is simple and it does work BUT do not pay more than a few bucks for it or make your own.

All the device does is set off all 4 flash bulbs in a common flash cube at one time, usually with a flashlight type reflector to "aim" the light burst.

If you have had one flash bulb go off directly in front of your face you can easily grasp the idea of 4 times that flash...

It ain't goin' kill anybody, but on the other hand it does take a few minutes for the old eyes to recover enough to cause any real help to the rest of the body...

Negative part of the idea is that you better have the unit out and ready to go BEFORE things reach that point of no return.

If you draw for the old flasher and he draws for the old 45...

You lose...

However if you suddenly let loose a blinding flash of light at an unsuspecting recipient it will give you time to follow up.

If you have made a mistake and just blasted your spouse sneaking up on you, no permanent damage has been done.

Also works on people teargas will not...

PINS AND NEEDLES

A number of possible offensive and defensive weapons that are both deadly and available fall into this genus.

HYPOS

The common hypodermic needle is legally available, without a perscription in the US. It can contain any liquid from drugs to poison, is easily carried and easy to use...

The device can be discouraging or deadly, depending on what it contains and how it is used.

The hypo, sans needle, can be used to squirt liquids (i.e., formaldehyde) into an attacker's face with an effect that makes tear gas seem lame by comparison.

With needle it can contain anything from vinegar to the above mentioned formaldehyde to cyanide or other poisons.

The unit must be carried in a safe fashion as not to drip out dangerous contents and still be brought into action at the proper moment.

If a small guage needle is used with a non-oil chemical it is possible to inject someone so that no notice will be taken of the injection, especially if the target is distracted by a quick step on the toe or slap on the back.

KURT SAXTON in his fine newsletter, THE WEAPONEER, designed a more sophisticated version of the hypo loveingly known as the fang...

More Go

Propelled needles are one of man's oldest weapons. When a thin projectile is propelled by a strong enough force it takes on some unusual characteristics...

One of the more unusual weapons is the blow-gun. This is simply a hollow tube equipped with a mouthpiece and darts.

Utilized by many native types around the world, a good blowgun will spit a dart several hundred feet and stop, or kill small game.

The range and stopping power of a blow-gun is determined by the length of the barrel along with the design and caliber of the projectile.

Most "modern" blow-guns come in a take down arrangement that allows for several different barrel lengths by simply sticking the tubes together.

Blow-guns can be made quite easily but they are so cheap it is usually easier to purchase one.

Unless, of course, one lives in California where everything is illegal...

The darts are usually assembled by the blower out of stiff wire and plastic beads. This system works but the higher priced dart with a small plastic cone increases both range and power considerably, be certain to purchase a number of these extras...

Tricks

Darts, arrows or bullets can be treated in a number of unsportsmanlike ways to increase their effective stop rating.

An oft used way is to bend the tip of the dart back about 1/4 of an inch and then sharpening it with a grinder. This barb will make it very hard to pull from anything's flesh.

If one is employing a separate point simply wrap it on the wire shaft with scotch tape so it will imbed as usual, but will separate in the target's tissue when the dart is pulled backwards.

This will leave the tip deep in the target's flesh.

These suggestions are even more effective if the darts are posioned...

To make a poison dart it is best to have more surface area than the usual wire dart affords. This can be accomplished by cutting a coat hanger into four inch lengths, pounding the tip flat with a hammer and then filing two notches part way down the tip and directly across from each other.

This forms a sharp, broad point that will contain a fair amount of poison and be difficult to remove.

Now if the wire is cut in half just aft of the tip and the two units taped together one has a real poison dart...

The tip can be coated with a number of substances from riacin to cyanide or rat poison to psychotropic drugs.

The chosen compound should be secured to the dart with common mucilage, a substance which will bind it but still allow the compound to be released into the victim.

If the compound (like cyanide) is subject to moisture the darts must be wrapped in some sort of airtight wrapping such as a plastic sandwich bag prior to use.

Any blow-gun thusly equipped is a silent, deadly weapon of high accuracy and fair range. A short practice period will allow the user to pick off beer cans, or other offensive objects, at 60-100 feet with every shot.

Most targets will not become upset at the prick of the dart, writing it off to some idiot...

Capture Darts

Vets (as in animal, not 'Nam) employ special darts that contain up to several cc's of liquid (usually a knock-out compound) and have a power head to inject said contents upon arrival at the target.

These darts are normally propelled by a CO2 or blank .22 charge.

For our purposes it is possible to modify a commercial hypo dart to be kicked out by a blow-gun, arrow, cross bow or slingshot.

Of course, the original gun can also be utilized.

We have listed the best supplier of these items; CAPCHUR EQUIP...

They also supply the knockout chemicals...

Fletchettes

As mentioned elsewhere, these small, finishing nail size finned darts achieve fantastic speeds when propelled by a gunpowder charge.

When utilized in Beehive shells in Nam these darts cleared a path through the enemy often pinning their weapons to their bodies.

SGT SANDY carries fletchettes designed to be loaded into a shotgun shell whereupon they will shread a bulletproof vest or destroy almost anything in their path.

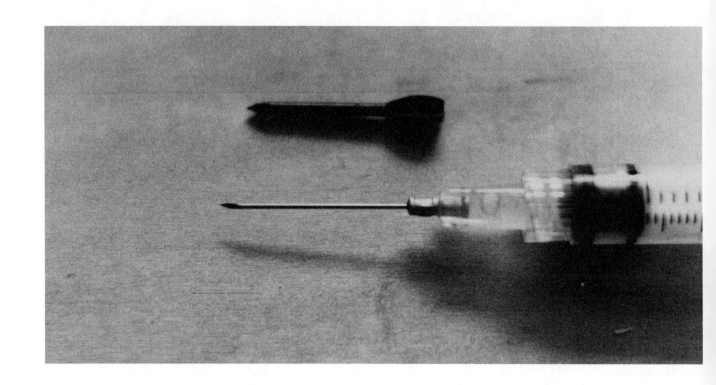

TWO DEADLY POINTS AND ONE EAR

A flechette lying above a common hypo needle. The flechette is the type used in our Nam cluster shells and as such should be coming on the surplus market.

The ear is a "Hunter's Ear", this one of the Double Farfoon variety that survived our trip through the jungle.

GREAT WESTERN
1709 Girard Blvd, N.E.
Albuqueruqe, N.M. 87106

XLR CAP-CHUR KIT FOR ANIMAL CONTROL DEPARTMENTS
EXTRA-LONG RANGE (POWDER) PROJECTOR
(FOR DOG CONTROL)

IS PROJECTOR HAS AN EFFECTIVE RANGE OF 60 YARDS AND IS RECOMMENDED
R DEPARTMENTS IN RURAL AREAS OR IN COLD CLIMATES.

 i Extra-Long Projector with adaptor, practice syringes, positioner and instructions
 2 Power Loads   (.22 Blank Loads) 50's   (1) Very Low (1) Low
 1 Jar Plunger Lube
10 1cc Syringes complete with NC1 Nose Plugs
 2 2cc Syringes complete with NC2 Nose Plugs
 2 CAP-CHUR CHARGES 50's   1cc-3cc
 1 2cc Hand Syringes (for measuring solutions)
 ~~1 CAP-CHUR SOL.   30cc Bottle~~   30   ~~10 pound dogs~~
                                              15 pound dogs
                                              20 pound dogs
                                              25 pound dogs
                                               0 pound dogs
                                               0 pound dogs
) pound dogs
                                               pound dogs
                                              ~~pound dogs~~
                                     ...g,.cc for 95 pound dogs
 ~~1 SOL.   30cc Vial (For Humane Death of Animals)~~
 1 Case for Extra-Long Range Projector

(handwritten, overlaid:) We will notify you when these drugs are available. In the meanwhile, perhaps you may want to consult a veterinarian for possible alternative drugs.

We regret any inconvenience this may cause you.

CAP-CHUR KIT FOR MEDICATING AND IMMOBILIZING CATTLE

GREAT WESTERN makes the best animal immobilizing equipment and drugs available. They sell three systems for short, medium and long range injection of any liquid drug. Thre first two systems, starting complete at $125 are CO2 powered, the long range rifle (not shown) utilizes a .22 blank.

Their syringes, whether shot from their weapons or not, range in size from 1cc to 15cc and inject their contents as soon as they pierce the skin of the target.

GW also sells various knock out serums for different sized animals. or you can inject your own selection.

INJECT IT

A very interesting series of weapons involves placing one or more chemical compounds underneath the skin of a target.

For years the various intelligence agencies have used hand held hypos or gas injection systems to knock out, irritate, or kill their counterparts across the fence.

A simple hand held doctor's hypo will allow the sudden implementation of a variety of substances into the muscle tissue of anyone who wanders within arm's length of a properly equipped reader...

There are several more sophisticated versions including Saxton's "Fang", a interesting spring loaded injector designed by Kurt Saxton.

In order to extend your threat zone range some sort of proplusion system must come into play. One of the best is borrowed from the role of "Wild Kingdom", you remember where they were constantly shooting carefree animals with hypo darts loaded with some form of tranquilizer in order to render them helpless long enough to implant some sort of transmitter or camera to record the number of times Mr. Elk paid a conjugal visit to Ms. Elk's bedroom...

Talk about violating something's civil rights....

Anyway, a specially prepared "remote injection weapon", such as the one we looked at from GREAT WETERN SERUM CO. will throw an aluminium hypo dart up to 60 yards with very little sound or effort and chemically inject your favorite chemical into the target in one fell swoop.

GWS makes a couple of models including a CO_2 powered pistol and a C_ _red rifle that will toss the magic dart 13 and 35 yards respectively.

These weapons shoot a 1-3 cc hypo and come complete with all n_ ssaey pieces and carrying cases for $125 and $225 and do NOT require a license of any sort...

For those extra special operations, they also make a .22 blank powered rifle that tosses the dart up to 60 yards with fair accuracy and checks in at $275.

This latter unit does require a firearms control license prior to ordering.

What do you load your new toy with?

Any liquid from vinegar (which causes extreme pain when injected but will not kill) to animal tranquilizers which will knockout a horse in a couple of minutes to poisons which, well you get the idea...

In the good old days I knew of a couple of folks who used to use a hollow pellet arrangement to inject a drop of pure LSD into their favorite victim.

Made for an interesting day or two.

Great Western even sells knockout drugs for animal control if you are not creative enough to think up your own version.

Our old friend, SGT. SANDY offers an alternative to the low powered, light weight hypo dart; he (they) sell a 12 guage shot insert that will throw a heavier model dart even longer distances...

ELECTRONIC WEAPONS

The days of Buck Rogers may be here for the US and Russia with charged particle beams that can reach out from space like some god driven raygun and zap missles before they get out of their silos, but few people realize that, on a smaller scale, even you and I can play Star Wars.

In the last couple of years several electronic weapons have appeared on the market. At least three different types of technology is involved with the new toys, but they each have the same end result in mind.

To incapacitate an attacker, and several of them do it damn well.

NOVA TECHNOLOGIES
13470 Research Blvd Bldg O Suite 1
Austin, Texas 78750

NOVA has pioneered the first cheap, practical electronic weapon for anyone. Known as the XR-5000 it is a hand held, plastic bodied, stun wand.

It is a capacitor discharge type weapon that throws 50,000 volts between two probes that are placed 2 inches apart on the front of the weapon.

The current is low, but actually set by the amount of resistance between the two probes.

The unit does not just "shock" the target but actually releases a series of on-off pulses of a certain frequency and duration designed to interfere with the synapse response of human muscles.

When the unit is activated, by pressing the side "trigger" a chain of lightning like arcing crackles between the probes.

When the unit is applied to a human the instant reaction, and I mean instant, is to "freeze" the muscles, causing a "let-go" reaction.

If the target is drawing a gun from a holster when the voltage is ap[plied he will NOT clear the holster. The muscles simply no longer work as directed but are over ridden by the new command.

A short shock of 1/2-1 second will cause this "let-go" effect, hurt, and disable anyone for a short period.

Over 1 second will drop the subject to the ground and 2-5 seconds will produce a very disoriented subject who will not be able to get up under his own power for up to 15 minutes.

Even when the target is able to return to his own power he will NOT feel like fighting.

This is due to some strange medical effect that uses the muscle's laetic acid as if the target had just run a marathon race in 5 seconds. It will leave him physically worn out and mentally disoriented.

Yes, it works. After I got up off the floor, some minutes later, (I swear that SOB not only left it on for far more than the 1 second we had agreed upon, he got a kick out of it as well) all of the above facts seemed very, very true.

This device was designed to replace the use of the classic police come-along choke hold after a number of lawsuits about excessive violence.

It does not exactly produce a come along effect, it produces a carry along effect...

But it works.

The entire unit costs about $65, plus one of three holsters ($5-$20) as well as a recharagble battery for about $20.

The effect works through clothes, including leather jackets and and in the rain. One burst of the arc is often enough to discourage a potential attack from man or beast.

NOTE: IN ALL THESE WEAPONS IT IS NECESSARY TO USE A RECHARGABLE BATTERY. A nive volt type is required and the power cycle of an alkaline will NOT produce the same results.

Also some rechargeable batteries do not produce 9 volts but closer to 7...These should be avoided also, use the one the manufacturer's battery or he suggests.

This weapon is sold to the general public through a number of sources and is probably the perfect defensive weapon except for the fact that one has to touch the target for it to be effective.

TASER A number of gun dealers or: QUALITY CREATIONS 2801 Biscayne dr

Youngstown, OH 44505

The TASER has been around for a few years, so needless to say, it is outlawed in California...Well, actually it is classified as a pistol and falls under the same laws.

Most states still consider it a defensive weapon and allow the average citizen to purchase and/or carry it.

The TASER is a rechargable flashlight with two "pods" located directly under the bulb. Square plastic cartridges fit into these pods and are aimed by pointing the beam at the target.

When the trigger is pressed a small powder charge inside the capsule explodes shotting out two tiny barbed darts that each trail a thin wire behind it.

If either dart lodges into the target (or his clothes) an immediate charge of 50,000 volts (much as the same as in the NOVA unit) is transfered to the target with the same results as with the XR-5000.

The obvious advantage to the TASER is the 15 foot range afforded by the darts. As their are two capsules in the "gun" one gets two shots, or four darts.

Once the dart hits home additional charges can be added at any time by repressing the trigger.

A set of telescopic "rabbit ears" can be substituted for the powder pods turning the TASER into a "touch" weapon instead of a shooter.

The TASER will set you back almost $400.

THE TALON GLOVE

A leather glove with a built-in shock device. The battery pack and power source are strapped to the wearer's wrist and two contact surfaces are placed in the palm of the glove.

When the glove is placed on the neck of the target 800 volts flows between the contact.

This approach tends to freeze the immediate area muscles and provide an effective "come-along" hold.

The device is rechargable and quite easy to conceal.

The TALON sells for $175 ONLY TO LAW ENFORCEMENT PERSONNEL and needs skin contact to work effectively.

THE SOURCE UNIVERSAL SAFETY CORP
12450 Ulmerton rd
Largo, FL 33544

A combination flashlight and shock baton utilizing the same principles as the NOVA.

It well take any suspect, is strong enough to be used as a normal riot baton and provides the "kicker" at one end.

Hard to tell from a regular flashlight, rechargable and sells for $150 ONLY TO LAW ENFORCEMENT PERSONNEL.

CATTLE PRODS-

Various dealers

Lack of control is the problem here; each pulse is a hot shot discharge that can burn skin and may or may not take someone down.

Each shock will cause someone to back off, make no mistake, but each pulse can be severe enough to do real damage or just severe enough to piss someone off even worse.

Usually priced around $50, not an advisable purchase.

BLS1
INFORMATION UNLIMITED-
see suppliers section

An interesting unit, sold as a kit or completed baton this shock rod uses the usual 9 volt battery along with an inversion circuit to build up a hell of a DC (unlike the above units that use AC) charge in a large capacitor,

A sharp, pin like rod extends from the end of the rod to form one pole of the circuit while the circular end of the rod forms the other.

To use the unit one presses a button which causes the charge to be built up in the storage cap. From that point on anything that contacts the two poles will cause the DC, plasma charge to discharge.

With a bang.

In fact the unit, with the correct battery, will punch a hole clean through a beer can.

Believe me this will impress your friends, and enemies...

The sharp point must contact the target, however it will go through most clothes quite easily as well as thick fur.

As in a big dog. As in this damn German Shepard that lived, lived to make my life misrable. Hid behind objects you would never think of a dog being creative enough to hide behind...

One blast of the rod, I even said "go ahead, make my day." I swear I did.

And he did.

And it did...

Note this is not a "come-along" type unit but actually releases a plasma discharge that can burn the hell out of someone and really hurts.

One blast and you would have no desire to repeat the experience without a .45...

Just a demo discharge will stop almost anything dead in its tracks.

The unit is well made and does just what they say it will do. My main bitch is the size, which is about that of a four D cell flashlight.

If it could be made a bit smaller it would be hanider all the way around, but this is a totally different concept and is the best around at what it does.

ELECTRONIC SHIELDS

A device one expects to see Dr. Spock operating; like the legendary force field of tv fame an electronic "riot shield" is a device which sets up a energy line and dares anyone to cross it...

TEC-SUPPORT INTERNATIONAL GROUP
PO Box 8470 STN. F.
Edmonton, Alberta Canada T6H 5H3

Makes a riot shield designed for repeling persons and crowds of persons from a control line or group of officers.

This shield has the following effects:

1 second-person recoils 2 seconds-involuntary muscle contractions 3 seconds-dazed effect, drop to knees 4 seconds-75% immobilized 5 seconds-95% immobilized

Also causes "psychological fear" by using a person's "natural fear of electricity"

How popular will this new crime deterrent become?

The company is now sending out xeroxes of their fact sheet because they have run out of color copies due to the demand.

Watch for it in your area soon...

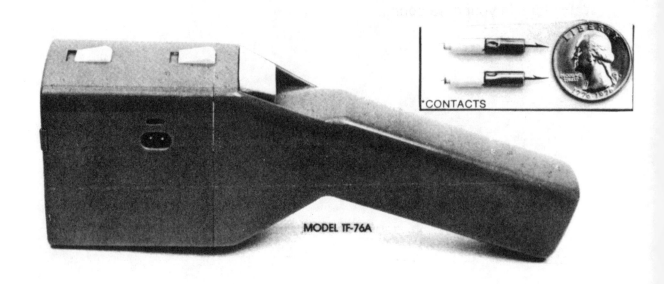

MODEL TF-76A

*CONTACTS

STUN GUNS

A look at the TASER (top) and the NOVA XR-5000 electronic stun weapons.

THE NOVA XR-5000

A FLASH IN THE DARK

A rather unusual photo taken in a dark closet of the BLS1 Electronic Shock rod from INFORMATION UN—
LIMITED at the moment of discharge.

Even with the slightly out of focus art deco look produced by my trying to hold the camera still on a 2 second
shutter speed while touching off the rod on a beer can I couldn't even see, you can see the power of the
plasma discharge as it punches a hole in the can.

Kind of awesome...

SOUND POWER

In the Big Brother Game, Scott mentioned that some countries in Europe use modulated ultrasonic sound to disrupt and "control" crowds and that anti burglar devices were available that would cause the intruder to become physically sick and vacate the premises.

So far these devices are still legal in America, although difficult to find on the commerical security market.

INFO UNLIMITED sells about six kits or ready made devices that use this principle to good effect.

Their smallest unit is just a 9 volt powered unltrsonic generator that produces a mild signal that drives dogs crazy and produces reactions in humans ranging from a bit of discomfort to headaches and vomiting.

I know, I use it in my lectures (Scott).

These units work better on some targets than on others; usually women retain their sense of hearing to a higher degree than do men and may be more affected, but the more powerful units will bother anyone.

I have seen these units used as anti-entry devices in vans and apartments to great effect, I have also seen the French police use them instead of tear gas to break up demonstrations.

I would prefer a more direct weapon if facing one very mad assiliant, but for general use these devices are nothing short of amazing;

They are especially effective if the target does not know they are in use..It seems to become an unbareable pressure inside one's head that simply induces the strong feeling of getting the hell away from there...

FOR RESEARCH AND ACTIVE PROPERTY PROTECTION

IPG5 — INVISIBLE PAIN FIELD GENERATOR — This small shirt pocket-sized electronic device generates moderately intense directional ultrasonic accoustical energy capable of **warding off aggressive dogs and other animals.** Unit is slightly larger than a king-sized **pack of cigarettes** running off of a standard 9-volt battery. Frequency **can** be controlled from 16-21 Khz allowing a setting that produces **maximum** effect on certain target subjects. Care must be taken to **avoid** directing toward people as most will experience intense pain and discomfort from this device. Prolonged use can produce nausea, **eyes** watering, headaches and many other discomforting symptoms.

> **PLEASE NOTE THAT THIS UNIT COULD BE USED TO DISCOURAGE CERTAIN UNWATNED PERSONAL ENCOUNTERS. HOWEVER, DUE TO THE UNKNOWN NATURE OF A PARTICULAR SITUATION, IT IS NOT ADVISED.**

IPG5	PLANS	$ 7.00
IPG5K	KIT	$39.50
IPG50	ASSEMBLED & TESTED UNIT	$59.50

PPF1 — PHASER PAIN FIELD — This device has recently been developed and patented in our labs and is presently being evaluated by state and government agencies for **riot and crowd control.** It is not **available** but soon will come under the jurisdiction of **weapons** and **infernal machine** control, making it unavailable to the public. The device consists of an array of 4 transducers that are powered by a **programmable** source of ultrasonic energy between 10 and 22Khz. Unit **automatically** sweeps between preset limits at a preset programmable rate. Produces a directional field of ultrasonic energy at **125db plus.** Unit is 7" by 7" x 11" and can easily be hand-held similar to a **megaphone.** It can be powered by a 12-volt source such as an auto **cigarette lighter** or internal Ni-Cad batteries. Similar, but more powerful unit is our PCC1 that contains 8 transducers in an array.

PPG1 — PHASOR PROPERTY GUARD — This all new modern device prevents unauthorized intrusion by creating an invisible field of highly **irritating** and **uncomfortable** ultrasonic accoustical energy at high sound pressure levels. Basic unit consists of a centrally located power/frequency controlled oscillator module whose output can be programmed to continually change in tone at adjustable sweep rates. This module feeds 2 to 6 remotely located ultrasonic transducers, positioned for maximum effectiveness of the area in question. The unit can be made to automatically turn on via simple detection circuitry so that an unauthorized intruder entering an area would immediately encounter this pain producing energy field, steadily increasing in frequency to an uncomfortable feeling occurring in the back of his head. System can also be adjusted to produce a high volume audible alarm at the low frequency end for further effect producing the **usual paranoia and intense nervousness** necessary to cause an immediate vacating of the premises. **Frequency limits and sweep times** are easily controlled via the front panel knobs along with an **AUTO/MANUAL SELECTOR SWITCH** that enables either a steady or constantly varying field. System also contains on/off switch, indicator lamp, fuse and convenient connection point for remote control and connection of transducers on rear of unit. Power requirements are about 60 watts at standard 115VAC. Completed unit and kits are supplied with 4 transducers. 100 feet of hook-up wire and all necessary hardware for installation. This system is not to be confused with the motion detectors where low power ultrasonic are only used as a means of sonic radar.

PPG1	PLANS	$ 15.00
PPG1K	KIT	$175.00
PPG10	**ASSEMBLED & TESTED UNIT**	**$250.00**

CROSSBOWS-SILENT DEATH

When it was invented, by a group of engineers and scientists, the best in their fields, it was called the weapon to end war forever.

It was feared by both soldiers and citizens alike, and groups materialized to attempt to outlaw the fearsome device.

Everyone knew, at the very least it was the ultimate weapon, one which would scar the very face of war forever.

And it did.

Sound familiar? It's true; at the time of its genesis the crossbow was as dangerous and as sweeping of a change from the usual means of waging war as is/was the A/H bomb (s) today...

The crossbow was more accurate, shot so much further (than most bows of the time) and penetrated the armor that soldiers came to depend on as the ultimate defense that it altered the course of battles for centuries to come.

For the first time in history a very small force could attack and defeat a larger force simply by the use of a different weapon and different tactics.

It scared the living hell out of people...

Technology has finally come to the aid of this ancient device. Modern crossbows borrow much of their design from rifles, compound bows and steel/nylon materials.

Their advantages lie in quiet operation, accurate shooting, extreme penetration and amazing stopping power.

An interesting experiment is to take a modern crossbow, arm it and shoot the bolt (arrow) into a block of ice. Then take a high powered rifle with a jacketed bullet and do the same procedure.

The arrow will penetrate 2-3 times as far...

Horton Safari Magnum Crossbow- A very interesting bow, imported from England and differing from the local products in several respects.

This bow is constructed from a modern, high impact type of plastic, giving it a very nice power-to-weight ratio. It looks and feels like a rifle, making the learning process quite natural in approach.

Unlike most other bows available the Horton employs a rear "v" notched sight that has range/windage adjustments much like a rifle.

It has no front sight.

The bow, like all the crossbows tested, is a bitch to cock. The Horton includes a rope helper to ease the chore somewhat but the purchase of a cocking lever is strongly advised.

Accuracy is very good. The arrow trough is smooth, straight and well constructed. The arrow sticks well enough to allow the bow to be transported and aimed with no loss of sighting.

The power is sufficient for almost any application and the operation is straightforward.

As one of the lowest priced bows on the market the Horton is a very good buy.

SUPERTECH DEATH

As with guns, bows have undergone many dramatic improvements since their invention. Some of the major upgrades in bows/crossbows have been the re-curve, allowing for a much higher draw weight by forcing the tips of the bow to actaully be drawn back against the natural curve of the bow.

The materials involved evolved from wood to composite space age fibers giving better draw and more consistent power.

The compound bow, using pulleys to redistribute the pull tension (a bit harder at the beginning when your arm muscles come into play and smoother at the end when the muscles are weakest) and provide a smoother, more accurate throw at the release is one of the most important inventions in bowdom.

All of these have been incorporated into the crossbow design.

It is good to look at the realistic advantages and disadvantages of the crossbow as compared to the bow.

A pull strength of X pounds in a normal bow is a fair bit MORE POWERFUL than the same pull in a crossbow because the arrow will be much longer and heavier than the crossbow bolt will be.

Yet bow can take years to master while anyone who can shoot a rifle with any degree of accuracy can pick up a crossbow and become a weapons system.

The bow is faster to reload and may be easier to draw.

The crossbow stays cocked after drawing with no further effort on the shooter's part and allows a greater freedom of movement.

The crossbow has better sights and is more accurate and can be fired from a horizontal position with less position give away.

TESTING

We tested a number of modern crossbows and discovered several interesting facts. First of all:

M&M ENTERPRISES
Special Weapons
PO Box 445
Island Lake IL 60042

Was very helpful in loaning us toys and supplying information. They also seem to have the lowest prices on every model we tried as the owner is very interested in his items and selects what he feels are the best fromt he world over.

We started out with the SCORPION, a conventional wooden stocked crossbow that was fairly heavy to use but did come with a detachable handle for cocking.

A necessity...

M&M also sells a separate cocking rod for use with most bows. BUY IT.

This bow sports a rear peep sight. I didn't like it, too slow in aiming, nice for still targets only.

On the plus side, a cheap, effective weapon.

FOXFIRE

Oh, yes, a steel bowed, hollow framed compound bow with a foot assist cocking lever.

Rear site mounted for right hand shooter (I am left), three pin front site that allows one to preset three range settings with colored coded pins which only need to be aligned on the target to place the bolt exactly there...

Very smooth trigger pull, great controlled release of the bolt.

Very accurate with an almost frictionless bolt release system. We clocked the bolt under full pull at 245 feet per second (using a radar gun). I got an accurate range of 100 yards.

This means a possible killing shot at the length of a football field and/or the delivery of a poison tip (held on with glue) or injectable dart IN TOTAL SILENCE!

Remember, even silenced guns, unless they have a deadened bolt noise and a subsonic bullet make noise.

A bolt is a whisper of death...

BALISTA II

Looks like a skinny crossbow the BALISTA is actually a modified speargun. The "bow" does not provide the actual power, the drawstring runs through two pulleys and then down the length of the unit to provide a long throw in a short (cross section) unit.

Uses a fixed rear sight with a nice cocking idea that actually breaks the unit in half to provide leverage in loading.

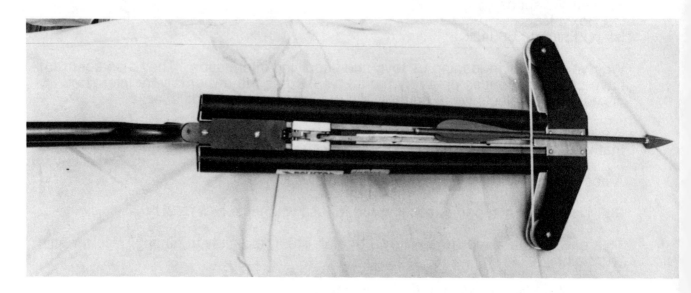

Two Mean Ones

Top is the BALLISTIA, bottom is the FOXFIRE compound crossbow. Both from M&M (see supplier's section). Note the speargun like approach to the BALLISTIA, the power bands actually extend all the way down the side tubes for a longer throw.

Quiet death.

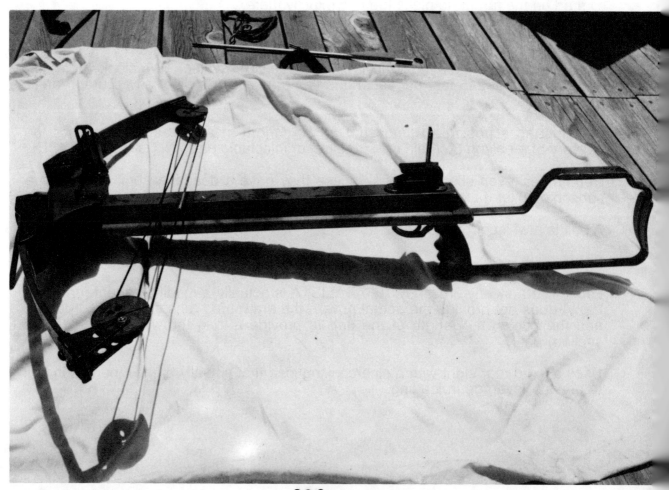

The unit is lighter than the FOXFIRE but not quite as powerful. It is easier to transport , cheaper (about $150 vs $350) and fun but lacks the extreme range of the more expensive units.

TRICKS

A number of tricks come to mind with this unique weapon;

Telescopic sights- Yes, available in 2X-10X ranges. Niether of us liked them. Hard to use, better groupings with the open pin front sight arrangement. Low power model okay but not worth the money,

Arrow dropping units-Available on some units. Great idea, makes re-loading faster.

Cocking aids-Necessary as the strain of loading is hard on the hands and also lessens accuracy of the next shot from frozen muscles.

Night Sights- Oh hell, we jerry-rigged our Univerisal NVD on the Foxfire and I could still pick off anyone at 50-75 yards in total darkness and in perfect silence.

It seems like something out of a fairy tale when the most ultra-modern electronic device can be taped to one of the world's oldest weapons and have the ability to take out a sentry with more deadly power than a million dollar engineered rifle....

Well it makes one wonder.

There is no reason an infrared sight could not have been attached to a CB, we just did not have the time.

Look for light frames, compound arrangements, nylon draw strings, some sort of cocking helper, pinned front sights and good dealer support.

Combined with chemicals and or delivery systems these units make one feel like a certain comic book hero of days past that could do wonders with his magic bow and arrows.

Without Marvel and company behind one...

SLINGSHOTS

Long gone from a child's collection of toys, the modern slingshot can be a potent weapon. From my first Wrist Rocket, a Whammo based weapon that used surgical rubber bands for extra pull and then braced the tail end against one's wrist for more leverage, I have understood the potential of these devices.

I believe that understanding came at the hands of one Sarge Lewis of the Detroit police department.

Bless his scary little soul, wherever it may rest today...

Since then folding models have made an appearance (the Maxima Folder) , sling postols and the best little rock thrower (joke, never use rocks...), the Com Bow Sling.

This latter device looks like a Wrist Rocket type unit but shares some design characteristics with the Balista; the latex bands run around pulleys and down the entire tube frame of the unit giving it much more pull strength.

This unit comes with the standard pouch/pocket arrangement for shooting ammo plus a band that accepts a shortened arrow with a notch cut out directly under its point.

Said notch is hooked over the band and the mini-arrow is fired like a conventional sling shot.

The Com Bow can be equipped with a 30 pound draw weight band (the "hunting band") which allows a 34 inch draw and will send a wooden arrow a powerful 35-50 feet.

Equipped with a razor edged hunt tip, barbed tip, poison, or inject dart it becomes a silent, small deadly weapon.

Note I like this $40 unit better than the $100+ "wrist cross bows" (see any of the Mad Max movies) which simply do not have the necessary throwing power.

Even slingshot ammo has taken leaps and bounds. One can still employ the usual steel ball bearings or even purchase shot shells (paper containers that open up in flight to release a shot spread) to bring down pigs on the wing...

A real weapon.

BEATERS AND BREAKERS

A number of batons and rods are available on the open market. Most of these units collapse into themselves and then opoen with a flick of the wrist.

Sort of like the good old days when you were a kid and you broke off a car antenna to have a fight with a rival gang, oh, well most of you probably didn't grow up in Detroit anyway...

The idea is a good one; the telescopic action provides much leverage in a fairly compact package.

INCO INC
PO Box 3111
Burbank, Ca 91504

Sells several models of batons (most of which are included in our photo) such as the SIPO, BLITZ and NI.

Some copywriter they got, huh?

The SIPO is actually a three sectioned spring that is covered in rubber. One flicks it outward from the 5 inch rod into a 13 inch heavy spring and then whips it at said attacker.

It hurts.

Besides extending your reach 13 inches the whip spring really delivers a stunning blow. INCO says it will not break bones.

Okay, but it hurts..

The BLITZ (6" closed, 16" open) is a bit more lethal and will break bones.

The real toy, the NI is a spring loaded telescopic wand that is made from heavy steel tubing. One presses a spring release and the rod shoots forward to 20 plus inches.

Shoots, forward. I have seen one break a 1/2 inch sheet of plywood. It also has a handguard in case one's enemy has a sword...

If the internal spring is replaced by as heavier model the "punch" becomes stunning indeed. Then, if one, as a student I met at a ninja conference had done, sharpens the normally blunt steel point, it will pierce about 5 inches of solid muscle...

The problem with our hybrid weapon is that in order to close one has to slam the point into heavy rock to compress the spring.

As one would suspect this does the point very little good.

We took a bit of our Friendly Plastic (see supplier's section) and molded a heavy duty slip-on tip to allow slam-closing without tip damage.

Mean device.

The Rolls Royce of these devices is the COBRA wand from our friends at ASP (the pistol people). This baton is used by the Japanese police force and a bit of practice shows the reason...

Perfectly balanced with a strong rubber coated non-slip grip the rod extends instantly with a nice click, locks in place and is very strong.

I could take a house apart with one of these rods. I probably could do the same thing with my hands given enough time, but I would never type a book again...

The ASP folks advise you not to strike bones or vital areas, just tissue...

Right, "here, Mr. mugger, hold out you fleshy tissue, oops, missed and broke both your arms huh?

Sorry..."

A real easy to carry, viable, deadly weapon.

Don't believe me? Read the novel Black Heart...

HANDHELD STOPPERS

Top to Bottom:

1. SIPO from:

INCO PO Box 3111
Burbank, Ca 91504

2. BATON.
M& M ENTERPRISES (address in supplier's section).

3. NI BATON
INCO OR M&M

4; COBRA BATON
ASP (address in supplier's section).

5. KEY HOLDER OR PAPERWEIGHT (brass knuckles).
M&M ENTERPRISES

6. EXTEND—A—CHUCK
M&M ENTERPRISES

See text for reviews and prices.

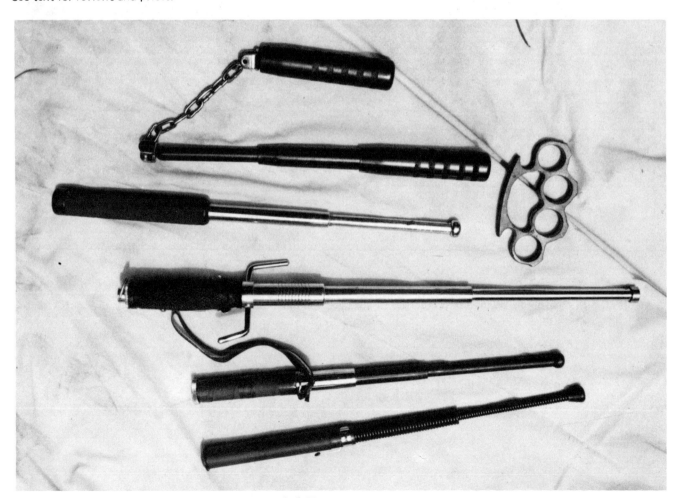

FOXFIRE STEEL CROSSBOW

A nice photo of the camo colored, all steel, compound Foxfire crossbow. Note elevation sights visible at the mean end and windage at the nice end.

Model is actaully Lee in a ninja disguise.

He's got a nice smile, doesn't he?

BLOW IT

Blow guns have been a popular method of death and mayhem for many years in the less "civilized" portions of our world.

They are now coming of age in the era of technological death.

Blowguns are simply hollow tubes with a mouthpiece. A dart of some sort or another fits into the tube and is ejected by a hard puff of air down the shaft.

The range and stopping power depends on the blowee, the fit and shape of the dart and the length of the tube.

It is quite easy to construct a BG from "common household parts" as the ads always say, but they are sold so cheaply it is easier to buy from one of the many suppliers in our delightful book or SOLDIER OF FORTUNE mag..

Except- Be sure your ad says the gun is:

A "take down", meaning the three pieces all fit together to make a multi-lengthed weapon.

Is ALREADY CONSTRUCTED! At least one company sells you a piece of hollow tubing and tells you to get a hacksaw...Real creative..

Order the extra "velocity cone darts"; most darts are simply wire you heat up and stick through a plastic bead. This works but does not air seal as well as the plastic cone dart and the latter even comes with a plastic hunting "razor" point..

By following the instructions elsewhere herein one can razor the darts, barb the darts, detatch the darts or poison the darts.

Commerical drug darts can also be "blown".

Silent, accurate, short range.

KNIVES IN GENERAL

We are going to look at two types of knives herein; survival (utility) and fighting.

In the Rambo movies (First Blood) Mr. Rambo managed to break out of jail sew up a major arm wound, threaten a cop to the point of heart attack, catach several fish, set a snare or two, light a fire, and find his way through the dense forest with a single knife.

Sort of true. The knife was made by:

Jimmy Lyle
RT 1
Russellville, AR 72801

and sells for about $200. It is one of the best hollow handled survival type knives I have ever seen and worth its custom price.

On the low end of the scale is:

THE LIFE KNIFE

This is the one we took to Africa and is the one item I had stolen from my bags during the entire trip..

A nice testimonal.

The LIFEKNIFE may not be quite as custom or the steel may have a trife less carbon but it WORKED. You can see the contents of the survival handle plus sharping stones and steel saw/garrote contained in the sheath.

This may be the best deal on the market for the money and could easily save one's life.

The handle is rugged, the blade good and firmly implanted, the saw teeth work the leather is heavy and blackened.

Other choices in this category are:

FLOAT KNIFE
ALSO FROM LIFEKNIFE

More of a water area weapon, it floats, has rescue flares etc. Same price range.

AITOR JUNGLE KING
PO Box 153505
Irving TX 75015

A bit more sophisticated with a built-in "harpoon" for lashing onto a stick and spearing that damned trout that just won't take the hook, a pair of latex bands and a pouch that converts it into a slingshot, can opener wrench (well, maybe your ATC broke down), etc.

Nice with about the same hardness of the LIFEKNIFE (not too brittle to break, hard enough to saw).

$90.00.

Others are available at every price range but these three pretty well sum up the choices...

FIGHTING KNIVES

Fighting knives differ from utility knives by blade design, blade hardness, handle construction, weight, color, holster and price.

Either can kill, make no mistake.

First of all lets dispel one rumor (that many readers are not going to be happy about my dispelling) do NOT throw your knife.

Do NOT buy a knife for throwing (except to impress people at casual parties). Most knives simply do not have the weight and force to penetrate any sort of medium to heavy clothes and inflict a fatal injury.

And once you have thrown your only weapon, you better pray it inflicts a fatal wound...

If you are really into throwing buy some ninja throwing spikes from one of our suppliers, their added weight helps with stopping power and you get more than one chance...

Fighting knives come in an endless variety of sizes and shapes from custom to common and all work.

If you want to go first class write:

RANDALL KNIVES
PO BOX 1988
Orlando, FL 32802

Mr Randall is known for making of the best custom knives in every shape/usage from sporting to modified Bowies'. His units are one of a kind and he will make them for anyone in a combat situation first, so they may be a bit of a wait, but it will be worth it...

Prices are very good, that being far less than most custom designers such as ANDERSON (also great knives, two year wait for some models) and each model is worth its tag.

Remember you may use a knife more than any other piece of sporting gear, take your time and pick it out correctly.

GERBER KNIVES
14200 SW 72nd av
Portland, OR 97223

Is another personal favorite with semi-custom blades in the semi-custom price range. Well designed.

When we fall into the "cheap" well there are still some great deals to be had.

WESTERN CUTLERY
1800 Pike
Longmont CO 80501

Makes a couple of boot clip models that I love. The blades are hard enough to hold a good double edge, yet not brittle and the boot clip design makes them very hidden and still very easy to get at in a sudden situation.

Inexpensive and they work.

If you don't wear boots (what kind of a man are you anyway?) you can do a belt clip arrangement or even substitute holsters for a mid back (very hard to find in a frisk) or upper thigh (well, maybe you wear a skirt..Afterall, you don't wear boots, right?)

COLD STEEL
2128 Unit D Knoll Dr
Ventura, Ca 93003

Specializes in low priced fighting knives. Many of their models, such as the Urban Skinner are actually push daggers, designed to be pushed into meat with one or two hands, doing a maximum of damage on the trip.

Their models are also known for clever sheaths; at least two fit into/become a belt buckle, some are boot and some belt clips.

Mean little buggers.

This brings up an interesting point; using a knife is not just the old overhand-slash-and-die that Hollywood promotes.

The ninja method (one of them) is to always use the BODY weight behind the blade by pushing with both hands in a stab or bracing with an arm and pushing (with A SINGLE EDGED WEAPON OF COURSE) for real penetration.

Think it's easy to cut some one? Fine hang up a canvas bag filled with old rags or newspapers, or nail up thick cardboard.

Now step in and slash at it.

See that little cut? Going to make the other son of a bitch mad isn't it?

Like any other form of fighting knives require PRACTICE AND TECHNIQUE.

A favorite of mine is a Wing Tsun technique wherein the single edged knife is held backwards (handle in hand and pointing outward) blade hidden back against the wrist/arm.

Now the entire arm can be brought into play by turning it outward and in front of your body pointing the until-now-hidden knife directly at the attacker and then the body backup is used to stab deeply or cut across a neck.

A SHOOTER'S KNIFE

The Russians have come up with a winner. After inventing the automobile and the electric light, they have developed a unique knife.

One that cuts, stabs, fights and shoots...

Right, shoots.

The folks at FLORIDA KNIFE COMPANY have borrowed the Russian's design (now there's a switch for you) and improved upon it.

The Florida Knife, known as the Pilum, is made from 4140 steel with a hardness factor of 56 and sports a 4.5 inch blade. Both the handle and sheath are constructed from black anodized knurled aluminum.

Both the handle and the sheath are round; the blade fits into a rubber holder in the tip of the sheath.

When closed the unit becomes a solid baton 9.5 inches long and can be used as a helper during any fighting situation.

When the sheath is pulled off, the blade is exposed and the Pilum is a solid fighting knife.

Now, suppose one's attacker also pulls out a knife at this point, say, for fun, a machette, or even a gun. Besides the usual defense (saying,"yes sir, take what you want"), is there any effective attack technique?

Yes. Remove the safety pin and press the trigger. A STRONG 11.5 inch spring propels the blade forward.

How forward?

We (see photo) shot it through 3 inches of salt pork on the first try...

Read three + inches of flesh and bone...

FNC rates the effective range at 30 feet. I would dispute this slightly, although we could hit a target at that distance, the blade had lost much of its penetration ability.

Then again, how many knife fights take place at thirty feet?

At 5-10 feet this is a DEADLY weapon. At 10-20 it may or may not be, depending on what the target is wearing, etc.

There are a couple of minor setbacks; you get one shot, loading is a learned process that takes a few seconds and can hurt (see below), it is not totally silent, and may be considered a concealed weapon in some states.

A couple of things we would change; installed a longer screw to hold the spring in, would drill a hole in a 4 inch square block of wood to hold the handle while loading...

But overall this is a hell of a product.

Impressions

The first loading process is a BEAR. It took two of us, struggling, to compress that bitch of a spring, but this eases up after the first shot.

One person can easily load the unit if the instructions are followed to the letter, i.e., press the plastic tip onto a wall and use one's hip to press the spring/sheath into position.

I had so much fun shooting the Pilum into the wooden fence, boxes, melons, and so on, that I bruised the hell out of my hip...

USE BOTH HANDS TO SHOOT! This transfers maximum power to the blade, prevents jump aiming and saves the hand. My one single handed shot tore the hell out of the webbing between my thumb and fore finger.

ALWAYS PUT THE SAFETY-COTTER PIN IN PLACE AFTER LOADING. Failure to do so will allow the blade and sheath to shoot at unplanned times; we have a half inch dent in the fence to prove the worth of this suggestion...

Use snap shoot aiming techniques and practice before use.

This is a device that can be used, at a moments notice, in three or four different ways, to knock out any attacker. A very realistic, useful, personal weapon that does not require any license or permit to own.

About $80 from:

FLORIDA KNIFE CORP
Box 1630
Merritt Island, FL 32952

FLORIDA KNIFE CORP's (see text) unusual shooting knife. A direct copy of a Russian weapon now being employed in "hot" areas.

First photo are the main pieces, unassembled.

Second is the blade going through 3 inches of salt pork (still in package, had it the next day for lunch) from a distance of about 7 feet.

Can be used as a baton, knife, or he pulls out the sword....Bang! He has 3 inches of blade shot into him...

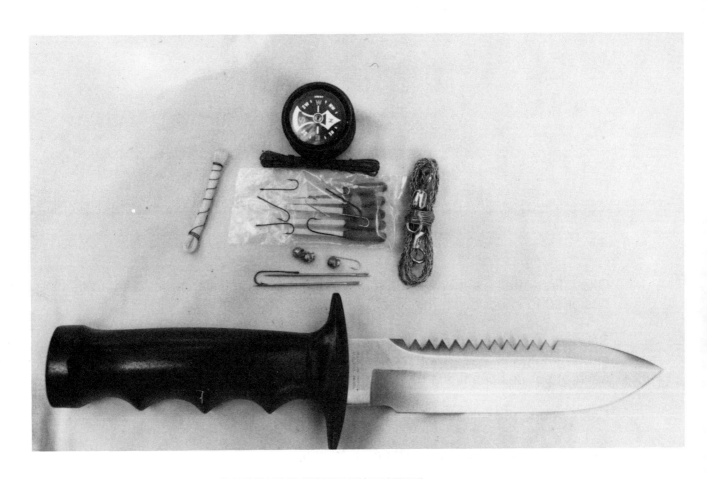

INEXPENSIVE KNIVES THAT WORK

Top is our LIFEKNIFE survival weapon with its component parts (excepting the sheath and sharpening stone) laid next to the blade, bottom is a nice push dagger (see text) and the WESTERN CUTLERY clip-on boot knife.

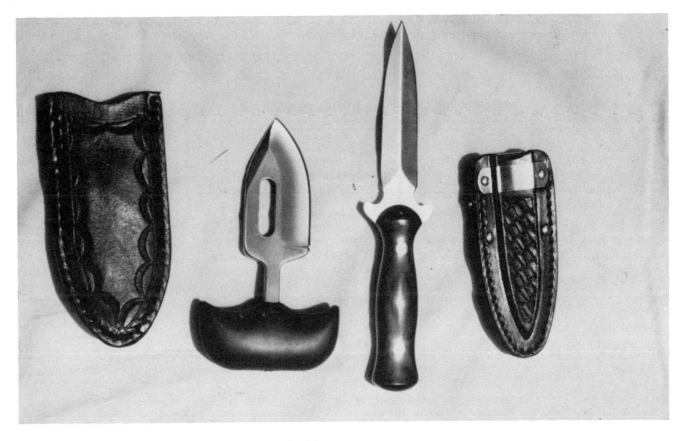

THE FIVE MOST DANGEROUS GUNS
IN THE WORLD

Okay, first of all we mean guns that are available to civilians, not electric gattling guns designed to shoot down missiles...

Second, each should represent a special type of weapon, it would be easy to say 5 10 guage shotguns loaded with double ought... This might be true in some situations, but each of our choices fills a certain need.

Each weapon is still available as of this writing.

Each can be used with a minimum of training.

Each must be affordable, even if expensive.

How did we pick these subjective units? We consulted the best people in the field, we tried things out, we talked to mean people who stake their life on their weapons, on both sides of the law and then we acted like kids in a toy store and decided what we would want to defend our last stores of canned quail eggs in the bomb shelter from our maddened neighbors and massed junkies...

Fun.

If one or more of these pieces won't set you at ease, see the section on id's and get the hell away.

BIG MAC ATTACK

Configured after the German machine pistols of WWII The MAC models are steel alloy framed machine pistols with several unique advantages over most semi-automatic pistols.

The units were light in weight with an extremely high rate of fire, held 20,30,40 or even 50 round magazines and came in either 9mm or 45 caliber.

The barrels were threaded to accept "caps" to keep the dirt out, or screw-on supressors in a matter of seconds.

With one of the suppressors sold through the mails in kit form (elsewhere in this book) the MAC 10 9mm became a whisper shooter.

The next interesting step is that they were/are the easiest guns in the world to make into full automatic fire.

In fact, many gun nuts were quick to pick up on the fact that a piece of hard rubber, or even a broken off pencil placed behind the trigger caused the semi version to become full auto...

After firing the weapon I would estimate the ROF to be about 600 rounds per minute with very little recoil.

A quick, quiet, deadly weapon that could be made legal in a few seconds.

Because of this fact the BATF closed down the MAC plants making the models 10, 11 and 11a rather hard to find. The plant has now reopened for business making a model known as the MAC INGRAM which is NOT nearly so easy to convert over to full auto.

The orginal guns can still be found in swap ads and at gun shows and I predict the price will head straight upward. The new models can be found (with some searching) for about $325.

Remember California outlaws ANY silencers, FFL or not, but some states do follow federal guidlines about ownership and some states like Nevada and Arizona are lax enough to allow full automatic ownership with a minimum of hassle.

The UZI is another of those wonderous Jewish weapons that work oh so well..

Sold to you and I it is a semi 9 mm accurate rifle/carbine that accepts different barrels with a simple screw on effort. Easy to silence, at this time one part (drop in) in available for under $20 which makes it fully automatic...

Easy to silence, mean, rapid rate of fire, little recoil.

Remember ALL FULL AUTO WEAPONS ARE IILEGAL WITHOUT THE PROPER FFL LICENSE!!!

Auto parts, silencer parts, etc. available from SGT SANDY'S, SWD, ETC.

PENGUN

In one sense they are not efficient weapons; they are single shot, usually small caliber, have no trigger and certainly do not look like a gun...

On the other hand, they don't look like a gun, can be very deadly at close range, can be silenced and can be purchased through the mail...

Used throughout history the tubegun, or pengun has proven to be a very effective, close range backup weapon that will often pass a harmless device during a not-too-intensive search, much less a causal glance.

They have been used by most intelligence agencies, by portions of the army during WW II (the MAC "Stinger") and in a number of James Bond type movies.

They work...

Tube guns have also been incorporated into other devices such as cigarette lighters and lipstick containers.

They are also simple enough to make instead of buy...

With a couple of notable exceptions, most penguns are .22 caliber. This choice provides enough accuracy and stopping power for close range shooting and has almost no recoil.

As you no doubt realize, no one can legally sell handguns through the mail within the US.

Back to the science of semantics...

Two commercial penguns are sold through the mails as I write this. The first, which we purchased and tested, is by COVERT ARMS. They make 3 models; a .22 short (fairly useless), a .22 long rifle which also accepts .22 magnums, and a .410 shotgun model which comes complete with a plastic full-hand grip and will do an amazing amount of damage at close range.

How to buy a gun through the mails?

Right, Covert does not sell guns...They only sell internal pengun parts, no tubes...

Yes, they do include an address for a tube supplier...

We ordered the .22 LR/Mag model. It comes in a kit version that requires a screwdriver and about 15 minutes to assemble. The parts are made from blackened steel and go together as the instructions say they will...

The end product looks like a real pen, including clip. The "barrel" (non-rifled, a bit over one inch long) unscrews to allow the seating of one cartridge.

The internal "hammer" is cocked against a spring and slipped into one of two grooves for safe or fire position.

To discharge the weapon one simply clicks the firing knob from it's slot allowing the spring to snap the firing pin onto the rim of the cartridge.

We experienced no misfires after correct seating and were generally very impressed with this blue steel, 5", 2 1/4 ounce close range weapon.

We also felt it was just a starting point for more sophisticated versions, see the following pages.

Price for the COVERT version is about $75 including separate tube.

The other model shown operates on the same principles but is a trifle fancier with chrome plating and such. It does resemble a pen to a greater degree but shoots only .22 LR's.

The main problem with this model, as far as most of us are concerned is that it is ONLY sold to law enforcement personnel.

This model is sold to be used as a back up weapon in case the officer is disarmed of his normal pistol. One can also guess it may end up planted on a dead suspect on occasion...

I did not inquire if they would sell to other security (private) individuals but I would doubt it by the the various "law enforcement only" warnings.

Remember that the completed weapon will fall under various concealed weapon laws and is going to be ILLEGAL TO CARRY without the correct license.

We have also included plans for a homemade model, however it should NOT be attempted by anyone without the correct knowledge and tools and will be governed by the same laws as the commercial versions.

GYROJET; An Idea Ahead Of Its Time?

About 20 years ago a unique idea appeared on the market; a rocket gun. The gyrojet was a pistolized affair that operated like a subminiature bazooka, firing 12 or 13 mm (diameter) projectiles upon request.

The gun's inventor came up with a solid fuel that seemed to have enormous potential; during tests a straight pin sized rocket, shot from a drinking straw bounced off a wall and hit the inventor in the arm.

Breaking said arm...

The first units were actuated by an electric igniter that lite the fuel sending the "rocket" off. Later models employed an interesting arrangement which placed the "hammer" in front of the "bullet". When the trigger was pulled a powerful spring jammed the projectile back into a firing pin which set off a more or less conventional primer.

The hammer then remained in front of the projectile until the burning fuel created enough pressure to overcome its spring, forcing it to recede into the body of the pistol. This arrangement allowed the pressure to become great enough to provide for decent flight.

Advantages to the gun were several; silent, hit with the force of a .45 using a much smaller "bullet" and the projectile left behind no case (the entire unit served as combination slug and case).

The gun worked well enough for the era. A fair number were sold to collectors and sportsmen and a few new models are still on the market (the one in the photo is $500), however no more 12 mm ammo is available.

A bit of the larger ammo can still be had.

Disadvantages were several and all related to one overlying problem; namely the projectile was still burning its fuel as it left the barrel and for a ways beyond.

This meant maximum force was NOT reached until some distance from the gun, close shots lacked the speed and penetration of normal bullets and accuracy left a bit to be desired, especially in windy conditions as any outside influence affected the projectile to a much higher degree while it was still in the burning stage.

The time and technology of this invention were wrong, the idea and potential benefits were right..

Many of today's bazookas (such as the Isreali model the US is considering adapting) burn their entire fuel BEFORE ever leaving the tube, solid fuels have come a long way, baby, considerably more "punch" could be incorporated into a bullet sized package today.

Rocket accuracy is far, far better due to such inventions as spring retention fins and would now equal most bullets...

A silent, accurate pistol that has more stopping power than comparable bullets and leaves behind no cases or rifling marks on the projectile itself?

I've always thought we had some of the most intelligent readers going, somebody who has more time than I might think about reinventing this useful little gadget and making some money on it...

Don't mention it...

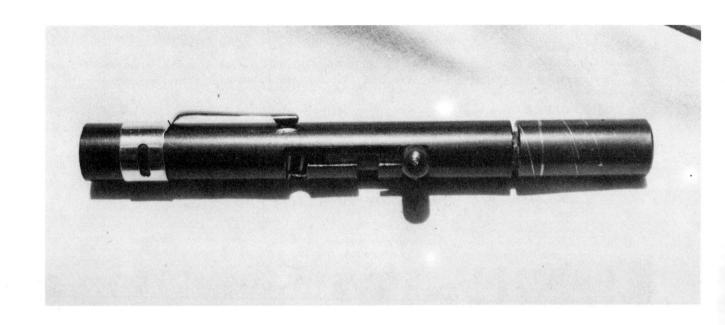

TWO UNUSUAL WEAPONS

The COVERT ARM's pengun we constructed from the kit (.22 LR and Mag) and one of the last remaining examples of a virgin GYROJET rocket pistol.

Gyrojet courtesy of the San Francisco Gun Exchange.

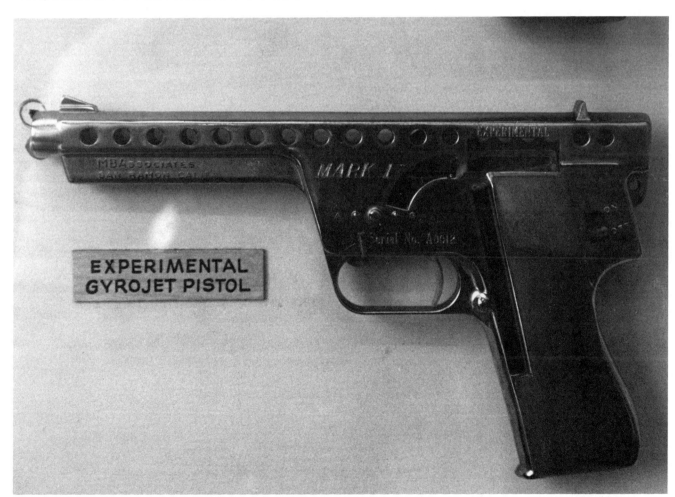

TWO TUBES

Examples of the best "penguns" on the market today. Note the CA is sold as an inactive kit which requires NO license (tube sold elsewhere) while the PENFIRE is restricted to law enforcement personnel.

COVERT ARMS
PO Drawer 31190
El Paso TX 79931
Aprx. $60.00

TUBES
PO Box 31276
El Paso Tx 79931
$10.00

PENFIRE
2114 Douglas
Loveland Co.
80537 $125.

MODEL 2A-K INACTIVE PARTS KIT

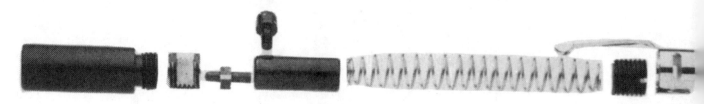

Handles all .22 Cal. including .22 Magnum

Completed
Model 2A-K

MODEL 3A .410 GA

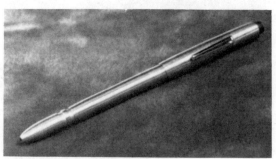

Price: $129.00

PenFire is a dependable, safe .22 Mag firearm (convertable to .22 LR with the new Optional Barrel). It is also a fine writing pen made from the highest quality Stainless Steel.

PenFire
was conceived by a Police Officer and designed by an experienced tool designer to be used and sold **only** to Police Officers.

PenFire
is an ultra-concealable, last resort defensive weapon. It can be carried by an Officer when no other weapon would be practical.

HIGH SCHOOL AGAIN

For those of you who miss your old high school zip gun, or those of you who would rather build a kit car than go out and buy a Corvette, here are the plans for a one shot pen gun, complete with silencer.

Again, remember owning a silencer without the proper license is illegal.

This is stolen directly from a newsletter entitled THE COMMUNIQUE which is not publishing at this time. When they were in biz it was the best spy type newsletter around. If they decide to re-start, or make back issues widely available we will give the address in the upcoming spy school report.

THE TECHNICAL DIRECTORATE

.22 CALIBER PEN GUN WITH SILENCER

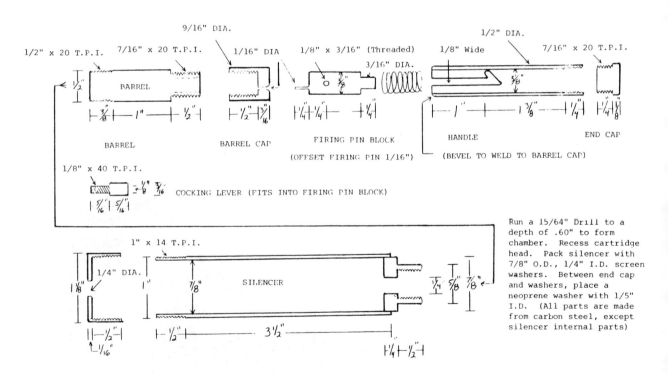

Run a 15/64" Drill to a depth of .60" to form chamber. Recess cartridge head. Pack silencer with 7/8" O.D., 1/4" I.D. screen washers. Between end cap and washers, place a neoprene washer with 1/5" I.D. (All parts are made from carbon steel, except silencer internal parts)

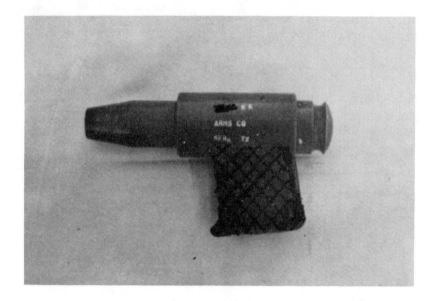

Based on the WW II tube guns used by the British commandos, among others, this single shot .357 mag uses a special, highly souped up cartridge, also made by KK can do some amazing things:

Be fired under water or in mud
Penetrate 1/8'' steel plate with a 2'' hole
Go thru 50 plys of bullet proof cloth
Be fired while still in holster
Etc.

This particular model was being modified as this is being written so it may differ slightly by our printing, but it appears to be the perfect weapon for frogmen, shark hunters, or as any kind of clandestine weapon. Recoil is quite low...

About $500.

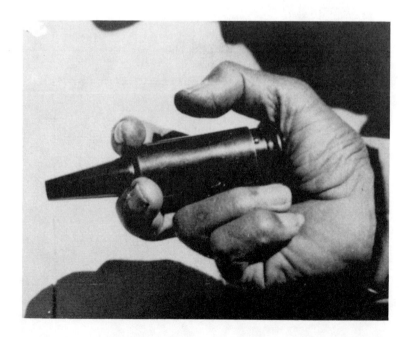

SUPERGUNS

There is simply no other word for these CIENER (see supplier's section) conversions. How about a fully auto M 16 (or 15) BELT FED, 500 round mag with brass catcher for firepower?

If you are being chased by 12 dogs plus an entire company of trained killers the above weapon just might not be enough. Move to the M16/15 over under with a semi or full auto Remington 12 guage riot or full barrel shotgun.

Both weapons are aimed, as in any good over-under, at the same aim point.

If these won't stop your troubles, don't call me...

I don't want to know.

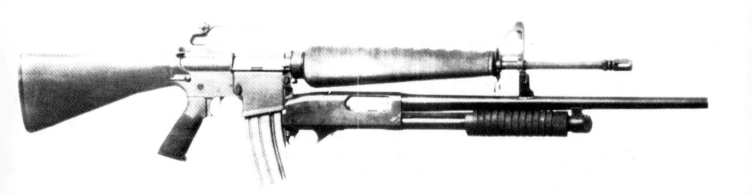

THE MOST SOPHISTICATED PISTOL IN THE WORLD (?)

Every device that is mass produced, from cars to toasters, is designed for the "average" person, right? Pay attention, we've talked about this before and there maybe a test... This means certain features must conform to the norm, be safe, reliable and set up for the person in the Pinto with Firestone 500 tires...

Even guns, good, expensive guns have got to be made with the average idiot in mind. They must function, but not too well or too quickly as to let the weekend shooter blow a toe off and sue the manufacturer.

This means a compromising situation EVEN ON A GOOD WEAPON!

If you are serious about shooting/surviving it is possible, as we have shown, to change certain characteristics of a commercial weapon to better suit the situation in which one expects to use the gun.

A total customizing job is expensive and difficult to have one person perform, no matter how good his gunsmithing talents.

On the other hand, certain firms concentrate on one or more weapons, spend money and time to engineer certain weapons to fit certain situations and then offer the conversion.

This is the story of the one we feel is the best example and quite possibly the best handgun available for CERTAIN SITUATIONS.

ARMAMENT SYSTEMS AND PROCEDURES (ASP) will take your model 39 Smith and Wesson semi-automatic 9 mm pistol and modify it into something called, oddly enough, an ASP...

We sent ASP a brand new 39 and asked for the conversion.
It took a while, but a weapon arrived that bore little resemblance to the original gun.
At the risk of sounding flip the ASP is a close combat weapon where the 39 was a general pistol.

Differences?

212...

Yup, 212 modifications to the original weapon that makes it into a 100% reliable professional pistol. Frills are taken off, improvements are added...

The ASP is designed for speed on target from a concealed position. The frame is computer designed to cut down on weight, yet allow less misalignment from recoil.

This is accomplished by centering the mass in the meat of the hand as well as extending the magazine as to let the little finger grip the magazine base, adding support.

The grips are changed to allow correct firing in a panic draw situation by close hand fitting. They are also made transparent as are the 3 clips so one can instantly see how many cartridges remain to be fired, a great idea...No more counting shots in a real life situation.

The entire weapon is disassembled and coated with Teflon. This prevents jamming, even with a dirty weapon as well as allowing the gun to be drawn free of clothing or of a holster with no "grabbing".

The sights are very unique; no front sight and a bright yellow "v" shaped gutter sight which allows both-eyes-open-instant-on aiming.

A special forefinger trigger guard allows two hand shooting with no mid-draw grip change.

The barrel is throated and the magazine well is beveled for quick/load quick/shoot.
All springs are rewound for maximum seating and feeding.

Trigger pull is lessened and evened out to create the best tracking I have ever experienced.

The hammer spur is removed for less binding in the draw, the magazine safety and the hammer safety are REMOVED!

This means it fires every time BUT can discharge if dropped with a chambered cartridge.

This weapon is designed to act as a subconscious extension of the person wielding it; it is a survival at close range edge.

It IS a defensive tool, if one is planning an assault take an AR-15, or a 12 guage shotgun, or, or...On the other hand for a reaction weapon that fits in with most actual fighting situations the ASP excels.

This combat piece is reworked to provide the ultimate in reliability, controlability, and rediness. It is a short range weapon, as is any pistol with the exception of a .44 mag with a scope sight...

Each ASP has at least 100 rounds put through it before it leaves the factory. Each is tuned until it will feed an empty round.

The unit does NOT come with the now popular double magazine as it is designed to be hidden in one's clothes with a minimum of bulk and mass.

It is odd to shoot a ASP and then a normal 39; the ASP is much lighter and smalller than its country cousin, yet seems to have less recoil due to the new balance and grip. In some ways one feels it is a mere .25 rather than the much more powerful 9 mm.

One Aberdeen Proving Ground test showed the 9 to be second ONLY to the .44 mag in relative stopping power.

This does not take into account the use of special ammo such as the Glaser...

The US army is just now joining NATO in switching from the old 45 caliber to the 9 mm as the standard side arm.

Even dry firing the ASP proves to be a totally different operation than handling any other 9 mm. The butt, slide, stop, safety and tang are all reduced to improve handling characteristics.

The damn thing fits in your hand like it was born there.

Trigger pull, either single or double action is smooth through the entire throw and requires just the right amount of force.

Leaving both eyes open and sighting down the guttersnipe trench sight seems very strange to me, and I can stand up with almost anyone in a range shoot, but when you get the trick and compare the aim with one eye shut it is dead on every time.

Even racking the slide is unusual as the springs have a different tension; one leaves the slide hand stable and pulls the frame rather than the other way around.

Even a complete dry follow through from draw to lock on and fire is a different and almost effortless action.

The ASP is designed to be the smallest and best weapon of its kind.
Is it?

ASP suggests one put at least one hundred rounds through the weapon prior to any serious firing. This is to let one become familiar with the difference in this weapon including the fact that 2 safety mechanisms are removed and the gun must be handled and treated like no over the counter pistol.

Playing with the unit in the living room is great, now let's go to the range and compare it with a 39...

ASP POWER

(top) Our ASP lying under its former form, the S&W 39. More differences than meet the eye.

(bottom) A two handed grip using the ASP's unique trigger guard and extended magazine for a steady shot.

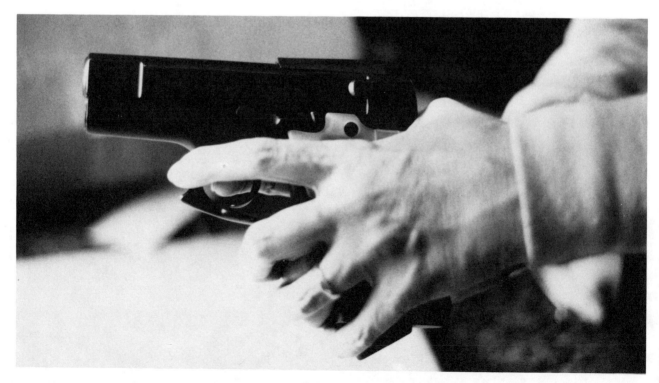

SUPERRIFLE-

The Poor Man's Sniper/Assault System

For this section we gave two of our favorite gun types free rein to use the latest technology in order to construct a Rifle Super System.

We asked for a three fold configuration:

1. An accurate, medium to long range sniper's tool with a heavy percentage kill range.

2. An automatic, multi-shot, assault rifle.

3. A close to medium range, silent compact killer.

Oh, yes, and we demanded it be done as cheaply as possible...

Our new editors argued, drank, bitched, spent money and tested. Finally they came up with a system that we felt met the demands.

Our system is based on one rifle and a series of modifications and add-ons. Each system uses some of the previous systems' high points and then adds those developments which will make it unique for its new role.

CHARTER ARMS

The basic weapon chosen for each system was a Charter Arms AR-7. This little gem was originally designed to be the ideal survival weapon. It utilizes the versatile .22 long rifle cartridge, allowing for a high number of cartridges to be carried in a small light package, but still offering enough killing power for survival purposes.

My uncle has bagged several bears with a .22 handgun...

Besides there are ways to increase this kill percentile as we shall see...

The AR-7 is ideal for a survival weapon as the entire gun breaks down into four main parts, three of which fit into the fourth (the stock) for easy carrying.

The entire assembly is a mere 16 and 1/2 inches long when collapsed into itself, a neat trick with a 16 inch barrel, and weighs in at 2 and 1/2 pounds.

It even floats.

It features a reliable recoil operated semi-automatic action with adjustable front (by tapping) and rear sights allowing for windage and elevation adjustment.

The gun will operate with standard or high velocity ammunition.

Price? Just under $100, complete.

Because of the 7's unique breakdown action it has appeared as the villain on many tv shows and movies, usually being shot by some no-good, commie type sniper.

A nice starting place.

The AR-7 floating survival rifle as it comes from the factory. Note that the entire barrel/receiver/mag fits inside the hollow plastic stock which is then closed off by a rubber butt plate.

The entire rifle can be purchased for just under $100 at any respectable gun dealer and works quite well as a survival or plinking gun with no modifications.

The package will fit into a backpack, take great amounts of abuse and stay on top of the water, in a very Christian manner, should it fall overboard.

.22 LR caliber.

AR-7

One of the most basic and most effective improvements one can make on any semi-automatic rifle is probably the one actually done the least.

As in cars, any rifle is made to accommodate a variety of shooters, conditions, and circumstances. No matter what type of weapon (semi-automatic) there are always some compromises built in to the design that will affect the accuracy of the unit.

In addition to this is the fact that a rifle is designed by one or more engineers and like any other complicated object there is often room for improvement if a certain aspect is studied by other engineers involved in only that area of design.

Take, for example, high performance engines; any competent race mechanic or speed designer can coax double or triple the available horsepower out of any engine by seemingly minor modifications that do not detract much in the way of reliability.

This same approach works with guns.

Most shooting, except strict bench rest target practice, is actually dependent upon a combination of factors. The average shot is not steadied upon a target for any length of time but is aligned with the target only briefly.

A good shooter will apply partial pressure during the entire sighting process and then increase the pressure to th firing point as the target and sights fall into direct alignment.

Professional shooters do not consciously "know" when the gun will actually fire as the pressure should be increased so gradually the weapon discharges without a last trigger jerk to throw the sights off the target.

This is a fairly effective method of shooting except that several mechanical factors come into play depending on the type of gun involved and the time necessary to achieve the ideal sighting.

As aim time increases both finger and arm muscles become strained and no longer will provide a steady, constant pull needed to release the sear at the precise moment the target comes into proper alignment.

This is complicated by the amount of trigger pull (measured in pounds) needed for the actual release as well as the distance the trigger must move to cause firing (trigger creep).

As any muscle becomes strained it requires more time to accomplish any given task and will not perform the task as smoothly as a fresh muscle will.

In guns this is further helped along because most triggers and pistol grips are simply not designed with the correct shape to enhance smooth pull.

A gun that requires 8 pounds of pull to disengage sear (fire) when measured with a mechanical device may actually require 2-3 more pounds MORE when actually pulled by a human finger simply do to trigger shape.

In addition most stocks and grips position one's finger so it lands in the center of the trigger, an area which stresses the finger 25% MORE than a tip position does.

Most pistol grips place the hand in a position of non-support when the trigger is gripped correctly adding to muscle strain and release time.
So what does this add up to?

Simply that there are certain "engineers", or gunsmiths that specialize in minimizing trigger release weight, trigger creep and reshaping triggers for maximum efficiency.

One such firm is:

> Williams Trigger Specialities
> RR 1 Box 26
> White Heath, Ill 61884

They will alter any semi-automatic rifle, whether single stage or double stage trigger release, to utilize the minimum trigger pull and creep possible while still maintaining a degree of safety.

This modification procedure includes polishing and reshaping trigger/sear parts and sometimes replacing the trigger itself.

The net result of such work is a much quicker release time requiring less effort and producing much less much tension.

Note this procedure does not increase accuracy of the weapon. It does, however increase the APPARENT accuracy by letting the shooter actually use more of the weapon's capabilities.

It also allows a shooter to utilize a slightly different technique when shooting anything but bench rest position. This technique is known as the "compressed squeeze" because one can now simply apply ALL the pressure needed AT ONE TIME when the target/sight come into alignment.

This is possible because of the reduced effort and lack of jerkiness required to actually shoot.

Of course, one can still utilize the "surprise" method and will still experience higher accuracy because of the lessened effort and muscle strain encountered.

How much more accuracy?

We shot our project AR-7 from a solid bench rest position at 50 and 100 yards and then at bipod 50 and 100 yards and then repeated he effort at the same ranges from a freestanding position.

Tried again with a modified model with no other changes.

Believe it or not we got a consistent increasy in BENCH accuracy of nearly 20% (averaged out)!

Pod and freestyle averaged out to a remarkable 70% and 145% INCREASE IN ACCURATE HITS!!!!

Remember this is a $35-$40 modification with NO added parts or gimmicks. Nothing fails, gets in the way, breaks or hangs up on tree branches. It simply makes the gun appear to be much more accurate under ANY shooting condition from sniper to assault...

It is the first and one of the most important additions to our or any super rifle program.

2. Explorer II scopemount. An inexpensive mount from Charter Arms which allows mounting of most standard telescopic sights. Installs without special tools. About $12.00.

3. Magazine. The standard AR-7 magazine is an 8 shot capacity, blued steel magazine. It works well enough as is but does not provide the firepower necessary for any sophisticated weapons system.

> Ram-Line Inc
> 406 Violet st
> Golden Co 80401

Makes a high impact, light weight magazine that snaps into the AR-7 receiver with no mods. This magazine holds 25 rounds with an anti-jam design that we found both easy to load (easier than the factory model) and reliable under field conditions.

A bargain at $16.25.

4. Stock. The supplied stock for our 7 is a black plactic affair that is hollow to contain

the other components. It incorporates a hand adjusted nut to lock the receiver/barrel assembly into place and a snap on butt plate (rubber) to hold everything in safe storage.

The idea works well but is a compromise at best because of the necessary bulk required to contain the rest of the unit when broken down.

It also has some minor problems (at least with our crew) in the area of comfort and shoulder fit.

Morgan Arms Co. Makes a replacement stock which is marketed by:

Wilkerson Firearms Co
6531 Westminster Blvd
Westminster Ca 92683

The stock is collapsable, controlled by a knurled knob and made from hollow steel. It measures a compact 7 and 1/2 inches when folded and extends to 12 inches when locked out.

The shoulder contact plate is curved and small enough to fit nearly any shoulder. It sports a swivel connector for sling hook up.

The Morgan stock also adds one other important feature; a pistol grip. This addition makes a real difference in quick aiming as well as steadiness.

The stock fastens with two allen screws and the pistol grip with one more.

This add-on kit adds stability, cuts down on weight and reduces the visible cross section of the entire unit.

Price is $60.00.

5. Binocular Sights. Of course you are at least somewhat familiar with telescopic sights, unless you live in a very small cave, but there is one advance you may not be totally at home with.

The binocular sight was invented to fill a definite need; that of a quick, accurate available light sighting condition. It is not, per se, a telescopic sight, rather it uses an occluded eye collimated lens system.

Sounds good, huh?

Basically the difference is that the binocular sight uses BOTH eyes at the same time, thereby making accurate shot bursts much quicker than with a telescope device.

The main hangups with a normal scope are that it cuts down on light, requires one eye to be shut during use, and by very design requires time and effort to find and then recognize a portion of the target.

This idea works very well on still targets in good lighting conditions and is still the best technique for sniper/standing-deer type conditions, but is not the best for low-light or moving target conditions...

An occluded sight is one that blocks one eye with the aim point and lets the other eye focus as normal. This means one can raise a weapon, keeping both eyes open and focused normally, find and hit a target within 1 or 2 SECONDS!

This is one of the easiest sights to use and will engage the target in the shortest time available. A good OEG (Occluded Eye Gunsight) will work in dim or worse lighting conditions as well as it does during the daytime.

When operated correctly the sight is raised and pointed towards the target keeping both eyes in focus. This provides a good field of vision without the necessity of focusing and unfocusing to bring a scope or iron sight into the correct range.

At once a bright red dot appears in sharp focus in the target area. It is in focus because the sight actually "simulates perceived distance".

Now the shooter simply places the red dot on the target to get a hit.

This is almost instinct shooting, it allows the shooter to engage several targets in the space of a couple of seconds as well as track a moving target in nil-light conditions.

A couple of notes:

We found the sight to be very effective on semi or even bolt action rifles, but the improvement was even more apparent on full automatic rifles firing in a burst pattern.

The dot is very obvious even in dim light.

The OEG works almost as well on an accurate (in our case the ASP) pistol as it does on a rifle.

Some people thought the term binocular sight ment the device had two "tubes" as in a binocular. It does not, this word refers to the use of both eyes in the aiming process.

One must have binocular vision (as most of us do), if a person is affected with a manifest ocular vision problem (ask your ophtalmologist) this technique will not work due to the problem of focusing both eyes at the same time.

This sight makes training non-shooters (wives, children, mother's-in-law) much easier as the idea of where-the-red- dot-grows-the-bullet-goes is an easy one to grasp.

Everything is in focus, there is no blurred front or rear sight or blurry target to deal with.

This idea works with either right or left handed shooters. In either case the "weak" eye sees the target, the strong eye sees the dot, the bullet hits...

If used in a static position for any length of time the dot can became tiresome. A quick blink cures this minor problem.

Vision disparities (most of us have a slight one) are automatically compensated for, unlike a fixed scope sight.

Long range/use a scope; short to medium real life conditions/use a bino... We tried an:

ARMSON, INC.
Box 2130
Farmington Hills, MI 48018

model, which is a bit expensive, but works with a built-in "energy cell" which lasts a couple of years and then is replaced, cheaply, with a new one.

It does work very well in low light conditions as well as full daylight. The sight is built of rugged materials and did not fail in any of our tests.

This device is good for many assault type weapons including the UZI, MINI-14, H&K MODELS, handguns and shotguns as well as our AR-7.

A great invention for those that deal in death...

6. Laser. Invented in the late 50's/early 60's the LASER has done much to work it's way into our lives. One of the more unusual uses of this coherent light device was discovered in the 70's when small models were attached to rifles and shotguns to aid in aiming.

Today's laser sights are smaller and more powerful versions of these early tests. Normally they attach either above or below the barrel of the weapon and throw a visible red dot 50-100 yards onto the intended target.

Laser sights are designed to be used in low light conditions or even complete darkness.

Many police departments have employed these sights with some success, mainly due to the psychological impact. It is hard to disobey someone's commands when you see a bright red dot on your chest and a shotgun backing it up...

For this type of application the unit is very good. For normal shooting conditions we found them to be a trifle inaccurate, limited to low light conditions, and over priced.

They operate for about 1 hour on a three hour recharge and weigh enough to make sighting a light gun such as our AR-7 rather slow and clumsy.

Our shooters scored more hits with low light and red dot sights than they did with the laser under the same conditions.

The red beam also makes it easy for the other guy to aim down your sight and shoot back...This is amplified by any NVD and would pose a real danger in combat conditions.

Commercial laser sights run in the $2,000 range and are available from:

> Laser Arms Corp
> Box 4647
> Las Vegas NV 89127

However there is an alternative; INFORMATION UNLIMITED stocks laser gunsight kits at a much lower cost and MEREDITH also features several lasers that could be used for sights.

See the supplier's section.

7. Twilight Scopes. One sight all of our testers liked was the low light telescopic sight. This is a passive, non-powered device that is coated and designed to pass the most light available, yet work in normal daylight conditions.

This device works as a "normal" scope but allows you to extend your shoot time into dusk conditions.

The best deals we found were from WILLIAMS GUN SIGHT CO. (see suppliers section).

8. Lite-Site Scopes. Another interesting idea is to incorporate an electronically powered LED into a scope giving a bright red dot at the center of the aim point.

This method works well in daylight conditions, allowing a fast access, aim/point time on most targets as well as allowing some tracking of moving targets.

In low light conditions the dot becomes almost magic. While the ambient light is not improved, the aim point becomes much, much easier to see and accuracy is improved by the same degree.

The LED consumes very little current and is lightweight, batteries last for quite a while.

Probably the most popular LED scope is the BUSHNELL selling for about $180-$200 from various dealers. It is a worthwhile buy at this price, but: FEATHER ENTERPRISES features a do-it-yourself LED kit which will adapt to most scopes for only $19.95!

This mini device attaches to the side of any 1 inch fixed or variable powered scope and via fiber optics places a bright red LED at the scope's aim point.

Well worth the money.

9. Bipod. Scaled after the military example, our test nylon/plastic bipod clipped directly onto the AR-7 barrel and provided a stable support for accurate-prone shooting.

It will clip onto almost any rifle and is a bargain at $10-20.

Available from FEATHER ENTERPRISES, and several other suppliers.

10. NVD Scopes (s). Not to run the subject into the good earth, we did test a couple of Starlight-type, Night Vision Devices including the one from STANO and a quick shot at a new LITTON version.

They work and will extend the night time range of an accurate weapon up to 200-400 yards. Of course, prices range from $1450 (STANO) to mid-$5,000's for different versions and generations.

They are a bit bulky, do not work (make that cannot be used) during the daytime, and are more fragile than iron sights, but for their application they cannot be beat.

See the see-in-the-dark section for a more complete look at NVD's.

11. Assisted NVD's. A brand new field of killing you can be in on the ground floor for...

This thrill requires a starlight scope mounted as the rifle's sight and then an assist by an infrared light source hung below the barrel.

We started out by trying a filtered light source simply taped on the underside of the 7. This worked, but the added light really did not increase the range of the NVD sight unless a super powerful light source, such as our Streamlite was used.

These sources tended to be fairly heavy for the lightweight AR-7 but did provide more night time accuracy.

Another try had us mount an IR viewer on the top and the source on the bottom. Also worked, even in total darkness, but had some alignment problems as the viewers were not designed to be utilized as a rifle sight.

We found the IR devices to be most useful in a total blackout situation when using automatic burst fire patterns.

The real breakthrough came when we mounted a small IR diode laser under the gun and a starlight on top.

Suddenly we had accuracy to 1/4 of a mile with fantastic resolution. A good marksman could hit the middle number in a license plate from almost that distance in almost total darkness.

With a good IR laser the light source is totally INVISIBLE to the naked eye but will throw a four foot circle of light on a subject hundreds of meters away in ink-blackness.

Good lasers from a number of commercial suppliers, cheaper models from MEREDITH and INFO UNLIMITED.

Read the in-the-dark section...

This lovely toy will start to appear on both the military and civilian markets in the near future, mark my words...

12. Twilighter. After looking at the most exotic and expensive sights on the market today, let's return to reality for a minute and look at a nice, under $20 low-light sighting tool.

The Twilighter, also known as the Nightsighter, is a small front sight attachment that is made for most popular guns including our beloved "7".

The device consists of three metal parts; the battery holder and LED mount, a battery cover and a clamp designed to fit the barrel in question.

Two mini watch batteries are placed in the holder and the cover is pushed into position completing the circuit. The sub-miniature LED (red) then lights up.

The entire unit is then clamped on the barrel, pressing up against the normal "iron" front sight blade.

All of a sudden the shooter can see where the barrel is aimed in dim light up to and including total darkness, making otherwise questionable shots well within the relm of reason.

This device was well accepted by all of our testers, the only minor notes offered were; hard to see the LED in bright daylight (although it can be removed in a few seconds and does not alter the normal front sight), sometimes needs minor adjustments in order to insure accuracy.

The power cells last about 3 years in normal use, or equal to the shelf life of the batteries...

A great buy ($17.95 postpaid) from:

Light Enterprises
PO Box 3811
Littleton Co 80161

13. Silencer. Use of the SWD silencer and replacement barrel. Found effective range cut down to about 50 yards and some loss of velocity, but still very adequate for most silenced needs.

See the section on silencers for more details.

14. Automatic Fire. Full auto conversion has come along way from the days when I filled the sear down as a kids. PALADIN PRESS carries about the best collection of books on do-it-yourself conversions for most popular rifles.

We had a gunsmith friend do our conversion but it would have been possible to do it in a home workshop.

Full auto works well on the 7 as there is enough recoil (especially with high velocity shells) to prevent jamming, but not enough to cause climbing of the barrel as in higher powered calibers.

As with most autos the best results were established by burst firing, rather than holding the trigger until the clip was empty.

Note this conversion IS ILLEGAL UNLESS YOU HAVE A CLASS 2 FFL!!

15. BMF Activator. Suppose there was a reliable device that sold for about $20 which would turn your semi-automatic rifle into a 500 round a minute "automatic", yet was completely legal?

The BMF activator is a hardened plastic and metal affair that clamps onto the trigger of your rifle. It can be mounted on either side of the trigger, allowing for right or left hand operation.   A small plastic activator bar extends from the BMF to the trigger. This bar is connected to a small plastic crank via a cam. When the unit is installed correctly the activator bar takes up much of the trigger slack.

Every time the crank is turned the bar pushes the trigger 4 times. Note, the gun is still semi-automatic, the BMF simply pulls and releases the trigger at a higher rate of speed than the human finger can.

Should the cranking exceed the gun's ability, the trigger simply "floats" until the next shot.

This device has been ruled by the Dept of the Treasury as not changing the classification of a weapon from semi-automatic; meaning it is not illegal.

The BMF works well, one can blow enough rounds to overheat the barrel, just like a auto, or do a controlled burst of 5-10 shots for better accuracy.

Originally designed for .22's only the BMF is now available for most semi's.
It does work rather nicely, with larger calibers a bipod is almost mandatory, but in .22, freestanding bursts are quite accurate.

The BMF does not change the working of the weapon, can be installed and removed quickly, and has built in safety features.

The final proof of the pudding is the fact that at least one police magazine has written an editorial against the BMF...

BMF ACTIVATOR
PO Box 12039
Houston, TX 77017

16. Electric Activator. Our never-say-die staff has taken the semi and/or auto BMF one step further.

You will notice that the plastic crank is screwed onto the activator by a removable metal bolt. If this is unscrewed the cam is easily accessible.

What if, instead of a hand crank, an electric motor was coupled to the cam?

Oh yes, does it work...

One of our weird boy whiz kids secured a fairly low rpm, battery powered motor (surplus stores, EDMUND SCIENTIFIC, etc), coupled it to the now exposed camshaft with a short metal or plastic tube and some super glue, or even threaded both so the unit can be unscrewed in short notice.

The mini-motor was attached directly onto the cam and then the wires run to the stock where a battery pack for the motor was located.

Between the battery and the motor a variable resistor (potentiometer) was added to control motor speed (in our BMF set-up each rpm means 2 shots) plus a single contact, spring loaded push switch.

These last items were clamped or taped onto the stock of the weapon allowing for finger or thumb control of shot bursts.

The Electric Legal Automatic . . . .

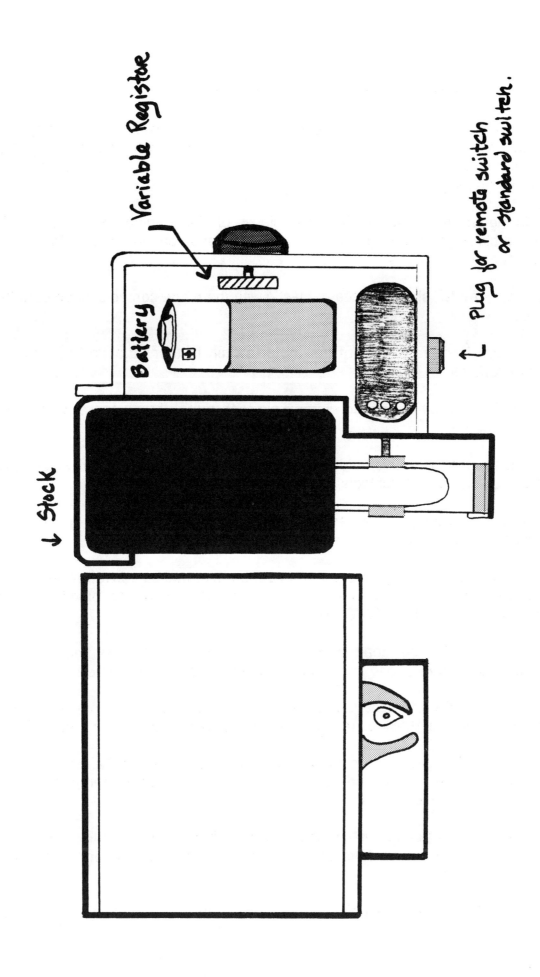

Variable Register

Battery

↓ Stock

↳ Plug for remote switch or standard switch.

379

With a bit of practice and parts substitution it works.

Now we can even take it one step beyond. Since the switch does nothing but close the circuit the switch can take any form from a boobytrap where something is opened or closed, setting off the entire clip to a very special personal firing mechanism known as the mouth trigger.

This trigger can be formed from two pieces of plastic joined at one end to form a "V" with a block glued between them so the open ends cannot touch without considerable pressure.

Or from one "U" shaped piece of plastic with the metal contacts glued onto the ends as shown.

One wire from each side of the motor switch is then attached to each end of the potentiometer.

Sometimes a spring loaded clothes pin with metal thumb tacks is substituted for a plastic switch.

In either case the unit is held in the mouth until firing is desired at which time the jaws are shut, closing the contacts and shooting the gun.

This unusual trigger has several good points; no mis-aiming due to arm or hand tension, instant reaction time and better accuracy.

It also has a few bad points; not too comfortable, makes conversation difficult, hard to explain wires running into your mouth, and for the peace of mind of your fellow comrades DO NOT CHEW GUM!!

17. Ammo. The one area that probably provides more room for improvement than any other is probably the one most overlooked by the average shooter.

The right choice of bullets can quiet the weapon, increase its power, up the stopping power or make a 100% kill ratio from a gun usually thought of as a rabbit killer...

a. CCI Stinger. This is the fastest (read most powerful) .22 ammo available on the general market. Improved stopping power as well as better accuracy over most distances. Hard to silence.

b. Hollow points. A non-jacketed lead bullet with a hollow core that expands upon impact doing more tissue damage (with less penetration) than a comparable jacketed bullet.

c. Glaser slugs. Simply the most deadly bullet available. Not made in .22 caliber at the time of this writing. See the glaser section.

d. Shot shells. Not real effective in .22 caliber, these mini-shotguns become much more dramatic as the caliber size increases. A shot shell contains a group of lead shot, usually about #7 in size and actually makes any weapon into a scattergun. Range and pattern are determined by the barrel length and the weapon chosen.

A good shot shell has several advantages to indoor combat; difficult to miss the target, great stopping power at close ranges (remember the stopping shock increases lograrithmcally with the number of hits, i.e., 2 hits has the power of 4 single shots, 3 is 9, etc.), not much penetration so they rarely go through the walls and kill four or five of the neighbors...

e. Tracers. Usually homemade, sometimes commercial or surplus in the larger calibers. A ideal method of actually figuring out where your bullets are hitting and allowing for real time corrections.

f. Explosive. Again usually homemade in the smaller calibers, available with the correct license, in larger calibers. These bullets provide a massive shock wave in tissue as the bullet fragments over a wide area making the impact that of a shot gun plus the actual explosion of the bullet.

Rivaled only by the glaser in killing power, explosive bullets are dangerous to handle, occasionally go off in high heat or in the barrel of the weapon, are dangerous to make and do not have as much stopping power against a bullet proof vest as a jacketed slug does.

These bullets, if constructed correctly, will actually explode a bit under the target's skin causing massive cavity formation plus heavy shock waves and blood contamination making them very destructive to both muscle tissue and bone structures.

Not to mention the fragmentation factor that tears tissue to shreads.

President Reagan was shot by Mr. Hinkley using a type of explosive bullet known as the DEVASTATOR (.22).

Why did he suffer only minor damage?

Because Mr. Hinckley, a $4.00 an hour security guard did not have the sense to realize these bullets take about 1100 feet per second of velocity to actually explode.

He shot them from a short barreled handgun which did not give the projectile enough time to gather the necessary speed, had he shot them from a rifle or long barreled pistol, Mr. Bush would have been president...

g. Incendiary. A bit safer to make and handle than the explosive models these are usually employed to cause fires or explosions in volatile materials. Often used after a couple of jacketed rounds to first puncture the tank or storage container and then the incin rounds to set it afire...

Also fairly bad in human flesh.

h. Poison. Not considered quite cricket in modern warfare, poison bullets are fairly easy to make and provide a 100% kill ratio when done correctly.

i. Multi-strike. An unusual compromise between glaser type slugs and single slug cartridges is the multi-strike concept. We tested a 9mm version of Multi-strike ammo because no one makes a .22 caliber multi-strike ammo at this writing. Our 9mm version contained 3 separate slugs layered one on top of the other. Each slug is fired by the same explosive charge and is spun by the barrel's rifling as it exits.

This results in an accurate pattern of about 4-6 inches at 20 yards.

Needless to say this 3 shot pattern both invokes the god of logarithms to increase the hitting force as well as the god of aiming to create a larger strike zone.

Another version of multi:-hit ammo is marketed by ONSLAUGHT AMMUNITION CO., in the Onslaught version 7-9 lead wafers (depending on the caliber employed) are stacked in the "slug".

We found the MULTI-STRIKE to be a bit more accurate, but the ONSLAUGHT to deliver a larger and more effective pattern.

Both types of ammo are available through normal gun dealers.

REMEMBER SEVERAL OF THESE ALTERATIONS ARE ILLEGAL IN THE US INCLUDING SILENCERS, AUTO CONVERSIONS, AND (in some states, notably California) EXPLOSIVE OR ALTERED BULLETS.

You must find out for yourself what is and what isn't legal in your area.

If you live in sunny California forget it, everything is illegal unless it is between consenting adults of the same sex...

CHARTER ARMS ONE BETTER

This is a look at ONE version of our do-it-yourself AR-7 update project. This would be used as a fairly close in in, rapid fire, assault rifle.

Note the following changes:

Trigger pull adjustment
Rubber pistol grips
Telescoping stock
25 round bananna mag (or two regular mags taped back to back for double loads)
BMF activator
Motor pack for BMF for full/semi auto fire (mouth switch not shown)
SWD silencer with barrel
TWILIGHTER LED front sight (plus normal SWD front sight)
Instant on plastic tripod
Optional camo cloth

A highly effective, silent and dangerous weapon.

CUSTOMIZING YOUR HANDGUN

As with most things, commercial handguns are a compromise at best; most will have a trigger pull that is strong enough to discourage early firing among those who shouldn't be shooting anyway (fast draw experts who can't shoot, buyer's who have fired three rounds on their new toy and now consider themselves gun experts, drunks, etc.), barrels and sights and magazines that may be a compromise between design/tooling costs and perfection.

A more expensive gun should not have as many faults, but a surprising cross section of " professional gun" owners find faults with their weapons that need correcting before they can shoot as well as their skills should allow them to.

If you can afford a full blown custom job like our ASP (see article) great,if you can't quite kick up the bread, there are other routes to attend to...

Some of these modifications will apply to either revolvers or automatics, but most automatics lend themselves to a customizing process better than do most revolvers.

That can be translated to read that automatics have more inherent problems than do said revolvers.

In whole a custom operation can be completed by a good gunsmith for about $150 max...

Trigger

The first and probably the most important modification is to have the factory trigger pull lessened from the up to 16 POUNDS some units come with, to a flawless 4-6 pound squeeze.

This change alone will increase accuracy and make a major difference in operations

Sights

A good set of sights; be they fixed or adjustable, is a very important part of any handgun. Handgun sights contain a built-in variable that adjusts for range and handgun kick/flick.

A handgun will rarely shoot exactly the same from a solid bench rest position as they will from any handheld stance.

The sights must be right-on for you as well as being aligned correctly on the gun.

Have the sights checked and or replaced if they are not doing what they should for you.

A good night sight, usually meaning only the front sight on most handguns makes your weapon a much more versatile weapon under changing combat conditions.

Several companies offer a good night sight conversion that transforms a target type weapon into a defensive unit that will point out the target under a variety of different background and ambient light conditions.

For those people who enjoy working with their hands;

Flying H Enterprises makes a conversion kit for sights. This kit consists of two small plastic cups of chemicals, reminds me of a girlfriend's cooking but that's neither here nor there...

These chemicals are applied to either/or front and rear sights in any pattern desired. Suggestions are two vertical dots, three horizontal dots or a small triangle on the rear sight with a dot on the front.

The chemical compound, once dried, becomes "charged" with exposure to light, either sun or lamp-flashlight and then glows in the dark for some time...

This method allows low cost custom sights that will greatly improve low light or dark shooting abilities.

At the minimum a brilliant orange front sight will make an improvement, a powered sight will accomplish even more.

Ejection

Most jamming occurs when a semi-automatic pistol will not totally rid a certain cartridge case from the port before the cocking slide closed.

Opening up the ejection port slightly will cure many of these problems, as well as allow the ejection of loaded rounds.

Magazines

A factory magazine can often be modified by varying spring rates, correct maintainance or modification so it will feed on a constantly reliable basis.

A good mag should also be funneled slightly to accept fast reloading.

SILENCERS

One of the most least understood and most glamorous weapon modifiers is the silencer. As taught by every movie and tv show that drifts out of Hollywood this wonderful device makes and gun in the world from .44 magnums to anti-aircraft batteries totally silent and maybe even more accurate.

As you have probably guessed this is not quite the way it is...

First of all even the best silencers simply quiet the expanding gases from the barrel of the gun. This means you cannot silence a revolver under any circumstances.

It also means this device only lowers the noise of the gases (most of the initial "bang"), it does not stop the loud "crack" made by the bullet as it breaks the sound barrier.

Most professional silencers replace the weapon's barrel with a shorter version designed to let the gas escape into the padding of the silencer at a much earlier rate than the stock barrel would allow.

A shorter barrel decreases the power of the projecting gases and lowers the bullets speed.

As the silencer is larger than the original barrel (to contain the necessary mufflers) most do not have a front sight thereby reducing the effective range of the weapon.

It must be pointed out that silencers are illegal (see the section about federal gun licenses) under all but a few special circumstances, and the bust is a severe one.

There are ways to overcome these small problems...

Stopping The Sound Barrier Noise

This is easy; simply use a sub-sonic cartridge. The easiest two calibers to reduce to a sub-sonic level are the .22 and the 9 mm Luger (automatic).

In the case of the lowly 22 one can simply look at the velocity chart and choose a bullet that is already within the sub-sonic perimeters.

For the 9 mm, it is normally necessary to remove some of the propellent (gunpowder) from the case, thereby reducing the force of the explosion as well as the bullet speed.

The other possibility for these, and several other calibers is to purchase cartridges that are already doctored by a professional supplier to react in the sub-sonic strata.

One problem with consulting bullet speed listings is that the type of weapon involved can make a large difference in actual, real world speed.

Many 9 mm cartridges are actually sub-sonic in handguns, but will break the barrier from MAC, or UZI type pistol/carbines.

Lowering the bullet speed can also cause tumbling with a loss of accuracy and varied damage.

One such cartridge that has taken this into account is the WHISPERLOAD made by:

American Ballistics Company,
PO Box 1410
Marietta, Ga 30061

Their solution is to use a 130 grain FMJ bullet in order to keep pressures at a level that will cause the projectile to travel properly, albeit at sub-sonic speeds.

We tried this load out in a MAC 10 and it worked and worked and worked...

However any reduced load bullet may not have the gas pressure necessary to operate the action of some automatics. The solution is to test any combination of cartridge and weapon before its use becomes necessary.

Any of these methods DO REDUCE THE POWER OF THE CARTRIDGE! The addition of the actual silencer may even reduce the output a hair more.

So why even think about the poor little 22?

Anyone who doubts the power of this cartridge should take a 22 Stinger and fire it into a block of soft modeling clay (see photo) or into a block of pine...

And watch it chop through 8 or 9 inches of solid wood...

The CIA and Mossad have been using silenced 22 pistols as "termination" devices for years with much success.

Remember a silenced weapon is by nature, only a close range unit. There is no reason to silence a long kill as the noise is too far away to be a threat anyway.

The clever English service even uses a 22 pistol completely encased in rubber that is totally silent.

There are various levels of silencers ranging from quickly devised one shot methods, to exotic copper wool gas mufflers. Each type will act differently on each weapon.

All good silencers have several facts in common:

Barrel attachment is by a threaded connector

The outer tube holds the internal equipment in close tolerance
Internal expansion is controlled by a baffling material

Rubber or plastic discs (wipes) are placed between baffles to restrict gas flow. These discs will wear out and need replacement every so often

The exit hole is kept to the size of the bullet

One Shots

A favorite of the IRA is to simply take a rather large potato, cut off the end and jam it onto the barrel of a pistol.

This is a fairly short range technique and also covers the target with mashed potato.

Not totally effective, but in Ireland there is always a potato somewhere in the vicinity...

A much better idea is to take a commercial adapter (about $10), screw it onto the end of your barrel and then screw a 2 liter plastic soft drink bottle onto the other end of the adapter.

This is a fairly good method for a single, close-in kill.

Another quick idea is to mount several baby bottle nipples, one on top of the other to the barrel so the bullet passes through the tip of the nipple on it's exit route.

Again, simple and quick, lacking is sophistication and not totally quiet by any means, but better than nothing.

COMMERCIAL VERSIONS

As any self respecting gun type knows, it is against federal law to buy/own a silencer. This sort of thing is punished by the ATF agents with much diligence (of course this does not apply if you have the correct FFL, but many people who own FFL devices do not want government agents dropping by).

It follows then that it is impossible to purchase a silencer through the mail.

Now I'm going to show you how to purchase a commercial silencer and have it actually delivered with the compliments of a government agency (the post office...).

In order to get around the law we come to the science of semantics; it's not what you say, but how you say it...

You see, you can buy a complete, commercial grade silencer EXCEPT for the outer tube. Note you have NOT purchased a silencer, simply all the internal "replacement" parts for the same device.

SWD Inc
1872 Marietta Blvd
Atlanta GA 30318

Sells, among other things, the internal parts for a complete silencer for the AR-7, a .22 High Standard pistol, and a couple of 9 mm Macs/UZI's...

These are top quality silencers that include a complete rifled, replacement barrel that bolts into the weapon WITH NO MODIFICATION!

This barrel then screws into their silencer for a tight fit.

All internal parts are included (see photos) including copper baffles, spacers and threaded end pieces.

Again note they sell only replacement parts and will disavow and or get pushed out of shape if you ask about "silencers".

This gives the hobbist a complete silencer sans tube.

Now what?

One can either purchase a 1" OD diameter aluminum tube and have the ends threaded at a machine shop to match the enclosed end caps, or:

Arm-Tec Box 401 Antioch, TN 37013

Just happens to sell complete, threaded tubes for SWD parts...

Prices are $15.00 and $24.00 for the High Standard and AR-7, in that order.

The parts are then assembled inside the tubes, the end caps screwed on, the barrel attached to the weapon and the complete assembly screwed onto the receiver.

Total assembly time about 10 minutes...

Fit, perfect...

How do they work?

With both .22's we could hear the bolt working after the shot.

That's all folks...

They don't make the gun quiet, they make it absolutely silent.

When I shot the first test shot I actually thought it was a miss fire until I looked at the target and saw the neat little hole...

Of course accuracy is reduced due to the shorter length of the new barrel, see the article on our AR-7 conversion for more details.

A commercial grade silencer for about $65.00...

While on the black market they can go for an easy $500.

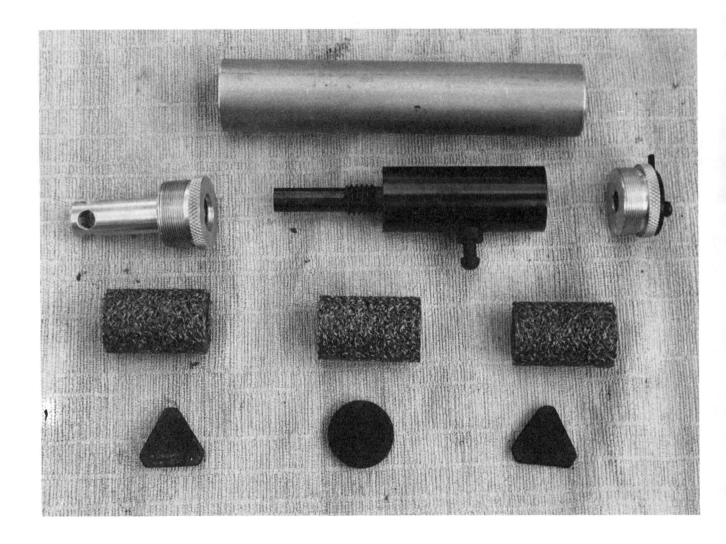

A look at the S.W.D. silencer replacement part kit, with external tubes, for the .22 High Standard pistol.

As one can see the barrel length is quite reduced but is engineered for a drop-in fit. The three baffles are made from copper mesh and the wipes from solid rubber. Both end pieces screw onto the tube and the first one also onto the new barrel.

Note a front sight, of sorts, is even included with the end cap.

POPSHOT

Another one or two shot silencing device that has appeared on the marketplace within the last couple of years is a steel unit which screws directly onto a two quart, plastic, soft drink bottle and then into a threaded barrel.

The most obvious use for this is the Mac series with their already threaded barrels. The unit we tried was from SWD and did fit both ends as advertised.

So what happens if one doesn't own a 10?

I took a Ruger .22, wrapped the barrel in a tapered fashion with fiberglass strap tape, cut the threaded portion of the plastic bottle off so the front sight would slip into the bottle, and then slide the barrel into the bottle as far as possible.

More strap tape was added to prevent back gas kick and the entire comical looking unit shot at night.

Effect?

It ain't no substitute for an SWD pro silencer, but it does kill the flash almost totally, and the noise down by about 2/3 rds.

Translated: no neighbors calling cops, accurate within a few feet (ever try to aim thru a two quart plastic bottle?) and one or two clean hits...

Cheap and easy.

Top is the internal parts kit from SWD with outer tube set up for use with our pengun. While not as quiet as the commerical, High Standard version, it will deaden the noise of your one shot to a very tolerable level.

Below is a makeshift replacement for the SWD 2 liter plastic bottle adapter. In this case the .22 (Ruger) is simply fiberglass taped with a couple of rubber grommets to make an effective seal onto the bottle neck.

This will also give you one moderately quiet shot although aiming is a bit difficult as one can see...

JONATHAN ARTHUR CIENER
Rd 2 Box 66Y6
Titusville, Fl 32780

The Ferrari of gun dealers; a legit class II manufacturer they sell full autos, over under's, (as detailed elsewhere) quick change suppresson barrels for .22's, AR15 and M16 suppressors, 170 round mags for full auto .22's, AR-7 conversions, etc.

In short the deadliest, quietest weapons one can purchase in this country.

Note they only sell legally, no tricks, no half kits.

Also the neatest T-shirt in the whole book, trust me; $7.95 PP size and color (red, white, blue or tan), catalog $4.00.

WALTHER PPKS

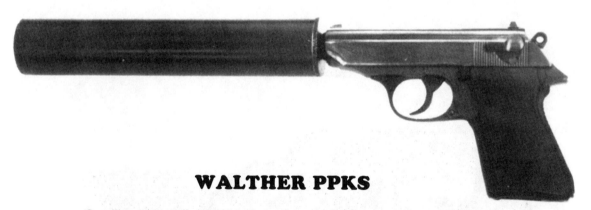

Quality and craftsmanship have long been synonymous with the Walther line of automatic pistols. Shown here is our unique larger caliber automatic suppressor fitted to the .380 PPKS. We also offer units designed for the PPKS, PP and TPH in .380, .32 Auto and .22 calibers.

Walthers are especially suited for being fitted with a suppressor due to the ease with which the barrel can be removed and our specially manufactured suppressed barrel installed. Order the suppressor fitted to your gun or a complete package.

This automatic pistol suppressor can be custom fitted to many other automatic firearms. For more details on custom suppressors, see page 13.

SUPERSONIC FALSIES

As a projectile exceeds the speed of sound (about 1100 feet per second at sea level) it creates an effect known as a bow wave.

This is the wave produced by a supersonic aircraft and travels away from the bullet at the speed of sound. If the bullet is actually moving faster than this speed the wave will be pushed back, or, more to the point, the air producing the wave will be pushed back forming a cone shaped area angling backwards from the projectile itself.

The faster the bullet, the more pronounced this effect is; i.e., if a bullet is traveling twice the speed of sound the actual slug would travel (assuming a constant speed, of course) 2350 feet while the bow wave would travel 1125 feet.

Since the velocity is not constant the difference in bow wave and slug will increase up to full speed and then begin decreasing.

Because of the dynamics of sound energy if the bullet passes near a person the bow wave noise will be much louder than the actual muzzle report of the weapon.

This fact coupled with the increasing range difference between the bow wave and the actual bullet adds to the confusion of the person hearing the reports.

Because of this quirk of physics many victims or near victims of long range sniping attacks will feel the secondary bow wave was the actual muzzle report (which often sounds like a quick, but fainter echo of the bow wave) and will place the sniper at 10 degrees up to a full 90 degree angle from where the shot was actually fired depending on speed and distance from the rifle.

The most important fact that arises from this discussion is that one cannot be certain from exactly where the shot was fired so INSTEAD OF TRYING TO RETURN FIRE, it is usually better to protect oneself from ALL directions and then attempt to separate the actual muzzle report direction from the bow wave effect.

To Tell The Truth

It is possible to determine the actual direction from which a shot was fired by analyzing the acoustical error involved with the bow wave/muzzle phenomenon.

For a quick and dirty shot (no pun intended) face the direction in which the bow wave was heard and extend both arms to the one's sides and then angle them a bit forward.

The shot will have come from one of those directions and the necessary defense or search and destroy missions can commence.

If the muzzle report was also heard and the actual direction noted, one can instantly establish which of the directions is the true point of origin.

This same technique can be performed after the area is declared safe by drawing the target's position intersected by a straight line towards the direction he "heard" the bullet come from.

Now draw the same scene on a sheet of tracing paper with the addition of the cone shaped bow wave pattern (as shown). When the tracing paper is superimposed on the original and rotated at right angles, both possible true trajectory paths will become clear.

Understanding the bow wave effect is important for two reasons:

1. Only when the true direction of the bullet's path is clear can the intended target take cover which will protect him from further shots.

2. After the attack the correct area can be searched for any evidence left behind by the sniper.

Subsonic

Remember the bow wave effect exists only when a bullet is super-sonic and will not exist on low velocity cartridges or when the distance from the muzzle is great enough to slow the projectile below the speed of sound.

When a subsonic bullet passes by a target the sound heard will often be that of a buzz or hum AFTER THE INITIAL MUZZLE BLAST IS HEARD.

Remember in SUPERSONIC firings two separate reports should be heard EXCEPT at distances under 100 yards where the two reports may come so close together they will often be perceived as only one sound.

At twice this distance the bow wave will actually be 100 TIMES louder than the muzzle report, giving rise to the mistake of interpting the actual muzzle blast as a mere echo.

The bow wave will often sound like a whip being cracked near one's head...

In these situations if you hear the bullet, you lived though it...

ONE SHOT-ONE KILL

It sounds like something out of a science fiction movie; a bullet that kills almost every time it is fired...

And it's legal.

This little known real life killer is named the GLASER SAFETY SLUG and is available at many gun dealers for (suggested retail price) about $2.50 per bullet in 9 mm.

It is made by Glaser Safety Slug Inc., PO Box 8223, Foster City, Ca. 94404.

The cartridge is made in 12 different calibers from the little .25 ACP to the mighty .44 Mag and includes both 308 and 30-06 rifle sizes.

This bullet has a 90-95% kill rate...

This means that 90-95% of the time the target dies. This includes times when the target is hit in the hand, leg or toe...

Hard to believe? The federal government rates the Glaser slug #1 in RI Index (relative incapacitate) in every caliber, and just a hair below the .44 magnum in stopping power.

That is, the 9 mm Glaser is just a hair below a 44 mag in stopping power...

Why does this phenomenon occur?

The Glaser slug is composed of the case, powder and primer and then a special, thin-walled copper jacket that contains #12 chilled lead shot suspended in liquid Teflon contained by a frangible plastic tip.

This unique construction allows the pre-fragmented projectile to actually penetrate the target in one piece. Pressure on the tip prevents the fragmentation of the slug until the tip goes through the target surface.

At this time pressure on the tip is suddenly relieved and the bullet disintegrates BELOW THE SURFACE, releasing over 330 sub-projectiles in a cone shaped pattern of destruction.

This causes "massive trauma and instant incapacitation", according to a government study.

And believe me, it does just that...

See the photograph of our test.

This unique fragmentation action transfers 100% of the available energy to the primary target. This is the only bullet that actually does that...

Most people die almost instantly, even from hand wounds that would be only a minor problem in other bullets, due to the extreme shock and loss of tissue.

This particular construction gives the Glaser some other unique characteristics; the bullet simply does not ricochet, thereby protecting bystanders from secondary strike harm (a normal .357 magnum can ricochet 3/4 of a mile).

The flat-nose truncated-cone projectile will allow the bullet to penetrate steel automobile panels and yet will fragment in 1" or less of tissue, releasing the shot into the target.

Recoil is less that half that of conventional ammunition allowing for less anticipation and better accuracy.

The Glaser is a very reliable bullet and operates all automatic weapons to nearly 100% of their capicity.

Because of the bullet's lighter weight, the front sight on pistols with a normally fixed front sight may have to be lowered to take advantage of the cartridge's extreme accuracy.

Remember this is NOT a shot shell; it is a single projectile that must hit the target as a regular bullet to be effective.

The summary amounts to; incredible penetration in solid objects, immediate fragmentation upon perforation, no over penetration, immediate stopping power, no ricochet, less recoil (equaling faster target acquisition in rapid fire sequences, same range as conventional bullets but better accuracy and to top it off it's legal under the Geneva convention and can be purchased both in the US and Canada.

For now.

This amazing bullet has all the earmarks of a "prohibited except for law enforcement use" object...According to French's First Rule anything that is effective and comes to be used by the police will soon be outlawed to the general public...

Buy some.

PICK YOUR PORK

These two pieces of salt pork (chosen for the close consistency to human flesh) were both shot with a 9 mm bullet.

The piece on the right suffered a direct hit from a hollow point "normal" bullet. It tore through the meat and did considerable damage.

The left hand chunk was taken out by one Glaser slug. As you can see it exploded the meat, turning it inside out and tearing it to hell and back.

One shot-one kill...

GLASER DEATH

Clay on left was shot with a normal 9mm ball round; same size piece on right was shot with a 9mm GLASER slug. Which would you prefer to face?

Bottom photo is a vest thick piece of KELVAR fabric that has taken a direct hit from the 9mm GLASER.

One hit...

EXPLOSIVE AND INCENDIARY BULLETS

As touched upon previously, bullets can be made to explode almost assuring of a lethal wound. The commercial versions of these cartridges work well but are illegal without an FFL.

It is possible to make homemade explosive bullets but the procedure is extremely dangerous and should not be attempted by anyone who is not an experienced reloader.

Even under experienced conditions one should never deal with explosive chemicals and metal bullets without wearing protective clothing including a welder's jacket, gloves and a shatterproof face mask.

I am not going to go into exact details as this is just too bloody risky unless you already have the necessary knowledge to fill in my blanks.

Suffice to say the bullets are usually machined down from a larger size, hollowed out, and then loaded with black powder and magnesium.

A primer is then placed in the tip of the bullet, face down. A hit in flesh and bone, along with the correct velocity will set off the primer and explode the bullet.

The shock wave, gas bubble and fragmentation will gouge out a large cavity and create heavy damage.

INCENDIARY

This one is a hair safer but still NOT for construction by amateurs. Again the bullet is machined and hollowed out and then the point filled with a normal lighter flint.

A drop of super glue is then added to hold the flint in place.

If fired against a hard surface this bullet will spark and ignite flammable materials. It has no real advantage in flesh wounds.

A more sophisticated version is prepared with a mixture of double base powder and zirconium wire (extracted from an unused flashbulb).

The powder is chopped (5 grains) into a fine powder and mixed with 2 grains of wire. This is an extremely unstable mixture that can explode if mixed in larger quantities or ground together.

If it is placed in an enlarged hollow point and a percussion cap (inverted) is sealed on top the unit will flash/explode upon impact.

Never shoot in a gun with a tubular magazine as the pressure may cause detonation.

Again these are DANGEROUS AND ILLEGAL.

POISON

A modern day version of the poison arrow, a hollow point bullet can be further hollowed out by using the tip of a ball point pen and one of several poisons inserted.

The tip is then sealed with super glue or sealing wax.

This makes a very deadly, very unsportsmanlike bullet.

Illegal.

MULTIPLEX-THREE STRIKES AND THEY'RE OUT

As anyone who has ever fired a shotgun loaded with 00 buckshot knows, the impact power of multiple projectiles is awesome.

Double buck is roughly equivalent to .38 caliber pistol bullets in individual pellet size, yet the total impact damage is worse than could be expected with an equal number of .38 hits...

Due to a strange mathematical effect the impact force transmitted is in a logarithmic progression. This means that 2 hits with a pellet (or bullet) hits with 4 times the force of a single strike. Three hits equals 9 singles and so on.

Multiple Munitions Industries, Inc (distributed by Silent Partner, Inc., Gretna, LA, 70053) has brought this concept home for the handgun user.

The MMI .38 special is a single cartridge that contains 3 separate bullets in the same package. As it is fired the slugs separate allowing each to engage the barrel's rifling.

At 20 feet one shot will give three hits within a 2 inch grouping. At 75 feet the group will be about 17 inches across.

In essance this means any .38 can have the stopping power of a .45 automatic, while a six shot .38 revolver can actually deliver 18 separate slugs into the target!

Available from many gun dealers and soon to be out in .357 as well as other calibers.

It works, note the test photos.

AMERICAN BALLISTICS
Box 1410
Marietta Ga 30061

As they so aptly phrase it; some situations require special ammo...   Manufacturers of sub sonic, armour piercing and super sonic match grade cartridges in most popular rifle and pistol calibers.

Will sell direct in large lots, or can be found at better dealers everywhere, as they say on tv...

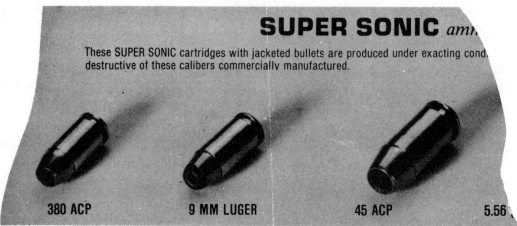

SUPER SONIC *amm*

These SUPER SONIC cartridges with jacketed bullets are produced under exacting cond. destructive of these calibers commercially manufactured.

380 ACP   9 MM LUGER   45 ACP   5.56

SUB SONIC *Whisperload®* *am*

These SUB SONIC Whisperload cartridges are designed to function quietly, reduce muzzle flash, and give subsonic velocity with a high degree of accuracy, consistency, and reliability.

M11/380 ACP 9mmk   M10/9MM Parabellum   45 ACP TUNGSTEN   5.56 (.223) Sniper
Military Cartridge SMG   Cartridge SMG   SHOT Cartridge SMG   Cartridge

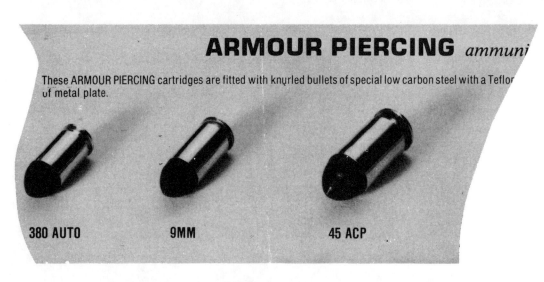

ARMOUR PIERCING *ammuni*

These ARMOUR PIERCING cartridges are fitted with knurled bullets of special low carbon steel with a Teflor uf metal plate.

380 AUTO   9MM   45 ACP

NORMAL SHOOTING TECHNIQUES

Double Action Revolver

This is the typical weapon of any trained handgun fighter due to their ease of use, safety, accuracy and non-jamming characteristics.

Double action revolvers have a cylinder that holds six rounds; to fire one simply pulls the trigger. Modern weapons have a plate in place which will prevent accidental discharge if a chambered weapon is struck on the hammer or barrel without being cocked first.

Good basic revolver shooting includes at least the following steps:

Grab the weapon firmly, holding the handle in the web of skin between the first finger and the thumb.

Use a natural stance, i.e.., feet about shoulder width apart with your weight divided between the two, unless you are trained and comfortable with another stance.

Draw the revolver from the holster and hold it at eye level while aligning the sights with your strongest eye and the target.

Support your shooting hand with your other hand by wrapping it around the stronger hand so the fingers fit into the grooves made by the other hand's fingers. Always put the index finger of the supporting hand under the trigger guard, not around it.

Pull the trigger in one steady squeeze throughout it's entire pull.

Automatics

Most modern automatics (which, of course, are actually semi-automatics in real life) are of the double action variety. This means the weapon is usually fired by loading a live round in the chamber, pulling the trigger to fire the first shot, which will in turn, chamber and cock the hammer for each subsequent discharge.

It is also possible to chamber and cock the double action, making it, in effect, a single action weapon for the first shot.

Double action autos cannot be placed into the "safety on" position with the hammer cocked.

Automatics generally carry more rounds than revolvers but are prone to jamming and are limited in barrel length; hence accuracy.

If you are engaged in a firefight and have another loaded magazine handy, depress the magazine release with the non-shooting hand ALLOWING THE MAGAZINE TO FALL CLEAR, grab the new mag with the same hand, put your index finger along the front edge of the magazine and insert it into the weapon.

Release the cocked slide and re-engage the target.

Commercial Speedloaders

One disadvantage to the revolver is the comparatively slow process of reloading. This can be brought up to almost automatic standards by the use of a speed loader.

This device holds six rounds in a separate unit that are spaced to fit directly into the weapon in use. A center mounted knob turns about a quarter turn to instantly release all six cartridges into their respective chambers.

To operate a speedloader effectively transfer the revolver into the nonshooting hand, release the cylinder and push it out with the middle fingers. Now use your thumb to push down on the ejector rod.

LET THE SPENT CASES FALL CLEAR.

Place the speedloader into the weapon and release the new cartridges.

Close the cylinder, re-aim the weapon and re-engage the target.

SNAP SHOOTING

A few years ago the army began testing a program that taught people to shoot both handguns and rifles in a natural fashion that seemed to be the most effective method of speedily teaching very accurate shooting techniques.

This technique, known as snap or instinct shooting, combines the body's natural abilities with a mechanical device to provide dramatic results...

To learn snap shooting begin thusly:

Quickly point your index "aiming hand" finger at any object within handgun range. Do this with both eyes open in a natural, relaxed stance.

Now check over your finger by sighting in a normal fashion and you will find you are right on target...

Why?

Because your brain automatically averages out the the difference between your eyes and "aims" on target.

Repeat this movement over and over until you are satisfied that you can accomplish it in one even fast motion every time.

Now take a gun, this can be any type of handgun, air pistols work just as well to learn on and don't cost much nor kill the neighbors...

I am going to assume you understand how to use a pistol correctly and safely, if you do not, learn that first...

Place the gun in your best hand, grab it tightly, but do not over tighten your hand as to strain the muscles herein.

Now smoothly point the weapon in the exact same fashion as you did with your finger.

Check the aiming and you will find you are on target or barely off. Repeat this movement until you can lay it directly on target every time...

Once you can do this with accuracy,, every time, try dry firing both single and double action revolvers and semi autos.

Do not attempt blinding speed and accuracy at the same time. Concentrate on the accuracy and the speed will come.

Keep in control at all times, but repeat and repeat, repeat, you get the idea...

Once one is comfortable in this position move on to an airgun or a .22. Use a good backdrop and keep the range down to about 15 feet.

If this seems impractical remember that about 90% of all handgun battles take place within this range. In fact history shows us that the great cowboy fast draw battles were usually under 10 feet...

Remember to hold the gun the same way every time you pick it up in order to maintain continuity.

Now try the same technique firing from the hip. Again bring the gun up smoothly to a perfectly level position. Your upper arm (bicep) should be directly horizontal; at a 90 degree angle to the ground, the elbow is held tightly against the body.

When gun "feels" aligned with the target, shoot.

Use a natural pointing motion that brings the pistol up towards the center mass of the target at the same time it is coming forward from a low position.

Some people find it is best to slightly rock the pistol forward and lock it in at the final split second before firing.

Try to always keep the wrist totally straight throughout this entire motion. A locked wrist will prevent most wide misses right off the bat.

There really can be no side to side movement in this type of shooting or there will be problems in correction.

Understand and use your natural center line, when you have this down pat the rest of the corrections will be vertical and fairly easy to allow for.

When you begin practicing with live rounds keep your index finger out of the trigger guard; this gives you the advantage of still using the point system with the finger as well as preventing any accidental discharge from the weapon.

This position will take some practice so it is wise to use a low powered gun without much kick as well as one that is cheap to burn rounds through.

Does instinct shooting work?

Yes, yes and yes. It will NOT match the squeeze the trigger after aiming with one eye closed method, but it can develop amazing accuracy.

The army used it first with rifle training and within 1/2 hour of practice had people shooting coins and even aspirin tablets OUT OF THE AIR.

It is designed for close situations wherein one second can easily make the difference between walking away and being carried away.

If you have ever been involved in a close encounter of the deadly kind you know that time seems to enter the twilight zone; even race car drivers have usually been through one or more crisis situations where time seems totally disjointed.

You must perfect this technique for close in situations.

Once you have mastered close range snap shooting begin trying the same technique with multiple targets; two shots to each central mass area and then two to the next and then spin back to the first to sense damage/movement.

When double and multiple shooting be sure to bring the wrist up and fire LOCKING it in the same position for the follow up shot.

Remember to repeat the point/lock and fire procedure for EACH target, do not "swing" the weapon around, spin the body and follow the correct technique with the arm for each target.

This will still take only a split second for each target, giving a much higher percentage of hits than the more accurate two hand stance or sight-and-aim method WHEN VIEWED WITH A TIME FACTOR IN MIND.

I can, and have, shoot and hit with an olympic medal winner and stayed in the same groupings when I have had time to aim and squeeze, of course I owned my first .22 when I was 5 years old...

I have also snap shot with street cops that could put four bullets into me before I could have gotten the correct eye shut...

Makes you think...

The most widely accepted shooting system in snap shooting is at least two shots to the main mass of the body and then stop to see what happens...

It is generally unwise to shoot for anything except center of mass unless you know the target is wearing a vest.

One should get the skill to hit a playing card from the hip at 10-15 feet every time with a medium barreled .22 long rifle...

Once the accuracy is there, try for speed. Bring the pistol up quickly, using a break-front holster if you want to practice drawing, and fire at the time it "feels" correct.

You will be surprised.

This same technique should be applies to rifle firing. Start with he finger, go to dry firing after bring the rifle into position smoothly and quickly and checking the sighting.

Again an air gun is best to start with, be certain both front and rear sights are held perfectly horizontally, a turned rifle is one of the most common reason for misses with snap shooting.

Work at fairly short range, but slowly decrease the target size and increase the speed. Your "inside" accuracy will amaze you after a few hundred rounds...

Any of these techniques will work better for someone who is used to guns and can already use them in the conventional fashion than it will for a pure beginner, but it can teach anyone to shoot with confidence and accuracy in a short time.

Practice and practice until it becomes no effort. Snap shooting should be a zen like movement that is performed without conscious thought.

Form becomes no form, thought becomes no thought.

Instinct.

POINT/COUNTERPOINT

The following is a summary I had with one of the top pistol experts in the United States. He has won numerous awards, teaches on his own and with Jeff Cooper and has "invented" several useful techniques.

We (the two of us) and Mike disagree on several points. Due to his expertise it seems wise to present his point of view on a number of subjects.

Remember this whole field is subjective and open to change. Ninja means adaptation to win.

Mike has suggested several pistol techniques that Steve Hayes is incorporating into his ninja teachings...

This is my memory of a spoken conversation after a party for some ninja students in San Diego, I had had a couple of beers and apologize for any misquotes that appear.

MIKE-"I do not believe in trick bullets. True they can fit in with some certain situations, but few people can predict when the next time they will have to fire a gun in anger.

Glasers tend to explode on contact with heavy clothing or armour, wafer bullets give an unpredictable pattern. Shot shells may not stop your enemy.

Most real tissue damage occurs with hydrostatic shock and that only occurs at speeds of mach 2, pistol bullets won't reach that level, 9 mm is just about mach 1, so use something with more mass and stopping power. I prefer the .45 as the best all around pistol bullet.

Shotguns are NOT the ideal home defense weapon. In the typical firefight, 10 feet or less, 00 buckshot has a spread of just a couple of inches, where's the advantage in that over a supersonic bullet that will keyhole and cause massive damage?

Besides many women (and men) will hesitate to fire a shotgun due to the recoil and so on. The gun itself is unwieldly and hard to keep handy. The barrel is too long for in home use.

I use several guns including a mini 14; little recoil, much damage, easy to point and shoot, lots of cartridges.

ME-What about the neighbors?

MIKE-Use the correct technique; first draw a rough picture of the inside of your house marking the choke (ambush) points. You will know where he is, he will not know where you are.

LIE DOWN, shoot upward from a prone position. This makes it difficult to be targeted and if you hit the enemy and the bullet passes through him it will exit through the roof, missing the neighbors.

Besides, if it comes down to it, who would you rather have shot, you or the neighbors?

Contest and most range shooting can be compared to traditional karate, fun, works under a given set of rules but bears little resemblance to a real life situation.

Point shooters use light bullets and light loads for high point ring shooting. This is not valid in combat, one needs stopping power and LESS ACCURACY.

Two hits in a small grouping, against a moving target who may or may not have body armour on, can be useless. Two hits 6 inches apart are much more likely to stop somebody.

Always shoot two shots at the center of mass and then check it out, FIRE AGAIN IF NECESSARY.

As in ninjutsu one needs the intention, intelligence and physical follow through. I would rather be backed by a combat shooter than a great (target) shooter in any real situation. I know he will not hesitate to fire when necessary, when a quarter of a second can be life or death.

Train with real loads and multiple targets. One good technique is to load with alternate rounds; one ball, one wad cutter.

Shoot two shots into each target and then check the holes. This will reveal if one has the tendency to lock on with the first shot and then pull off from recoil or next target anticipation or if the first shot is fired before the target is locked in and then the second is more carefully placed.

An alternative technique is to load an automatic with a clip full of ball, except for one wadcutter in the last position, fire at multiple targets, chamber the last round and slam a new clip in loaded with wadcutters, continue firing at the same targets.

This will show if you reload and relock correctly or if you have a tendency to pull in any direction.

Oh yes, shoot the second clip with your weak hand to see the difference...

Remember when monday morning quarterbacking about vest disfiguration and tissue damage that it is damn hard to hit a mean, moving target twice in the same area so it becomes a moot point...

Practice, practice and learn to control your field of interest. I have three loaded pistols in different places in my house at all times...

THE HARRIES FLASHLIGHT TECHNIQUE

Many pistol firefights actually take place in low light or no light conditions, usually at short range. The following method is, in our humble opinion, the best all around technique available, it is being taught in some of the best combat shooting courses in the world (including Jeff Cooper's) but has never appeared in print before.

It is an excerpt from an upcoming book by Mr. Harries which Crocker- Edwards hopes to publish in the near future.

The need to shoot during the hours of darkness, or in very dim light, IS...absolutely necessary in the real world!

And no group, organization, or individuals concerned with training, will disagree on that point.

In fact, it is probably THE ONLY concept with all around agreement between--The Police; Military; and the "Private" sector (different shooting schools, and instructors).

You must identify your target to shoot safely OR effectively. In the first place, you don't want to shoot someone on "your" side. (Team member--Partner--Family) and just as important; you can't afford to wait for the "Dark Shadow" to fire several rounds in your direction...to "prove" he's the bad guy!

Remember, at night--and at the close range you are likely to be--if you "see" a shadowy form in low light, or in the darkness--YOU ARE AT POINT-BLANK RANGE! This means; even a poor shot (which criminals usually are) can hit you, and at close range...things happen FAST!

Unless you're wearing your "mummy-style" body armor; you'll probably take some hits; BECAUSE of the close range--IF--you wait to until hostile action is taken against you, before you know who's there.....What can you do?

YOU MUST I.D YOUR POSSIBLE THREAT FIRST!

We know already that it is bad news (for yourself, and others) to shoot at targets you haven't identified as friend or foe. This is a problem even in daylight, at night, the problem is compounded.

WHAT TO DO?.....WHAT TO DO?

O.K. we've established that we can't afford to "take-fire" to locate the bad people.....and we don't want to shoot anyone except those we have decided that need to be shot.

What now?

WE MUST LEARN TO USE A HANDY, PORTABLE, LIGHT SOURCE. TO AID US IN IDENTIFYING FRIEND OR FOE.....AND AS AN AID TO SHOOTING.

THE FLASHLIGHT

HISTORY

Back in the late 60's and early 70's when I started in Combat Pistol Shooting--I saw, and used many "trick" flashlights. 'V' blocks of angle iron screwed to the magazine; Belt packs with cords to "adapted" miner's lights; Lanterns of all sizes and shapes. (Mine was one with a mercury switch, set up to go on, as I brought it on target.)

And in later years, the type of flashlight used by most of the competitors as the "Hot Set-up" was one that throws a beam that looks like a WWII searchlight! I've seen some very powerful, wide-angle lights that people switched on, and then "dropped" or set down quickly near them. The light was so bright that it lit up the country side, (not to mention the targets on either side) even when they stuck it under their arm, pointing at the ground out in front, there was enough light to shoot by!

CONTEST VS "REAL WORLD"

(the technique development)

WELL ....that works in certain "contest" situations when you have a chance to "practice and refine" the problem. Most of us who are dealing with "real world" survival...just don't have the right "trick" gear for each and every situation, because we never know ahead of time, what kind of confrontation, or fight we may be in. Which means we need ALL-PURPOSE GEAR!

Which leads us to my thinking on the problem: I decided, many years ago, that a technique should be developed that took several things into consideration:

1. The technique should not differ greatly from the "normal" shooting stance.

2. It should offer control of both Pistol and Light. And be usable for both searching areas, and from the draw (Pistol; Light; or both) .

3. The Flashlight should be a "practical" everyday type [standard C or D cell, cylindrical and common] .

4. The sum total of the Flashlight; the Technique; and the Shooter--should be at no real disadvantage at getting HITS, EVEN in a contest.

The idea that you should use one type of Flashlight and Technique for a contest, and something else for the "street" DOES NOT RING TRUE!

If you are to be effective in saving your life, you must practice in a manner suitable for a great number of situations. You can't afford to limit your practice to situations in which your "special" gear will allow you "to-get-by"...YOU HAD BETTER BE GOOD WITH SIMPLE GEAR!

We're talking about Flashlights in particular, however, this type of thinking [also known as the K.I.S.S. principle] can apply to most Weapons in general.

Some of my friends in Law Enforcement have those Flashlights that are combination Clubs; Arc-light; Flamethrower; and walking stick! They will blind Elephants a block away, and you can take home movies with them. And yes, THEY do carry them every shift, and put them on the charger regularly. So if you live with your "super-light" 24 hours a day, by all means, use it!

For the rest of us, $ expensive $ trick gear is just going to get in the way of good sound tactical thinking.....For example; Who really carries a $500 or $1000 boot knife? I've seen them, and I would even like to have one...BUT SO WHAT! I wouldn't dare carry it where I though it might get lost, stolen, or scratched up!

THE POINT I'M MAKING......IS

DON'T THINK A HIGH PRICED PIECE OF GEAR WILL MAKE UP FOR A LACK OF SKILL OR PRACTICE!!! [if this is all you ever remember from all of this...it just might save your life someday!]

 AND...if you have several flashlights...

YOU WILL BE MORE LIKELY TO HAVE ONE AVAILABLE TO YOU, WHEN YOU NEED IT!

Remember.....a small 110 camera in-your-pocket, is worth many "fancy" 35mm jobs...complete w/tripod and telephoto lenses, if they are "back at the ranch"]

Practice, Practice, Practice, and then practice some more! Being able to shoot in low light, or darkness, is one of the most practical skills you will ever learn.

YOU MAY BET YOUR LIFE ON IT....SOMEDAY!

Looking with the flashlight (pistol still in holster).

On decision to draw; gun hand contacts pistol; flashlight goes vertical and then starts downward.

Gun arm extends and flashlight arm swings upward as flashlight starts pointing to the front.

Draw starts forward; flashlight extends down and at arm extension, begins to whip inside and underneath the gun arm.

Flashlight arm should touch slightly and "slide" forward into "lockup"; the edge of the flashlight hand is pressing into (and just slightly upward) the back of the shooting hand. Left elbow down as in next photo with HARD ISOMETRIC TENSION.

Final lock. Both hands are pressing against one another providing great stability. A tiny bit of the flashlight beam should touch the shooting hand. NOTE: During the draw and lock steps the muzzle DOES NOT point at your hand, arm or the flashlight AND even a long 5 cell light won't be hard to manage IF you practice this technique step by step until it becomes a fluid process.

The flashlight shown with Mike is a cheap 3-D cell Everready available at drug stores coated with about 50 cents woth of black tape. Any light will do...

ITR   WILLIAMS GUNSIGHT CO.
PO Box 557   7389 Lapeer rd.
Maricopa, AZ 85239   Davison, MI 48423

ITR makes an AIR GUN (caliber .428 and up) that has the stopping power of a .243 Winchester! The ram shown was killed by a single shot. Which is good as you only have one...No gunpowder but in the fine print one sees it takes 200(!) pumps to get up to full power. Not much less noisy than a "real" rifle.

WILLIAMS stocks sights, rifles, bows, gloves, reloading equipment, replacement barrels, ammo, camo and coveralls. Great prices, wide selection.

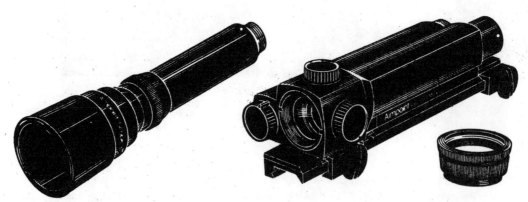

Aimpoint 3X Scope Attachment   Aimpoint Mark III Sight

AIMPOINT

AIMPOINT is unbeatable for hunting as you are on the mark immediately The dot is on target all the time with unbelievable quick shooting as a result. Because it does not magnify and is further away from the eye, it is much easier to get your bearings, even in dense undergrowth and even if your prey comes a little too close. This sight reduces the risk of wounding game because you get more time for precision aiming. You see the dot immediately and your field of view is unbroken wherever your head is.

BULLETPROOF CLOTHING

The Facts, Madam, Just The Facts...

As most of you know, DuPont developed a fabric named Kelvar, some years ago while looking for a long lasting tread substitute for rubber on high speed tires.

It did not work out.

It did stop bullets, however, by adsorbing, or spreading out the impact shock over a large area while also providing a number of "hard as steel" layers to "catch" the actual bullet.

Some problems occured with the orignal units; physical weight, sweat retention, disfiguration upon the first impact which allowed the second slug to slip through, waterproofing trouble, and so on.

All of this not withstanding, they did stop bullets and saved several hundred lives while the construction process was being refined to overcome most of the problems.

The bulletproof clothing we experimented with (at least the commercial variety) was supplied by SECOND CHANCE, INC., the best selling brand on the market.

We also asked SILENT PARTNER for a chance to test their fabric and products and were informed they did "not wish to participate nor be mentioned in any such tests in our publication."

Okay, take it for what it is worth...

In the next few pages we are going to review and test the available fabrics and vests as well as show how they can be made better, self-built and even defeated...

Vests And Such.

Most bullet proof, or to be correct, bullet resistant, clothing falls under the term "vest" even though in real life it may be a shirt, jacket, or series of panels designed to protect the body's various high threat zones.

In fact very few BP units are actually made into vests. Rather, most are "threat zoned" with high priority areas such as the chest, back, and often the the groin given heavier protection than the less deadly targets such as the side, arms and legs.

Every piece of resistant clothing provides only so much protection depending on how many layers of top grade, woven Kelvar are utilized in the construction of the item.

Clothing is usually made by inserting nylon covered Kelvar pieces into shirts, jackets, or custom constructed body coverings.

One should attempt to match the amount of protection with the amount of threat. Although, in theory, it would be simpler to wear as many layers of protection as possible in all high risk areas, this is not so in the every day world.

Kelvar is not light, it does tend to prevent body breathing and can amplify heat levels rapidly, is a bit bulky and somewhat of a hassle.

If you are playing Clint Eastwood, running heroin, trying to get Nixon back into main stream politics, or lying to the IRS, a heavy duty threat level is probably worth the sweat and tears, to avoid the blood.

One should not make the mistake of thinking a Kelvar garment stops all injury; IT DOES NOT!!

Blunt trauma, or in lay folks terms, massive bruises plus shock and sometimes broken bones can and often does result when a Kelvar protection garment receives one or more large caliber bullets.

Kelvar does spread the shock wave; it does not magically get rid of it. One is likely to fall back and down when taking a Kelvar helped hit, a condition that probably helps in some cases by stopping a follow-up shot from the bad guy.

It can easily put you in the hospital BUT YOU ARE ALIVE.

Following the ever so popular laws of physics the amount of protection required depends exactly on the mass and velocity of the projectile.

Large caliber cartridges and heavy powder loads (magnums) quite simply do more damage than do their lighter cousins.

With or without a bulletproof garment.

One system to enhance the protection level of any bullet resistant garment is to include one or more panels of hardened steel or hardened ceramic designed for stopping armor piercing bullets over heavy threat areas.

This technique will abruptly increase both the weight and warmth qualities of the garment, but will stop bullets which would pass through the normal "bulletproof" garment.

A Interesting Note

An interesting note is that most Kelvar garments will NOT stop the thrust of a knife or other, thin, sharp object. In fact ice picks or our ninja ESCORT will go through most thick vests if applied with enough force behind them.

Many vest wearers are not aware of this fact and several HAVE DIED because of it....

When we tested the SECOND CHANCE Kelvar material (at the thickness used for the vest we used) we were able to put both the ESCORT, and our ninja claws through the vest to some degree.

Enough to at least hurt if not kill...

BULLET RESISTANT GARMENTS: IMPROVING, MAKING, AND BEATING THEM

Improvement.

There are a couple of methods of improving on the commercial bullet resistant garment:

Penetration/Blunt Trauma

First of all, most people are shot with .22, .32 or .38 caliber handguns, NOT with .357 KTW mags or .44 mags. These smaller calibers ARE effectively contained by a good Kelvar garment such as the SECOND CHANCE model we tested.

The larger, or coated bullets we tried did create enough bruise/nerve damage to injure, or perhaps kill someone without much bodily fat and/or muscle.

On the other hand, no protection would have killed the above without much problem.

If you have a commercial garment that is rated towards a low threat level, and you are nervous...It is possible to purchase an addition insert plate of armor stopping steel or other material, and sew an insert pocket over the heart/heavy kill areas.

This is often done with velcro, to allow quick on-off applications of the additional armor.

Armor plates are available from several of the suppliers we have listed at the end of this interesting chapter.

If the existance of blunt trauma worries you we have discovered a method to cut down on blunt nerve damage to a great effect...

As far as I know, as of writing, no one else is using, or has suggested this method, although I am certain it will appear in a commercial version in the near future.

Sorbothane a newly developed (for the space shuttle program) rubber based shock absorbing compound will combat the main thrust of blunt trauma.

When we tested SC Kelvar with foam cardboard book bags as a backdrop it was possible to cut out 50-85% of the secondary damage due to blunt trauma...

This stuff is a miracle, it can and will make the difference between injury and no injury or death versus injury.

It can also provide the chance for return fire from the victim, who may have otherwise been incapacitated.

One can purchase this magic shock destroyer at most large outdoor sporting goods shops (used for taking the shock out of hiking or jogging in boots and running shoes) or from our buddies at EDMUND SCIENTIFIC.

It does not breathe well, and does increase the sweat factor although it is light enough to not add much weight to the entire resistant garment.

Sew, or tape, or glue a few thin sheets of this space age helper to the back of your protector.

Again, realize that any cartridge/barrel combination (a longer barrel produces higher projectile speeds than a short barrel does) that will beat an average bullet resistant garment (threat level II is about average for most law enforcement officers) will penetrate and do considerable damage.

This effect does require a sniper type rifle and/or some sort of penetration ammo.

One cannot not hide a .223 M16 or .06 rifle in a belt holster...

Concerning the SECOND CHANCE Kelvar armor; IT STOPPED EVERYTHING IT SAID IT WOULD STOP WITH NO EXCEPTIONS.

When the SC vest was coupled with a K-47 armor insert it stopped a .223 (5.56 mm) ball round WITH VIRTUALLY NO TRAUMA DAMAGE TO THE BACK UP BAGS.

Any protective material will cut down on the both the blunt trauma and the penetration potiental of a bullet and may well save a life.

Making Your Own

It is possible to make-your-own bullet proof garments in almost any threat level, by one of several available processes.

1. One can purchase the necessary Kelvar and/or armor plating from the suppliers listed and then simply take any heavy duty pull over shirt, sew two pockets, one in the front and one in the back to contain the Kelvar, and have a "vest" that will match many of the commercial models for 1/3 to 1/2 the price.

2. Purchase a down vest kit from an outdoor supplier MINUS the down filling. This gives a nylon vest-cover that is ideal for taking Kelvar while NOT showing the give-away outline of a bulky "hidden" bulletproof garment.

3. Purchase a ready made, commercial flak vest WITHOUT FILLING (source shown) or down vest and remove the filling replacing it with available Kelvar panels.

4. Sew your own (or have it sewn) garment from the drawings we have shown, or from DANGEGELD ARMOR's free (when you buy Kelvar) garment plans.

Any of these ideas will save one mucho pesos while allowing custom threat design.

Overcoming Bulletproof Garments.

There are a couple of known methods for defeating bulletproof garments;

1. If one knows a garment is likely to be involved simply shoot for unprotected areas, such as the head (unless an armored hat or helmet is used) and/or legs.

2. Employ armor piercing bullets such as the infamous KTW Teflon coated bullets (available in many handgun and rifle calibers). This bullet, along with standard military armor piercing ammo, and speciality ammo like that made by some of our suppliers, will enhance the penetration quality of any bullet, raising it one or more threat levels above its unarmored cousins.

The KTW bullet is hardened and then coated with a blue Teflon coating. Although some dispute the ability of Teflon to actually help pierce armor, this bullet works quite nicely when attempting to pierce Kelvar. It is not a miracle cure, but does raise the penetration level at least one threat level...

At least one bill has been introduced in Congress to outlaw the KTW "cop killer" (not one police or federal agent has been killed by a KTW bullet as of this writing; over 95% of their stock is sold to overseas agencies to combat terrorism) but has been defeated.

After receiving huge amounts of publicity, the KTW question was put to several thousand police officers in a trade journal survey.

They voted, overwhelmingly, to KEEP THE KTW LEGAL AND AVAILABLE!

Why?

Simple, too many bad guys are starting to wear vests...

The cops would, however, approve a bill to make any bad type caught wearing a Kelvar garment, during the commission of a crime, to be guilty of a felony and sent to prison...

Yes, KTW's help beat vests, but "normal" armor piercing bullets also slip through Kelvar when backed by the correct charge and barrel length.

We discovered another method...

As mentioned elsewhere, when we shot a Kelvar/nylon protection "plate" with GLASER slugs (from a 9 mm auto) the first shot tore the Kelvar to ribbons and the second, GLASER or otherwise, penetrated the vest with ease...

This is not a well known fact.

See the photos...

BULLETPROOF VESTS

To begin on a typical negative note; there is no such thing as a bulletproof anything. As we have pointed out, big enough bullet, hole through anything...

Second of all the term bulletproof vest does not really describe the products we are going to look at.

Body armor is the actual term which covers these products, or perhaps ballistic protection devices.

As there is much misconception about these products we are going to go into them in some detail including:

    Standards
    Stopping power
    Wearability
    Improving a vest
    Making your own body armor

Most soft body armor is made of Kelvar a fabric invented by Du Pont for use in auto tires. Pound for pound it is five times stronger than steel.

Most armor is made from a number of layers of this fabric glued together. The more layers, the more stopping power.

Protection is also dependent upon type of fabric, weave, and garment design.

At the time of this writing the best Kelvar for body armor is Kelvar 29, 31 x 31 count, 1000-denier Zepel waterproofed fabric.

Do not hesitate to inquire what type of Kelvar has been utilized in any armor your are interested in.

The government has established standards for classification of Kelvar armor. Manufacturers of vests have also published their own tests. We are re-printing those standards.

We also conducted our own tests in which a couple of interesting facts not included in the other studies came to light.

First off we would like to thank SECOND CHANCE for providing us with a sample vest as well as several different thickness samples of vests for our testing purposes.

We also asked POINT BLANK, another manufacturer for samples and were told that they did not wish to participate in any such testing.

Okay.

Rather than using clay for backing in our tests we used padded mailing bags as to see the degree of blunt trauma (we'll get to that in a minute) easier.

We used a model Y2 Second Chance vest for our tests as well as several different samples. This vest was supposed to exceed class IIA ballistics.

We used .22, .38, 9mm, and a .44 mag for our test weapons. Rather than go through each single shot I am going to state that the vest did what it was advertised to do. The .38's and .22's bounced off, some, like 9mm 112 grain imbedded but did not penetrate. The 44 jacketed mag from an 8 inch barrel went right on through....

The vest weighs in at 2 and 1/2 pounds and is fairly comfortable, although warm and a trifle bulky.

Now, we did say the vest lived up to its published results with regard to stopping power. If you look at our photos you will notice major damage done to the backing bags in several of the shots.

This is the result of blunt trauma, the energy dissapated from the impact spreads throughout and through the vest and can cause injury to the wearer even though the bullet did not go through the vest.

The smaller calibers will not cause much BT, the larger ones will do damage.

Well, better damage than death...

Earlier Kelvar tended to disform after one or two hits and not always stop the next hits. This problem has been pretty well solved with the newer versions.

One problem that does still exist is wet Kelvar loses much of its stopping power. You can buy waterproofed armor but it quickly becomes uncomfortable to wear.

Moist Kelvar is fine, soaking wet Kelvar is not fine...

IMPROVING ON SOFT ARMOR

There are several things one can do to improve the effectivness of soft armor. Many models have an area where the user can insert extra layers of Kelvar over "vital" areas, this increases the survivability rate.

To further this process actual armor, hardened steel plates can be insterted. With the Kelvar these will stop 30-06 armor piercing rounds, not to mention anything lesser...

If the vest does not have an insert, sew or glue one in.

Now for an interesting improvement that I have yet to see on the market, there is a new material, made for the space program called sorbothane, that absorbs shock better than any material ever has....

It can absorb up to 90% of any shock applied to it. This material is available from a number of sources, sold as running shoe inserts, shock absorbing material, etc.

When we placed it behind the vest and in front of the bags the damage was reduced significantly. This could easily mean the difference between three broken ribs and you just getting knocked on your ass.

It is much easier to return fire when you are knocked on your ass and mad than when you are nursing broken ribs...

Yes, it does make the vest hotter, but glue some between the insert and the vest or the vest and you....

You will start to see this on the market... Remember if you are shot and survive your first and only concern is to take out the other person. Now. Quick.

Never mind the bruises, pains, shock, take him out!

A shock is a shock, TAKE HIM OUT!

Unload the entire clip.

These vests are not invisible and if one is looking for signs of a person wearing one they are fairly easy to see.

This has brought out fears that criminals will start to try and beat the body armor concept.

There is some validity in that concept.

BEATING BULLETPROOF ARMOR

Several television shows and magazines have brought out the fact that anyone can purchase bullets which will go through most vests.

The most famous is the KTW, a Teflon coated, armor piercing bullet that will go through 36 layers of Kelvar like a hot knife through butter.

This brought out many cries about outlawing the bullet, however a police survey showed most cops do NOT want it outlawed...

Too many bad guys wearing vests these days.

A lesser known armor piercing slug is made by Winchester-Western will also go right on through most soft body armor.

A much more likelihood is a bad guy shoooting at a cop's head than buying and carrying KTW bullets.

In our tests we discovered another unknown vest beater; when we fired Glaser slugs into a Kelvar vest, the bullet would enter the vest, then "explode" the enclosed shot into the fiber, tearing it to shreads.

After one or two Glasers into a vest we found almost any slug would then pass through the ripped up fabric. If a gun was loaded with a couple of Glaser's and then jacketed slugs...

Another interesting fact is that Kelvar will not stop thin, sharp pointed objects. Some knives will be deflected but items like the Escort will go through easily.

So will fletchettes, thin, needle/arrows shot from guns...

The only source in the US at this time is Sgt Sandy's which sells fletchettes to be loaded into shotgun shells.

A 12 guage shell stuffed with these needle sharp min-arrows will tear anything they encounter into shreads, amassing massive tissue damage. They are deadly accurate within normal-to-slightly less than normal shotgun pellet range.

Single fletchettes as small phongraph needles encased in plastic which peeled away after the unit left the barrel (allowing the needle to be rifled by the lands and grooves of the barrel) have been used by the CIA and other such groups for assisination. They were even tested for more general use in Nam, but as with any super fast, low mass unit foilage penentration was not too good. This tiny sliver traveled at a fantastic rate of speed, was very accurate and caused a "keyholing" effect when it struck a mass of tissue.

Keyholing is the means by which small mass/high velocity projectiles rid thier energy. In reality it means the fletchchette often tears throughout the targets body bouncing off bones and ripping a ragged destructive path.

Sgt Sandy's steel arrows are a bit larger, giving them better penetration.

Ice picks and thin knives also go through soft armor vests quite well. When we took our Shuko (hand claws) and thrust at our Y2 vest, they did penetrate to some degeee, but not enough to cause any real damage, and not enough where I would not have fought back...

MANUFACTURING YOUR OWN BODY ARMOR

Soft armor can range anywhere from $100 for the small, thin, T-shirt type to well over $500 for fancy safari type jacket armor.

However one can manufauturer one's own version of soft or hard, or combination armor. Kelvar can be purchased from several sources, the one we like best is:

> DANEGELD CO;
> Box 2734
> Manassas Va 22110

Besides Kelvar which they sell by the yard, they sell insert plates, almost every sort of camo fabric your can visualize from Tiger stripe to snow, and include free patterns/instructions when you purchase Kelvar fabric.

These patterns include vests, groin protections, kill area inserts, and so on.

A good company that responds to your questions, charges minimal prices and provides good service.

Another way to create a "bulletproof" coat or vest is to purchase a army suprlus flak jacket from which the cermanic panels have been removed (they did not stop many bullets anyway...Several of the suppliers we have lilsted will sell these surplus jackets.

A commando stylc vest, one wihc will support loaded clips, knives, and various other equipment and has space for soft (or hard) armor inserts is sold by:

> THE BUNKER
> 903 Warrior River Road
> Hueytown, Al 35023

This handyvest comes with a variety of pocket sizes (for different weapon mags) and sells for about $70.

A final option is to purchase a sew-it-yourself down vest kit from many outdoor supply shops or from:

FROSTLINE

Box 2190
Boulder CO 80302

Sew the kit (or have some friendly young lady friend sew the kit if you are as inept at sewing as I am) and instead of down (or, for cold weather wear, with the down) insert glued layers of Kelvar.

These methods give you the option of customizing your protection as well as saving you money in the process.

Remember, heavier Kelvar or hard armor stops thngs better but is both harder and heavier, will make you quite hot on a warm day and is hard to conceal.

This last point is quite an important one. If I can tell you have a vest on under your shirt guess where I am going to aim for...

Any modern PI, law enforcement officer or ninja should think about this sort of protection very seriously.

Shell

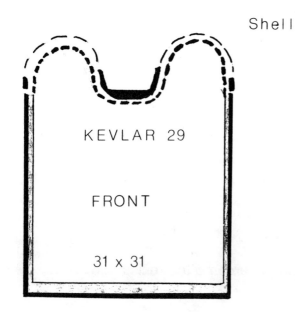

KEVLAR 29

FRONT

31 x 31

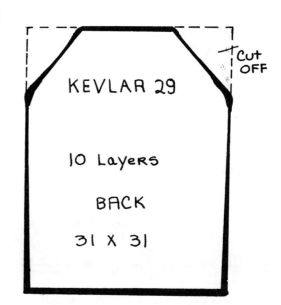

Cut OFF

KEVLAR 29

10 Layers

BACK

31 X 31

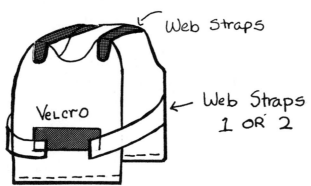

Web Straps

Velcro

Web Straps
1 OR 2

Sew straps on before Inserting Kevlar pads.

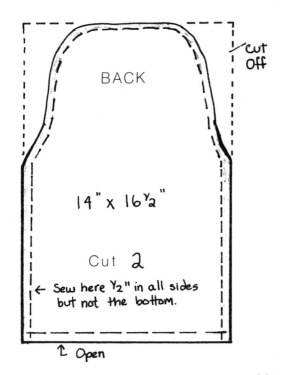

Cut Off

BACK

14" x 16½"

Cut 2

← Sew here ½" in all sides
but not the bottom.

↥ Open

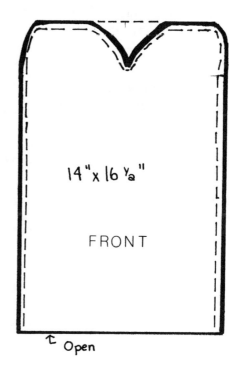

14" x 16½"

FRONT

↥ Open

437

ARMOR PIERCING BULLETS AND BULLETPROOF VESTS

As we have seen from looking at bulletproof vests, the term "bulletproof" is a relative judgement.

Nothing is bulletproof, not even Russian multi-layered tanks.

One simply has to fire a big enough bullet to overcome the resistance.

A more accurate term would be bullet resistant.

For maximum penetration we need the opposite characteristics in a bullet as we would demand for the best stopping power and most damage to the target.

A hollow point, or even jacketed lead bullet spreads out with impact creating a wider area of shock and tissue damage than a solid projectile does.

This very mushroom factor spreads the force of the impact over a wider area which a vest or armor plate can dissipate preventing penetration.

A solid brass bullet distorts less under impact and provides a much more difficult task for a vest.

A few years ago the media discovered solid bullets coated with one of the world's slickest materials; Teflon. These bullets, made by KTW, will pierce even the thickest vest with ease, as shown by the very fact that KTW uses Kelvar targets to advertise their product.

These "cop killer" bullets soon became a buzzword, although as I write this there is no incident on record where a cop has died because of teflon bullets...

Laws were suggested to stop the manufacture of KTW's, but, oddly enough, most cops (shown by surveys) do NOT want them outlawed.

Think about it.

More and more crooks are wearing Kelvar vests giving them the edge in "warning shot" confrontations.

A smarter move would be to make it a federal offense to wear a bulletproof vest during the commission of a crime... Besides, the majority of KTWs are actually shipped overseas, often to anti-terrorist organizations, and now that Russian soldiers are starting to wear Kelvar vests...

It should be noted that normal armor piercing ammo will also pierce most Kelvar vests almost as easily as KTW's.

In our vest-tests we came up with another interesting fact. When a GLASER slug was fired at the Kelvar it would rip part way into the fiber and then "explode" its shot load into the vest.

This cut the hell out of the Kelvar fiber.

No, the Glaser did not go through the vest, however it distorted and tore the Kelvar up so badly the next 9mm jacketed bullet went through like it was fired into jello.

See the photo.

This boils down to the simple fact that one or two Glasers can be fired quickly followed by one or more normal slugs with a good chance of going right on through the vest.

Of course this does not work on an armor plate-reinforced vest as the Glaser disperses upon hard surface impact.

AMERICAN BALLISTICS CO. also makes Teflon coated AP bullets.

DANEGELD VEST SPECIFICATIONS

As for the penetration rating for Kevlar, there is no government rating for penetration alone, i.e. ratings are for stopping penetration with an acceptable amount of backface deformation. Such ratings can only be applied to the finished protective garment or panel, as backface deformation will vary with the size, configuration, and construction, within a small but significant range. Three layers of the Kevlar that Danegeld sells would stop penetration on any level I threat bullet, but the impact would not be spread over a large enough area. One vest mfg. uses seven layers of this type of Kevlar with a little glue in between the layers ("micro-lamination") to stiffen their armor up to get a Level I rating for penetration & deformation with those seven layers while most mfgs. use eight, nine or as does Danegeld on this t-shirt armor, ten layers, to meet the deformation standard (our t-shirt would have met with eight, but we used ten for an extra margin of protection which would very likely stopped virtually all Level IIa and Level II threat bullets from penetrating, although blunt trauma from those higher threats could still have posed some danger with a Level I armor).

I tend to get suspicious when a mfg. talks too extensively about test results, independent lab tests, etc., because there is no monitoring or inspection of the armor or manufacturing processes, and therefore nothing to stop someone from having a specially made item tested, and then using inferior materials or different standards of quality control for subsequent production. Danegeld Kelvar is the standard type used in ballistic protection, and is the top quality of that type.

NILECJ STANDARD FOR THE BALLISTIC RESISTANCE OF POLICE BODY ARMOR

A Voluntary National Standard Promulgated by the
National Institute of Law Enforcement and Criminal Justice.

Following a Congressional mandate to develop new and improved techniques, systems, and equipment to strengthen law enforcement and criminal justice, the National Institute of Law Enforcement and Criminal Justice (NILECJ) has established the Law Enforcement Standards Laboratory (LESL) at the National Bureau of Standards. LESL's function is to conduct research that will assist law enforcement and criminal justice agencies in the selection and procurement of quality equipment.

In response to priorities established by NILECJ, LESL is: (1) Subjecting existing equipment to laboratory testing and evaluation and (2) conducting research leading to the development of several series of documents, including national voluntary equipment standards, user guides and technical reports.

This equipment standard is a technical document consisting of performance and other requirements together with a description of test methods. Equipment which can meet these requirements is of superior quality and is suited to the needs of law enforcement agencies.

The necessarily technical nature of this NILECJ standard, and its special focus as a procurement aid, make it of limited use to those who seek general guidance concerning body armor. The User Guide Series is designed to fill that need.

NILECJ STANDARD FOR THE BALLISTIC RESISTANCE OF POLICE BODY ARMOR

1. PURPOSE

The purpose of this standard is to establish minimum performance requirements and methods of test for the ballistic resistance of police body armor.

This standard is applicable to armors intended to protect the torso against gunfire. Many different types of armor are now available; they range in ballistic resistance from those designed to protect against small caliber handguns to those designed to protect against high-powered rifles.

Personal protective armor manufacturers make a great variety of armors, many to special order, but production is currently concentrated in six classes designed to resist the following threats:

22 LRHV, 40 gr RN lead (1050 plus or minus 40 fps); 38 Spec., 158 gr RN lead (850 plus or minus 50 fps); and 12 gauge #4 shot.

357 Mag., 158 gr JSP (1250 plus or minus 50 fps); and 9 mm, 124 gr FMJ (1090 plus or minus 75 fps).

357 Mag., 158 gr JSP (1395 plus or minus 20 fps); and 9 mm, 124 gr FMJ (1175 plus or minus 75 fps).

44 Mag., 240 gr JSP (1425 plus or minus 50 fps).

30 Carbine, 110 gr M-1 (1950 plus or minus 50 fps); and 12 gauge rifled slug (1600 plus or minus 50 fps).

30-06 rifle, 166 gr AP M-2 (2750 plus or minus 50 fps).

The ballistic threat posed by a bullet depends, among other things, on its composition, shape, caliber, mass, and impact velocity. Because of the wide variety of cartridges available in a given caliber, and because of the existence of hand loads, armors that will defeat a standard test round may not defeat other loadings in the same caliber. For example, an armor that prevents penetration by a 357 Magnum test round may or may not defeat a 357 Magnum round with higher velocity. In general, an armor that defeats a given /leadcore round will not resist penetration by an identical round with an armor-piercing core.

Classification

Police body armors covered by this standard are classified into five types, by level of performance. Table 1 /summarizes the protection they afford.

2.2.1 Type I (22 LR-38 Special)
This armor protects against the standard test rounds as defined in paragraph 5.1.1. It also provides protection against lesser threats such as 12 gauge No. 4 lead shot and most handgun rounds in calibers 25 and 32.

2.2.2 Type II-A (Lower Velocity 357 Magnum--9mm)
This armor protects against the standard test rounds as defined in paragraph 5.1.2. It

also provides protection against lesser threats such as 12 gauge 00 buckshot, 45 Auto., 22 caliber Long Rifle High Velocity (rifle), High Velocity 38 Special and some other factory loads in caliber 357 Magnum and 9mm, as well as the threats mentioned in paragraph 2.2.1.

2.2.3 Type II (Higher Velocity 357 Magnum--9mm)

This armor protects against the standard test rounds as defined in paragraph 5.1.3. It also provides protection against lesser threats such as 12 gauge 00 buckshot, 45 Auto., 22 caliber Long Rifle High Velocity (rifle), High Velocity 38 Special and most other factory loads in caliber 357 Magnum and 9 mm, as well as the threats mentioned in paragraph 2.2.1 and 2.2.2.

2.2.4 Type III (High-Powered Rifle)

This armor protects against the standard test round as defined in paragraph 5.1.4. It also provides protection against lesser threats such as 223 Remington (5.56 mm FMJ), 30 Carbine FMJ and 12 gauge rifled slug, as well as the threats mentioned in paragraphs 2.2.1, 2.2.2 and 2.2.3.

2.2.5 Type IV (Armor Piercing Rifle)

This armor protects against the standard test round as defined in paragraph 5.1.5. It also provides at least single hit protection against the threats mentioned in paragraphs 2.2.1, 2.2.2, 2.2.3 and 2.2.4.

2.2.6 Special Type

A purchaser having a special requirement for a level of protection other than one of the above standards should specify the exact test rounds to be used, and indicate that this standard shall govern in all other respects.

2.3 Configuration

Police body armor is offered in a variety of configurations. All makes and models offer protection for the torso front. Many models also cover the back, and some offer additional protection. Police body armor may be specified to contain armor parts to cover the:

      (a) torso front, or front and sides
      (b) torso back, or back and sides
      (c) groin,
      (d) coccyx (end of spine)

or any practical combination of these, as required.

3.2 Backing Material

A block of non-hardening, oil-base modeling clay, 45 cm by 45 cm by 10 cm thick (18 by 18 by 4in), placed in contact with the back of the armor test specimen during ballistic testing.

3.3 Deformation
The maximum momentary displacement of the back surface of the armor test specimen caused by a fair hit that does not penetrate the armor.

3.4 Fair Hit
A bullet that impacts the armor at an angle of incidence no greater than 5 degrees, no closer to the edge of the armor part or to a prior hit than 5 cm (2in), and at an acceptable velocity as defined in this standard. A bullet that impacts too close to the edge or a prior hit and/or at too high a velocity, but does not penetrate, shall be considered a fair hit for the determination of penetration but not deformation.

3.5 Full Metal Jacketed Bullet (FMJ)
A bullet made of lead completely covered, except for the base, with copper alloy (approximately 90 copper-10 zinc).

3.6 Jacketed Soft Point (JSP)
A bullet made of lead completely covered, except for the point, with copper alloy (approximately 90 copper-10 zinc).

3.7 Lead Bullet
A bullet made of lead alloyed with hardening agents.

3.8 Penetration
Complete perforation of an armor test sample by a test bullet or by a fragment of the bullet or armor, as evidenced by the presence of that bullet or a fragment in the backing material, or by a hole which passes through the backing material.

3.9 Strike Face
The surface of an armor designated by the manufacturer as the face that should be worn away from the body.

KILL ZONE PROTECTION KIT

THE KILL ZONE PROTECTION KIT is very easy to make into a light, comfortable, yet very effective ballistic protection garment.

MATERIALS INCLUDED IN KIT;

Kevlar ballistic material, instructions, 1 cutting pattern for Kevlar, 1 cutting pattern from outer coverings, 1 cutting pattern for carrier pocket.
OTHER MATERIALS & ITEMS NEEDED;

Outer covering material 1 ft x 2 1/4 ft, material for pocket (see "Materials & Cleaning Instructions"). If you are attaching the KZP with a Velcro strip, you will need a 10" long Velcro fastener (two halves, each 10", sold together as one item), and a piece of material, that matches the garment you wish to attach the KZP to, 1 ft x 2 1/2 ft. You also need a t-shirt or other garment to use as the base garment, a good pair of scissors, thread, a needle or a sewing machine, a pen or felt tip pen, some pins or tape.

The first step is to cut the Kevlar fabric. You will have a piece which is 50" or 51" wide x 24" long. Using the "Kevlar pattern", mark out ten, 10"x12" rectangles as shown at the left. Cut the Kevlar with a good pair of scissors (dull scissors won't work at all), it will go slow, but you should be able to cut it without any problems. The cut edges will unravel some, but that is natural for this fabric. (If you want to make stronger edges and save yourself some cutting, instead of cutting each rectangle, cut three pieces 10"x24" and two pieces 12"x20", fold these to the proper size and when you stack them up alternate the folded edges around the sides of the stack.) Now take the pieces of Kevlar and stack them up. They should all be the same size and the edges should be fairly even.

Next, take your outer covering material, (see Materials & Cleaning Instructions"), and place the "Outer Covering Pattern" on it and trace the outline of the pattern. Cut the piece of cloth out. Fold this piece of cloth in half with the side you want to end up on the outside, facing in. Place the stack of Kevlar inside, all the way to the fold, and centered between the two side edges. On top of the cloth, draw lines at the sides just outside (closer to the edge) of where the Kevlar is underneath. Take the Kevlar out, and sew the two sides of the outer covering. Put your hand inside this "bag" and turn it inside (right side) out. Slide the stack of Kevlar inside, it should lay flat and none of the

445

layers/corners should be bent over. If you are going to put a Velcro strip on this (see instructions below) you will want to put it on now. Next, take the outer covering with the Kevlar inside, fold in the top edges and sew the top shut. Your ballistic insert is now complete.

Now you are ready to make a carrier pocket on a t-shirt or other garment. Take your pocket material, (12"x15") (if you are attaching this to a t-shirt, you can use a piece out from an old t-shirt) and place the "Pocket Pattern" on this, trace the outline, and cut the pocket material. Refer to the "Pockets" instructions for the general procedure of sewing on a rectangular pocket. Put your garment on (on a t-shirt, for the greatest concealability, you may want to put the pocket on the garment in the proper position. Sew the pocket on the garment (if you are using a sewing machine, you might find it easier to cut the t-shirt open on both sides, sew the pocket on, then sew the sides of the shirt closed-don't try this unless you know a bit about using a sewing machine). Be sure that the pocket is on strong (use double stitching at the top). The top of the pocket which you left open is where you insert the KZP ballistic insert.

If you want to make your KZP insert to attach to a garment by means of a strip of Velcro fastener, you have a couple of choices. You could make the outer covering from a material that matches your uniform, and sew on the Velcro strip before you sew the top closed. However, if you are going to use a heavy material, or if you will be getting the garment dirty, you will probably want to make a second outer covering to go over the first. Sew the one half of the Velcro fastener to the top of this second covering, and then don't sew the top completely, but leave an opening of about 6" through which you can put the Kevlar insert, and take it out when you want to wash the second covering.

Hold the insert with the Velcro strip attached up to the garment you wish to use it on (you should have the garment on when you do this). Mark where the other piece of the Velcro fastener needs to be attached to the garment. Take the garment off and sew on the Velcro. On a garment with a front that zips or buttons, cut the Velcro into two pieces and sew them on both sides.

The KZP is very versatile. You can use it on the front or back of any garment by using one of the methods above, or you can use it as the back protection in combination with a F&S kit by following the directions in the "Straps & Fasteners" section. If you are using a F&S with the two t-shirt method, you can make a pocket on the back (between the shirts) for the KZP. If you are making a F&S or B kit, you can attach a pocket to the outside of these and use the KZP for extra protection over the vital areas. If you carry a notebook, portfolio, or even a clip-board, you can carry the KZP in it as emergency protection. In fact, you can do many of the above things with just one KZP insert since it is so easy to slip out of one carrier or place of use, into another.

EVERYBODY DESERVES A SECOND CHANCE

While there are a number of bulletproof "vests" on the market that are good at what they do, we sincerely endose the SECOND CHANCE line.

Why? Because they were not afraid of being tested and supplied all materials asked for, their products lived up to their own advertising in our tests, they offer a wide variety of protective garments to match various conditions, they sell hard armor inserts, the vests fit and are well manufactured.

SC prices are about the best around for pre-made garments and they have a hell of a record, and a very sexy catalog...

Besides the standard vests one can purchase additional side panels, groin guards and two different hard plates for high threat zones.

SECOND CHANCE
PO Box 578
Central Lake, MI 49622
800-253-7090

Special SECOND CHANCE *Features*

- ♥ **SECOND CHANCE** now offers the six-point-adjustable closure system (SPA) whereby the two shoulder straps and the chest and abdominal straps are adjustable to the figure of the body armor wearer. This system is standard with all Second Chance cotton cover carriers.

- ♥ **SECOND CHANCE** RK-30 metal plate protection is standard with all SPA carriers. Plate width is seven-inches with the depth varying according to the panel depth purchased.

- ♥ **SECOND CHANCE** now offers ballistic panels that are interchangeable with either the Deep Cover II carrier or the new SPA carrier. This feature extends the wearer's flexibility in choice of carrier.

- ♥ **SECOND CHANCE** ballistic panels are completely removable for easier laundering of the cotton carrier. The ballistic pads should be cleaned according to the instructions sewn on each of the panels.

- ♥ **SECOND CHANCE** offers separate components for soft body armor, i.e. side panels, shirt tails, groin guards, interchangeable carriers, etc., making it unnecessary to purchase a complete unit for just one of the many features you enjoy.

- ♥ **SECOND CHANCE** offers a heavy duty Cordura nylon carrier, in Navy and OD, for all three panel configurations to handle the K47-30 extra protection insert combination.

- ♥ **SECOND CHANCE** offers all levels of ballistic protection (Model Y2, Model Z, and Model Z9 and Model "B" Series) in each of the three design configurations.

- ♥ **SECOND CHANCE** soft body armor is available in white, light blue, tan and navy washable cotton carriers as standard.

- ♥ **SECOND CHANCE** can, and will, work with the individual customer to satisfy the particular need for ballistic protection. Any vest which does not fit properly can be exchanged.

- ♥ **SECOND CHANCE** offers soft body armor in the design configuration to fulfill your every need.

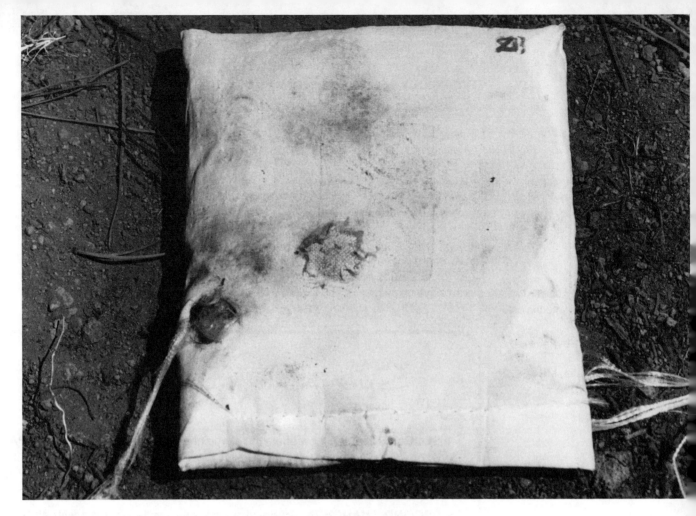

KELVAR CONTROVERSY

Top photo is the reverse side of a SECOND CHANCE vest after being hit with a 9mm ball and a .44 Special (not a mag). Note there is NO penetration, but a fair amount of blunt trauma.

TO WHOM IT MAY CONCERN:

Up until nation-wide publicity affirming the deadly force of the KTW bullet, there were only a relative handful of 'gun expert' type people who knew about the existence of the armor piercing handgun ammo.

I am probably in a position to be more sensitive than anyone to the reports of KTW or other armor piercing ammo being used by criminals. Until this exposure, it just hasn't happened!

The manufacturer of KTW told me that over 95% of every KTW he makes is 9mm for export to European law enforcement agencies. In Europe, the 9mm submachine gun is used in situtations where Americans would use handguns and shotguns.

For decades Winchester-Western has produced a .357 magnum metal piercing bullet. It is not quite as effective as KTW, but it will still penetrate almost any soft body armor. Yet I know of no case where a cop was shot with it. You would need a Second Chance Model Z9 (36 layers) to stop it. The Model Y has 18 layers and the Model Z has 26 layers of Kevlar.

Our Second Chance K-30 inserts will enable your Model Y or Z Second Chance to stop 9mm

KTW, .357 KTW, .44 magnum KTW as well as .30 carbine FMJ. It will also stop certain foreign military surplus steel jacket 9mm's, usually Czechoslovakian import, which soft body armor will not usually stop.

The Second Chance Model Y or Z will stop the .45, .380 and .44 Special KTW.

My general feeling is that there is approximately a hundred times greater chance of a policeman being killed by a head shot due to this vest publicity than there is by a criminal seeking out exotic armor piercing ammo and then deliberately shooting a policeman with it. If a pure and simple killing of a policeman is the desired effect, this can be much more easily accomplished with a high-powered rifle from a distance, or with a sawed-off shotgun in the face from close range. It has been our experience that the vast majority of cop killings are the unplanned result of a small time criminal suddenly being confronted with capture... a situation we call "the cornered rat syndrome".

The preceding is a synopsis of the testimony given by Richard C. Davis, President of SECOND CHANCE BODY ARMOR, INC. to the U.S. Congressional Sub-Committee on Crime on the date of 30 March 1982.

WHEN YOU ARE SHOT

Always remember these three words: SHOOT! SHOOT! SHOOT! Unless the shooting was an accident, or there were other extremely unusual circumstances – DO IT!

As soon as his gun goes off, the suspect is no longer a simple purse-snatcher or traffic violator. He is a [c]op killer. You must act with all the professionalism of the [M]arines on Iwo Jima. Have the kindness of a wounded [gr]izzly bear and the restraint of a starving tiger!

[I]f this sounds blood thirsty consider: "If he shoots you [on]ce, will he shoot you again?" The answer is usually "yes"! [E]ven though your Second Chance will withstand a whole [gu]n-full of .45's or .357's, getting shot isn't really fun. More[o]ver, having a nut jerking rounds all over town could easily [co]st the life of your partner or an innocent bystander.

When shot, most Second Chance 'saves' have said the [no]ise and surprise tended to shock them more than the [bu]llet's sting. Don't let your mind be distracted by thoughts [of]: "Am I going to die?" If you are conscious enough to worry [ab]out dying, you probably aren't. But even if you are, [G]ET HIM!

[Ef]fective March 1, 1983, SECOND CHANCE innovation [in]troduces interchangeable ballistic panels, in updated levels [of] protection, which will fit the DEEP COVER II carrier as [w]ell as the new Six-Point-Adjustable (SPA) cotton carrier.

This offers the officer flexibility to be able to change [ca]rrier styles without buying another set of ballistic [pa]nels. The features of DEEP COVER (i.e. feathered [ed]ges and higher back and better clavicle coverage) [ar]e now standard in all Second Chance soft [bo]dy armor.

Check out the easy step-by-step measuring method [an]d ordering system for Second Chance body armor [in] the enclosed 4-page price list flyer. Order your [bo]dy armor today from America's leading body [ar]mor manufacturer...Second Chance... [fir]st in innovation and first in 'saves'!

THE TRUTH ABOUT "BLUNT TRAUMA"

by R.C. Davis, Inventor of Second Chance

If I were taking a "word association" test and the given word was "Blunt-Trauma", the first word I think of is: "Bullshit".

Casting all pretext of modesty to the wind: 1) I have been shot more times than any (living) person. 2) Second Chance has saved far more policemen than all other body armors combined. I know more about: "soft body armor trauma" than **anybody**. More than Doctor Snowjob, the FBI, the CIA, the KGB, your mother, or the Lone Ranger.

In a nutshell: **Don't worry about it!** The average cop is being shot with junk: .22's, .25's, .32's, and .38's. The biggest trauma danger here is psychological.

With the .357's and .45's there is a **possibility** of internal injury, primarily in skinny people. (**Without** Second Chance, there is a **probability** of internal death.) The Second Chance Super Featherweight has saved 9 American policemen from .357's, .45's and 12 gauge shotguns. **None** of the men suffered any serious "Blunt-Trauma" injuries. **All** 9 of them killed, wounded, or captured their attackers. **No Second Chance vest has ever failed in use.**

In these cases the men wore a soft body armor weighing 2½ to 3¼ pounds, for a vest which covers a 12½ x 14 inch area front and back. A two pound vest (10 to 15 layers) could very well be another story.

To prevent all reasonable possibility of injury from a .44 magnum or 12 gauge slug, you'd have to have about a six pound vest. **But,** any vest **over 3½ pounds** creates a **far greater danger in its inherent loss of comfort and concealability**. I know of cases where departments bought 4 to 5 pound imitations of Second Chance and later had officers killed or crippled by common .22's and .38's; because the vests were just a little too thick, too stiff, and too heavy to wear.

THE MOST IMPORTANT THING YOU SHOULD WORRY ABOUT IS NOT WHETHER YOUR VEST STOPS NON-EXISTENT .44 MAGNUM, BUT: WILL YOU **WEAR IT** ON THAT FATEFUL DAY TWO WEEKS OR TWO YEARS FROM NOW WHEN YOU DON'T THINK YOU WILL BE SHOT.

449

NON—RIOT/RIOT HELMET

For the well dressed bullet resistant person some sort of unobtrusive head covering is a real requirement. Riot helmets rarely go with designer clothes and most will not stop a bullet anyway. Here's an alternative you can even attend a baseball game in...

SILENT PARTNER
230 Lafayette st.
Gretna, LA 70053
$60.00

COMMAND CAP. Pat. App.

*On the range
a head shot
is worth 3 points . . .*

*. . . On the street
it's worth your life*

Silent Partner proudly announces our state-of-the-art flexible armor head protection, the Command Cap.

To the potential attacker, Command Cap appears to be nothing more than an ordinary SWAT style cap. However, beneath that plain black or camo exterior is a Silent Partner ballistic insert of 16 layers of Zepel-D treated (waterproofed) Kevlar 29 — the same style and weave used in our famous T-shirt armor!

The Level IIA (penetration resistance) armor panel is encased in a sturdy Cordura nylon carrier concealed within the cap, guaranteeing the maximum in comfort and front head protection. Although not intended to replace the helmet, Command Cap is the logical alternative for those occasions when "hard hat" ballistic integrity is not practical or available. Conventional uniform hats offer no protection from a felon's bludgeon or bullet. Command Cap can substantially reduce the level of damage from a blow or bullet to the head.

WARGAMES

As I write this article a man, one Cliff Johnson, from Stanford University has just lost a lawsuit in the California courts to prevent hookup of a system he was hired to design that would automatically start a nuclear war in response to a foreign attack WITHOUT HUMAN CONTROL.

This device is known as a launch-on-warning-command system and could and would launch our MX/Minuteman missiles if the computer sensed a missile attack from another country.

Johnson pointed out the fact that a computer error could start a war by accident.

His case is to be heard by the California appeals court in the near future.

Does this remind anyone out there of a certain popular movie or is it just my imagination?

Hello Joshua...

MISCELLANEOUS SOURCES

SPOTLIGHT COMMUNICATIONS
PO Box 3047
Greenville, NC 27834

Guarantees the lowest prices on Regency scanners or they will give at least $5.00 off any competitors's price.

Also descramblers, some frequency directories and filters.

ELECTRA CO.
300 East County Line Rd
Cumberland, IN 46229

Makers of Bearcat scanners; they do not sell direct but will forward information and direct you to your nearest dealer.

Or call at 800-SCANNER

JC LABS
PO Box 183
Wales, WI 53183

Scanner helpers including a $40 all electronic VOX logging unit.

MORNING DISTRIBUTING CO
PO Box 717
Hialeah, FL 33011

Very inexpensive antenna tuner, vhf converter, receiver transmitter and voice descrambler kits.

ETCO ELECTRONICS
North Country Shopping Center
Plattsburgh, NY 12901

ETCO is still around and still selling a good selection of electronic kits, small transmitters, batteries and general elect- ronic supplies.

ELECTRONIC SUPERMARKET
PO Box 988
Lynnfield, MA 01940

Miscellaneous electronic supplies.

If you are anywhere near our ages you remember the great fun you had as a kid when the world war two junk hit the surplus market. Surplus stores were full of amazing items from C-rations to tanks...

Electronic parts bins were crammed full of items that looked so interesting, but rarely worked after living in Valvolene and possibly going through several invasion attempts...

I spent many happy hours trying to get a simple pair of tube walkie-talkies to work.

Well for those of you into your second childhood, Vietnam surplus is just now hitting the marketplace.

And there are some bargains to be had...

SCIENTIFIC RADIO SYSTEMS
367 Orchard st
Rochester, NY 14606

Is selling the SR-MP-25 (Shrimp 25) switchable 6 and 25 watt transceiver that uses frequency synthesized operations to tune between 2 and 15 MHz.

The unit operates off batteries or AC, has internal compression and is even waterproof to 1 meter.

A nice dependable unit that is illegal to operate without the proper FCC license.

AMC SALES INC
9335 Lubec Box 928
Downey,Ca 90241

Still provides some of the most inexpensive VOX recorder controls, drop-out relays and converted recorders.

GRR-R RECORDS
357 MacArthur Blvd
Oakland,Ca 94610

One of my personal favorites; they will supply records or endless loop cassette tapes of "Sebastian" a German Shepard watchdog, plus instructions on hooking him/them up to a timer.

All of the fun of your own trained guard dog with none of the hassles of buying food or shoveling shit...

COMTEC
226 Robbins Ave
 Philadelphia, PA 19111

Several models of voice activated two way radio systems.

REDI-SET TARGET, INC.
PO Box 23084
Jacksonville, FL 32241

A unique, all steel, counterweighted target system that will stop and contain all handgun, carbine and .223 bullets.

The target surface is spray painted any color desired and then fired upon. The unit will take sustained fire and automatically resets, instantly, for the next shot.

Target alone $60, stand (if desired) $65.00.

With a suitable backdrop this is an excellent system for increasing shooting skills at distances of 15-100 yards.

DAVIS COMPANY
3942 Trust Way
Hayward, CA 94545

Custom pistol grips made from energy absorbing "santoprene" for better hand placement and natural shooting.

DAVIS LEATHER CO
 3930 Valley Blvd. #F
 Walnut, CA 91789

Not the same company, just a clever tie in with "see above".

Nice holsters for all types of handguns.

HOGUE COMBAT GRIPS
PO Box 2038

Atascadero, CA 93423

Very nice fiberglass reinforced nylon handgun grips.

See above...

BOZ CUSTOM GUNS
2933 East Bay Dr.
Largo, FL 33541

Basic to full house conversions for semi-automatic handguns and revolvers.

DENNY'S RELOADING SHOP
531 Pine st.
Osage, IA 50461

Custom reloading and custom bullets...

JET LOADER TICO INTERNATIONAL
PO Box 2668
San Francisco, Ca 94126

A unique speed loader for revolvers, the JET LOADER is spring loaded and will power cram 6 cartridges into a revolver in any position and without turning any knobs.

The speed of this system could mean the difference between life and death in a combat situation.

About $7.00 each, a couple of different carriers are available.

ADVANCED .45 TECHNOLOGY
1031 Elder st.
Oakland, CA 93030

An amazing kit that includes an air cylinder that screws onto a .45 instead of the regular barrel, hoses, connectors and a CO_2 tank.

When installed the shooter can "dry fire" his weapon with the same feel as actually shooting. A fountain soft drink sized bottle of gas will give 50,000 shots!

The savings in money is nothing short of amazing when compared with live ammo plus the unit can be used anywhere.

A portable bottle may be belt-carried to allow realistic combat type firing.

MARYLAND GUN WORKS
26200 Frederick rd.
Hyattstown, MD 20871

Custom handguns for all applications.

COMBAT EQUIPMENT SALES, INC.
PO Box 1348
Tyler, TX 75710

A tactical, load bearing harness you can design from their components to fit your particulars; rappelling gear, packs, ammo carriers, utility bags and other goodies.

LL BASTON CO.
2101 N College
El Dorado, AR 71730

Nice parts to detail your handgun including shock absorber inserts, match triggers, high visibility combat sights, etc.

A FRIENDLY PRODUCT

A group of, let's see how to phrase this, "friendly" folks in the new life hippie capitol of the free world, Boulder Colorado, have come up with a unique product.

Called, you guessed it, FRIENDLY PLASTIC, this wonder product comes in inexpensive bags containing 4.4 ounces of a white granular plastic compound with some interesting properties.

When placed in boiling water it combines and expands to make a solid, extremely flexible product that can be shaped like modeling clay.

When it dries (which can be helped along with a cold water dunking) it hardens into a non-brittle heavy duty plastic good for a myriad of unusual uses...

One evening when we had nothing better to do we, in the space of 20 minutes, designed a pair of plastic "brass knuckles" with built in metal screws on the knuckles, a mean, bladed ring, customized hand grip for our ninja claws that greatly improved their performance by stopping sliding and fitting the wearers hand perfectly, rigging temporary sights on silenced weapons, and hiding several, ah, small objects we did not wish found by incorporating them into my abstract "sculpture".

The plastic can be remelted and remolded at the user's whim.

FRIENDLY PLASTIC
2888 Bluff st # 233
Boulder, CO 80301

In this case, do not mention this book as your source; the friendly folks are not big on thier product being applied to weapon uses...

Oh, yes, you can custom make a weapon handle easily with this product as well as hide/pot a surveillance transmitter...

GUN GOODIES

ARMSON, INC.
PO Box 2130
Farmington Hills, MI 48018

SGT. SANDY'S
PO Box 6
Westminster, SC 29693

ARMSON makes the most complete line of O.E.G. gunsights around plus publishes the instructions to make one into a quick combat shooter.

SGT. SANDY'S is simply the neatest place around for anyone who spent their childhood digging through surplus stores. They stock every gun item available from auto parts to slings, to fletchettes (I would love to re-print the letter about their supply problem because the government didn't want them ordering from a particular ''pinko'' county, but the language is a bit rough on the edges for a family book).

Prices are great, their stock constantly changes and they will even trade goodies.

SHOWN BELOW - INSTALLED ON AR-15 SPORTER WITH ABSOLUTELY NO MODIFICATIONS TO YOUR RIFLE (1 MINUTE INSTALLATION)

"SPECIAL"   "SPECIAL"   "SPECIAL"   "SPECIAL"

BRAND NEW "IN THE WRAPPER" M-16 MILITARY 30 ROUND MAGAZINES!

CONSOLIDATED
827 Pacific Ave No. 507
San Francisco, Ca 94133

Unusual professional source for two of the best transmitters we have tested for both size, stability and range. C-1 voice, C-2 telephone line; both check in at $120 each.

Also some Japanese equipment, belt buckles that undo handcuffs (you never know), belt buckles that hide Charter Arm's guns, other neat stuff.

Catalog $3.00

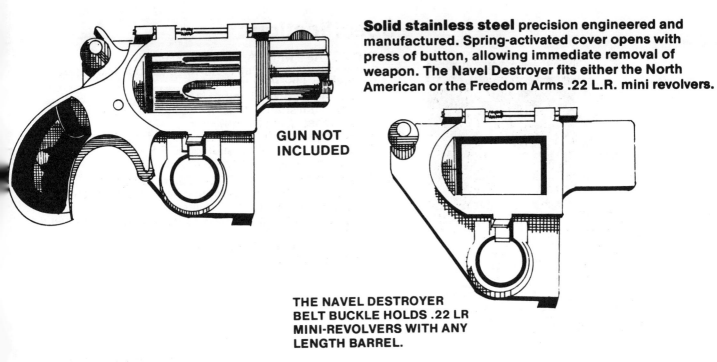

Solid stainless steel precision engineered and manufactured. Spring-activated cover opens with press of button, allowing immediate removal of weapon. The Navel Destroyer fits either the North American or the Freedom Arms .22 L.R. mini revolvers.

GUN NOT INCLUDED

THE NAVEL DESTROYER BELT BUCKLE HOLDS .22 LR MINI-REVOLVERS WITH ANY LENGTH BARREL.

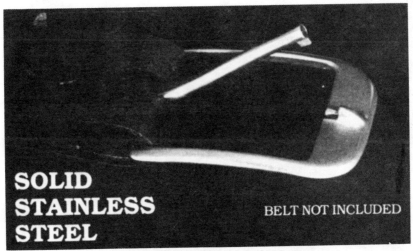

SOLID STAINLESS STEEL

BELT NOT INCLUDED

The Brannigan Back-Up

SPECIAL WEAPONS PRODUCTS
Bldg 601 Space Center
Mira Loma, CA 91752

NEOTERIC, INC.
6622 N 57th dr
Glendale, AZ 85301

SPECIAL WEAPONS makes some of the best designed nylon holsters we have had the opportunity to test. Their small caliber ankle rigs are outstanding and their 24 hour rig (not shown) is our official ASP carrier. This latter design is a cross shoulder harness that counter balances two extra mags under arm are with a large caliber pistol under the other. It is very comfortable and really can be worn 24 hours a day, although sleeping is a bit strange...

NEOTERIC makes the Riot Staff (see text), powered by compressed air it can turn any 98 pound weakling into the Hulk. Will knock anybody on their ass..

I guarantee it.

24 HOUR HOLSTER — This shoulder rig is designed for the professional who is required to carry a firearm concealed for extended periods. The harness features soft 1½" wide nylon webbing that molds to your body and does not bind or chafe. The holster is made of ballistic nylon and features an exclusive Velcro® adjustable, metal reinforced thumb break retention system. The holster is adjustable for right and left handed use, features an adjustable belt tie-down and will accept most medium and large frame autos, and small, medium and most large frame revolvers. The magazine pouches will accept double column 9mm magazines, .45 magazines, and strip style loaders for revolvers. Speed loader pouches are available as a no cost option. The pouches also feature an adjustable belt strap for weight equalization and belt loops for use on trouser or web belts. This holster fulfills the design concept of comfort, speed and security for the 24 hour professional.
No. 1201 Holster with magazine pouches
No. 1201 SL Holster with speed loader pouch   **$44.95**

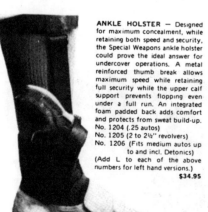

ANKLE HOLSTER — Designed for maximum concealment, while retaining both speed and security, the Special Weapons ankle holster could prove the ideal answer for undercover operations. A metal reinforced thumb break allows maximum speed while retaining full security while the upper calf support prevents flopping even under a full run. An integrated foam padded back adds comfort and protects from sweat build-up.
No. 1204 (.25 autos)
No. 1205 (2 to 2½" revolvers)
No. 1206 (Fits medium autos up to and incl. Detonics)
(Add L to each of the above numbers for left hand versions.)
          $34.95

Specifications

A. RIOT STAF® with KA-1 Barrel Assembly
1. Length: 31-inch Patrol Barrel; 34½-inch Riot Barrel
2. Weight: 4 lbs loaded
3. Minimum strike distance: 2 inches
4. Maximum shaft extension: 18 inches (Patrol Barrel); 22 inches (Riot Barrel)
5. Average effective strike range: 6.2 feet; 6.8 feet
6. Average working pressure: 350 P.S.I.
7. Average shaft velocity: 25 ft/sec

B. Construction Elements: KA-1 Barrel Assembly
1. Impact Shaft: molybdenum nylon; stainless steel
2. Power Bearing: teflon; stainless steel
3. Support Bearings: UHMW (ultrahigh molecular weight) compound
4. Recoil Springs: stainless steel
5. Barrel: polycarbonate

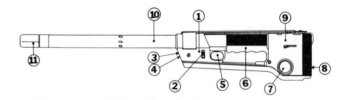

#118 MILITARY SMOKE GRENADES (M-18)

Brand new G. I. — straight from the factory. This grenade is used to produce dense clouds of smoke for signaling and screening movement of small units. The smoke from military grenades is designed to cling to the ground rather than rise into the air. The average soldier can throw the grenade a distance of 35 meters. Burn time 50-90 seconds, fuse delay 1-2 seconds after handle is released. Weight 19 oz. Available in White, Red or Yellow. Please specify color when ordering. You may mix colors as you wish.

Price: 1 or 2 grenades $32.50 ea.
       3 thru 11 grenades $30.00 ea.
       12 or more grenades $27.50 ea.

PHOENIX SYSTEMS
PO Box 3339
Evergreen, CO 80439

Smoke grenades, trip flares, auto conversion parts, trip wire, camo make up, etc.

R6727 Camo. Fatigue Shirt. Woodland pattern, 50% poly. 50% cotton, first quality. Sizes: XS-XL. $18.95

ADVENTURE UNLIMITED
PO Box 20138
Affton, MO 63123

A complete outdoor gear supplier with many camo items, knives, boots, bags and so on.

SURVIVAL OUTFITTERS
PO Box 594
Festus, MO 63028

They sell many interesting items including guns by mail for 5%-10% over cost, replacement barrels to change calibers, sub-inserts for shooting smaller (cheaper) ammo in large bore guns, stocks, bows, flash suppressors, etc.

**New 12 Guage Insert Barrel Shoots Tranquilizer Darts
In Any 12 Ga. Break-Open Shotgun:**
Single, double, O/V, or combination. Uses industrial 22 blanks (Ramset) for propellant.
12 GA. Tranquilizer Dart Insert Barrel Complete With Reusable Dart . . . **65.00**
20 GA Tranquilizer Dart Insert Barrel Available On Special Order **85.00**
Extra Tranquilizer Darts (Fit 12 or 20 GA Models) **9.00**

461

M452 "STINGBALL" RIOT CONTROL GRENADE

The M452 "Stingball" Riot Control Grenade is designed to provide a less lethal alternative than bullets for crowd dispersion or suspect apprehension.

The M452 has a short (approximately 1½ second) delay fuse which both prevents throwback and enables the user to easily achieve air bursts without having to undertake the dangerous practice of holding an activated grenade for a short pre-throw countdown. The short delay also makes possible a more accurate and timely delivery to the target area.

The M452's body is composed of thin soft rubber to help lessen the danger of fragments when the grenade bursts. The bursting (or more accurately the propelling charge) is located in a small, soft rubber container in the center of the grenade, while the payload of "Stingballs" is loaded in the space between the inner and outer containers.

The "Stingball" loading consists of a large number of marble sized soft rubber "Stingballs." When the grenade explodes the central propelling charge will burst the outer shell and eject the "Stingballs" outward in a radial pattern at a velocity of several hundred feet per second. The blast effect of the

M452 is quite similar to the M429 Stun Grenade.

The physical impact of these "Stingballs" is similar to a point blank hit from a sturdy slingshot. It is quite painful, but considerably less damaging than a blow from a lead bullet.

To help lessen the chance of injury, the metal fuse mechanism is designed to be ejected from the grenade body a short time before the grenade explodes. This prevents the grenade fuse from becoming a dangerous fragment due to the explosion of the central propelling charge.

This grenade is also available in a M452C "Comboball" loading which includes both "Stingballs" and powdered CS tear gas to provide a dual effect.

Accuracy Systems, Inc.

2105 S. Hardy Drive
Tempe, Arizona 85282
(602) 966-5064

ASSAULT LINE™

A must in tactical usage is minimal elongation under rappelling load, high abrasion resistance, high strength, and non-kinking flexible deployment. Our Bluewater II® 100% nylon Kernmantle® static line is technically the perfect rope for rappelling. Tightly braided sheath covers braided core strands. Specs: Diameter ⁷/₁₆″ (11mm). Tensile strength: 7000 lbs., Elongation w/200 lb. load—1.6%, Elongation at rupture 20%, shrinkage 5—8%. Load absorption 1450 ft/lb. UIAA test falls survived—2. Hank size 150′.
Colors: NEW! (1)Camo, (2)Olive Green, (3)Black. [8 lb. 3 oz.]
Reel size: 600′ [40 lb.].
RAP-2150(   ), Assault line, 150′ **$94.95**
RAP-2600(   ), Assault line, 600′ **$369.95**
RAP-2X(   ), Assault line—cut to your length, 150′ or more **$.65/ft.**

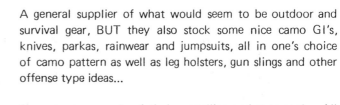

BRIGADE QUARTERMASTERS
266 Roswell st
Marietta, GA 30060

A general supplier of what would seem to be outdoor and survival gear, BUT they also stock some nice camo GI's, knives, parkas, rainwear and jumpsuits, all in one's choice of camo pattern as well as leg holsters, gun slings and other offense type ideas...

Shown are a couple of their rappelling and rope tools. All prices are in line and service is very good.

They even have dog tags...

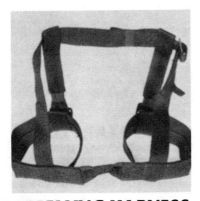

RAPPELLING HARNESS

One Size-Fits-All Adjustments.
Made with Mil-spec parachute harness webbing rated to 6000 lbs. Exceptionally comfortable. Designed primarily for rappelling—lower hookup for better balance. A must choice for all rappelling uses—police, military, and pleasure.
(2)Olive, or (3)Black. [13 oz.].
RAP-H2(   ), Rappelling Harness **$27.95**

DELTA PRESS LTD.
PO Box 777
Mt. Ida, AR 71597

COBRA
PO Box 30035
Midwest City, OK 73110

DELTA is a publisher and bookseller, kind of the competition...Their decals and signs are worth the $1.00 catalog alone.

Ever since we put up our "Is There Life After Death? Trespass Here And Find Out" sign, salesmen have dropped to a bare minimum.

COBRA carries a number of custom gun accessories, slings, ammo holders, folding stocks, etc. Nice stuff.

WS #7

WS #8

WS #9

WS #10

WS #11

WS #12

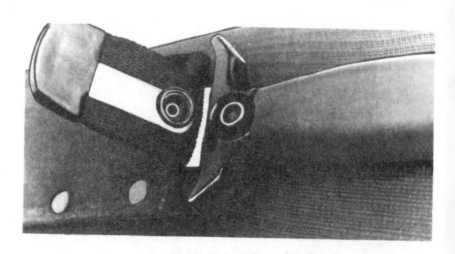

A male snap is recessed into the handle of the knife. The quick release tab breaks the snap loose in an instant without feeling around for it. This allows the fastest draw possible and there is no danger of cutting the strap as would usually happen with conventional cross-over straps.

On the following pages are shown some of the custom knives available from COBRA.

PARELLEX CORP
1285 Mark st
Bensenville, IL 60106

A general supplier for knives, crossbows, camo suspenders (!), flashlights, holsters, and outdoor gear.

A neat camo bulletproof vest, some nice velcro ammo holders and even a gas mask.

A real slick catalog in the fashion of EDMUND.

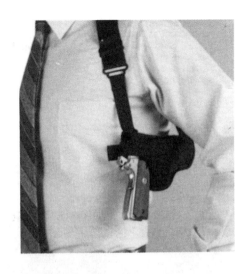

Turn Your Lens Into A Spotting Scope!

Tele-Optics unique tele-converter turns your 35mm SLR camera lens into a spotting scope/telescope. Ideal for target spotting, nature studies, bird-watching. You'll even want to bring it along on your hunting trip for game spotting. Interchangeable eyepieces for a variety of magnifications. It's as easy to use as attaching your lens to your camera. Fits standard ¼" tripod mount. Extremely lightweight and compact. Rugged high quality construction and optics throughout. Available in Right-Angle model—ideal for the astronomer and Straight-Through—ideal for the shooter. 18mm eyepiece is included. Fits Nikon **(1)**, Canon **(2)**, Minolta **(3)**, Olympus **(4)**, Pentax K **(5)**, Pentax Thread **(6)** and T-Mount **(7)** lenses. Specify camera lens when ordering.

11 The Sword And The Pen

Who needs it? International travelers, businessmen, and government representatives visiting unstable countries could find this executive pen set a lifesaver. Legitimate 6" long ballpoint pen with replaceable ink cartridge sheaths a 3-sided, 2½" razor sharp blade mounted permanently in the handle of the pen. You can mince more than word with this exceptional personal defense product.

Executive Pen Set
174100 $35.00

ARMAMENT SYSTEMS PRODUCTS, UNLTD.
PO Box 18595X
Atlanta, GA 30326

Still one of the more interesting suppliers around, NOTE this is not the same company as ASP that did our gun conversion.

ATTACHE ARMOR PAD
Code: AAP

Instantly transferrable from most popular sized attache cases to folios, our AAP provides ballistic protection from most handgun calibers. Nine layers of bullet resistant Kevlar are fitted into a black nylon chamber pouch that can be worn under clothing in emergency situations.

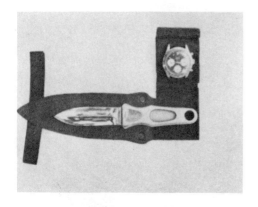

BANDIT
Code: BDT

A speciality rig combining a watchband and a knife sheath constructed to be worn on the inside of the forearm. It is designed for concealment rather than speed and accommodates the A.G. Russel "Sting 1a" and other similar low profile edged weapons. The BANDIT is available in black only; please specify wrist size: S(6½"); M(7"); L(7½"); and XL(8").

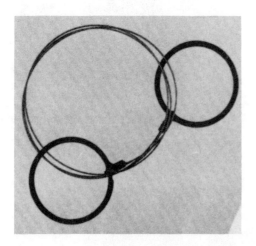

GODZILLA'S DENTAL FLOSS
Code: GDF

. . . .an updated version of the knotted silken cord or hemp rope, the garotte is an unusual weapon, guaranteed to turn heads. The two rubber coated loops cushion the finger while the steel cable cuts through the problem when someone's stuck their neck out.

BUDGET COUNTERMEASURES

CAPRI ELECTRONICS
Route 1G
Canon, GA 30520

A line of very inexpensive rf detectors (the TD-17 shown) that will track from 1Mhz to 1,000 MHz with an adjust for sensitivity and LEDS help track down nearby transmitters.

The unit show works very well for the money (under $100). It is not a spectrum analyzer by any means, but makes a nice unit for double checking on unusual signals.

Also some inexpensive line checking gear.

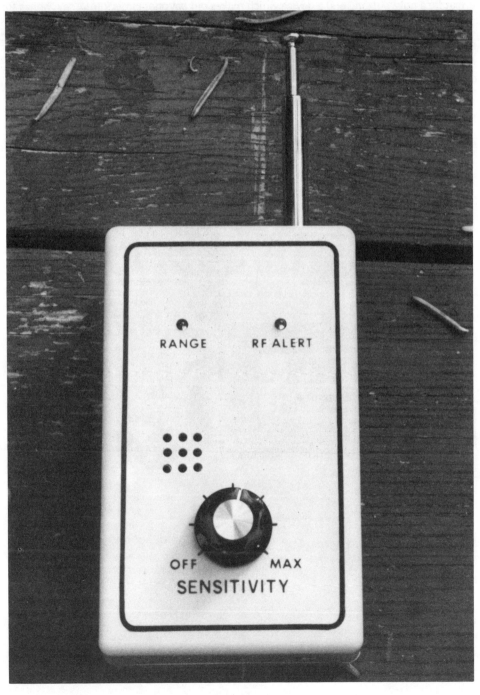

IE, makes, or carries, whatever the case may be, a nice line of inexpensive telephone "helpers". The items pictured here are their TELEGUARD, a lockout system which allows (like several others from VIKING, ETCO, etc) the owner to make one phone the master so no other extension, or PBX can listen in to any conversation unless the master phone aloows it.

They also make a toll restrictor that lets you control any DIAL (not touchtone) phone so no long distance calls can be made without the owner's knowledge and a TAP DETECTOR which will alert one to the addition of unwanted, simple, taps or extension phones added to the line. A A light and tone comes on at any unwarranted voltage drop.

They also feature a hold button, and a device which makes old payphones back into payphones for home use.

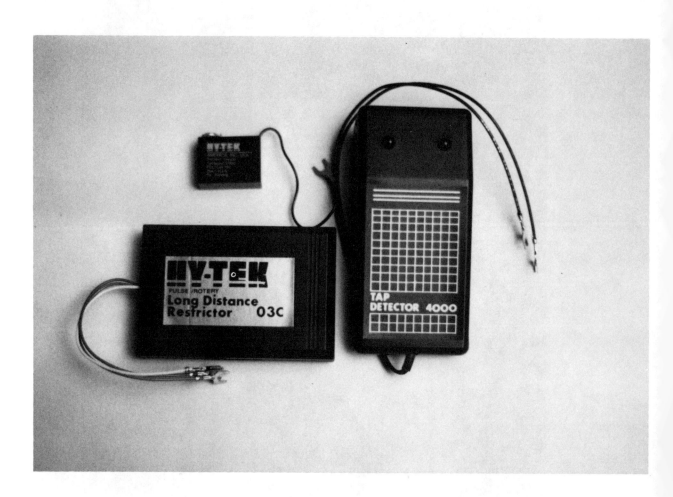

ESS LABS
5955 S Campbell
Chicago, IL 60629

ESS specializes in countermeasure gear ONLY and they make some original nicely priced packages including;

A Total Sweep Package, Executive Analyzer, End User Phones with anti-tap and detection circuits.

They appear to be an alternative to the higher priced, more commerical packages on the market and offer many of the same options.

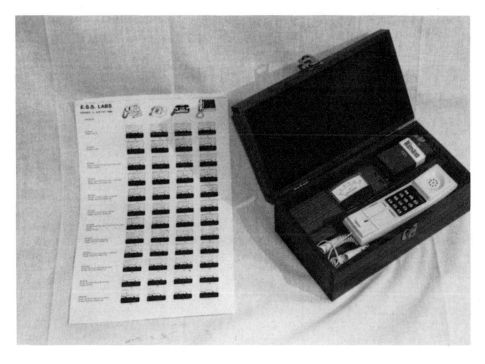

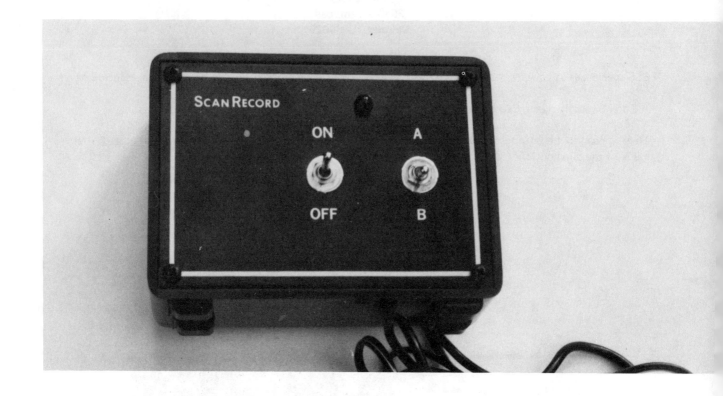

LOGGER AND PEN

The scanner to tape recorder VOX logging unit from CAPRI ELECTRONICS (top), an inexpensive unit that will turn any recorder on only when voice is present from a scanner receiver, allowing unattended recording of any transmitter.

Also a typical pen transmitter (this one Japanese, available over the counter in the international duty free area of Japan's largest airport).

Operates in the commerical FM band with a range of about 100-300 feet. Microphone fairly sensitive if clipped down to prevent cloth rustle, or left out on a desk.

The pen also writes...

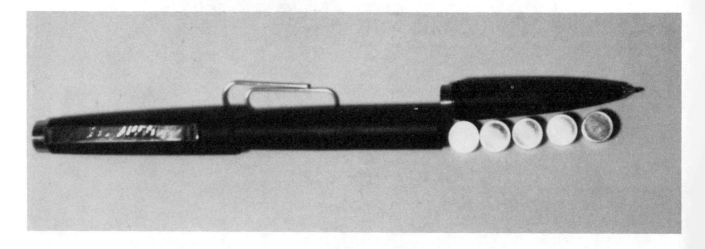

TWO HEAVYWEIGHTS FROM THE AXIS

Problem: Sie benötigen einen Überwachungssender, der jederzeit über einen Hand-sender ein- und ausgeschaltet werden kann.

Lösung: Fernsteuer-Überwachungsanlage PK 945 (Nur für Export)
Ein selektiver Fernsteuerempfänger schaltet über einen Handsender den Überwachungs-sender nach Ihren Wünschen „Ein" oder „Aus".
Technische Daten: Fernsteuersender: Abmessungen: 100 x 70 x 30 mm. Gewicht: 350 g. Stromversorgung: 8 x 1,5-V-Batterien. Frequenz: wird aus Sicherheitsgründen nicht be-kanntgegeben. HF-Leistung: 2 W. Gehäuse: Metall. Reichweite: 300 m. **Überwachungs-sender mit eingebautem selektiven Fernsteuerungsempfänger:** Abmessungen: 75 x 65 x 20 mm. Gewicht: 135 g. Stromversorgung: 2 x 1,5-V-Batterien. Frequenz: 3-m- oder 2-m-Band. Reichweite: 500 m. Betriebszeit: 1½ Jahre.

Problem: You require a monitoring transmitter which can be switched on and off by a portable transmitter.

Solution: PK 945 Remote-Controlled Monitoring System (for export only)
A selective remote-controlled receiver switches the monitoring transmitter "on" and "off" according to your demands via a portable transmitter.
Specification: Remote control transmitter: Dimensions: 100 x 70 x 30 mm. Weight: 350 grams. Power Supply: 8 x 1.5 V batteries. Frequency: is not given for security reasons. RF power output: 2 W. Housing: Metal. Range: 300 m. **Monitoring transmitter with built-in selective remote-controlled receiver:** Dimensions: 75 x 65 x 20 mm. Weight: 135 grams. Power Supply: 2 x 1.5 V batteries. Frequency: 3 metre or 2 metre waveband. Range: 500 m. Operating time: 1½ years.

PK ELECTRONICS
2000 Hamburg 13
Badestrasse 36
GERMANY

ASIAN MERCANTILE CO
Box 1584 CPO
Tokyo 100-91
JAPAN

PK is still one of the major manufacturers of electronic surveillance gear in the world. One can purchase every-thing from bugs that are as small as a grain of rice and fit inside elctronic components to the $25,000 LASER bug that our model is based upon.

Around for years they have a very good and very expensive reputation.

Okay, ofr all of you that wrote me the "yeah, it's a great book but where the hell has CONY Corp gone?" After the publication of How To Get Anything On Anybody, I FOUND THEM FOR YOU!!

The same bargain basement prices on the same unbelieveable transmitters and phone taps that we raved about in the last book are now carried by ASIAN MERCANTILE.

If you read the last book there is no reason to go on about this company...

Some of their gear also available in the US, no customs and legal to order, from CONSOLIDATED.

If they change again I don't want to hear about it.

It can pick up mutual telephone conversation

471

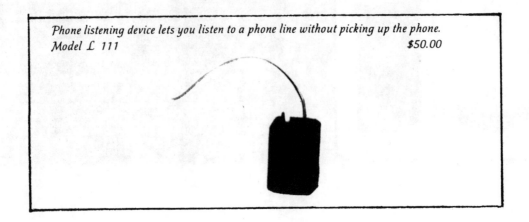

Phone listening device lets you listen to a phone line without picking up the phone.
Model L 111 $50.00

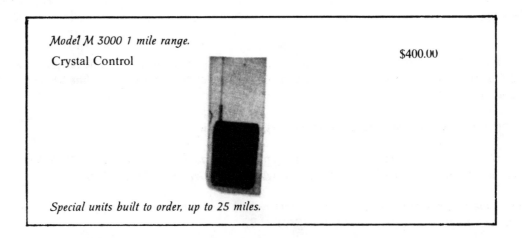

Model M 3000 1 mile range.
Crystal Control $400.00

Special units built to order, up to 25 miles.

WYNN may be out of business due to a Federal visit. They hand-design and build some of the best-for-the-money surveillance gear in the U.S. Their catalog has expanded to include some rather inexpensive transmitter locaters and sweep devices. They will still custom engineer almost anything at the best prices around. Catalog at this time is $4.00.

ELECTRONIC TRACKING DOG

While it is true that electronic beeper tracking devices have been around for quite a stretch, most have several drawbacks including reaction to bounce and miltpath signals, lack of attenuators, two antennas required, lack of portability, and so on.

ESC (see supplier's section) has come up with the best model we've seen. Using a recharageable magnetic attatching transmitter (good for up to 30 hours use), and one antenna the receiver is portable and can be mounted under a dash, carried on a bike or cycle, or even in its own shoulder strap harness arrangement to track on foot.

12 LED's and a meter give an accurate idea of direction and range, 4 seperate switches for attenuation allow following from a few meters up to 3-5 kliks in town and 10-15 out of town or when the receiver is mounted in a permanent base arrangement with a yagi antenna.

Some practice with this system and one can follow anything and guess at the tracking distance with a fair amount of accuracy. A very nice unit for about $2000 for one and less for quanity (3 and up) buys.

ESC
MODEL 3090 ᵀ·ᴹ· VHF DIGITAL TRACING SYSTEM

ESC
TL 100 ^{T.M.} TRANSMITTER LOCATOR

ELECTRONIC SECURITY COUNTERMEASURES is also still around and also has expanded their catalog to include some really nice items. They also seem to have lowered their prices on several things, a nice surprise.

Several new transmitter locators, the MASON type phone anaylzer, anit-spy phones, night vision equipment, eyeglasses with little rearview mirros on the inside edges like they used to sell in Superman comics, satellite receivers, the whole spectrum...

An interesting idea That has been used in a number of undercover operations I know about, including one where a group of Stanford students put themselves through school by the use of a computer, radio transmitter and the roulette wheel at several Vegas casinos. One can attempt their own construction by simply wrapping fine wire in a loop around an-in ear earphone and a larger loop of the same wire to be held on the body. Feed the output of a receiver directly into the large induction loop. This model available from PK.

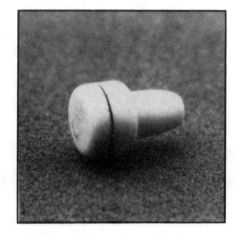

Technical Specifications:

Dimensions	:	35 x 8 mm
Weight	:	28 g
Power Supply	:	1,5 V button cell
System	:	magnetic

Forbeing able to work discreet on monitoring operations, our technicians have developed a wireless earphone. TRM 0020 works together with an induction coil, worn under the jacket on your shoulder, which transmits all signals to the earphone inductively. TRM 0020 does not depend on other power sources as it has its own power supply.

MICROTRON
42 38th st
Wheeling, West Virginia 26003

Still a consistent supplier of various surveillance and anti-surveillance gear. I don't believe MICROTRON makes their own gear, but acts as a distributor for low to medium priced selections from all over the world.

THE XZ84 IS THE MOST DEPENDABLE AND STATIC FREE MONITORING SYSTEM IN ITS CLASS.

Designed for security applications that require long term Surveillance, the XZ84 features a custom matched set that includes a wireless FM Transmitter and a portable base receiver. These components are installed by simply pluging them in any regular AC (120v,) electrical outlet in your home or office building. For example: "A store detective may monitor the stock room located in the basement of the building from his office which is located on the tenth floor. **No** batteries to run down. Since this system operates on the regular 120 V. line, any building in the vicinity operating on the same power transformer shall be a potential target for security monitoring, while virtually eliminating the possibility of an accidental 'overhear' from local radios. The transmitter may be easily installed inside lamps or other appliances on your property. The XZ84 is shipped ready for immediate deployment. Excellent results! Warning: The use of this system for eavesdropping is punishable by a fine and (or), imprisonment. Sold as a security system only.

(In stock, immediate delivery.)

| VOLUME DISCOUNTS |
| AVAILABLE |

ELEKTRON
Route de Fontblanque
84210 Pernes
FRANCE

A greatly expanded catalog of gear that includes some items rather hard to come by on these shores.

They even claim to be developing a "microphone" killer, this device is usually based on two untrasonic outputs that beat against each other to produce a harmonic that would override any other noise right at the microphone of any recorder or transmitter.

A nice theory but several American firms have tried it over the last few years and you will notice it is not on the market...

I'll believe it when I see it...

Catalog in French and English. A tip: if you order anything from overseas have it shipped over by international courrier service. They put on their own custom's stickers and pass right through.

In most cases.

TSU 3000

ELK 3011 - VOICE CHANGER

This unit has been designed to permit telephone conversations to be made, without the possible recognition by your correspondant, of your own voice. A special « custom built » integrated circuit (LSI) has been developed just for this unit. Surprising results may be obtained, such as changing the sound of a mans voice for a womans, or the inverse. Thus the original tone may be kept, altered or radically changed.
The unit can be fitted to any type of telephone, anywhere It should be noted that when used for the reception of incoming calls, the correspondant will not know who is answering, which permits known but unwanted callers to be dismissed without suspicion. (see picture on the back)

2200

ELK 2018 - PEN SIZE « BUG »

*This apparently innocent-looking pen contains a VHF microphone « bug », capable of transmitting up to 150 yards. Used with our **ELK 2020** « U » radio recorder, the pen size « bug » can be left almost anywhere to pick up conversations in its surroundings.*
Its inconspicuous appearance and absence of aerial, makes it easy to use in almost any circumstance.

2201/GP

High power (1 watt) transmitter, powered by the car's battery, giving a maximum range of about 30 miles, 100 miles with a plane.
Size : 110 × 60 × 30 mm.
Weight : 150 grams.

2018

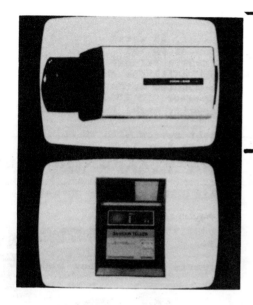

SPECIAL SURVEILLANCE APPLICATION LENS - Long Range 14:1, motorized, auto iris, focus, zoom, 12VDC, 25mm to 350mm, f/3.5. Minimum object distance 1.7mm. Total weight 3.0Kg. Ideal for those medium to long range applications. With 2X extenders, 50mm to 700mm, f/7.0.

ATM VIDEO SURVEILLANCE - consists of right angle auto iris WATL 190, f/4.8 lens to provide proper lensing for installation in the tight areas of ATM machines. Video tape documentation is made via the latest time-lapse/time-date generator and VCR's. This surveillance system allows for the positive identification needed to effectively expose and prosecute fraud..

VISUAL METHODS INC.
35 Charles st
Westwood, NJ 07675

The most diverse line of optical surveillance devices we could locate. Both the rigid and the flexible (fiber optics) lenses we tested were of the highest quality and did exactly what the ads say. They also stock camera, complete ABSCAM briefcase kits, transmitters etc.

For anyone who has ever wanted to look through a keyhole, under a door, through a grill, in the dark, in full color, on film or video, at something they weren't supposed to be able to see...

Call VISUAL METHODS...

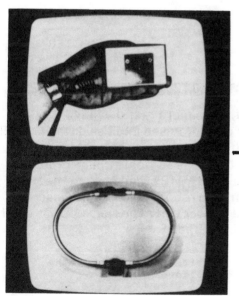

SMALLEST COLOR TV CAMERA - VMI's new TV 321 is the smallest solid state color camera head available on the market. Its length from the front of the lens to the rear of the camera is only 3/4". The total size of the camera head is 1-3/4" x 3-1/2" x 2-1/4". This solid state charged priming device (CPD) in a 2/3" vidicon format has a picture quality equal to the standard sized color cameras available. In addition to small size, this camera has long life, high reliability, minimal lag, and the ability to operate on both 12VDC or 117AC. The TV 321 comes with an 11mm focal length, f/1.8 pinhole lens and can be used in applications where cameras must not be seen. Camera head can be located 20 feet from its electronics via cable supplied.

DUAL IMAGE FIBER OPTIC - Two different views can be recorded simultaneously using Visual Methods' dual imaging fiber optic lens. This lens has been designed for use with any "C" mount CCTV or 16mm camera. The model FO1402 allows the user to obtain two side-by-side images of different views with equal or different magnifications. Each of the 100cm (3 foot) flexible fibers has a resolution of 400 lines, 360 degrees flexibility, with a minimum bend radius of 4 inches, and an f/4 aperture. The dual image fiber is especially useful in difficult situations where cameras will not fit, and in non-destructive testing applications.

477

SAS OF AMERICA INC.
950 NE Hiway. 10 Suite 203
Minneapolis, MN 55432

One of the most complete, state of the art, law enforcement type suppliers. Very fancy catalog with anti-bomb gear, non-lethal projectile guns riot shields, LASER sights, FANG road blocks, shock batons, vehicle armour kits, miniature solid state surveillance cameras, room bugs, on and on and on.

Not cheap, but very high quality.

PIGSTICK IN POSITION

Mobile Tracking Syste

STOCK CODE: 006/001

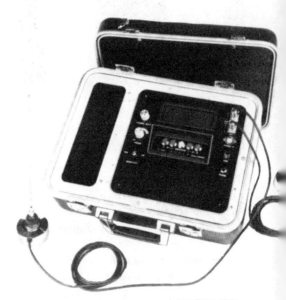

RECEIVER
STOCK CODE: 006/101

TRANSMITTER
STOCK CODE: 006/201

THIS IS A LOW PRICED ALTERNATIVE TO THE SA94 PIGSTICK DISRUPTER

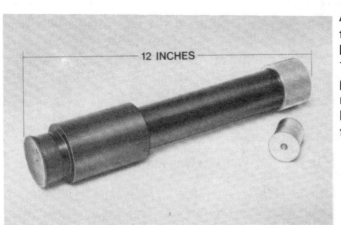

12 INCHES

A lightweight, aluminium 'gun' designed for the disruption of Improvised Explosive Devices (IED) by firing a high velocity charge of water .
The Disrupter can be fired from either a ground position using the SA91B stand or from the HUNTER, remotely controlled robot vehicle. A 12v car battery, or the Hunter's own power supply is used to initiate the cartridge.

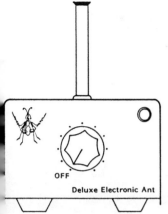

EA-14 RF PREAMP/ELECTRONIC ANTENNA

If you can't (or don't want to) install an outside antenna, let the EA-14 DELUXE ELECTRONIC ANT™ pull in those weak signals for you. It amplifies signals 12 to 20 dB over the built-in whip that comes with your scanner.

Two units in one — the ANT can also be used as a preamplifier for your outside antenna. Covers 30 - 1,000 MHz with 20 dB gain on VHF and 12 dB on UHF. Noise figure under 2 dB. Convenient front panel gain control allows you to select the amount of gain you need. 50 ohm input and output impedance. Motorola jack input, Motorola plug output (other plugs and jack can be furnished on special order at additional cost).

Requires 12 to 16 VDC @ 30 mA. Furnished with a DC power cord for those who have their own 12 volt supply, or order an A-01 AC to DC adapter (listed elsewhere in this literature). Also includes a 33" telescoping whip antenna. Unit measures 3¼"w x 4"d x 2½"h.

CAPRI ELECTRONICS
Route 1
Canon, Ga 30520

CLIFTON CO
11500 NW 7th Ave
Miami, Fl 33168

CAPRI (top) and CLIFTON (bottom) are two companies we have covered before...But each has added to its line and both still represent two of the best bargains in the electronic surveillance world today.

CAPRI sells scanner to recorder relays, de-scramblers, antenna boosters, filters and auto gain controls, among other trivia. They also handle kits for pre-amps, amsp, filters, etc. Lowest prices around, great for any automatic scanner-recorder or relay stations.

CLIFTON deals in countersurveillance only, from their now famous "Hound Dog" rf locator to a number of fairly crude looking telephone testers that sell for a fraction of their slick looking competition and allow one to put together a complete phone tester for thousands of $ less than the fancy models.

A 50-wire extension cable is supplied. It connects from here to the main phone cable →

Meter reveals any parallel connected bug by the amount → of leakage on the phone line

Switches test from parallel to series to determine if any → bug is in series on the line

Reverses polarity of the test in case a polarized bug has → been attached to phone line

ONLY **$295**⁰⁰

MASON ENGINEERING INC.
1700 Post rd
Fairfield, CT 06430

Miniature Probe Receiver System
20 KH_z – 1 GH_z WITH VISUAL DISPLAY

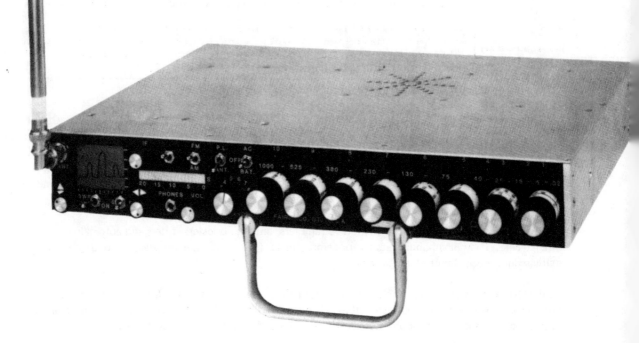

- Full frequency coverage to 1000 MHz
- Spectrum analyzer display
- Easy effective operation
- No technical background needed
- Comprehensive step by step RF countermeasures sweep instructions
- Small, light weight
- Integrated package, no "plug-ins"

- Battery portable mode for transmitter location
- LED Signal level meter aids transmitter location
- Detects low frequency power line type transmitters
- Large speaker for feedback detection mode
- High level performance specifications found only in very costly "rack mount" equipment.

MASON is one of the oldest and one of the best operators in the anti-surveillance field. They have good, real, electronic engineers that design some of the best "sweep" equipment available, do good work themselves, and they give reasonably priced seminars.

Not cheap, but you get what you pay for...

PK 385 - MICRO DIRECTIONEL. Modèle permettant l'écoute et l'enregistrement jusqu'à 75 m, avec volume son ajustable, 2 entrées : écouteurs et enregistreur. (Voir data technique ci-dessous).

PK 385 - DIRECTIONAL MICROPHONE. PK 385 is equipped with a special directional microphone and a very sensitive amplifier. This design allows absorption of disturbing noises which are not originating from the direct required direction. It is ideal for natural scientists and reporters. Socket for connection of a tape recorder is provided. Sound transmission is performed with a headset. The amplification is variably adjustable. Dimensions : 650 x 50 mm diameter. Weight : 240 grams. Power supply : 9 V. battery. Amplification : 80 db, 10 000 fold. Operating time : 50 hours.

MATERIELS SPECIAUX
INFOS A 1 International
BP 127
75563 Paris Cedex 12
France

From what I can tell they don't really make anything but do search the world over for some good surveillance gear, combine it under one roof, so to speak, and offer it from France.

Against the law?

This is the country that sold A-bombs to the PLO...

Probably gets through customs easily, prices are so-so, I can't read how much the catalog costs...

PK 360 - APPAREIL PHOTO A DECLENCHEMENT PAR ONDE RADIO. Ensemble comprenant émetteur : portée 1000 m, fréquence 27,12 MHz, 200 x 150 x 60 mm, 500 g. ; récepteur : 130 x 90 x 70 mm, 380 g. ; appareil photo : objectif Tele-Xenar 1:3,8/75 mm, capacité 50 photos 24 x 24 mm, déclencheur variable à partir de 2 photos/sec. Alimentation batterie 12 V D.C. avec rechargeur secteur.

PK 360 - CAMERA WITH REMOTE CONTROL UNIT. Everywhere where a direct triggering with a switch or by a person is impossible, the PK 360 can be used. This special system for wireless remote controlled triggering can be operated from a distance of up to 1000 m. Transmitter : dimensions : 200 x 150 x 60 mm. Weight : 500 g. Output power : 100 mW. Frequency : 27.12 MHz. Receiver : Dimensions : 130 x 90 x 70 mm. Weight : 380 g. Antenna : telescopic. Camera : Exposures : 50, size 24 x 24 mm. Lens : Tele-Xenar, 1:3.8/75 mm. Power supply 12 V D.C. battery and charger. Triggering : adjustement of up to 2 exposures/sec possible.

BI-SOURCES

Bi, in this case at least, means swings both ways...LEA is one of the biggest suppliers of both sur and counter-sur gear in the country. Reading their catalog is better than most spy novels. Bug finders, metal detectors, full spectrum sweepers, riot gear, transmitters, and anything else you can think of.

USI is a little brother; again they appear to be a supplier rather than a manufacturer. Some of their items one could find elsewhere for less, some seem to be nearly unique. Both offer custom designing.

LEA
700 Plaza dr
Secaucus, NJ 07094

USI
PO Box 2052
Melbourne, Fl 32901

LONG RANGE HF RADIO SYSTEM

Incredibly compact! A versatile, multi-function radio station that actually stores away inside its own high-impact, protective suitcase. Operates absolutely anywhere — car, office, home, hotel room, boat. Plugs into 120-230 VAC 50/60Hz mains, or operates from any 12VDC power supply, including the optional battery pack. Just open the case, plug it into the power source. Select SSB voice modulation or CW code operation and you're on the air! Antenna supplied consists of a coaxial-fed dipole of adjustable length for the frequency you are using. Converts to a long-wire antenna with ground lead, or to a counterpoise where good grounding is unavailable. In either configuration, marking bands indicate optimum length for each frequency. A special antenna tuner with field-strength metering is built in. Broad range of operating frequencies, gives continuous coverage of 1.6 to 30 MHz band in precise 100Hz steps. In any frequency range, receiver sensitivity is .35 microvolts for 20dB of quieting. Other Outstanding Operational Features: ●frequency-scanning mode for band surveillance ●secure voice transmission available as an option ●front panel reduction of radiant power on SSB or CW to avoid overload at nearby reception points ●fast/slow tuning dials. In addition to the dipole/long-wire antenna and coupler-tuner, the entire system comes complete with these accessories: ●lightweight headset ●microphone ●CW code-key ●AC and DC power cords ●universal power supply and ●fitted carry-case of tough, molded high-impact plastic, with two latches and combination lock. Meets IATA standards for under-the-seat airline carry-on luggage.

An optional 12VDC battery pack in its own briefcase, rechargeable sealed acid 'Gel Cell' batteries is available. Provides hours of continuous operation at full 100-watt output. Much longer charge-life at lower power demands. Built-in 115/230 VAC 50/60Hz recharger brings batteries back up to full charge wherever AC is available.

Long Range HF Radio System   No. 6750   **Portable Battery Case   No. 6750-005**

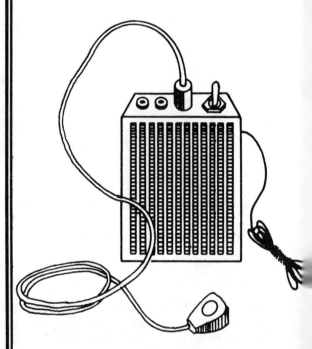

For picking up sound vibrations hundreds of away through most any type of barrier.

ISA
38 Settlers Trail
Stamford, CT 06093

The MR-1 and MR-2 MiniReceivers

The MiniReceivers are highly effective broad range receivers which are used to detect eavesdropping transmitters. An indication of the RF field strength is given by the LED bargraph on the front panel. Power is supplied by a standard 9 volt battery.

The MR-1 is a desk model, which will alert the executive to the fact that a transmitter has been turned on in his office, or that someone has entered his area with an operating transmitter. It also gives an indication of a transmitter that has been placed in the area after business hours.

The hand-held MR-2 detector is used to sweep an office to determine if there are any eavesdropping transmitters present in that room.

SA-1, SA-2 Special Audio Amplifiers

Used in special situations when a pair of wires cannot be traced to the source. The SA-1 will quickly determine if there is audio on the pair or not. It will also supply an activating voltage if it is suspected that a carbon microphone may be located at the end of the pair. Battery powered. The SA-2 is the SA-1 amplifier supplied with contact microphone for stethoscope use. The contact microphone is used to determine the vulnerability of walls, windows, air ducts, doors, etc. to audio intrusion techniques.

SS-1 Sound Source

Designed to furnish a known sound inside an area that is being "swept" for eavesdropping devices. The sound is an intermittent "chirp" and can easily be recognized even when other sounds such as music or voices are present on nearby broadcasting stations. Supplied with a DC power pack for plug-in to standard AC outlets.

SS-2 Sound Source

Same as above except supplied with battery and recharger for use where AC is not available.

WT-1 Wire Tracing Kit

The WT-1 Wire Tracing kit is composed of a specially designed tone source, matching detector, accessory cables and complete instructions. It is used to trace wires and cables. It will locate the distant end of a specific pair of wires such as telephone lines or a pair of wires which have no apparent function. This is especially important in determining if certain critical telephone pairs have been bridged or coupled to another pair of wires.

The same folks that brought you the non-linear junction detector (finds diodes, transistors, IC's through walls even if the bug is long deceased) for a mere $15,000 now offer a more complete line of anti-surveillance gear including the good old MASON type phone analyzer, tape recorder detectors, and a very nice chart recorder that sweeps the rf spectrum and draws a permanent record of each signal for follow-up operations.

Also do on-site sweep services.

Good engineering, not cheap, I would trust them as much as anyone else in this crazy business...

TACTIX
1075 Old County Rd
Belmont, Ca 94002

Very nice countermeasure gear which closely resembles another manufacturer we have listed...Suspect they are just an "area rep", but worth keeping track of.

They may have added other lines by now or come up with orginal products...

WIDE BAND SYNTHESIZED COUNTERMEASURES RECEIVER SYSTEM

- **PROFESSIONAL INTEGRATED COUNTERMEASURES SYSTEM**
- **DETECTS SPECIAL MODULATION TECHNIQUES (SUB-CARRIER, SINGLE SIDE BAND, CONTINUOUS WAVE, PULSE CODED MODULATION, SPREAD SPECTRUM)**
- **FULL COVERAGE TO 1,300 MHZ**
- **HIGHER FREQUENCY COVERAGE OPTIONAL**
- **CARRIER CURRENT DETECTION**
- **AUDIO FEEDBACK TRANSMITTER LOCATOR**
- **CODED TONE VERIFICATION/ DEMODULATION CIRCUIT**
- **FULLY SYNTHESIZED 20 CHANNEL PROGRAMMABLE SCANNING RECEIVER COVERS 25 MHZ TO 550 MHZ FREQUENCY RANGE**
- **LIQUID CRYSTAL DISPLAY FREQUENCY READOUT**
- **STANDARD ACTIVE ANTENNA PROBE FACILITATES RAPID DISCOVERY AND LOCATION OF EVEN LOW POWERED MILLIWATT TRANSMITTERS**
- **VISUAL AND AUDIO ALARM FEATURES**
- **RUGGED ALUMINUM CONSTRUCTION PREVENTS RF INTERFERENCE**
- **RECHARGEABLE 12 VOLT POWER PACK WITH BUILT IN CHARGING CIRCUIT**

PROFESSIONAL CARRIER CURRENT
AND SUBCARRIER DETECTOR
Now you can detect those hard-to-find bugs!
BE SURE YOUR KIT OF
DETECTION EQUIPMENT IS COMPLETE!

Discover a world of hidden transmissions using the CD-01 Ca'
Detector. With the CD-01 you can quickly check power lines
business for hidden "wireless intercoms" or "FM room mo'
can also be checked for carrier current transmitters. Wh
radio receiver you can even demodulate hidden subcr
along with the main carrier.

The CD-01 has a sensitivity of 6 uV, which al'
miss. It can tuned from 10 KHz to 690 KP
carrier current/subcarrier frequencies
be switched in to reduce or elimina'

Power lines can be easilv '
turining the unit ON
through the tw-

Ph-

VIKING INTERNATIONAL
PO Box 632
Newhall, Ca. 91322

VIKING has always been high on our list and remains
there. They do employ their own engineers who come
up with some of the best and lowest priced snoop and
anti-snoop toys around, yet they will stock other
people's items when they met their spec's.

VIKING's owner spends a great deal of time traveling
around the world testing possible inclusions.

I still stand on their surveillance recorders as being the
best around and each new piece of gear excites me.

Catalog $4.00 I believe.

COMPRESSION MICROPHONE
PREAMPLIFIER

The compression microphone preamplifier Model 12B is used to
make recordings of sounds occurring in a large area where only one
microphone can be installed.

The compression amplifier provides a constant output level over a
wide range of varying input levels (weak and strong sounds).

It can be used with a dynamic microphone or with one of our
subminiature electret mikes (M1 series).

Specifications:
Gain: 30 dB typical
Compression: more than 20 dB
Output level: 80 mV rms typ.

Model 12BD *for dynamic microphones or electret mikes with their own power source.*

Model 12BE *for use with our subminiature
electret microphones, M1 series.*

SECURITY AND MILITARY PRODUCTS

ALCAN WHOLESALERS. INC.
PO Box 2187
Bellingham, WA 98227

A unique combination of military type gear including camo suits, sweaters, packs, battle vests, Kelvar helmets, knives, flashlights, exploding targets (hit it with anything larger than a .22 and a large explosion follows) and CS tear gas gernades.

Also features several nice minature transmitters, phone taps, anti tap gear, drou-out relays and the Nova stun gun.

Their prices seem to be among the lowest on most items.

SuperBug Transmitter

The SuperBug Transmitter is a powerful electronic transmitting device. It has a transmitting range of up to an incredible 6500 feet (according to local conditions). Use it as a component of your home or business security system where audio activity in areas of potential intrusion on your property can be monitored and/or recorded, especially in larger areas where extended transmitting range is required. The SuperBug has no wires to connect; just turn on the switch, place in desired location, and it's ready to go. It has a built-in ultra-sensitive filterized electret capacitor microphone, capable of clearly picking up conversations held up to 30 feet around it. The SuperBug has a stabilized frequency control and the frequency range is 88-109MHz (adjustable with trimming screw). Its transmissions can be received on a standard FM radio. The SuperBug is powered by one 9V alkaline battery, which fits inside the unit. Includes antenna. Quality Israeli manufacture. Dimensions (in inches): 1.4 x 1.5 x 2.3. Regularly priced at $295.00, the SuperBug is now at the special price of $195.00 for a limited time. Notice: Due to the powerful transmitting capabilities of this device, FCC regulations should be consulted and obeyed before use. WARNING: Because of the capabilities of this device, it is possible that it could be misused for the unintended purpose of surreptitious monitoring. Federal law prohibits the use of such devices for the purpose of overhearing or recording the private conversations of others unless such use is authorized by all parties engaged in the conversation.

AS-1203 . . . . **SuperBug Transmitter** . . . . **$195.00 ppd.**

ROOM & TELEPHONE TRANSMITTER

This device transmits both room and telephone conversations. Constant power for the various operations is supplied by the built-in electronic automatic governor. No batteries are needed to operate this device, giving it unlimited operational capability. It is ideally suited for situations in which both room and telephone need to be monitored, but there is only one opportunity to enter the room and none to change batteries. The AS-4116 will function as a room transmitter normally, and also as a telephone transmitter when the telephone receiver is off the hook. It can be installed inside the telephone or anywhere along the telephone line in the room to be monitored. All elements are cast with silicone caoutchouc to make them resistant to tropical climate and vibration. Quality Israeli manufacture. Transmitting range: up to 900 ft. (according to local conditions). Frequency range: FM 88-108MHz, adjustable with trimming screw. Installation: in parallel with the telephone line. Dimensions (in inches): 0.9 x 1.2 x 2.0. (Specifications subject to manufacturer's changes.) NOTE: Sold to professional law enforcement personnel only.

AS-4116 . . . . **Room & Telephone Transmitter** . . . . **$295.00 ppd.**

SHEFFIELD ELECTRONICS
2057 E 75th st
Chicago, IL 60649

Manufacturers of some very sophisticated gear for those on both sides of the fence.

Catalog comes in English, Spanish and French in case you are involved in almost any war, at least one spec sheet should be just what you need...

Haven't tested their gear, but looks good.

PHANTOM ZERO.
The model PZ-T6 is a series connected high security telephone monitoring FM subcarrier transmitter that receives its operating power from the telephone line. It is installed, either inside of the telephone or on the line, with two non-polarized wires and transmits both sides of a conversation only when the telephone is used. The PZ-T6 will accommodate all multiline telephones. Transmitter is waterproof.
Transmitting range: 150 to 275 meters (500 to 900 feet).
Dimensions: 53 × 31 × 15 mm. (2.125 × 1.25 × .625 in.).
Frequency: withheld for security reasons.

The model PZ-T10 is a battery powered parallel connected high security telephone monitoring FM subcarrier transmitter that transmits only when the telephone is used and can be connected at any point to the line. Solid-state on-off switching is used instead of a relay to eliminate all associated relay problems. The power supply is external and uses 12 standard 1.4 volt "AA" size mercury or alkaline batteries. Peak performance transmitting time is 60 hours of telephone use. Transmitter is waterproof.
Transmitting range: 300 meters to 1.2 kilometers (985 to 3937 feet).
Transmitter dimensions: 45 × 35 × 17 mm (1.75 × 1.4375 × .6875 in.).
Battery case dimensions: 95 × 68 × 50 mm (3.75 × 2.625 × 2 in.).
Frequency: withheld for security reasons.

Transmitting distances were measured using our model AR-55 receiver and will vary according to conditions at hand. Open air line of vision distance measurements are greater than those specified. Our equipment does not interfere with television reception worldwide.

INFORMATION UNLIMITED
Box 716
Amherst, N.H. 03031

Always one of the most interesting suppliers of electronic projects, usually in kit form, IU has broadened their selections to include more ready made items at low prices.

Probably the most complete LASER supplier around they also specialize in ultra-small transmitters, gain antennas, stun rods, and have added some very inexpensive infrared night vision gear to their lineup.

Always a prompt supplier they will also answer questions and help with any problems arising from their sales.

PHASOR STUN WAND/BLASTER

Produces explosive or burning plasma discharge capable of puncturing a beer can. These devices are labeled as **dangerous**.

PSW3 .... BURNING WAND PLANS	**$7.00**
PSW3K .... KIT/PLANS	**$39.50**
PSW30 .... ASSEMBLED	**$59.50**
BLS1 .... BLASTER WAND PLANS	**$10.00**
BLS1K .... KIT/PLANS	**$69.50**
BLS10 .... ASSEMBLED	**$89.50**

LONG RANGE VOICE TRANSMITTER

Clearly transmits all voices & sounds well over an honest mile. Tunable frequency between 88-115 MHz. Optional power supply or battery operated.

MFT1 .... PLANS	**$7.00**
MFT1K .... KIT/PLANS	**$49.50**
OPTIONAL AC POWER SUPPLY	**$19.50**

TECHNICAL COMMUNICATIONS CORP.
100 Domino Dr.
Concord, MA 01742

Not a small entry; TCC has built cryptographic systems for 123 countries...They have now moved into the private sector, offering very high level "scramblers" for all types of radio gear (fixed, mobile, portable, hand-held), telephone systems and even digital data channels.

They utilize non-linear digital codes AND ciphers to provide about the highest security one can purchase.

Their ciphering is controlled by exact synchronization between two units that switch at between 150 and 350 times per second with an 8 bit code preamble.

This gives about 18 billion possible code combinations. Yes, one could sit down for 1,000 years (skipping meals and bathroom visits) and perhaps break the code.

Yes, NSA may be able to crack a recorded conversation with their advanced computers, I don't know. Short of that kind of effort one's converations are fairly secure.

Not cheap.

Try not to piss off the NSA or KGB and you should do okay...

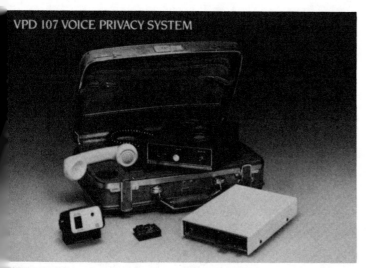

VPD 107 VOICE PRIVACY SYSTEM

CSD 909 SERIES STRATEGIC MULTI-DIMENSIONAL CIPHERING SYSTEM

APPLICATIONS
- Radio (UHF and VHF)
- Radio base, mobile, and hand-held
- Telephone, fixed and portable
- IMTS and cellular radio telephone

FEATURES
- Medium security level
- 125 code combinations
- Half duplex or full duplex operation
- Clear voice override
- Easy to install and operate

The VPD 107 series Voice Privacy System provides a medium level of security using a combination of frequency inversion, tone masking, and sideband masking as a means of scrambling. One of the largest IMTS systems in the world is secured by TCC's VPD 107 series. The units feature automatic synchronization and clear voice override.

APPLICATIONS
- Radio (UHF, VHF, HF-SSB)
- Radio base and manpack
- Telephone, fixed and portable
- IMTS and cellular radio telephone
- Facsimile (Group I and II)
- Radio teletype and SSTV
- Satellite, COMSAT, MARISAT
- Low-speed data

FEATURES
- Maximum cryptographic security
- 1.27×10^{89} key combinations
- Code (key) depth over 100 years
- Unique reset key entry memory circuit
- Superior recovered voice quality
- Excellent operation on HF-SSB circuits
- Operates over any narrow band communication channel without external modems
- Designed to MIL-SPEC standards

The CSD 909 series uses a complex multidimensional polycipher technique for ciphering. Analog signals are digitized and encrypted by a unique transformation algorithm which conserves bandwidth. After encryption, the digital bit stream is converted back to an analog signal for narrowband transmission. The versatile field-proven CSD 909 series will cipher radio, telephone, facsimile, and low-speed data links. It is ideally suited for military and top level government applications requiring strategic long term security.

MICROTEK
PO Box 2101
Sheffield Lake, OH 44054

At least one cute product, maybe more by the time this is published...

Their MT-100 is a pocket-sized, crystal controlled transceiver that, under ideal conditions, can hit up to 1,000 miles away...

The catch?

It is a CW (morse code) unit only. This means one needs a few hours of practice to utilize it and, by law, one should have an amateur FCC license to operate the unit.

Trust me, the FCC is so understaffed and swamped these days, they really don't have time to search out a 5 watt CW unit that is just used on occasion...

One can even order the unit equipped for use outside the normal amateur bands for more security.

A great survival device or emergency communications transceiver.

Cheap at $100...

SPECIFICATIONS

Frequency - 7.0-7.3 MHZ
Power output - 5 watts RMS
Operating Voltage - 12 VDC
Size - $3\frac{1}{4}$" x 2 1/8" x $1\frac{1}{4}$"
Antenna - 50 Ω
Receive Sensitivilty - 5 µv
Crystals - 1
Current Consumption - Rec. 20 ma.
                                    Tran. 750 ma.
Price - $100

A LAST PLUG

UNIVERSAL TECHNOLOGIES
PO Box 38169
Dallas TX 75238

Simply the best made and by far the cheapest NVD gear we could find. As I mentioned, we bought our demo 'cause we liked it so much...

Scope from the $2500's with all goodies, goggles about half of what everybody else charges IF you are law enforcement or can convince them you have read this book and deserve the break.

OFFICIAL POLICE MODEL OP

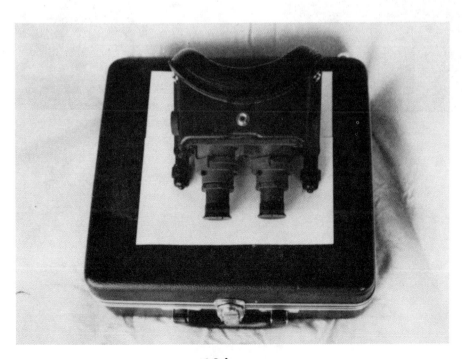

ROSS ENGINEERING ASSOCIATES, INC.
68 Vestry st
New York, NY 10013

Jim Ross has been known in the business of electronic surveillance and countermeasures for some time. He teaches seminars on the subject, which, unlike some others in this field, do not appear to be for the sole purpose of selling his equipment and services.

He also carries some very nice looking equipment that is NOT the stock stuff offered by 10 other firms and utilizes some interesting principles. Ross publishes a newsletter on surveillance and telephone related items.

Shown (below) is the Datotek scrambling system used with a transceiver, briefcase with acoustic coupling and on a modified office phone.

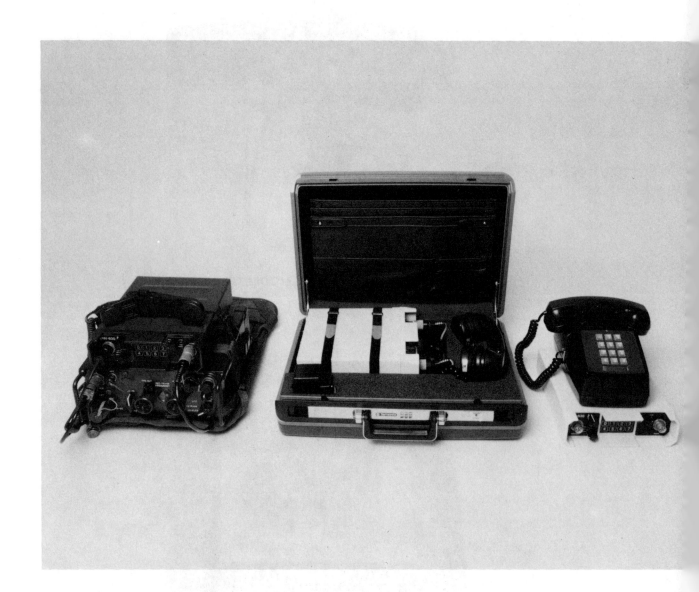

CIRCUITS

The following circuits are presented for informational purposes only UNLESS you have a warrant or proper legal use for any of these devices. THIS IS UP TO THE USER TO DISCOVER!

We take no responsibility for the construction, certification or use of any of the following devices.

If you do construct anything in this field remember a few basic rules:

Do be familiar with normal construction techniques and always use a solder station not a super hot wood burning iron.

Watch for cold solder joints.

Slways tune any transmitter with a plastic tuning wand (diddle stick) NOT a metal screw driver.

Use the tips in How To Get Anything On Anybody for tuning and placement of any transmitter.

Watch for correct polariaty of any component.

Most of these transmitters can be tuned above or below the normal FM band allowing for more selective reception. If not, vary the Q of the tank circuit.

Use as short of connecting wires as possible.

Coils can be would on wood screws or drill bits of the proper diameter and then soldered. The screws/bits are then removed to leave an air core coil.

It is also possible to measure the current being drawn from the power supply for tuning for maximum output, see HTGAOA.

When tuning a transmitter watch you are not tuning a harmonic instead of the main frequency, check up and down the band.

To adjust an FM receiver to pick up 109 Mhz instead of 108, carefully adjust the trimmer cap located on the main tuning capacitor and "walking" a known station down a number or two. The entire band will now be re-adjusted...

Parts can be gotten from a number of radio suppliers in the back of electronic magazines plus Radio Shack, Information Unlimited, or from Circuit Specialities, Box 3047, Scottsdale, AZ 85257.

This weapon is fast, silent, clean and deadly. It is also concealable, being only 5 3/4 inches long. Being composed of plastic and paper, with two small metal springs and a thin needle, it will not register on metal detectors set to ignore belt buckles and various small clothes fastenings.

Since it is in a tube with a half inch diameter, the needle will not bend if the tube's tip is placed firmly to the body surface before pressure is applied. It will go through any clothing. The only drawback is the thickness of the clothing. Since the needle protrudes 1/2 inch out of the tube, if the victim is bundled up, the needle may not penetrate. Both needle and plunger retract automatically.

The model I built the fang for is the LUER-LOK TIP 5570 B-D 3cc 256 5/8. A different size syringe and needle will need different specifications. But you should be able to make one to accommodate what you can get most easily.

This model is concealable and nondescript. It doesn't look like much of anything. Indeed, this keeps it from drawing attention to itself.

But it is amazingly effective. A quick thrust, less than a second of firm pressure, and the deed is done. It can be carried in pocket or purse with no fear of harm to the owner.

Materials for my model are:
One twistee balloon, 10 inches long and bought at any grocery store, 8 per package. The mouth end is cut off and it is split down both sides to make two thin rubber strips, 7 1/2 by 3/8 inches.

The tubes are made from a brown grocery bag. Cut off the bottom, slit the side and iron flat. Mark off 3 1/2 by 12 inch strips. I got 13 strips so one bag goes a long way. The two springs are model C-668 from most hardware stores, made by Century Spring Corp., Los Angeles, CA. They are 3/16 of an inch in diameter by 1 1/2 inch long. I suppose other companies turn them out and maybe they don't have to be exact. However, you should make sure that whatever syringe you use, the springs are about the same diameter.

For the end plugs you can use either thick cardboard, plastic or wood. I used a 5/8 inch dowel for the top part and a 3/16 inch dowel for the tip. Dowels slightly larger can be ground down with a file or grinder.

Since I meant to make several, I put the 3/16 inch dowel in the vise and tapped a depression in its exact middle with a nail so the drill bit would stay put. I used a 3/16 inch bit and drilled as deep as it would go. Then I had several tips after hacksawing them off the dowel, each 1/8 inch thick.

The best glue for making the tubes is Carter's Rubber Cement. Although you should use Elmer's Glue-All for holding the wooden ends in the tubes, rubber cement helps in rolling the paper, as it doesn't set up so fast and can be manipulated until the tubes are as wanted. Also, rubber cement bonds well with the balloon rubber.

To begin, cut off the projections from the top of the syringe, as they are not needed. Since the syringe needs sliding space, take a five inch strip of 3/4 inch masking tape and wind it around the syringe at a steep angle. Let it overlap a little. This will provide about two

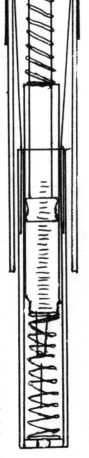

thicknesses of tape. Now when you roll the paper around the syringe and glue it, it will leave enough room for the syringe to slide in easily but won't let it rattle around.

The same principal applies to the outer tube. The outer tube must be loose so the rubber will not be caught between it and the inner tube. But it must not be too loose or it might push the syringe at a slant, preventing the needle from going through the hole.

To keep the outer tube loose, but not too loose, roll a separate tube of paper around the inner tube, exactly three paper thicknesses. This is easy to do. Just count the rolls and match the end of the first roll with the beginning of the first and cut it off and glue it there. Don't use so much glue that this three-roll tube sticks to the inner tube. It is just a form.

To glue the rolls, start rolling the paper around the syringe. Neatly apply glue all along the top side just a bit from the edge. Roll the paper forward until it connects, making sure it is perfectly even. Wait a few moments for it to set. Then roll it all the way. If it is uneven, you can remove it from the syringe and tamp it even before glueing the end of the paper.

For the inner tube, it is easier to cut three inches from the paper. When the nine inches are rolled and glued, glue the strip of rubber 1 inch on either side of the top. Then glue the other three inches of paper on, starting at the glued end. Use enough glue so that both sides of the rubber strips are glued so they won't come out.

Next, make the three-roll tube form. Then roll a 12 inch strip over it and when set, slide it off and slide the three roll form off the inner tube.

After making sure the holed tip fits into the lower end of the inner tube, glue around it and gently push it in flush with the tube. Give it a couple of hours to dry.

Remove the plunger from the syringe and put a spring over the plunger. Put the plunger into the syringe and push it all the way in. Put the other spring into the tube and push it in with the needle.

Now, put the rubber over the end of the plunger and push it through the outer tube. Put in the cap, making sure the rubber is at both sides. Pull the rubber so that the plunger is taut against the cap. Then cut the rubber in the middle, glue both ends and press them back along the outside of the cap. Cut a strip of paper about one by two and a half inches and glue it around the top of the outer tube over the strips of rubber. Then put Elmer's Glue-All around the cap and gently force it into the top against the plunger head. Ideally, the plunger should project about an eighth of an inch above the top so when the cap is put in and held by a rubber band until the glue dries, there will be no slack.

Actually, only the spring the needle rests in is really needed. All the spring around the plunger does is keep the hypodermic fixed in place. However, even if you have used it twice and still have a half cc dose left, the hypo can be loose and the needle will still protrude and unload when the pressure is put on.

If a little give bothers you, when putting the baloon rubber in the tube, measure its length to fit the plunger completely pushed into the hypo. The tensile strength of the rubber is too weak to push in the plunger when it is withdrawn.

Taken from Kurt Saxton's WEAPONEER, great buy from PO Box 327, Harrison AR 72601. Kurt also publishes a $25 a year GREAT newsletter called GUN RUNNER.

The power supply circuit for the Info Un infrared viewer with a artists conception of the completed unit. See the srticle for construction details.

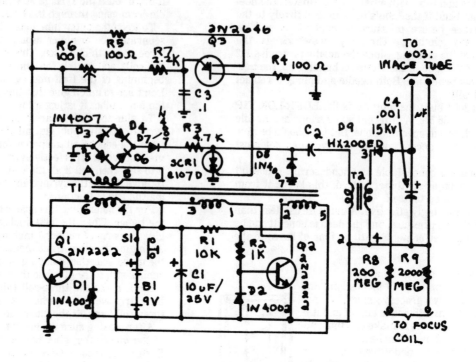

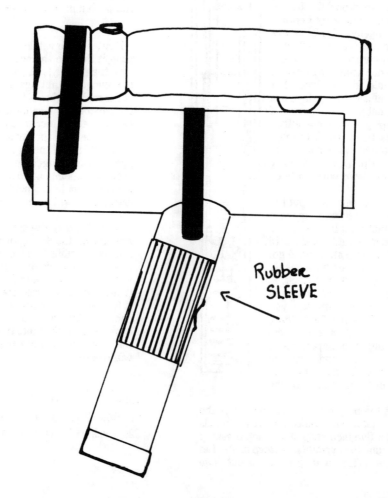

Rubber
SLEEVE

496

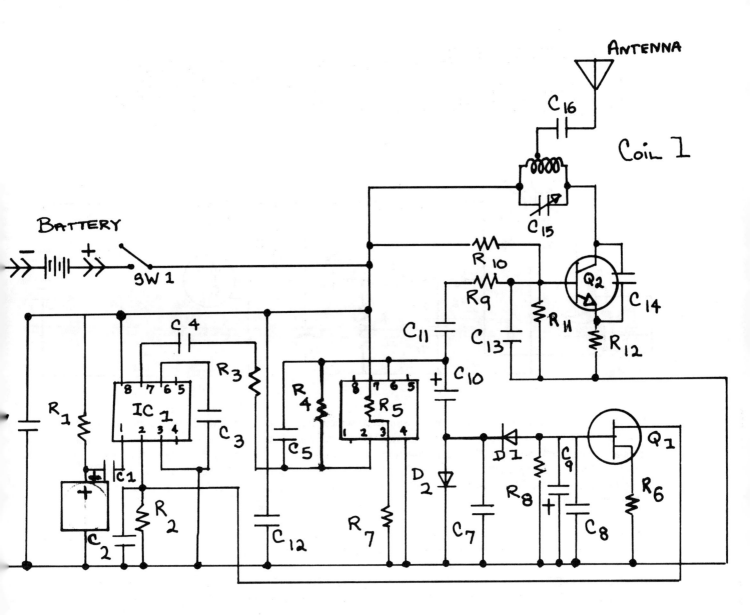

A most unusual electronic transmitter that incorporates an AGC stage to allow for differences in source volume. Medium range with a 33 hour battery life. Great for any application which may be exposed to both slight and loud sounds.

R1, R5, R7, 10K, R2, R10, 15K, R3, R6 1K, R4, 100K, R8 1 Meg, R9, R11 2.7K, R12 220 ohms all ¼ watt carbon. C1, 4.7 MFD 35 v electrolytic, C2, C11, C12 .1 MFD, C3 .001, C4 1 MFD 35 V Tantalum, C5, C7, C8 100 PF, C9, 22 MFD 35 Tant, C10 .22 MFD 35 Tant, C13 .047, C14, C16 10 PF, C15 5-60 trimmer cap, C17 470 35 v elect.

M1 electret mic Radio Shack 270-090, L1 4 turns of Belden 22 guage wire (wrap on 5/16 hex bolt and then remove bolt to leave air core) tap at 1¼ turns for antenna connection, IC1 RCA SK3891/Motorola MC3340P attenuator, IC2 LM 741 CP OP amp, Q1, RCA SK9164, D1, D2 SK3090 ger diodes, Q2 2N4124, SW1 slide switch, 9 volt battery, wire 22 and 18 guage solid insulated.

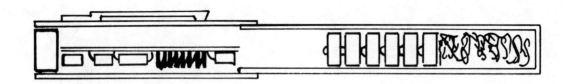

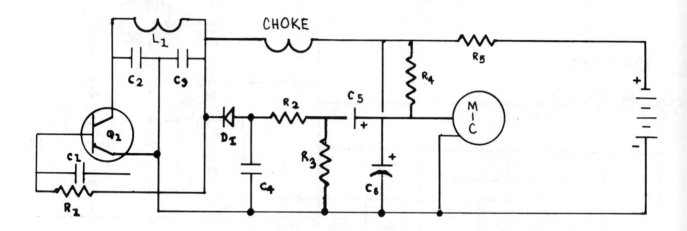

The top circuit is a simple one transistor transmitter designed to be wired on a thin PC board and then placed in a hollowed out fountain pen (see the photo). The batteries are button cells in series to reach about 4.5 volts and the switch can simply be the connection between the cap and pen body (if metal). Range is short but it works. R1, R2, R3 10K, R4 1K, R5 270 ohms, C1-C4 47 pf disc cap, C5, C6 2.2 uf tant cap, RFC 33 microhenry choke, Q1 2N3904 transistor, M1 electret mic RS 270-090, D1 MV2209, L1 8 turns No 24 wire 1/8 inside diameter air core.

One of the smallest telephone line powered bugs is shown in the bottom circuit. The diodes will allow quick placement, range is limited but entire device can be put together for about $6.00...

R1 470 ohms, R2 10K, R3 6.8K, C1-C4 47 pfd cap, D1-D4 1N4002 diodes, D5 Varacter diode 68pfd (MV2103), L1 4 turns No. 20 wire 1/8th air coil center, Q1 VHF transistor (2N2369A or equiv), ant 18 " insulated wire.

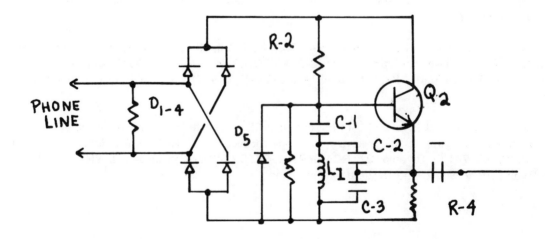

.5 MFD 100V Silicon Diode

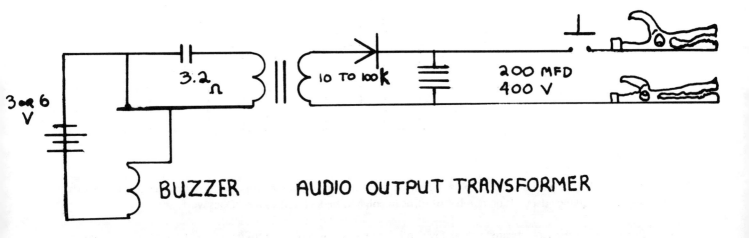

BUZZER   AUDIO OUTPUT TRANSFORMER

Two High Voltage Pulse units to "blow" bugs off a telephone line. Note the line should be closed off before any telco equipment or you will have a lot of explaining to do...

Bottom—R1 47K, 2 watts, R2, 100 K, R3 22K, R4, 100K C1 1,000 ufd (600 VDC). Use relay (such as automotive) that will handle 300 amps. B1 High voltage DC source..

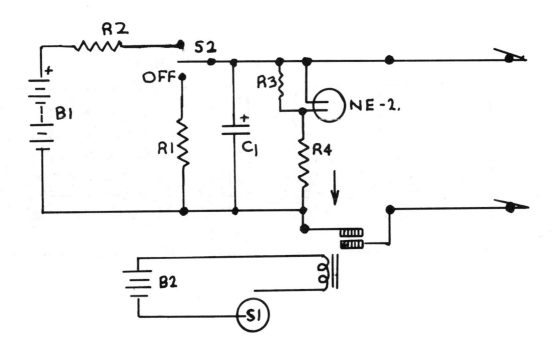

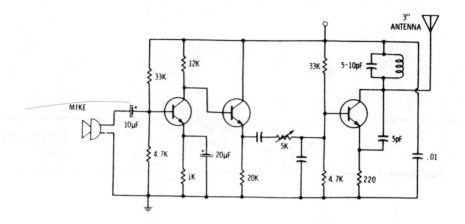

Top circuit is a general circuit for a typical three transistor miniature transmitter. Any general transistors will do, frequency depends on number of turns in coil and tank circuit values. Does work...

Bottom is a very sophisticated procject which is known as a telephone drop-in unit. The entire construction is done on a circular PC type board that will fit inside a "normal" carbon mic from the mouthpiece of a telephone. Build the unit than carefully take apart a real phone mic removing any fiber rings and leaving c clip ring, cover, case compression ring and2nd ring. The unit must now be placed back inside the case with the compression ring pressed against the board securely or soldered to it (it is a power source) remember the telco mic can be tossed out and the compression ring is the larger of the two rings. R1 1K, R2 220K, R3 4.7K, R4 100K, R5,R6 10 K, R7 2.2K, R8, R9 27K, C1 12uf mini tant, C2,C3,C4 8.2 uf mini tant, C5,C6 22 pf disc, C7 22 pf mini disc, D1-D4 1N4148 diodes, Q1-Q5 2N3904, L1 12 turns No 28 varnished wire on 1/8 air core, tap a center, RFC 1 mh chocke Mouser 43LS103, Mic RS 270-090 No 26 hook up wire, start with a Western Electric Phone Cartridge. The beauty of this unit is the two second unscrew-drop-in feature...

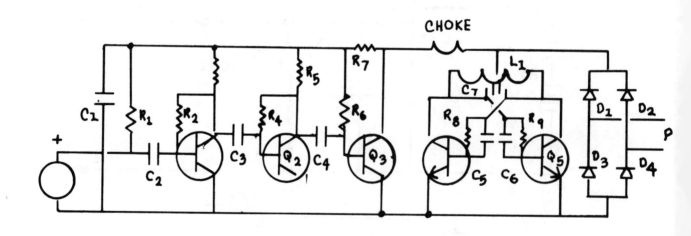

This unique circuit is a voice alteration device that is designed to alter the human voice in order to disquise it for speech purposes plus to render any taping non voice print analysis prone.

Most of these units operate by altering the waveform of the speakers voice by filtering and changing the magnitudes, phases and time factors present during speech.

This particular circuit acts as a variable bandpass circuit plus introduces some random changes that are nearly impossible to undo.

The various switches control the frequency passes of botht he Q and the center frequency within each range, (upper are centers, lowers are Q modifiers.)

One can also experiment with commerically available parametric bandpass and cut off filters, but this design is one of the best we have tried. I would use a good dynamic mic or our old Radio Shack electret standby for high quality. Type of speaker with also alter the operation; acoustic couplers from various suppliers can also be used for a better phone hook up.

IC is 1 LM324 are (])LM324's. experiment with different resistors for different results.

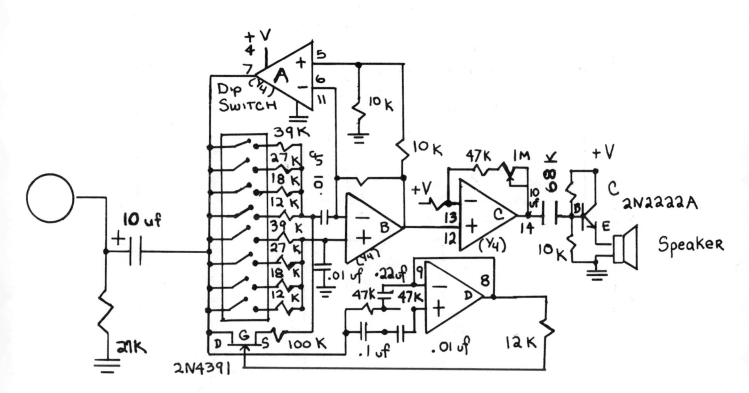

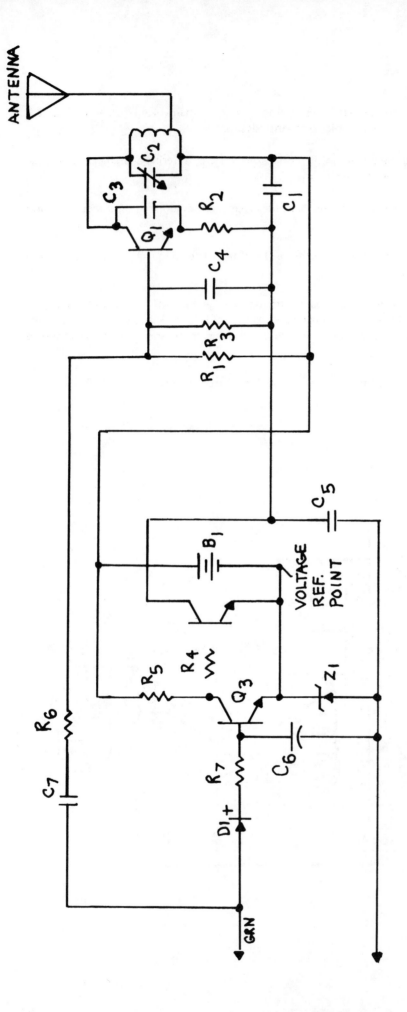

A polarized telephone line transmitter with good stability and fair range. Note the wires must be connected as shown, will operate only in an off-hook condition.

R1 15K, R2 220 ohm, R3 3.9K R4 2.2K, R5 3.9K, R6 150K, R7 100 K all ¼ watt carbon. C1 .01 mfd 50 v disc, C2 6-35 pfd trimmer cap, C3 5 pfd, C4 .01 mfd disc,C5 .1 mfd 25 vdc disc, C6 10 mfd 25 vdc elect, C7 .01 mfd. Q1-Q3 NPN gen purpose (PN2222), D1 50 v lamp rect diode 1N4002, Z1 1N5245 zener diode, L1 8 turns no. 16 would on a No. 8 wood screw and then air cored., 9 volt battery, clips, etc.

MUST READ BOOKS

Please note we didn't say "suggested." If you have spent thirty bucks for this book and you want to profit by it READ THESE BOOKS.

Stephen Hayes 1, 2 and 3 . . . (and any others he has out by now.)
> Do not read these to become a deadly fighter. Books don't do that (although some of the techniques WILL give you an insight to winning physical battles . . .). These books will reinforce and expound on what we are trying to cram into you: how to define real goals and accomplish them. How to win . . .

The Book of Five Rings
> You may get more out of this book on winning than any book you will ever read. You may not understand a word of it; we've both read it at least 20 times and are somewhere in between . . . Please don't fall into the popular bit of reading it once and telling everyone what a fantastic book it is and how you understand it all.

Ninja
> A novel. A very, very, good book. Some things are not true, some a bit off perhaps, but it contains some amazing history and philosophy fitting in with what we are writing about. Besides a hell of a story.

How to Get Anything on Anybody
> Lee -- Yeah, take it with a grain of salt because you know I am making money on every copy sold. But it is my best effort and has gotten great reviews . . .

Big Brother Game
> More salt. My book, but my favorite (except for this one) that I have written even though it got me in trouble, threatened by the US attorney general, hauled in by the FBI and is banned in several countries . . .

The following companies have gone out of business since publication of **SpyGame**:

Justin Concepts (p. 5)
Beaver Products (p. 5)
National Association of Private Investigators (p. 273)
Postal Mail Cover (p. 301)
Etco Electronics (p. 452)
Sgt. Sandy's (p. 458)
Parellex Corp (p. 465)
Wynn Engineering (p. 472)

The following companies have reported address changes since publication of **SpyGame**:

Nova Technologies (p. 320)
13706 Research Blvd.
Suite 100
Austin, TX 78750

SWD (p. 389)
1872 Marietta Blvd., NW
Atlanta, GA 30318
(No longer in sales; only repairs)

Davis Leather Co. (p. 454)
P.O. Box 2270
3990 W. Valley Blvd., #D
Walnut, CA 91789

Accuracy Systems, Inc. (p. 462)
P.O. Box 41454
Phoenix, AZ 85080

Brigade Quartermasters (p. 463)
1025 Cobb
International Blvd.
Kennesaw, GA 30144

Delta Press (p. 464)
P.O. Box 1625
El Dorado, AZ 71730

Elektron (p. 476)
P.O. Box 39
84210 Pernes
FRANCE

ISA (p. 483)
350 Fairfield Ave.
Stamford, CT 06093

Ross Engineering (p. 492)
7906 Hope Valley Ct.
Adamstown, MD 21710

All other companies and organizations referenced in **SpyGame** are either listed correctly or did not respond to the publisher's request for updated address information.